Instructor's Manual to Accompany DiYanni

LITERATURE

Reading Fiction, Poetry,
Drama, and the Essay

THIRD EDITION

JUDITH STANFORD

Rivier College

McGraw-Hill, Inc.

New York   St. Louis   San Francisco   Auckland
Caracas   Lisbon   London   Madrid   Mexico City   M
New Delhi   San Juan   Singapore   Sydney   Tokyo   Toronto

D1402859

This book is printed on recycled, acid-free paper containing a minimum of 50% recycled de-inked fiber.

Instructor's Manual to Accompany DiYanni
LITERATURE: Reading Fiction, Poetry, Drama, and the Essay
Third Edition

ISBN 0-07-016946-2

234567890 BKM BKM 90987654

ACKNOWLEDGEMENTS

I would like to thank my colleagues Kathleen Cain (Merrimack College) and Rebecca Burnett (Iowa State College) for their substantial contributions to Part Three, Drama. In addition, Jeanne Provencher provided valuable suggestions for the section on *A Raisin in the Sun,* and my colleague at the Rivier College Writing Center, Leslie Van Wagner, offered the insights and questions for *As You Like It*.

Judith A. Stanford

PREFACE

In *The Chronicle of Higher Education*, Marie Jean Lederman writes:

> The motivations for reading and writing are different for many of us, but they are born
> out of a passion for knowing oneself and for controlling an increasingly bewildering
> universe. Where are our passionate readers and writers now? More and more students
> march dutifully through the halls of higher learning to the thud of a vocational drum.
> How do we beckon them to the drumbeats they do not yet hear?

With his text *Literature: Reading Fiction, Poetry, Drama, and the Essay*, Robert DiYanni
provides an answer to Lederman's question. His careful explanation of the reading process
beckons students to those drumbeats they may not yet here. In addition, the Writing about
Literature chapter leads students to understand the connections between engaged reading and
thoughtful writing.

This instructor's manual is designed to support both processes: engaged reading and
thoughtful writing. Each part of the manual offers approaches to the readings, suggests possible
responses to the questions and discussion and writing topics in the text, and provides additional
subjects for writing or discussion. Whenever possible, I have suggested ways to connect
consideration of the reading selections to consideration of the students' own writing processes.
The writing topics in this manual provide many different kinds of assignments: literary analysis,
imitation, comparison, argument, personal response. Some assignments concentrate on the
content of the works being read; others require examination of their form. Several topics
encourage students to think about their own reading and writing processes.

As you use this manual, I expect that many of my "suggested responses" will be different
from your own and from those of your students. Both Robert DiYanni and I would be grateful
to hear your suggestions and to learn about your classroom experiences as you use this text and
instructor's manual.

ORGANIZATION OF THE INSTRUCTOR'S MANUAL

Frontmatter:

In addition to a brief Preface, the frontmatter includes the following features:

- *Thematic Contents* listings for each literary genre:
  Fiction
  Poetry
  Drama
  Essay

- *Additional Topics for Writing and Discussion—Across the Genres.* A list of topics that encourages students to see relationships among works from different genres.

Text:

- *Parts One through Four, composed of chapters corresponding to the text chapters, and organized by genre, like the text: Fiction, Poetry, Drama, the Essay.* Each chapter contains these features:

  1. Discussion to explain the reading process. Discussion of the literary selections. Possible responses to questions following the selections. Additional topics for writing and discussion.

  2. Additional topics for writing and discussion for the Collection chapters in each part.

  3. A list of writing topics that require making connections among the works in the discussion chapters of each part and the works in the Collection chapter.

- *A Writing about Literature chapter, with Suggestions for Writing and Discussion.*

- *An Appendix offering Suggestions for Teaching Critical Comments About Literature.*

Contents

Part Four, The Essay

Part Five, Writing about Literature

Appendix A

Appendix B

Additional Topics for Writing and Discussion—
Across the Genres

1. Write as if you were Antigonê responding to John Donne's "Meditation XVII: For Whom the Bell Tolls" (pp. 1545, 1585).

2. Explain why you agree or disagree that May Swenson's poem "Women" (p. 685) reflects the views of Torvald Helmer at any point in *A Doll House* (p. 1088).

3. Use e. e. cummings's "anyone lived in a pretty how town' (p. 659) as a reflection of views and behaviors exhibited by Torwald or Nora in *A Doll House* (p. 1088).

4. Explain how Blake's "A Poison Tree" (p. 422) reflects the feelings and experiences of Othello (p. 880).

5. Compare the decisions of the Sergeant in *The Rising of the Moon* (p. 790) and Bonaparte in "Guests of the Nation" (p. 29).

6. Would James Baldwin believe race was an issue in Othello's jealousy? What advice would Baldwin give Othello? (See "Notes of a Native Son," p. 1612, and *Othello* p. 880.)

7. What would Francis Bacon, who wrote "Of Revenge" (p. 1563), say to Iago about his motives for revenge and the crimes perpetrated? (See *Othello*, p. 880.)

8. How would Othello react to Robert Grave's poem "Symptoms of Love" (p. 1655)?

9. Read Raymond Carver's poem "Photograph of My Father in His Twenty-second Year" (p. 739). Imagine that you are Biff in *Death of a Salesman* (p. 1323) and write an essay about Willy as a younger man.

10. How does Anya in *The Cherry Orchard* (p. 1141) illustrate the theme of the illusion of immortality found in E. B. White's "The Ring of Time" (p. 1525)?

11. Imagine that you are Henry David Thoreau writing an account of the war in Shaw's *Arms and the Man* (p. 1178). Read first Thoreau's "The Battle of the Ants" (p. 1556), and look closely at Thoreau's notion of what is admirable in battle.

12. How does Virginia Woolf's "The Death of the Moth" (p. 1559) illustrate a view of fate similar to that found in Sophocles' *Oedipus Rex* (p. 806)? Consider in particular Woolf's choice of a creature as insignificant as a moth, and how that reflects upon the fate of a king.

13. Imagine a conversation between the E. B. White of "Once More to the Lake" (p. 1598) and Willy Loman (*Death of a Salesman*, p. 1323). How would Willy interpret White's story? What advice would White have for Willy?

14. Compare Ellison's "Battle Royal" (p. 286) with Baldwin's "Notes of a Native Son" (p. 1612).

15. Compare the theme of blindness in the following works:

    The Blind Man (p. 669)

    Cathedral (p. 331)

    When I consider how my light is spent (p. 557)

    The Blind Man (p. 669)

    Oedipus Rex (p. 806)

    Doc's Story (p. 340)

16. Compare Alice Walker's story "Everyday Use" (p. 346) with her essay "In Search of Our Mothers' Gardens" (p. 1644).

17. Read the following works and think about the pictures you are given of work and/or business. What responses do you have to these writers' views? Write an essay agreeing or disagreeing with one or more of the ideas you discovered in the works.

    A & P (p. 9)

    Reapers (p. 662)

    Lineage (p. 690)

    Death of a Salesman (p. 1323)

    Fences (p. 1460)

18. Compare the relationships of the wives and husbands in Susan Glaspell's *Trifles* (p. 1264), Kay Boyle's "Astronomer's Wife" (p. 40), and Nathaniel Hawthorne's "Young Goodman Brown" (p. 96).

19. Compare the themes of violence in "The Black Cat" (p. 80), "Guests of the Nation" (p. 29), *The Lesson* (p. 1231), and "No Name Woman" (p. 1636).

20. Compare *A Raisin in the Sun* (p. 1393) with "In Search of Our Mothers' Gardens" (p. 1644), and *Fences* (p. 1460).

21. Consider the theme of death and change in "A Rose for Emily" (p. 57), "The Metamorphosis" (p. 183), *Death of a Salesman* (p. 1323), "The Death of the Moth" (p. 1559), and "To an Athlete Dying Young" (p. 613).

PART ONE

Fiction

CHAPTER ONE
Reading Stories

The initial chapter on reading stories illustrates the process of reading—what we actually do as we read. Thus the "commentaries" in this chapter are not exhaustive interpretations, but demonstrations of how readers read. To the end, the comments on the stories in this chapter are open-ended. They invite student readers to decide what finally to make of the stories. The interpretive leads offered on each of the stories are just that—*leads, directions, approaches* that leave ends loose enough for students to tie up themselves.

In discussing all three stories in Chapter One, you may find it more important to get students to respond thoughtfully and attentively than to decide on a watertight or definitive interpretation. Class work can be directed toward the act of reading and interpreting itself— making students conscious of their own reading processes and providing them with interpretive guidelines, model behaviors, and strategies to become more attentive, reflective, and sensitive readers who value their previous experiences of life and language. A logical extension of directing students toward consciousness of their own reading processes is to suggest that as they become better able to understand and evaluate their reactions to what someone else has written, they should also become more sensitive to their own writing—both the process and the product.

Open-ended comments lead students to discover new ideas about the reading and writing processes; in addition, such a questioning approach to the literature encourages students to discern writing topics in which they are genuinely interested. Learning to ask significant and challenging questions—without the fear that they must lead to one "right conclusion"—is a powerful invention strategy that enables students to become engaged with their writing and thus to write papers their instructors can read with similar engagement.

You may also apply the teaching strategies of Chapter One by selecting works from Chapter Five, A Collection of Short Fiction, and asking students to read and respond to them with the three demonstration stories along the lines suggested in Chapter One. Although theoretically any story may be used in these ways, for convenience and efficiency short selections often work better than long ones. You can, for example, do an interlinear commentary as you read a story like "The Storm" or "The Boarding House." In doing so, you and your students would simply read a part of the story aloud in class, then jot down observations, responses, questions. Proceed part by part (you'll have to decide on the size of the parts), allowing time to write notes and queries after each section of reading. You can ask students to read their responses along the way, or wait until the end and ask them to comment on their experiences while reading the story or on what they think and feel on completing it. You might ask students to read their responses and observations aloud or in small groups. In a large-group discussion, you may find the class moving toward an interpretive consensus, or you may find a split in opinion. You may leave a series of unanswered questions up in the air. You can vary your approach as your pedagogical instincts dictate.

As students read selections, they will move through the stages of experience, interpretation, and evaluation. You may want to plan writing assignments that will encourage each of these stages. Journal writing or in-class warm-up writings call for experiential responses, while you may want to ask for interpretation and evaluation in more formal essays written as out-of-class papers or as midterm or final examinations.

"The Prodigal Son" • *Luke (pp. 3–4)*

In discussing "The Prodigal Son," you may find many students to whom it is new, providing the chance to discuss the different ways in which the parable might be interpreted both by people unfamiliar with its Christian context and by those who know the context. You can encourage students to discuss their different responses and suggest that they consider how their reactions to the parable have been affected by their varying religious backgrounds, ages, economic status, or by their own family relationships.

Additional Topics for Writing and Discussion

1. Write a dialogue that might occur between the elder brother and the younger brother in the early-morning hours after the feast has ended.

2. Write a letter the mother of the two boys might send to her sister in which she describes the feast as well as her reactions to her husband's decision.

3. Read the story of the prodigal son in the Bible (Luke 15). Does reading the other short parables that lead up to the story of the prodigal son (those of the lost sheep and the lost coin) change your response to the parable of the prodigal son as it is told here?

4. Create your own parable to illustrate a principle or idea you believe in. Imagining your audience to be young children, create this parable to convince them that they should behave, act, or believe in a certain way.

"A & P" • *John Updike (pp. 9–13)*

Although Updike's "A & P" is no modern supermarket and although Sammy may seem naive and immature to today's eighteen-year-olds, the decisions he makes and his conflict with authority demonstrate that some parts of growing up are timeless.

Possible Responses to Questions (pp. 13–14)

Experience

1. Some students may find the story outdated, but most will find Sammy an appealing character who has the courage to act on his convictions. Expect some pragmatists who think that Sammy is foolish to throw away even a cashier's job (and displease his parents) for a girl who barely knows he exists.

2. Some readers will object to the sexism in the story. Lengel looks at the girls as though they were sinful exhibitionists and the butcher, McMahon, pats his mouth as he "sizes up their joints." To McMahon, Queenie and her friends are no more than pieces of meat. Sammy seems to be their champion, yet it is hard to ignore his comment about girls' minds; "Do you really think it's a mind in there or just a little buzz like a bee in a glass jar?" (p. 9). Sammy stands up for the girls, but whether he respects them any more than does McMahon or Lengel is debatable.

3. Some students admire Sammy for his decision, believing that he comes to see the girls as real human beings and thus defends them. Others are disappointed in Sammy; they see his argument with Lengel as simply an easy way to quit a job Sammy didn't really like. Many students change their responses to Sammy.

Interpretation

4. Sammy is bright, ironic, witty. He has little respect for the people who shop in the store, characterizing them as "sheep," "winos," and "houseslaves." He obviously feels that he is superior to the customers as well as to the conventional, stodgy Lengel who acts as Sunday school superintendent whether he is in church or at the A & P.

5. Sammy's description of Lengel sizing up the girls' joints suggests that he is beginning to sympathize with them and to take their side against the older men who run the store. Also, as Lengel talks to Sammy after chastising the girls, Sammy thinks "No" and angrily punches his cash-register keys so that they play a sardonic counternote to Lengel's officiousness.

6. Sammy realizes that if he continues to act idealistically and romantically, he will have a difficult time in a world that values pragmatic hypocrisy more than honest disagreement. Sammy sees that he will always have problems with small-minded authority figures, and he is aware of the difficult times ahead.

Evaluation

7. The story almost certainly endorses Sammy's values. We see the entire scenario through his eyes, and Lengel and McMahon seem as one-dimensional to us as they do to him. Sammy's luscious descriptions of Queenie allow us to see his infatuation with such beauty and class in the midst of soap powders and women with curler-infested heads who yell at their children. As mentioned above, some students will see Sammy as foolish or wrong-headed, but the evidence in the story suggests that Updike admired his hotheaded romantic.

8. Responses will vary. Most students have worked in jobs where they have had to put up with less-than-competent supervisors. Nearly everyone has experienced a conflict with an authority figure. Discussion on this topic should be lively.

9. Responses will vary.

10. Responses will vary.

Additional Topics for Writing and Discussion

1. Why is Stokesie in the story? What would be lost if he were left out?

2. How important is the issue of class in this story? Is Sammy attracted to Queenie only because she is beautiful or also (or perhaps mainly) because of the lifestyle she represents? If he is attracted to her lifestyle, do you find his response to Lengel hypocritical?

3. Spend ten minutes observing a modern supermarket. How do the details you observe differ from those offered by Sammy?

4. Describe the final scene of the story as seen through the eyes of Stokesie or Lengel.

5. Do you think Lengel was unfair to the girls? Defend or argue against his actions.

"The Story of an Hour" • *Kate Chopin (pp. 14–18)*

Students have widely varying responses to "The Story of an Hour" and to Louise Mallard. Many feel that she is unfeeling and has "no right" to be happy that her husband's death gives her freedom. Students who feel this way often point to Mr. Mallard's apparently good behavior as a husband—he does not abuse or humiliate his wife, this argument goes, so she should be grateful and not angry. Other students may point out that we have no evidence Louise Mallard ever tried to explain her feelings to her husband, so that she—much more than he—is responsible for her own imprisonment. Many readers, however, sympathize with Louise Mallard and understand her marriage to have been a spiritual death.

Possible Responses to Questions (p. 18)

In discussing these questions with students, you might want to encourage a variety of responses and to forestall the search for a "correct" answer by having students write brief comments on each question. Students might then discuss their views in small groups, with one student acting as recorder to note the comments and reactions to comments and then to report when the class reconvenes as one group.

Additional Topics for Writing and Discussion

1. What do you think the author's attitude is toward Louise Mallard? Give examples of details that support your response.

2. Read each of the Comment sections following portions of the story. Find a comment, or part of a comment, that you find puzzling or disagree with. Explain the questions you have in as much detail as possible.

3. Both "The Prodigal Son" and "The Story of an Hour" tell about the unexpected return of a close relative who has been believed dead. Examine both the similarities and the differences in the two narratives. Consider as many details as possible—the action, the dialogue, the setting, the tone, the word choice, the use of repetition, the irony.

4. Explain your final view of Louise Mallard and then create a detailed character description of Brently Mallard to support your view.

CHAPTER TWO
Types of Short Fiction

The second chapter briefly outlines the different fictional genres. Parable is compared with fable, which is illustrated here in Chapter Two. The tale is also illustrated and compared with fable, parable, and short story.

Also discussed in Chapter Two are the short story and the short novel (see discussions of Tolstoy's "The Death of Ivan Ilych" [pp. 31–33 of this manual] and Kafka's "The Metamorphosis" [pp. 42–44]).

Because nonrealistic short stories break the conventions of traditional fiction, they are given special mention and explanation. Nonrealistic stories in this text include Borges's "The Garden of Forking Paths," Marquez's "A Very Old Man with Enormous Wings," Allen's "The Kugelmass Episode," Silko's "Yellow Woman," and Boyle's "Astronomer's Wife." These works vary, of course, in the degree of their nonrealism. A few of them might be taught together as variations on nontraditional departures from the conventions of realistic short fiction. Or they can be paired or grouped thematically with other more realistic works.
(See discussion of these stories later in this manual).

"The Wolf and the Mastiff" • *Aesop (p. 20)*

Aesop's fable is included here to illustrate the fable form; particularly, students should note that a fable states its moral explicitly. Fables concentrate on human failings, which are often satirically criticized through animals that are given human qualities.

Additional Topics for Writing and Discussion

1. Think of a human failing (perhaps a habit of a particular friend or relative). Write a fable intended to make fun of the failing and to suggest that the person should try to overcome it. Be sure to include a sentence at the end of your fable which clearly states its moral.

2. Read more of Aesop's fables, then write an analysis describing what kind of human failings he seems to criticize most often and most severely.

3. Fables usually state their moral in an absolute way—allowing no room for "maybes" or "what ifs." How might you argue with the moral of "The Wolf and the Mastiff"? Is there any justification for being a "fat slave" rather than a "starving free person"? Do you identify more easily with the Wolf or the Mastiff? Do you think that the majority of people you know fall into the Wolf or the Mastiff category?

4. Write an argument explaining how a pet owner might defend the Mastiff's point of view.

"The Widow of Ephesus" • Petronius (p. 21)

In discussing the Petronius tale "The Widow of Ephesus," it isn't necessary to arrive at interpretive unanimity in the class. In fact, students should see that a major difference which distinguishes the tale from the fable or parable is that the tale has a more open-ended quality. The tale, like its direct descendant the short story, is often ambiguous and invites a variety of interpretations.

Possible Responses to Questions

This series of questions is designed to stimulate many possible responses. None of the suggested interpretations is wholly correct or completely wrong.

Additional Topics for Writing and Discussion

1. Do any of the interpretations of "The Widow of Ephesus" offered on page 23 of the text seem persuasive to you? If so, explain which interpretation seems most convincing, giving evidence from the story to support your opinion.

2. Compare the reactions of the widow to her husband's death and the reactions of Louise Mallard to the news of her husband's death. As you study the reactions, what differences can you see between the presentation of emotions in the tale ("The Widow of Ephesus") and their presentation in the short story ("The Story of an Hour")?

3. Read some twentieth-century views of grief (see, for example, the works of Elizabeth Kübler-Ross or Harold Kushner). Then consider the stages of the widow's grief. How do her reactions differ from those described by modern theorists? How are they similar?

4. Write an account of the widow's story from the point of view of the maid who stays with her in the tomb.

CHAPTER THREE
The Elements of Fiction

This chapter includes the most traditional of our approaches to the study of fiction, and in it critical terms are defined and illustrated. By illustrating each fictional element through the stories included in Chapter One, students are made aware of how repeated readings or turnings back to a work further illuminate it. The references here to the Chapter One stories are brief and to the point. More extensive commentary follows new examples introduced at various points in the discussion, such as the Character section with references to, and quoted passages from, Kay Boyle's "Astronomer's Wife."

Each element of fiction is discussed to highlight its central features. Each is accompanied by a story that follows the explanation, with a question or two focusing on the element under consideration. Before we turn to each of the fictional elements singly and to their accompanying stories and questions, we should note that throughout Chapter Three the concern of Chapter One—reading stories—remains in evidence, though muted. In addition, with the discussion of each element, this manual will suggest ways to direct students' attention to their own writing process while they learn to read actively and to evaluate the writing of others.

PLOT AND STRUCTURE

The discussion of plot and structure focuses attention on the ways authors arrange incidents, on the dynamic nature of the story's developing action. Traditional questions can be raised here, such as: How are the specific incidents of the plot related to one another? Why has the writer arranged the incidents in a particular order? (For example, examine the flashbacks in "A Rose for Emily" and the "The Short Happy Life of Francis Macomber.") Reader-centered questions can also be asked: What effect does the story's action have on us at particular moments? What are the effects of the writer's plotting? That is, how does the writer arrange incidents to manipulate the emotions of readers?

As you discuss each rhetorical possibility, you might suggest that students consider implications for their own writing. In "A Rose for Emily," for instance, Faulkner manipulates chronological order (a pattern most students are familiar with), telling us about the smell (which turns out to be Homer's rotting body) before he tells us about Miss Emily's purchase of rat poison (with which she presumably killed Homer). Because the chronology of the story is unconventional, many readers come to the final gothic scene with no idea at all what horror lies in the upper bedroom. The discovery that Miss Emily has been sleeping with her lover's corpse thus delivers a shock that could not have occurred if the chronology of the story had been traditional or "logical." Students, in their own writing, can make the same kinds of conscious rhetorical choices. They can break the rules, but they need to be aware of the effect such choices will have. If they want to shock or surprise their readers, they might experiment with Faulkner's time distortion; if they want to present a straightforward, easily understood report, they had best consider keeping their chronology in order.

Similar analyses can be made throughout the text; any reader-centered question can be expanded to a discussion of, and application to, the students' own writing processes. For example, you may want to give some consideration to the structure of a particular story, to its shape as an artistic whole. Here we might be concerned less with the story's developing action and its changing effects on readers than with its organization—the relationship among its parts. We can ask students to identify and examine the parts of a story, considering its changes of scene, its shifts of focus, its variations in style or dialogue, or its changes in point of view or tone.

Guests of the Nation • Frank O'Connor (pp. 29–37

This story takes place in Ireland—an important point that many students miss. You might ask them to note references to local place names (such a Claregalway), to Irish dance songs ("The Walls of Limerick" and "The Siege of Ennis") and the Irish names (Mary Brigid O'Connell). In addition, in the first paragraph we hear one character shout, "Ah, you divil, you, why didn't you play the tray?" Most readers can't miss the Irish brogue in that line of dialogue.

Students may also find it hard to believe that prisoners of war could become friendly with their jailers, or that they would be able to fit into the culture of the captors. You may want to point out that even prisoners with far greater culture gaps than those which these Englishmen face have acted in a similar way.

Possible Responses to Questions (p. 37)

1. and 2.   Section I provides the *exposition* by introducing the five main characters, Donovan, Belcher, Hawkins, Nobel, and Bonaparte (the narrator). We learn the primary personality traits of each man, seeing each as a unique individual, yet also noting that the latter four share many common qualities while Donovan remains outside their group. The two British soldiers and their Irish guards enjoy playing poker and the four seem to see the war as distant and removed from themselves. Although they lose their tempers, Hawkins and Nobel argue about religion and war more as the verbal wrestling of schoolboys rather than as the angry exchange of enemies. Bonaparte observes Hawkin's conversation with the old woman about the root causes of the "German war" as a comic encounter where the glib British soldier is dazzled by "old girls" complex and original explanation.

In Section 2, Jeremiah Donovan plays a larger role and the narrator notes, in the first sentence, that Donovan has "no great love for the two Englishmen." This comes as a surprise to Bonaparte, who is even more astonished when Donovan later informs him that the English soldiers are hostages whom they may have to shoot. Section 2, then, introduces *complications* and suggests the moral dilemma that Bonaparte and Nobel will later face. The relationship between the prisoners and their captors shifts as the Irish soldiers face the possibility that they will be asked to kill men they have come to regard as comrades.

Section 3, like Sections 1 and 2, begins with the arrival of Jeremiah Donovan. This time, Donovan advances the plot and forces the *crisis* by informing Bonaparte that the prisoners must be shot. Donovan shows excitement, and perhaps even glee, when he urges his countrymen to do their duty and when he informs the British soldiers of their plight. Nobel and Bonaparte demonstrate their increasing horror at what they are being ordered to do, and Bonaparte asks himself questions that show he has now come to face and to challenge the assumptions of patriotic obligations during wartime.

In the final section, as part of the *falling action* the British soldiers try to argue their way out of the execution while Donovan shows himself more fully to be a single-minded, perhaps sadistic, pawn of the military. He sees none of the complications that the four other men express. The *denouement* comes when Donovan, assisted by Bonaparte shoots the two hostages. While the Bonaparte appears unmoved, Noble and Bonaparte are profoundly changed by their own complicity in their comrades' deaths; both young Irish soldiers are shocked and horrified at the realities of war. Bonaparte sums up the impact of the incident when he says, "Anything that happened to me afterwards, I never felt the same about again."

Additional Topics for Writing and Discussion

1. The central characters can be compared. On what basis? They can also be distinguished from one another. Explain briefly the identifying characteristics of each.

    [Nobel and Bonaparte are much like Belcher and Hawkins; they are willing to look for friendship across differences. Jeremiah Donovan, one the other hand, never gets too close to anyone and pays heed only to external laws, which he defines as "duty" or "loyalty to country." The two prisoners, Belcher and Hawkins agree politically, although Hawkins is the more talkative and argumentative in expressing what he calls his communist or anarchist ideas. Belcher seems to be the cooler and more collected of the two; he talks little during most of the story. At the end, however, Belcher becomes more like Hawkins and talks a great deal just before he is shot.]

2. The old woman clearly is a minor character. What does she contribute to the story? Donovan is more immediately necessary to the story's action; what is his function? Would the disappearance of either Donovan or the old woman significantly alter the outcome of events? Why or why not?

    [The old woman, with her references to pagan gods, suggests the blind fate that brings the two Englishmen to their graves. Donovan represents the unfeeling, self-important patriot who uses love of country to justify his own love for violence and cruelty. The disappearance of the old woman might not alter the outcome, but it would alter our view of the outcome. The disappearance of Donovan might significantly change the outcome. If there were not another "duty-bound soldier" around to watch over Noble and Bonaparte, they probably would let the prisoners escape. Noble and Hawkins have argued vigorously over politics, but in the end, the Irishman seems more likely than his English counterpart to have seen their connections rather than their differences. And, of course, Bonaparte tells us at the end of Section 3 that if the prisoners did make a run for it, he would "never fire on them."]

3. Even though the story has a sad ending, the earlier sections have a number of humorous elements. Identify some of these, explaining what they contribute to the effect of the story.

    [Much of the humor in the story is ironic. For example, the discrepancy between what we expect the Irishmen to know and what we expect the Englishmen to know is amusing: The Englishmen know the country side and its people better than the Irishmen do. Another example of ironic humor occurs in the never-ending card games: Belcher beats Bonaparte and Noble, but whatever they lost to Belcher, Hawkins lost to them—and Hawkins played with money that Belcher gave to him. The old woman is a wonderful comic character. Expecting a stereotyped little Irish peasant, Hawkins tries to shock her by using profanity against the war and inviting her to do the same. She turns the table, however, by solemnly blaming the war on heathen deities and "hidden powers." Because so much of the humor is ironic, it prefigures the darker ironies of the conclusion.]

4. The details of the execution in Section 4 are particularly impressively presented. Notice, for example, the different reactions of Belcher and Hawkins to the announcement of their imminent execution. What do we learn about each at this point? Look carefully also at the descriptions of Hawkins as he falls after being shot. What do they contribute to the feeling of this passage? Why do you think O'Connor included those messy details rather than describe a smooth, uncomplicated event?

[Hawkins remains much the same; he continues to argue about politics and religion, believing that he can convince his accusers to behave humanely and not to shoot him. We may be somewhat surprised that he offers to follow Noble's beliefs at the end, but if we look back in the story we see that Hawkins has always enjoyed argument for its own sake and that fellowship, not conversion, was his true aim. Belcher, on the other hand, starts to talk a great deal. He seems to learn at the end that he has left a lot undone and unsaid in his lifetime, and he tries frantically to make it up in his final moments.

We also learn certain facts about the doomed men: Hawkins carries a letter from his mother with whom he was "great chums," and Belcher leaves no close heirs, his wife having left him eight years before. The ugly details of the execution force the reader to see what was really is: pain, slow death, betrayal, fear, senseless sacrifice, and meaningless retribution.]

5. Compare the view of war in O'Connor's story with the view of war in one or two films or television series you have watched.

CHARACTER

The discussion of character raises the question of how effectively fictional characters can be compared with real people. Any number of stories can be approached with this consideration in mind, especially realistic stories. Beyond asking how we come to know fictional characters, the chapter discusses techniques of characterization from the writer's point of view. Both concerns as discussed in this chapter may be supplemented with the comments on *character* and *dialogue* in Chapter Fourteen on drama.

You may want to consider in more detail Joyce's characterization in "The Boarding House." Or you might consider discussing the character *relationships* in the work, bypassing the emphasis on technique. Not to be overlooked are minor characters, such as Polly Mooney's father, the one minor figure in "The Boarding House." Perhaps you might compare more generally the roles of minor characters in stories previously read. A useful and simple generic question is: How would the story differ (what would be gained or lost) if this or that minor character were omitted?

While you are discussing character, you might ask students to consider the character they project when they are writing essays, reports, or other creative work of their own. Fiction written in the first person is especially helpful for showing students how their own choices of time, diction, or subject create a picture of themselves for their audiences. (See, for example, "Araby" or "I Stand Here Ironing.")

"Astronomer's Wife" • Kay Boyle (pp. 40–43)

In "Astronomer's Wife" there are two major characters, Mrs. Ames and the plumber. They provide a perfect opportunity for students to see the contrast between a dynamic major character (Mrs. Ames) and a static major character (the plumber). Here the contrast is particularly important because the unchanging, steady, certain nature of the plumber is one of the things that enables Mrs. Ames to follow him down into the earth. In addition, Mr. Ames stands as a fine example of a minor character who is keenly drawn with one or two strokes of the author's pen. He also comes close to being a stereotyped academic—a scholar with his head almost literally in the clouds, unable to deal with the realities of day-to-day life and disdainful of those who do.

Possible Responses to Questions (p. 43)

1. The story's characters are sharply contrasted: the dreamy astronomer with the practical wife; the passive astronomer lying in bed versus the active plumber walking about the grounds seeking the source of the plumbing problem. To the wife, the plumber appears confident and competent—a man who knows how to get things done—unlike her husband who isolates himself from her and the children to think rather than to act. The wife seems bewildered by the plumbing problem. She seems to need far more understanding and reassurance than the astronomer realizes, reassurance and understanding that the plumber gives her.

   The differences between the astronomer and plumber are striking. Besides the contrasting nature of their work, there is the contrasting attitude toward Mrs. Ames. Ironically, the more common and less intellectual plumber sees more readily and clearly than the astronomer the kind of woman the wife is. Unlike the astronomer, he talks to her gently and lovingly. And we are not terribly surprised when she goes into the earth with the plumber, leaving the astronomer to his stargazing.

2. Mrs. Ames's primary role in the marriage seems to be that of mother to a badly behaved, although gifted, child. Professor Ames expects her to keep his household running correctly; she is to provide him with food, clean his clothes, and take care of any maintenance problems. Professor Ames, on the other hand, has no responsibilities other than to pursue his studies. He never praises Mrs. Ames and never talks to her except to complain about some need that has not been met or to make fun of her. When she is talking to the plumber he says, "Katherine! There's a problem worthy of your mettle!" And of course, like a typical badly behaved child, he expects to be able to stay in bed as late as he likes waiting for his "mother" to act responsibly.

Additional Topics for Writing and Discussion

1. Boyle presents the story from the point of view of the wife by taking us inside her consciousness and rendering her experience in language that reflects her essential self. Why are we not taken into the mind of the astronomer? If you were to rewrite the first page of the story from the astronomer's point of view, either directly in the first person or indirectly in the third, what differences would emerge?

   [The astronomer would, of course, be sympathetic to himself and would perhaps present us with information we do not have here that would justify his behavior and satisfactorily explain his attitude toward his wife.]

2. What are the symbolic associations of "up" and "down" in this story? Trace this spatial imagery from beginning to end and explain its significance.

   ["Up" is associated with lofty thinking, with cerebral activity, with the heavens, the life of the mind, and abstractions. "Down" is associated with the earth, with practicalities, bodily functions, and finally sexuality. The imagery is significant because, as Mrs. Ames begins

13

to understand "down"—which the plumber patiently explains to her—she is able to realize that the problems in her marriage do not come from her inability to attain the standards of "up." Instead, she sees her husband's detachment from things of the earth as a disability. She stops trying to deny the "down" part of life and follows the plumber.]

3. Reread the ending carefully. What does the plumber mean when he says, "There's nothing at all that can't be done over for the caring?" Notice how Mrs. Ames translates this statement into three concrete images. How do these images help us to understand her? What does she mean when she says "the trouble is very, very serious"? Why does she go with the plumber?

[The plumber could mean many things: that the plumbing problems can be fixed because he is a man who truly cares about his work; that Mrs. Ames's marriage could have been fixed if the astronomer had cared; that Mrs. Ames's sadness can be remedied if only she cares enough and has somebody to care for her. The word "care" is used both in the sense of wanting something, of being committed to it, and in the sense of tending or nursing someone or something. The three images that come to Mrs. Ames's mind are the power that comes from herbs to make a sick person well, the rain that stops a drought, and time that heals a broken bone. These images enable her to see that there is help for every trouble or problem; the solution lies in a power that heals, cures, "cares" for the sufferer. When Mrs. Ames says that "the trouble is very, very serious," she means on a literal level to tell the servant that the plumbing problem is critical (perhaps to justify her descent into the earth with the plumber). On the figurative level, of course, she means that the problem in her marriage, the problem with the lack of real love and understanding in her life, is "very, very serious." She goes with the plumber because he has offered her at least a look at a different way of life. When they go together into the "heart of the earth," they also take a journey into the human heart.]

4. Compare the wife's departure with the plumber with the experience of the woman and the ka'tsina spirit in Silko's "Yellow Woman."

5. Compare the male characters in "Astronomer's Wife" with those in "The Blind Man" by D. H. Lawrence. Look closely at the physical characteristics of each pair of characters; look also at their speech, their names, their jobs. In addition, compare the way each writer characterizes the male figures.

SETTING

The discussion of setting on pp. 43–54 of the text distinguishes between a story's milieu and its use of space. The first involves considerations of why the story takes place when and where it does, along with the significance of the cultural dispositions it reflects. The second involves consideration of spatial concerns like proximity, distance, inner and outer, higher and lower. Milieu invites historical speculation, spatial analysis, dramatic and even cinematic investigation, as suggested by "A Rose for Emily" and "The Story of an Hour."

Examining the importance of setting and the way authors use spatial relations to develop their themes and support their ideas should help students to think about the use of spatial order in their own writing. Setting—both milieu and use of space—may be important in writing projects as widely varied as a proposal arguing for the construction of a new shopping center and an essay examination discussing Doric architecture. Students should be encouraged to see that examining the way Mason uses setting is interesting and worthy of study for its own sake. But they should also be making mental notes for their own future writing projects.

"Shiloh" • Bobbie Ann Mason (pp. 45–54)

The title of this story raises the image of a battle, and indeed a battleground becomes an important part of the exterior setting. In addition, as we might expect, battles between and within the characters comprise the internal landscape of "Shiloh." You might ask students to note as many battles as they can while they are reading the story. Then have them meet in small groups to discuss the battles each person has discovered and to begin evaluating how, if at all, these battles are resolved. A speaker from each group should briefly summarize the responses for the whole class, thus providing a context for considering the conflicts in "Shiloh."

Possible Responses to Questions (p. 54)

Questions 1 and 2 are closely related; students' responses to the first question lead to the interpretation and evaluation required by the second question.

The Civil War battle to which the title refers began with Southern soldiers attacking the Union camp where the commander-in-chief was Ulysses S. Grant. Although General Grant and his troops eventually defeated the Southerners, the battle suggests a daring raid in the face of enormous odds. In Mason's story, both Norma Jean and Leroy seem to be waging just such wars. Leroy has always regarded history (in the public sense) as "just names and dates." As he thinks about the Battle of Shiloh, he realizes that he has also regarded his personal history—and Norma Jean's personal history—in the same way. As he runs through the significant events of Mabel Beasley's life (including the events of her daughter's life), he understands that "he is leaving out the insides of history." He has hoped for an easy solution to the problems of his own life and to the stresses threatening his marriage. But just as being at Shiloh has forced him to imagine the "insides of public history" (the effects of historical events on human beings), so too have his contemplations led him to recognize that he was being simplistic in searching for an easy reconciliation with Norma Jean. He now rejects the idea of building a cabin because he sees that "building a house of logs is . . . empty," just as his view of history has been superficial and external.

Additional Topics for Writing and Discussion

1. Whose point of view are we given in the story? How does point of view relate to the setting?

   [Because the story is told from Leroy's point of view, we see his conflicts most clearly. He is fighting his leg injury, of course, but more important is his struggle to understand what he wants to do with his life and what he wants from life. In addition, he is beginning to examine his marriage in a way he never did before, trying desperately to find a way to heal the old wounds he and Norma Jean have experienced over the years and to build a future for them together. It is interesting to note, as we think of Leroy's battles in comparison to Shiloh, that he identifies the Southern troops not with brave and stalwart warriors, but rather with Virgil Mathis, a "boastful policeman" who led a drug raid on the back room of the local bowling alley. When Leroy first thinks about the drug raid, he compares Virgil Mathis to his mother-in-law, whom he imagines storming through the front door to catch him smoking a joint. Leroy, then, sees himself as the victim of the raiders; if we pursued the analogy with the Battle of Shiloh, he would be identified with the ultimately victorious Northern troops rather than with the Southerners.

2. How is the setting of Shiloh significant to Mabel Beasley?

[Battles and battlefields surround Mabel Beasley, Norma Jean's mother. Mrs. Beasley constantly mentions Shiloh as a place Leroy and her daughter ought to visit. She sees the battlefield memorial as restful and healing. Her own marriage, rather ironically, took place in Corinth, the place where the raiders of Shiloh were ultimately defeated. Mrs. Beasley, who idealizes the battle site, spends a great deal of her life inciting battles. She constantly offers advice to her son-in-law, but far more damaging is her determination to keep her daughter dependent and afraid of her. She treats Norma Jean as though she were still a child and tries to control every aspect of her daughter's life.]

3. Describe the battles faced by Norma Jean and explain their significance.

[Norma Jean is fighting to become an independent, functioning adult, and she wages war on many fronts. She lifts weights and does leg exercises to build her body; she rediscovers her talent at playing the organ; she begins to speak up to her mother ("You ain't seen nothing yet," and "When are you going to *shut up* about Shiloh, Mama?"); she begins taking an adult education course in composition. Ironically, Norma Jean's fight to become independent directly opposes Leroy's struggles to bring them closer together. He wants to build a log house to keep them safe; she wants to walk away and explore her life on her own, just as she walks off in the final section to explore the battlefield and the river that runs through it.]

4. How important to the story is the death of Leroy and Norma Jean's infant son, Randy?

[Although Randy's death is mentioned only peripherally throughout the story, it is a dominant symbol of the conflicts the characters experience. We learn early in the story that Leroy believes that the "memories of Randy . . . have almost faded," and he feels lucky that he and Norma Jean are still together, because he read somewhere" or else he heard . . . on *Donahue*" that most couples who lose a child find their marriage destroyed. He wonders vaguely if his being around the house reminds Norma Jean too much of the early days of their marriage, but he dismisses his thought that "one of them should mention the child."

Later in the story, we see that Randy's death has weighed heavily on Leroy, as suggested by his compulsive retelling of his life story to the hitchhikers he picked up. Many things in Leroy's life trigger memories of Randy's death. When he meets Stevie to buy marijuana, he remembers that Stevie's father and he were in high school together, and thinking of high school leads him to remember his teenage marriage and fatherhood. It is interesting to note that although earlier in the story Leroy thinks of Randy's death as a faded memory, the reminiscence elicited by the meeting with Stevie brings back each part of the night Randy died as though it had just happened.

Like Leroy, Norma Jean is still deeply affected by the loss of her infant son. When her mother rattles on about the dog who has been put on trial for killing a baby and reports that "the mother was in the next room all the time . . . they thought it was neglect," Norma Jean covers her ears. Later she tells Leroy that her mother "just said that about the baby because she caught me smoking." Norma Jean still has unresolved (and almost certainly unjustified) guilt feelings about her baby's death. Yet even when she mentions her feelings to Leroy, neither of them is able to discuss what happened. They both avoid mentioning Randy or his death. They are, as Leroy realizes at the end, looking only at the surface of their relationship and ignoring "the real inner workings of a marriage."]

5. Consider the activities Norma Jean and Leroy pursue. How do these activities help to define their characters?

[Leroy's activities include sewing a *Star Trek* pillow cover and building models. The latter activity leads to his constructing a miniature log cabin. Leroy's hobbies suggest his desire to stay at home, to build a place where he and Norma Jean can be together and learn to know each other. Norma Jean, on the other hand, has begun to lift weights and to study English composition. Both pursuits suggest her desire to grow—physically and intellectually—and both indicate a need to find a structure for her life. Note, for instance, her faithful adherence to her exercise routines and her delight in outlining paragraphs.]

POINT OF VIEW

Point of view is the most technical of the elements of literary art to which we introduce beginning students. You might want to ask them about their responses to the narrators of particular stories and especially to account for those responses. If the narrator is "invisible," you can ask how the story would be different with a more noticeable narrator. Sometimes taking a brief passage and transforming its point of view is enough to suggest how a change in point of view alters a story's tone and resonance.

While you are discussing point of view, you might ask students to consider how viewing a subject or theme from various angles can affect their own approach to a writing assignment. Even formal business reports, which supposedly take an objective stance, are in fact often written to reflect one particular view of the subject. Understanding how point of view can be used effectively to communicate a particular idea and learning how to identify a piece of writing were point of view has been manipulated are valuable and practical skills. In addition, students may be encouraged to consider any writing topic from many points of view as a discovery technique. Many fine papers have resulted from the writer's ability to look at the familiar and recognize what no one has seen there before.

"A Rose for Emily" • William Faulkner (pp. 57–63)

To begin class discussion on this story, you might ask students to write a brief explanation of why they think the story is called "A Rose for Emily." Possibilities abound. Some critics think Emily is herself the rose—a flower of the Old South emblematic of genteel yet decaying womanhood. Another interpretation points to the rose imagery at the end of the story as the townspeople break into the upper bedroom. The most popular reading sees the story itself as a rose, offered to Emily, who although a deranged, broken woman who has been sleeping with a corpse, nevertheless represented to the townspeople (who are now telling her story) a symbol of the Old South which is fast passing away. My favorite interpretation was a suggestion made by a student: Homer is the rose—killed and preserved as a memento, the way a young Southern woman in earlier times might have preserved the rose she wore to a ball.

Possible Responses to Question (p. 63)

The narrator's view is complex and ambivalent. Emily is both admired and hated. She is admired for the stubborn pride, for her imperviousness and monumentality. She is hated for the aristocratic superiority she displays. She is affectionately remembered and respectfully memorialized on the one hand. On the other, she is portrayed as a rigid, eccentric woman unable to release her hold on the past and unwilling to change her ways. She's shown to be stubborn yet forceful, arrogant yet dignified, violent yet respectable.

The narrator's view reflects Faulkner's admiration for the Old South—for everything Emily Grierson and her house represent: an agrarian world in which manners and style, grace and civility, mattered, where tradition was valued. It conveys simultaneously, however, a critical stance that recognizes a need for change, since time does not stand still and since there were features of the antebellum South that were morally repugnant. The narrator seems to recognize the need for change while experiencing a nostalgia for the past—a double perspective that parallels the town's ambivalent attitude toward Emily herself.

Additional Topics for Writing and Discussion

1. What qualities of character does Miss Emily possess? How does Faulkner reveal them? In paragraph 3, Faulkner writes that "Miss Emily had been a tradition, a duty, and a care." What do you think this means? What might Emily represent?

    [These questions should help students formulate a detailed analysis of Emily's character. The quotation, in particular, focuses on the dual nature of Miss Emily and the ambivalent attitude the townspeople have toward her. She is described as a "carven . . . idol in a niche" (end of Section 4, p. 62), as looking "like a girl with a vague resemblance to . . . angels" (first sentence, Section 3, p. 60), yet also as a tough matron who refuses to admit the passage of time or to account for her motives when she buys rat poison.]

2. Examine the scenes in which Emily is shown dealing with other people, particularly the aldermen and the druggist. What would be lost if any of these scenes were omitted?

    [These scenes show Miss Emily's forcefulness and determination. They also demonstrate that even the most prominent of the townspeople can crumble under Miss Emily's icy stare and insistence on her right to do things as she chooses. The scene with the aldermen also shows readers Miss Emily's inability to accept the changes that come with time, foreshadowing her inability to give up Homer even when she knows he is dead.]

3. Look at the description of the Grierson house in paragraph 2. What parallels can you draw between the house and Miss Emily? In addition, explain the significance of the way the neighborhood has changed. Also explain the implications of the final sentence of the paragraph.

    [Miss Emily's house is described as "stubborn and coquettish," terms that certainly fit her in various parts of the story. The refusal of the old house to give up its grace and dignity in spite of the decay around it suggests Miss Emily's staunch determination to ignore the fall of the Old South. The Civil War graves surrounding Miss Emily, as well as the graves of the "august names of that neighborhood," also connect Miss Emily to the antebellum South; now she, one of its last representatives, is buried with that South.]

4. Read the end of the story aloud, from the words "The violence of breaking down the door seemed to fill this room with pervading dust." How many times does the word "dust" occur? And at what points within the sentences in which it appears? What symbolic associations are stirred up by this all-pervasive dust? What connections can you make between the description of the dust and the description of the house and cemetery?

    [The word "dust" occurs four times—three times at the end of a sentence, emphasizing its importance. Dust certainly suggests death and decay, but it also suggests dryness and lack of disturbance. In the upper bedroom, everything—including Homer—is left as it was in the past; but of course even Miss Emily cannot stop the effects of time. The dust covers the carefully arranged toilet articles, the clothes, the furniture, and Homer's corpse. The dust imagery also suggests the biblical "to dust thou shalt return," connecting the bedroom and house (both tombs of a kind) to the cemetery.]

5. What has decayed? How many different kinds of things suffer deterioration?

[The neighborhood around Miss Emily's house; Miss Emily's house; the Old South; Miss Emily; Homer's clothes and toilet articles; Homer; Miss Emily's pillow "yellow and moldy with age and lack of sunlight" (p. 62, last sentence in Section 4.)]

6. Explain what the story's point of view and its time scheme contribute to its effect. Why does the story begin after Miss Emily has died?

[The time scheme in the story is discussed in this chapter of the manual in the Plot and Structure section (see pp. 9–10). The point of view, like the time scheme, is essential to the story's overall effect and theme. For the reader to be convincingly surprised at the end of the story, the narrator cannot know what has gone on behind Miss Emily's door. We would not have the same story at all, for instance, if we saw these events through the eyes of Miss Emily—who would know, and would tell us, exactly why she was purchasing the rat poison and exactly what had happened to Homer. Seeing the story through the eyes of the towns-people also leaves the reader with some interesting puzzles that would be eliminated with, say, an omniscient author view. For example, why exactly does Emily kill Homer? And why does Tobe depart so abruptly after he lets the townsfolk into Miss Emily's house?]

LANGUAGE AND STYLE

The section on language and style offers a fine opportunity for students to consider their own writing decisions as well as the linguistic choices made by experienced authors. As students analyze the way Faulkner's sentence structure varies from Hemingway's or evaluate the diction James Joyce chooses for the opening section of "Araby," they might also think about their own sentence patterns and word choices. Looking closely at style—particularly at diction and the use of figurative language—helps students to recognize the value of concrete details.

For beginning writers, a passage such as the final paragraph in "A Rose for Emily" (p. 63) can help in understanding the difference between "telling" and "showing" a reader. Faulkner could simply have said that when the townspeople found Homer's corpse, they realized that Miss Emily had been sleeping in the same bed. That information could be read with surprise and shock, but the full impact of the horror comes from the details Faulkner shows us and the words he chooses to describe the macabre scene. The "dry dust" that is "acrid in the nostrils" puts readers right at Homer's bedside to discover with terror and revulsion the "long strand of iron-gray hair" that lies in the indentation on the pillow beside the grinning, fleshless skull.

"Araby" • James Joyce (pp. 66–69)

Most students will readily see that this story traces the narrator's steps to bitter disillusionment. Many first-time readers of "Araby," however, do not understand *why* the narrator is so completely undone by finding the bazaar to be shabby and banal. Asking students to look closely at Joyce's style will help them to comprehend the narrator's disappointment. First, you might ask them to estimate the narrator's age—he's old enough to be allowed out at night on his own, but young enough to be friends with boys who fight for each other's caps. He's proba-

19

bly about twelve or thirteen years old. Then ask students to look at the word choices and the way sentences are constructed in the story. Most readers will agree that a preteenage boy would speak much more simply and use more colloquialisms. Most college freshmen have read *Catcher in the Rye*, and they can quickly see the distinction between Holden Caulfield's voice and the voice of the boy in "Araby." Understanding that the narrator is an adult, looking back on a childhood event, helps to explain why the disappointment is described in such vivid and mature terms. The narrator says that he saw himself as a "creature driven and derided by vanity," but it is only as an adult that he can discover such sophisticated words and images to describe what he found to be a profound, although probably puzzling, sadness as a boy. The adult narrator is also able to explore the reasons for the disillusion which the young boy could not have understood so clearly. Each step of the growing infatuation with Mangan's sister is described in detail and accompanied by intensely romantic imagery. Although readers, and the older narrator, see Mangan's sister as quite an ordinary girl, the young narrator makes her into a goddess or an exotic princess. His disillusionment with the bazaar, which she believes—and has led him to believe—will be wonderful, signals his disillusionment with Mangan's sister and with the idyllic possibilities she represents for him.

Possible Responses to Questions (pp. 69–70)

1. The boy sees himself as a hero—perhaps a knight—on a religious quest. Mangan's sister represents a goddess or perhaps, in Christian terms, an angel. The boy sees himself as an instrument commonly associated with heavenly music and responds to every action of Mangan's sister as though she were the angel whom he can serve.

2. The conversation is trivial and silly. It represents the same sort of unimportant bickering the boy might hear every day on his way to school. He is deeply disappointed that a place he believed to be magical and even holy should prove to be so much like his everyday world, which he views as dark and sordid—filled with "drunken men and bargaining women."

3. The dead-end street is "blind" because while it seems to go somewhere, it in fact leads the traveler to an unproductive route. The boy finds himself having followed a path that he thought would lead to something wonderful, but instead he too ends up at an unproductive final setting. His eyes burn with anguish because he realizes that he was seeing falsely. What he thought he saw (a romantic goal to end a romantic quest) was not what he now realizes to be true. When he sees the reality of the bazaar, the truth blazes brightly but horribly before him. His eyes are now momentarily blinded by the truth; he must adjust to this new, harsh light and recognize that he has been fooling himself by seeing the world falsely in the soft glow of romantic vision.

Additional Topics for Writing and Discussion

1. Find examples of the boy's romantic view of the commonplace. Analyze and explain how Joyce's style suggests this view.

   [In addition to the fifth paragraph, which has already been discussed, see the final three paragraphs on p. 69, and the paragraph in the middle of p. 68, which begins "When I came home to dinner. . . ."]

2. In the first long paragraph on p. 67, the narrator describes his method to "annihilate the tedious intervening days." Most of us have tactics for getting through boring experiences as we wait for something more exciting to happen. Describe boredom-relieving tactics you have applied to a specific situation.

3. Examine carefully the words Joyce uses to describe a minor character in the story—for example, Mrs. Mercer, the aunt, or the uncle. How do the connotations of these words suggest the narrator's attitude toward them?

   [Mrs. Mercer: "garrulous woman," "collected used stamps for some pious purpose." The narrator clearly finds this woman to be a bore and a hypocrite; "garrulous" implies talking far too much, and "pious," used in connection with stamp collecting, implies that Mrs. Mercer carries her holy obligations to a ridiculous length. Similar evaluations can be made of the other characters.]

4. Consider the descriptions of Mangan's sister. How do we know that the adult narrator has a different view of her than the boy whose feelings he is describing?

   [A particularly useful passage to examine is the dialogue beginning at the bottom of p. 67 and continuing on to p. 68. The boy clearly sees Mangan's sister's conversation with him as far more romantic and exotic that it really is. The adult narrator shows us a conventional schoolgirl, passing the time with a very ordinary question, followed by a very ordinary expression of disappointment.]

5. Both Joyce (in "Araby") and Mason (in "Shiloh") make setting an important part of their stories. Compare the way these writers use setting, paying special attention to their choice of words, their use of figurative language, and their sentence structure.

THEME

Students often find it difficult to distinguish between subject and theme; you may help them to see the difference by comparing it to the distinction between subject and thesis in their own essays. For instance, they may decide on or be assigned a subject, but that is only the beginning of the planning process. They must then decide what they are going to say about that subject, and they must next formulate a tentative thesis. While writing and revising, they must make sure that each part of their essay—language, structure, point of view, etc.—supports and relates to their thesis. If they discover that they cannot support their thesis, they must revise it; their eventual goal is to produce a coherent piece of writing in which the parts work together to demonstrate the main idea. Of course, there are differences between writing to support a thesis and writing to reveal a theme. For example, fiction writers usually do not state their thesis. In spite of the differences between thesis and theme, the connections that can be made are often helpful to students as they come to understand their own reading and writing processes.

A Worn Path • Eudora Welty (pp. 71–76)

Encourage students to discover the legend of the Phoenix before they read this story. This miraculous bird, believed by ancient Egyptians to embody the sun god, was fabled to live for 500 years and then, after consuming itself in fire, rise newly regenerated from its own ashes. Often seen as a symbol of immortality, the Phoenix offers suggestive possibilities about Welty's character who bears its name.

For students who complain that literature is too sad and looks too much at the dark side of life, this story provides a fine antidote. Phoenix Jackson is a wonderful heroine whose shrewdness, humor, self-knowledge, and imagination affirm what is best in humanity.

Possible Responses to Questions (p. 76)

1. The challenging, difficult path Phoenix travels so many times to get the medicine symbolizes the pitfalls she faces when she wants to get anything from the white world. This path is traveled not only by Phoenix Jackson but by many like her who have learned how to protect themselves from bigotry and hardship, yet also know how to get what they need for survival—most particularly for the survival of their children who suggest hope for the future.

2. Responses will vary. You might encourage students to discuss their view of the story's theme in small groups and to develop a dialogue suggesting their interpretation to share with the class. As possibilities, mention that dialogues might take place between two of the people Phoenix meets or between any character and someone who does not appear in the story. Consider also a dialogue between Phoenix and a friend to whom she tells the story of her quest.

Additional Topics for Writing and Discussion

1. Describe the way Phoenix Jackson faces the first part of her journey—until the track goes into the road. What does your description tell you about Phoenix?

   [Phoenix faces the trail through the woods with courage, humor, and determination. She talks constantly to the animals and plants, fully respecting their right to be there, but also intent on making her own way. "Thorns," she says, "you doing your appointed work. Never want to let folks pass, no sir." And she tells the alligators, "Sleep on . . . and blow your bubbles." She sees the log laid across the creek as a challenge, and when she crosses successfully, takes time out to congratulate herself. We recognize her sense of humor when she worries about getting caught in the barbed-wire fence because "she could not pay for having her arm or her leg sawed off if she got caught fast where she was."]

2. Carefully evaluate the episode with the hunter as Phoenix Jackson leaves the woods. What do we learn about both characters?

   [Phoenix is knocked over by the black dog, but rather than being angry at him, she regards him as another natural obstacle to be overcome. The dog has his rights, she has hers. On the other hand, the white hunter—whose dog is chained, not free—immediately takes control and starts trying to run things. He patronizes Phoenix, then menaces her, asking if she isn't afraid of his gun. When she replies she's seen plenty of guns go off and is not afraid, he condescendingly praises her. The episode ends with the white man telling a mean and petty lie. He says he'd give her a dime, but he has no money. But a few minutes earlier, Phoenix has pocketed a nickel that the man accidentally dropped. She worries about the morality of stealing the nickel: "God watching me the whole time. I come to stealing." Nevertheless, she has learned to survive by watching white people carefully, appearing to follow their rules, taking her opportunities when she can, and maintaining a quiet dignity.

22

3. Discuss the significance of the big black dog.

[Phoenix admires the big black dog and may, in some ways, identify with him. She says, "He ain't scared of nobody. He a big black dog." Then she quietly sics him on the white man's trained hunter. Later the hunter echoes her description of the black dog when he tells Phoenix, "You must be a hundred years old, and scared of nothing.]

4. How is Phoenix treated by the people in Natchez? How does she respond?

[When she first arrives in Natchez, Phoenix prepares herself for her encounter with hospital personnel: She asks a young woman to help her lace up her shoes. "See my shoe. . . . Do all right for out in the country, but wouldn't look right to go in a big building." The woman helps her, and she moves on into the hospital, where the staff is helpful but impatient and unconcerned about Phoenix's feelings. One nurse says, "Tell us quickly about your grandson, and get it over. He isn't dead, is he?" Phoenix receives the medicine she seeks, but it is given grudgingly. Through all of this, Phoenix never loses her dignity; she sits "silent, erect and motionless, just as if she were in armor."]

5. How is the ending related to the rest of the story? Consider the action, the setting, and any possible irony.

[The ending episode reflects the earlier scene with the hunter. Here Phoenix must bargain with an attendant to get a nickel instead of a few pennies. We see the smallness of the attendant and the irony of her action. She says she wants to give Phoenix "a few pennies" because it is Christmas. At a time when the city is overflowing with expensive decorations and package-laden shoppers, the attendant thinks herself generous to offer an old black woman a pitiful few cents. Phoenix, however, once again shows herself able to cope. When she has her begged nickel from the attendant, she puts it together with the nickel the sportsman dropped and declares her intention of buying her grandson a paper windmill. Her generosity and determination cheer the heart, and the image she creates of herself marching "back where he waiting, holding [the windmill] straight up in this hand" is a picture few readers will forget.]

IRONY AND SYMBOL

Irony is a topic that requires careful attention. Most students either know or can easily learn the definitions of the various kinds of irony, and they can understand examples of irony which are carefully labeled and explained. Learning how to detect irony on their own, however, is not so simple. You may at this point want to teach Swift's "A Modest Proposal" (pp. 1586–91), doing a close, paragraph-by-paragraph reading to show students how to pick up the clues indicating that a writer is being ironic. (For suggestions, see the discussion of "A Modest Proposal" in this manual on pp. 265–66.) In addition, you might bring to class—or invite students to bring to class—examples of verbal and visual irony. They may also enjoy giving examples of irony they have seen on television programs or in films. Becoming sensitive to irony is a gradual process and one that seems to need much cautious encouragement. No one likes to feel that he or she did not "get the joke," so you may want to avoid a guessing-game approach and concentrate instead on group analysis where students freely offer their interpretations of cartoons, articles, books, etc.

Just as students have problems identifying irony, they also have trouble controlling irony in their own writing. Often the irony will be too heavy-handed, or, conversely, not clearly enough defined. As students read experienced writers who use irony, they should take note of those techniques that will help them should they choose to use this device in their own writing.

Inexperienced readers often have one of two problems with symbolism. Either they freeze at the thought of "hidden meanings" that lurk between the lines of the story to trip them up, or they become overly enthusiastic and see a symbol in every innocent piece of furniture or casually described animal. Helping students to follow the guideline questions on text page 265 should get them on the right track.

"The Black Cat" • *Edgar Allan Poe (pp. 80–85)*

This classic tale of horror and ironic retribution serves as a fine means for discussing Poe and introducing his theories about short fiction. Students may already know that Poe is regarded by many scholars as the father of the American short story and was the first to define the short story as a separate literary genre. As a literary form, the short story is still in its infancy— compared to the drama or the poem, for instance—yet students will notice dramatic changes in the genre since Poe first pronounced that the tale must have "unity of effect and impression." He went on to say that a "wise" literary artist does "not fashion his thoughts to accommodate his incidents; but having conceived, with deliberate care, a certain unique or single *effect* to be wrought out, he then invents such incidents—he then combines such events as may best aid him in establishing this preconceived effect."

Possible Responses to Questions (p. 86)

1. The central irony of the story concerns the relationship between the narrator and the black cat. The narrator desires pets because he craves the affection and happiness domestic animals afforded him when he was a child. The black cat offers him the "unselfish and self-sacrificing love" he desires, yet he is unable to accept that love. The narrator, who is in the grip of alcoholism, must destroy whatever gives him joy and pleasure. Thus that which he most desires leads him to hatred, misery, and ultimately death.

2. The story is filled with ironies. The first cat is named Pluto, an allusion to the Greek god of the dead. The name is particularly fitting, since the narrator tries to kill "death," yet is, in the end, brought to his own death by the second black cat, who represents a reincarnation of the first. An example of verbal irony occurs when the narrator's wife comments that black cats are witches in disguise. The narrator notes that this observation was not intended seriously, yet it is clear that he regards the animal with suspicion. The narrator also calls on God and describes himself as being fashioned by the "High God" when he compares himself to the cat, yet it is he who behaves as a savage beast, both to his pets and to his wife.

Additional Topics for Writing and Discussion

1. At the end of the story, the narrator blames the cat both for seducing him into murder and for consigning him "to the hangman." To what extent do you think the cat is to blame for any of the events in the story? What motives do you ascribe to the narrator? Why does he act the way he does?

[The cat serves as a symbolic alter ego to the narrator. Pluto was the speaker's original pet, a cat that was extremely attentive to his master. Pluto follows his master everywhere and their "friendship [lasts] . . . for several years." Then the speaker describes changes that begin to happen, both to himself and to the cat. The narrator's "general temperament and character . . . [experience] a radical alteration for the worse." Because he falls into the grip of "the Fiend Intemperance," he becomes "more moody, more irritable, more regardless of the feelings of others." In like manner, Pluto is "becoming old , and consequently somewhat peevish." The speaker's abuse of alcohol and the cat's increasingly quick temper are certainly parallel.

When the speaker first injures the cat, he says, "The fury of a demon instantly possessed me." And we cannot help but remember that earlier in the story the wife had suggested that "all black cats [are] witches in disguise." But because the cat itself is never seen doing anything demonic and the man is presented as a consistently unsympathetic character, we cannot read this as a horror tale in which the mind of an innocent man is slowly possessed by a demonic cat.

To the extent that the cat and the narrator are one, the cat might be seen as the demonic part of the man. but if we see the cat as actually separate from his master, we can hardly blame the murder in any way on the animal. The man becomes increasingly irrational, violent, and paranoid—presumably initially as a result of his alcoholism. His problems cause him to project meaning and causes on random, accidental circumstances. His house burns down and he projects (although he denies that he sees a cause-and-effect chain) that the conflagration has happened as punishment for his cruelty in hanging the cat.

As for the narrator's motives, it is never very clear that he has any. By the end of the story, he is more fully identified with the black cat than ever. He says, "And now was I indeed wretched beyond the wretchedness of mere Humanity. And a *brute beast*. . . ." His desire to destroy what he believes to be the reincarnated Pluto leads him to kill his wife while she is trying to protect the animal. He kills like a fiend who is completely amoral; and, while he attempts to blame his actions on alcohol, we have the feeling that he is controlled by a demon far more powerful than rum. The narrator is quite mad.]

2. At the end of the story, the narrator says that the murder of his wife "disturbed [him] but little." He further contends that he feels no embarrassment when the police search the house and he begins his final speech to them simply "to render doubly sure their assurance of my guiltlessness." Do you find this explanation of the speaker's words and actions convincing? Explain your answer.

[It is certainly possible that the speaker acts and speaks as he does because he is incredibly arrogant and self-confident. Yet why would he feel such a need to convince the police of his innocence when they have already started to leave? Perhaps a part of the human being remains, after all, and that small portion of decency is trying desperately to be assured that a horrible crime has not been committed. The man seems to be trying to convince himself as much as the police that nothing suspicious lurks behind his cellar walls. He is betrayed, of course, by the cat he has sought to destroy—and whom he calls "the Arch-Fiend." In one of the story's greatest ironies, he will now pay the penalty of hanging on the gallows as he once hanged the cat. Although he rails at the animal, we have a sense that the story has come to the only possible conclusion. The narrator's final ranting seems a frantic attempt to keep the officials in the cellar rather than allow them to leave. At the end, we could argue, he wants to be caught—perhaps to be brought to justice or perhaps to gain notoriety and recognition for his actions.]

3. In his definition of the short story, Poe said the author should have in mind a "preconceived effect." Does the story have such an effect which all the incidents contrive to support and reveal? If there is a preconceived effect, what is it, and when do we know for certain what it is?

[A likely *effect* for this terrifying tale is "the spirit of PERVERSENESS." Poe literally "spells out" this effect in the ninth paragraph and goes on to suggest the theme related to the effect. "Yet I am not more sure that my soul lives, than I am that perverseness is one of the primitive impulses of the human heart—one of the indivisible primary faculties or sentiments, which give direction to the character of Man." The events of the story certainly confirm that the main character is perverse, and his ironic fate suggests that life itself can extract retribution in terrible and perverse ways. Few readers will be willing to agree that they are in any way close to the narrator's perverseness, yet the question he asks as he unfolds his tale makes us all examine our own hearts and consciences at the very moment we are condemning his. "Who has not," the narrator demands, "a hundred times, found himself committing a vile or stupid action, for no other reason than because he knows he should *not*?"]

4. Do you feel sympathy for Pluto (and the black cat who takes his place)? Or do Poe's descriptions make the animal seem strange, threatening, and frightening? Find specific images and descriptions to explain your response.

5. Compare the narrators in Gilman's "The Yellow Wallpaper" (pp. 152–163) and "The Black Cat."

CHAPTER FOUR

Approaching a Story: Guides for Reading and Writing

This chapter summarizes the approaches to reading fiction which are explained in detail in earlier chapters. You may want to work through each step with your class, asking them to respond either in writing or through discussion to Luigi Pirandello's "War," before they read the commentary that follows the story.

You might remind students that these guidelines may be applied not only to the selections in the anthology section but also to any other fiction they may read. In addition, students may profitably use these guidelines to become more conscious of the various elements of their own writing as they become more knowledgeable about, and familiar with, the works of professional authors.

"War" • Luigi Pirandello (pp. 88–2)

The extended discussion following "War" (pp. 93–95) suggests several possible ways to approach the story. The topics below offer additional options.

Additional Topics for Writing and Discussion

1. Describe the setting of the story. Does it seem particularly appropriate to the characters, plot, and theme? Explain.

   [The opening paragraphs set the scene: a "stuffy and smoky second-class" train compartment in which "five people had already spent the night." We can imagine the exhaustion, weariness, and tension in that car, and the conflicts in the dialogue that follows are thus emphasized. The exchange of opposing views would not be the same if it took place in the clean sunny kitchen of one of the characters, or on a bright Sunday morning during a beach picnic. We get the sense of these characters being bound by the same circumstances quite randomly and without reason, being carried by the same power toward their destinations in life, just as they are bound together in the railroad car and carried to their destinations by the unseen engine and engineer.]

2. Choose one of the major characters and decide whether he or she is a dynamic or a static character. Explain your reasons, and if the character you chose is a dynamic character, discuss whether or not you find the change believable.

   [The grieving mother and the father who explains how he has dealt with his own loss and both major characters. Both are dynamic, and while we are more fully prepared for the change in the mother, the father's change is also believable. Since we have heard tremendous outpourings of grief, the father's philosophical approach doesn't quite ring true. When he is actually confronted with the loss—when the mother asks, "Then . . . is your son really dead?" (p. 90)—we can easily believe his stunned and grieving reaction. As noted in the commentary on the story, either character may revert to his or her earlier view, but certainly each has been profoundly affected and cannot return in the same innocent and unexamined way to their previous states of mind.]

3. Do you find any irony in the story? Explain how any examples relate to theme.

   [It is ironic that the philosophical father, after comforting the grieving mother and converting her to his point of view, suddenly finds himself experiencing the very feelings he has been arguing against.]

4. After you have read the commentary following "War" (pp. 93–95), choose any statement or idea that you question or disagree with. Or choose a statement that made you think differently about the story than you did when you first read it. Using details from the story to support your ideas, explain your question, disagreement, or change of mind.

28

CHAPTER FIVE

Topics for Writing and Discussion for A Collection of Short Fiction

"Young Goodman Brown" • *Nathaniel Hawthorne (pp. 96–104)*

1. The narrative of "Young Goodman Brown" divides into five parts. Define these five sections and explain what each contributes to the story.

[In the introductory section, we meet the main characters, young Goodman Brown and his wife Faith. In addition, the scene is set (colonial Salem), and we learn that the young husband feels compelled to embark on a hazardous and evil journey although his wife begs him to stay with her. The second part of the narrative introduces complication into the story. For example, Goodman Brown meets Goody Cloyse as he walks through the dark forest with the devil and then spies on the deacon and the minister. Next, as Goodman Brown looks up toward heaven, he sees pink ribbons (like those Faith wore in the first section) and hears unearthly cries. At this moment, we are taken into the climactic section of the story. Realizing that Faith has come to the forest, young Goodman Brown hurries to the witches' sabbath, where he stands beside his wife and pleads with her to resist the evil that surrounds them both. In the fourth section, Goodman Brown finds himself alone in the forest, not knowing whether his wife has obeyed his command. The story moves toward its resolution as he returns to the village and sees the "virtuous" townspeople of the dark sabbath once again in their familiar places. In the final, concluding section (the ending paragraph) we are not given an answer to Goodman Brown's quandary, but rather are told that his life was irrevocably changed by what happened that night, be it dream or reality.]

2. At what point did you realize that you were reading an allegory rather than a realistic story?

[The opening scene seems realistic enough, with its domestic details and Faith's gentle words. Anyone who knows the distance between Salem and Boston would certainly recognize the occult nature of the traveler who joins Goodman Brown when the strange companion mentions that he was in Boston fifteen minutes earlier. Even with today's means of travel it would be impossible to make the trip in that short time; only a supernatural figure could accomplish this feat. For those who do not know the distance, the suspicion should certainly come when the elder traveler begins to list the many people he has helped and to describe the evil ends he served. If any doubts remain, when Goody Cloyse acknowledges the traveler as "the devil," every reader should know the story is not realistic. Not all occult fiction, however, is allegorical. Recognizing the allegory comes from seeing that Faith's name is representative rather than individual. She is not merely a specific young wife, but rather a figure who represents purity, innocence, and belief in God; in like manner, of course, the devil represents evil (particularly sexual evil), while members of the community stand for various sins—they are hypocrites, gluttons, murderers, and blasphemers.]

3. Identify some of the story's ironies.

[When the devil says he would not wish "that Faith should come to any harm," he may seem to be simply lying. In fact, there is a greater irony. If Faith were to die entirely, the devil would lose much of his power, for he would no longer have any good to win over to his side. Ironies abound, of course, in the ranks of highly respected townspeople who attend the evil ceremony. When Goodman Brown sees Goody Cloyse, he exclaims, "That old woman taught me my catechism!" And the narrator tells us that "there was a world of meaning in this simple comment." The irony here is that Goodman Brown has not learned the traditional catechism, but he certainly has followed the deepest beliefs of his teacher. She has, in fact, through her hypocrisy, helped to bring him to the deep forest.]

4. How would you state the theme of the story? Consider what happens to Goodman Brown and why it happens as you consider this question.

[It's very easy to say that Goodman Brown loses his faith because he envisions (or perhaps really sees) his wife Faith consorting with the devil. But the story seems more complex than that. Why does Goodman Brown expect that his Faith will never be tempted even though he himself is tempted? He idealizes Faith in an unrealistic way, imagining her to be perfectly pure, innocent, and untried. Once he believes that she too might find the path to salvation stony and difficult, he becomes disenchanted and depressed. In the beginning of the story, Goodman Brown sets out, knowing he is looking for evil, yet promises that after this one night he will return to Faith and all will be well. He sounds like so many "sinners" who always look outside themselves (rather than within) for salvation. When he sees that even the greatest good (Faith) may sometimes come into and be tempted by the presence of evil, he chooses to give up and to lead a life devoid of the struggle toward belief and salvation. His unengraved tombstone symbolizes his empty earthly existence as well as the void he faces in death.]

5. Suggest the significance of setting in "Young Goodman Brown."

[The story has at least two settings: the "frame" setting of the realistic Salem village that opens and closes the tale and the surrealistic dark and twisted forest that serves as the background for the story's central action. The setting, of course, reflects the internal land-scape of the main character's mind. When young Goodman Brown is at home he sees things in a very different way than he does when he is in the deep woods with their flickering firelight and strangely perverted voices. The inner setting of the story and the inner part of Goodman Brown are both troubled, complex, and alienated.]

6. Read the footnotes to the story carefully. How does understanding the historical background affect your reading? Hawthorne lived and wrote in the nineteenth century, almost two hundred years after the setting of his story. How do you think readers of his century would differ in their response from the response today's readers might have?

7. Why do you think Hawthorne chooses to tell this story through the eyes of a third-person narrator? How would it be changed if it were a first-person narrative, told through the eyes of the title character?

8. What institutions and types of individuals does Hawthorne criticize in this story? What complaints does he have about these institutions and types? In what ways might his criticisms still apply?

"The Death of Iván Ilych" • Leo Nikolaievich Tolstoy (pp. 105–140)

1. What do the reactions of Iván Ilych's friends and family reveal about them? What comic elements appear in the first section? Would it make much difference if this section were placed last rather than first?

   [Iván Ilych's friends and family—with the exception of his schoolboy son—are far more concerned with themselves than with the dead man. Iván Ilych's wife is worried about how she can get more pension money from the government; Peter Ivánovich is worried about getting to his bridge game; his colleagues are worried about how they can use the appointment opened by Iván Ilych's death to further their own careers or those of relatives. The comic elements in the first section include the false grieving, the stereotyped comments of the mourners, and the widow's insistence that her own sufferings were far worse than the suffering of the dead man. If this section appeared last, the reader would not have nearly as much interest in learning about the story's main character; a funeral so devoid of real mourning is certain to pique nearly everyone's interest.]

2. Characterize Iván Ilych. What is the significance of his having been a middle son and a middling student?

   [Iván Ilych is an average, conforming man who tries desperately to live his life as an acceptable cliché—to walk the middle of the road, to straddle the fence. He does not excel in anything, but neither is he at the end of the line; he is squarely in the middle.]

3. Describe Iván Ilych's relationship with his wife. Why did they marry? How do they view each other? What keeps them together?

   [Iván Ilych's motives for marrying are described in the middle of p. 113. It is no wonder that he lost interest in his wife after she became pregnant and no longer made his life "easy, agreeable, gay, and . . . decorous." Each seems to view the other as a social necessity, and of course, for Praskóvya Fëdorovna, her husband is also an economic necessity. They apparently stay together because that is the easiest course and the course most acceptable to society.]

4. Explain Iván Ilych's attitude toward his work. What value does he attach to it? How are his work and his attitude toward it related to his attitude toward his family? What are his greatest pleasures in life?

   [The last part of Section 2 describes in detail Iván Ilych's growing alienation from his wife and children and his growing absorption with his career. His greatest pleasures in life are acquiring material possessions, playing cards with his cronies, and his work, including having power to "ruin anybody he wish[es] to ruin" (p. 114).]

5. Explain the connection between Iván Ilych's behavior and attitude at court and the doctor's attitude and behavior toward him. Explain the connection between Iván Ilych's attitude toward his wife and family and his wife's attitude toward his illness.

   [The doctor holds power over Iván Ilych just as he—as a judge—held power over the lives of the criminals who appeared before him. Iván Ilych comes to realize what the powerless feel like; he hates the doctor's half-truths and patronizing attitude. Iván Ilych has expected his family to be no trouble to him, to provide him only with pleasant moments. When he becomes ill, his family responds in kind. They do not like being disturbed by his demands or having to deal with the pain and ugliness of his illness.]

6. Explain Gerásim's function in the story. Contrast him with one or two other characters.

[Gerásim is a simple peasant who, in contrast to nearly every other character in the story, has no pretensions. He is able to give Iván Ilych comfort because, unlike the other characters, he sees death as a natural part of life. He is not afraid of death, and so is not uncomfortable being around Iván Ilych. Gerásim sees Iván Ilych's illness as part of the normal process of dying. He is able to respond to Iván Ilych's demands and to give him comfort because Gerásim realizes he does not have to—and cannot—cure Iván Ilych; instead Gerásim recognizes his ability to help Iván Ilych through his final illness. The servant eases his master's pain both physically and spiritually simply by being with him, listening, and responding to what he says.]

7. Why does Iván Ilych have difficulty accepting the implications of the following syllogism: "Caius is a man, men are mortal, therefore Caius is mortal"? How do details such as the smell of the striped leather ball he played with as a child qualify the idea of the syllogism?

[Like most people, Iván Ilych knows intellectually that all humans die. Emotionally, however, he cannot accept his own mortality. He clings desperately to his memories and the details of his surroundings, irrationally hoping that the unique aspects of his life will somehow grant him a dispensation from the fate of generalized and undistinguished humankind.]

8. Why does Iván Ilych resist seeing the truth about himself and his life? Why does it take him so long to face the truth? What does he finally come to realize about how he has lived his life?

[Iván Ilych resists seeing the truth because it is so painful. When he realizes he has led an empty life based on shallow values, he is terrified. He knows that he faces death leaving nothing of importance behind him. Section 11 details his realization and response.]

9. How does Tolstoy convey the sense of the horror of death? How does he counter that view with a vision of death as a triumph rather than a defeat?

[The horror of death is graphically presented in Section 12 as Iván Ilych lives through his final hours of pain. Yet at the end he sees death not as darkness, but as light. He has been fearing and resisting death, but at the end, death (in the sense of earthly fear) has vanished. "Death is finished," Iván Ilych says. "It is no more!" In its place is joy.]

10. Explain the function of Iván Ilych's son and daughter. What does each contribute to the story?

[The daughter, unable to forget the years Iván Ilych neglected his family, remains separated from her father. Iván Ilych's son, however, in the final moments of his father's life, comes to him and offers him love. When his son catches Iván Ilych's hand and kisses it, Iván Ilych feels as though he has "seen the light." He realizes that although he has not led his life as he should, he can still redeem himself by confessing—not to a priest, but to those who have been most injured, his family.]

11. What, finally, is our attitude toward Iván Ilych? Do our feelings about him change in the course of reading the work? Why or why not?

12. Has Tolstoy adequately prepared us for Iván Ilych's change at the end of the story? Is the ending of the story believable? Why or why not? What really happens at the end?

13. Elizabeth Kübler-Ross, a prominent psychologist and expert of death and dying, has suggested that people go through a series of identifiable stages when confronted with the fact of their own imminent death. These stages include denial, anger, depression, bargaining, and acceptance. How useful are these for understanding Iván Ilych's reactions?

14. In rewriting this short novel as a short story of perhaps ten to fifteen pages, what would you focus on? What would you omit?

"The Storm • Kate Chopin (pp. 141-144)

1. What is the significance of the title? What evidence do you find within the story to support your view?

   [The storm is both the actual rain-and-thunder event which provided the impetus for Alcée and Calixta to make love and the symbolic disturbance in the two marriages suggested by the final line of the story. In addition, the storm could refer to the storm of passion which Alcée and Calixta experience but which (the ending of the story implies) will end with no hard feelings and with no one being hurt.]

2. What does the language of the story suggest the author's attitude is toward the characters and their actions?

   [The language is sensual and joyous. For example, Calixta's flesh is described as being like "a creamy lily that the sun invites to contribute its breath and perfume to the undying life of the world," and her passion is described as "generous" and "without guile or trickery" (p. 143). The author presents this lovemaking in a sympathetic and good-humored way. Even today, such a lighthearted approach to sexuality is unusual; at the time Chopin was writing, it was almost unheard of, particularly in the work of a woman.]

3. What purpose do the opening section and the ending three sections serve? What would be lost if we were given only Section 2 along with a brief sentence letting us know that the two main characters were both married to other people?

   [The first section shows us Bobinôt and Bibi as caring and concerned husband and son. Bobinôt even buys a special present for Calixta. We therefore see Calixta's actions in Section 2 not as rebellion against a harsh husband or as despair over a difficult child, but rather as a separate choice having to do only with herself and Alcée. The final three sections suggest that Calixta will be able to continue being a good wife to Bobinôt and a good mother to Bibi, and that she and Alcée will be able to continue being lovers while his wife is away.]

4. What single element seems to be missing from Calixta's and Alcèe's marriages?

   [Sexual satisfaction and compatibility. Near the end of p. 143 we learn that Calixta's flesh knows "for the first time its birthright," and the ending of the story (p. 144) indicates that Clarisse Laballièrê, although devoted to her husband, "was more than willing to forego for a while" their conjugal life.]

5. Compare the marriages in "The Storm" to the marriages of Iván Ilych and Praskóvya Fëdorovna.

6. Write a scene showing the reunion between Alcée and Clarisse when she returns from Biloxi.

7. How do you feel about Alcée and Calixta? Plan an argument either defending them to their accusers or condemning their actions to those who would defend them.

The Man in a Case • Anton Chekhov (pp. 144-152)

1. Read the first eleven paragraphs of the story and list all the sentences or phrases that suggest enclosure or confinement. Then explain how these images reflect the story's theme.

[Sentences and phrases suggesting enclosure or confinement include the following:

Marva "had never been out of her native village"; for ten years "ventur[ed] out only at night." (para 1)

people . . . who are recluses by nature (para 2)

strive, like the hermit crab or the snail, to retreat within their shells (para 2)

never stirring out of his house . . . without an umbrella, galoshes and a padded coat (para 2)

His umbrella he kept in a case, he had a case of grey suede for his watch, and when he took out his pen-knife to sharpen a pencil, he had to draw it out of a case, too. (para 2)

Even his face seemed to have a case of its own, since it was always hidden in his turned-up coat-collar. (para 2)

He wore dark glasses . . . and stopped up his ears with cotton wool. (para 2)

. . . [W]hen he engaged a carriage, he made the driver put up the hood. (para 2)

Even the dead languages he taught were merely galoshes and umbrellas between himself and real life. (para 2)

Belikov tried to keep his thoughts in a case, too. (para 4)

The slightest infringement or deviation from the rules plunged him into dejection, even when it could not possibly concern him. (para 6)

At the meetings of the teachers' council he fairly tormented us with his circumspection and suspicions, his apprehensions and suggests (typical of a mind encased). (para 6)

[H]is home life was . . . the same story: dressing-gown, shutters, bolts and bars, a long list of restrictions and prohibitions. (para 9)

Belikov's tiny bedroom was like a box, and there was a canopy over the bed. (para 11)

Before going to sleep he always drew the bedclothes over his head. (para 11)

Chekhov's narrator piles detail upon detail to depict through comic hyperbole the irritating, yet pathetic, protagonist of his tale. Each image suggest that those who withdraw from the world, either physically or mentally, are to be both scorned and feared. Scorned because they fail to grow or to appreciate the world around them. Feared because their own paranoia and resistance to change often motivates them to be powerfully repressive forces.]

2. What is the effect of the frame-story device? How would the story be changed if we heard only of Belikov and Varya and did not meet Ivan Ivanich or Burkin?

[The high-school teacher who tells Belikov's story and the veterinary surgeon who listens to the story are extremely important. First, we have only Burkin's word for the peculiarities of his teaching colleague. Given Burkin's irritation with Belikov's teaching style, there is certainly the possibility of exaggeration. There are certainly scenes which Burkin could not have witnessed, yet he describes them as though he saw them first-hand.

Also, after Burkin has finished telling the story, Ivan Ivanich does not have quite the reaction Burkin apparently hoped for. Rather than laughing at Belikov or condemning him out of hand, Ivan Ivanich thoughtfully considers the implications of the story. In one of the most important passages of the story, Ivan Ivanich asks the storyteller a pointed question: "And is not our living in towns, in our stuffy, cramped room, writing our useless papers, playing vint, isn't that living in an oyster-shell, too?" Burkin shows that he is in a case of sorts himself when he avoids this query and refuses to consider the deeper implications of the story he has just told. Ivan Ivanich, however, pursues more possibilities, thinking about the shallow quality of human existence. He notes that the average person must "look on and listen to people lying . . . not dare to speak up . . . and all for the crust of bread and a snug corner to live in, for the sake of some miserable rank." He declares life to be "intolerable" and finds himself unable to sleep. Ironically, Burkin who, while telling the story has maintained his own superiority to Belikov, manages to settle down in his own comfortable (perhaps case-like) bed and fall asleep within ten minutes.]

3. How does Belikov's courtship of Varya embody the central conflict of the story?

[Just as Belikov stands for confinement, conservatism, and resistance to change, Varya typifies progress, risk-taking, and an open-mined approach to life. She does not mind singing in public, expresses her feelings with ease, and argues energetically with her brother about literature. Most shocking to Belikov, she rides a bicycle. Perhaps what really troubles Belikov is that Varya touches some desire within him to be more free. As he worries about proposing, he says, "I am somewhat alarmed—[she and her brother], their outlook, you know, is so strange, and then she is so sprightly. Supposing I marry and get mixed up in something. . . ." At the end of Burkin's tale, Belikov is soundly dismissed by Varya's brother, falls down stairs, and lands at the feet of Varya and two other ladies who laugh at him. His reported death in the aftermath of this encounter does not seem a tragedy, perhaps because Belikov in many ways seems already dead.]

4. Prior to the ending of the story, what hints suggest that the narrator is more like Belikov than he might realize?

[Burkin lives in the same house as Belikov, directly across the hall. He admits that they "saw quite a lot of one another" and in many ways he seems almost a double for Belikov. Their names begin with the same letter, they are both teachers, and they both focus on small details. Both men believe themselves to be holders of "truth" that others should live by. For instance, Belikov repeats clichéd mottoes such as "It's a very fine thing, no doubt, but . . . let's hope no evil will come of it." And Burkin is nearly always on the scene to prompt Belikov to go on when he doubts the wisdom of courting Varya. Listening to the exchanges of Belikov and Burkin reminds the reader of listening to an internal dialogue of two parts of one mind arguing with itself. Thinking of Burkin in this way makes the concluding dialogue gain new meaning. Perhaps Belikov represents a side of Burkin's self that he believes he has killed off through telling the story; yet his refusal to face the wider meanings that Ivan Ivanich poses shows that the case has not yet been successfully opened.]

35

5. Describe Kovalenko's view of life. How does he compare with Belikov? Which view comes closer to your own? Explain.

[Like his sister, Kovalenko represents an attitude of freedom and lack of restraint. He is Belikov's antithesis, and during their confrontation he points out in no uncertain terms his disdain for those who "stick their noses into my domestic and family affairs." While most readers will sympathize with Kovalenko's reaction to Belikov's prudery and extreme deference to authority and public opinion, some may note that, while he expects tolerance for himself, he shows little for others. For example he preaches to his colleagues, calling them "a pack of time-servers" and characterizing the school in which they teach as "having a sickly smell about it." He also loses his temper and throws Belikov downstairs, ignoring the possibility of injury.]

6. Write a dialogue between Kovalenko and Varya after their final encounter with Belikov.

7. Compare Chekhov's story with Wendy Wasserstein's play of the same name (text page 1513). (For a possible response, see this manual, pages 232–235).

8. Compare Belikov with Iván Ilych (text page 105). What similarities do you see in the lives? How does you response to their lives—and to their deaths—differ?

"The Yellow Wallpaper" • Charlotte Perkins Gilman (pp. 152–163)

1. Why is it necessary that this story be told from the woman's viewpoint and in the first person? Do we accept all that she says? Some of it? Explain.

[Since the woman is the only person who can see the figure behind the wallpaper, the story must be told from her point of view. Using first person brings the reader closer to the character's experience and allows the author to detail subtle and minor changes in the woman through her changing choice of words and mental images. We believe much of what the woman tells us concerning the way the house—particularly her room—looks.

We also believe some of the information she gives us about other people. We accept that John is a physician, that her brother is a physician, that both men want her to stop writing because they believe the writing is exhausting her. We may question some of her judgments. For example, she describes the room she stays in as a nursery because it has barred windows and "rings and things in the walls" (p. 154). The reader may make quite a different interpretation, seeing the room as one that has been used to house a person or people believed to be insane. In addition, the details at the end of the second section (p. 154) suggest a person who is not fully in touch with reality; the need to see patterns everywhere and the perception of a sinister threat in the lines of the wallpaper indicate that the woman is emotionally unbalanced. On the other hand, by declaring her need for work (p. 157) and recognizing that saying what she truly feels and thinks gives her relief (p. 157), she suggests a far more sensible process to regain mental health than do those who are supposedly trying to help her.]

2. What kind of relationship do the husband and wife have? Is there evidence to suggest that John is concerned about his wife and that he is doing all he can to help her get well? Is there evidence to suggest that he is the cause of her mental problems?

[John seems to be genuinely concerned about his wife, but his motives also tell us a great deal about their relationship. The woman points out that John feels professionally

36

humiliated because she doesn't get well. In addition, John tells her repeatedly that she must get well for his sake (p. 157) and for the sake of their child (p. 158); we are never told that he in any way understands the need to have a self to get well for. While John may not be the entire cause of his wife's problem, he certainly contributes to it. He refuses to let her write; he tells their friends that she could get well if she chose; he refuses to let her visit her cousins whom she longs to see; he leaves her in the company of his sister, whom the woman describes as "a perfect and enthusiastic housekeeper [who] hopes for no better profession" (p. 156).]

3. Many details about the husband characterize him: his name, his profession, his speech. Explain what John is like and why he thinks and acts the way he does.

[The name John is common, ordinary, and undistinguished. The husband in the story lives up to his name; he holds the opinions designated to be correct for his time and his profession (see, for example, his reference to Weir Mitchell's rest cure. There are many explanations for John's behavior, but the most general—and perhaps most fruitful—way to start discussing him would be to look at him as a nearly perfect stereotype of the "good husband" and the "respected physician" of his era. The question then becomes: How much is John to blame, both for his own actions and for his wife's condition, and how much of the problem can be attributed to the societal expectations of the time in which they lived?]

4. How ill is the narrator? How ill does she think she is? How ill does her husband think she is? What do John and her brother think will cure her? What does she think will cure her?

[The narrator has a serious mental illness which gets worse as the story goes on. She recognizes that she is very ill and repeatedly tries to explain her feelings to her husband (see p. 158, for example). John and her brother think complete rest away from other people, plus firm determination of mind, will cure her. The woman believes that "congenial work, with excitement and change" (p. 153) would help her. She especially needs to return to her work of writing and to be able to tell the truth about herself and her feelings. At the end of the story, she seems more and more concerned with the patterns in the wallpaper, with tearing it off, and with freeing the woman she believes to be trapped inside the wallpaper. Certainly these actions can be interpreted as increasingly frantic efforts to let her real self out into the world.]

5. What kind of room is the narrator in? What kind of room does she think she's in? How does she account for the bars on the windows and the "rings and things" on the walls? How do you account for them?

[See the response to question 1. In addition, note that the bed is permanently attached to the floor and that the bedposts have been gnawed. At the top of p. 162, the woman attributes the teeth marks to the children she imagines to have lived there, but only a few lines later she acknowledges that she herself has taken a bite out of the bedstead.]

6. Of what significance are the outcroppings of violence in the narrator's language, especially in her descriptions of the wallpaper? What does the wallpaper symbolize? Who is the lady behind the wallpaper?

[The wallpaper suggests the patterns of the woman's life, patterns that make no sense to her, that seem to go nowhere or create no beauty. The lady behind the paper is the woman herself, or perhaps her spirit. Her violent language indicates how angry she is at the confines of her life.]

7. Trace all the references to writing, imagination, fancy, and fantasy through the story. How do these references help you understand the difference between husband and wife? Compare this contrast of imaginative capacities with the contrasting imaginative abilities of the husbands and wives in "The Story of an Hour" and "Astronomer's Wife." Or you might compare the implications of the endings of the three stories—or their different tones and methods.

8. Research Weir Mitchell's methods of treating hysterical women, or read selected chapters of Phyllis Chesler's *Women and Madness*. How do these readings affect your response to the woman in "The Yellow Wallpaper"?

"The Open Boat" • Stephen Crane (pp. 163–179)

1. How are the sections in the story related? What does each contribute?

[Section 1: The opening section establishes the situation—four men are stranded in a small dinghy. They are distinguished primarily by their professions—"the oiler," "the captain," "the cook," and "the correspondent." The dramatic setting of the dangerous sea is established, and the men argue pointlessly about whether or not a house of refuge has a crew and whether or not a lifesaving station is nearby.

Section 2: As the men continue their battle against the elements, their dependence on one another becomes evident. The captain is injured, yet he has the knowledge and the authority to comfort and encourage the men. The oiler and the correspondent steadily cooperate on the rowing, while the "cheerful cook" follows orders to bail. Instead of arguing, they all strive to see the tiny point the captain indicates as the lighthouse and maintain their cautious optimism that they will make it to land.

Section 3: The first sentence affirms the theme that is built throughout the second section, "It would be difficult to describe the subtle brotherhood of men that was here established on the seas." The connection among the men and their ability to maintain humor and an ironic perspective build our sympathy and admiration for them as they sight land and begin to head for shore.

Section 4: The tension mounts as the men try to row to shore but are forced back by the raging surf. The men talk more, agonizing over whether or not they have been seen and then whether or not those on shore will come to rescue them. In the mind of each man, a sharp, poignant dialogue with fate questions why they have been allowed to come so close to land yet have been kept from salvation. The section ends with a surprising question as the cook asks the oiler what kind of pie he likes.

Section 5: The oiler and correspondent respond with agitation to the cook's question, providing a link between the two sections and suggesting how for these men time progresses seamlessly, with day and night melding into each other as easily as question and response. The men relieve each other willingly, cling together in sleep, and offer what comfort they can to each other as they continue to row. While the others are asleep the correspondent spots the fin of a shark cutting through the water, and this visible sign of death makes him long for the comfort of conscious human companionship. The sense of isolation and despair is acute.

Section 6: The men no longer speak except when absolutely necessary; exhaustion, despair, and cold have overtaken them. They sleep intermittently while the man tending the oars continues to be haunted by a shark circling around the boat. Still, occasionally a bit of the old spirit surfaces as they comment on their hatred of rowing and contemplate what they will do if anyone shows them an oar, or even a picture of an oar, should they make it safely to share.

Section 7: The men continue to row the dinghy and finally decide to head for shore, knowing that they will capsize. When the boat overturns, the men swim, and all reach the sandy beach safely except for the oiler, who is drowned. The final paragraphs are written from the correspondent's point of view, reflecting on the ironies of the tragedy and on the terrifying initiation to the power of the sea experienced by the survivors.]

2. Notice the use of figurative language in "The Open Boat." Cite several examples you find particularly effective, and analyze what they contribute to the story.

[The description of natural elements dominates Crane's story. The powerful opening line suggests how drawn the men are to the sea, and in the sentences that follow the ocean takes on multiple colors, with its waves depicted as sharp, threatening, and destructive. At the beginning of the second part, once again the language emphasizes the power of the sea, with its hill-like waves. A memorable sentence suggests the beauty that those who were not trapped by the ocean might find: "[The scene] was probably splendid. It was probably glorious, this play of the free sea, wild with lights of emerald and white and amber." With the repetition of "probably," Crane emphasizes that any beauty is hidden from the men in the boat, to whom the ocean represents the horror of danger and possible death. Note also the striking description in Section 1 where the boat becomes a bucking bronco and the men desperate rodeo riders.]

3. What is the significance of the poem about the soldier of the Legion (Section 6)? What does this section of the story suggest about the point of view?

[In this section we see very clearly that the correspondent's point of view dominates. Although we are sometimes told what the other men are thinking by the omniscient narrator, we are most often in the correspondent's mind. Here he imagines a nearly forgotten classroom scene from his childhood. He and his schoolmates had memorized lines about a soldier who was dying far from familiar circumstances. As a boy, he was unmoved and thought of the poem merely as an assignment; now he feels deeply the poet's words. (The correspondent's experience provides a perfect opportunity to discuss how we read texts differently at different times in our lives. Most of us will not, of course, lie "dying in Algiers" or be in a shipwreck, yet as we grow older, our ability to empathize with and take comfort from literary experience almost always increases.)]

4. What is the role of fate in this story? How does it relate to the story's theme(s)?

[Fate is pictured as an "old ninnywoman" who acts randomly, without either rancor or pity. She serves the "seven mad gods who rule the seas"; these "gods" apparently use their powers to torment their victims, allowing them to come close to shore only to drag them away to sea again at the moment rescue seems imminent. Through the story, neither fate nor nature shows any response at all toward the men. The only force they can count on comes from the bond that grows between them. In the face of an indifferent universe, strength comes only through human connection, the unity that Crane calls "the subtle brotherhood of men that was established here."]

5. What examples of irony do you find in "The Open Boat"?

[Irony abounds. The language of the narrator is extremely witty and ironic even in the face of destruction. For instance, he envisions the men thinking, "Was I brought here merely to have my nose dragged away as I was about to nibble the sacred cheese of life?" as they watch the shore vanish from sight. The men, then, become trapped rats or helpless mice, teased by the catlike fate. A comic image for a potentially tragic event creates an ironic tone. The initial sighting of land with the man who runs waving down the beach also becomes ironic when the men realize that he thinks they are simply on a lark and calls other vacationers to watch as the dinghy's crew curse and fume. The final irony is that the oiler, the strongest of all the men, is the only one not to survive, while the correspondent (an inexperienced sailor), the injured captain, and the hefty cook (who floats on a piece of life preserver) all reach shore safely.]

6. Identify examples of repetition. What purpose does the repetition serve?

7. What is the correspondent's response to the men and women who finally come to his rescue at the end of the story? How does this response differ from his reactions to the men who shared the boat with him?

8. How do both the seagull and the shark function as symbols to reinforce theme and characterization?

9. To what extent is the ending of the story happy? Can there be any happy ending when one of the characters dies? How would the meaning of the story have changed for you if the oiler had lived?

10. Stephen Crane actually lived through an experience similar to the fictionalized version in "The Open Boat." He, Captain Edward Murphy, William Higgins (an oiler), and the cook of the ship *Commodore* spent about thirty hours in a small boat after the ship sank. As in the story, Higgins was the only casualty. How does the fictional version differ from what Crane might have written if he had been doing a newspaper report? How does your response to the story differ when you know it is based on an actual event?

"The Boarding House" • *James Joyce (pp. 179–183)*

1. What aspects of Mrs. Mooney's character does Joyce emphasize? What is your response to, and evaluation of, her? What methods does Joyce use to create such an impression of Mrs. Mooney?

[Mrs. Mooney is a strong, determined woman who is able to act when she needs to. For instance, when her husband went after her with a meat cleaver, she left and established her own business. Joyce emphasizes the conniving and manipulative side of Mrs. Mooney and gives us a detailed description of her maneuvers to get her daughter married. We are not suppose to admire Mrs. Mooney, in spite of her strong and apparently admirable actions at the beginning of the story.]

2. What facts of Mr. Doran's life make it almost inevitable that he will do what Mrs. Mooney wants and expects? Of what importance is the fact that Mrs. Mooney rehearses these facts in her mind as she prepares to meet him for their discussion?

[Mr. Doran is a serious young man who has been employed for the past thirteen years in a Catholic wine-merchant's office. Mrs. Mooney knows that he would do almost anything to avoid a scandal. When we see her rehearsing the facts of Mr. Doran's life before the confrontation, we realize that she is a shrewd judge of character and that she takes a cold-blooded, practical approach to her daughter's "ruin."]

3. Joyce uses the word "reparation" to account for how and why things have to be settled in the way Mrs. Mooney has decided. What does the word mean? What are its connotations, both military and religious? Is either connotation relevant? Why or why not?

[The word means "to make amends." In a religious context, "reparation" indicates expiation for a sin. In a military context, "reparations" are materials and money paid by a defeated nation for damages to another nation as a result of hostilities with the defeated nation.

Mrs. Mooney sees Mr. Doran as an enemy who has committed a crime in his territory (his room) against her property (her daughter). Mr. Doran views himself as a sinner. Thus both connotations of the word relate to the meaning of the story.]

4. How does Doran react to his predicament? What does he feel? What would he like to do? Why does he act as he does? Look carefully at the passage in which he remembers the beginnings of his intimacy with Polly.

[Doran is frightened and ashamed. He is worried that his affair will be revealed to his boss, and in addition, he really feels that he has sinned. He would like not to have to marry Polly. He comments on p. 182 about her bad grammar and her vulgar behavior. When he thinks about the beginning of his intimacy with Polly, he remembers it as not having been entirely his fault. He sees Polly as a seducer and himself as an innocent celibate.]

5. Polly's brother, Jack, is a minor character. Is he necessary to the story? Why is he included, and what does he contribute?

[One function served by Jack is to supply a further motive for Doran to see himself as trapped into marrying Polly. Jack has threatened to beat up anyone who plays fast and loose with his sister and to put the teeth of the seducer down his throat (p. 183).]

6. Explain how the point of view shifts from one character to another. Explain the consequences of these shifts.

[The point of view shifts from an omniscient narrator in the first three paragraphs to Polly's and Mrs. Mooney's points of view in paragraphs 4, 5 and 6. In paragraphs 7 through 10 we are given Mrs. Mooney's point of view; Mr. Doran's contrasting view is found in the paragraphs that complete the first section (p. 182). The final section of the story is told from Polly's point of view. The changes of viewpoint show us how differently each character sees the affair and yet how each is concerned mainly with what personal satisfaction he or she can derive from it.]

7. In his letters, Joyce wrote that he was in part trying to capture the moral climate of Dublin in his *Dubliners* stories (from which "The Boarding House" comes). He also remarked that he wrote some of the stories in a style of scrupulous meanness. How do these remarks relate to what is revealed to us in "The Boarding House" about the emotional, religious, and social lives of the characters?

8. At the end of the story, Joyce indicates that Mrs. Mooney talks with Mr. Doran. Yet he omits any description of the scene. Why? Write a scene that fills in those details of action, gestures, and dialogue that Joyce left out. Try to make it fit logically and stylistically with what has gone before.

"The Metamorphosis" • Franz Kafka (pp. 183–213)

1. Summarize the essential plot events of each of the story's sections.

   [Section 1: The reader is introduced to the main character and his bizarre plight: Gregor Samsa, a traveling salesman, wakes up to find himself transformed into a giant insect. Gregor's relationship with his family soon becomes obvious. They are interested in him only because he supports them and takes care of their physical needs. He is paying off his father's debts, and his mother and sister are upset that he has not made the early train because they fear he will lose his job. Gregor struggles with the obvious physical difficulties of his situation; he does not seem yet to have faced the grave psychological problems that his insect form will cause. As he tries to get out of bed, to struggle to the door, to speak in his newly transformed voice, his main worries are for and about his family as well as his work. When the chief clerk from his office arrives, we learn that Gregor's job is in jeopardy, and when Gregor finally shows himself to his family, their darkly comic response (shooing him away like a household pest) emphasizes his lonely, isolated plight.

   Section 2: The second section of the story focuses on daily life at the Samsa apartment following Gregor's transformation. His sister Grete does most of the caretaking; she experiments with various foods until she finds what he will eat and also proposes moving furniture so he will have more room. No one speaks directly to Gregor, and it is clear that he has become an object, a burden to be tended but not considered as part of the family. We learn that Mr. Samsa exaggerated the state of the family finances after his business failure and that, in fact, some money remains. Gregor regards this information as a relief because he can be less worried about supporting his family, but the reader sees the bank account as one more piece of evidence that Gregor has been used and manipulated. The section closes with Gregor's mute protest against the emptying of his room. Although he sees he will be more comfortable without the furnishings, he clings to them as the last vestige of his old self. The family, misunderstanding his gesture, is appalled and frightened and his father forces Gregor back into his room by bombarding his son with apples.

   Section 3: The Samsas begin to take control of their lives. The family takes in boarders, and the father, mother, and Grete get jobs (although earlier in the story, Gregor had rationalized that none of them was capable of work). When Gregor frightens the boarders, the family has a violent argument, ending with agreement that Gregor must be dispensed with. Gregor, seeing that his family no longer needs or wants him, wills himself to die. His corpse is found in the morning by the charwoman. Mr. and Mrs. Samsa and Grete take the day off from work to recuperate from the ordeal of the past months. They take a trip to the country, where mother and father talk with happy anticipation of Grete's being married.]

2. How would you describe this story? Is it science fiction? Fantasy? Allegory? Or something else?

   ["The Metamorphosis" cannot be classified as science fiction because it does not concern itself with such matters as the process by which Gregor becomes transformed. The story addresses the inner changes of both Gregor and his family far more fully than it does the external changes. The category of fantasy can also be dismissed, since the only fantastic element is Gregor's transformation. In every other way, the story seems like realistic fiction. We get the details of the everyday life of the Samsa family, their boarders, their servants, and their employers. The figures in the story do not stand exactly equivalent to any particular human quality, so "The Metamorphosis" does not seem to be an allegory. Instead, Kafka's story is an example of experimental fiction, a genre that combines the real with the unreal as a means of confronting the absurdities of modern life.]

3. Explain the changing responses of the family members toward Gregor. How do these changes suggest a possible theme?

[At first the family panics because Gregor will no longer be able to support them. They seem helpless and despairing. As the story progresses, however, each member finds a way of coping with what seems to be an impossible circumstance. They all find their approach to Gregor. The sister makes caring for him an obsessive ritual; the mother ignores him as much as possible while protesting that she must see him; the father acts as an adversary, keeping the beast that he believes his son to be from the family. Because we, as readers, are inside Gregor's head, his family's actions seem wrongheaded and even vicious. Another view, however, shows people who have been nothing but useless leeches coming to terms with their lives and learning how to cope. When Gregor's sister leaves the warm tram, springing to her feet and stretching her body, we have the sense that another metamorphosis has taken place. Not only has the family escaped from the cocoon of their apartment, but also they are finally free of a crippling dependency.]

4. Compare "The Metamorphosis" to "The Death of Iván Ilych." In both stories, the main character dies. In both stories, we see the reactions of the family. What are the similarities and differences?

[Both stories offer a remarkable enactment of the dying process. The main characters go through stages of denial, anger, bargaining, and acceptance. In addition, the responses of the families are similar in many ways. Iván Ilych's family are dealing with a terminally ill person. They are variously angry, sad, or obsessed with caring for him. For instance, his wife insists on calling doctors to consult about her husband's ailment. In "The Metamorphosis" the family is supposedly dealing with a very different, surreal circumstance, yet nearly every reaction corresponds to those of people with a dying relative. Even the final scene where the family gathers to view the corpse seems eerily familiar. Now that the death has finally occurred, the survivors can step back from their exhaustion, anger, and grief and once more think about the person they loved. The illness may have transformed that person into a figurative "beast," but death restores, to some extent, humanity. And the cleaning lady who has arranged to get rid of the body is not unlike the modern funeral director who quietly takes care of the unpleasant details while the family gathers its strength to go on.]

5. Identify some of the story's symbols and explain how they relate to theme.

[The pictures of the woman with the muff becomes an important symbol to Gregor as he becomes less and less human. When his sister and mother begin to move furniture out of his room, he stations himself over the picture in a desperate embrace. The woman may be only a glass-encased image, but she represents his one link with the world he once inhabited. Through the window of his room, Gregor can see a hospital. Certainly this building emphasizes the motifs of illness and death with run throughout the story. When Gregor's father throws apples at him and one lodges in Gregor's back, the apple certainly takes on symbolic meaning. A fruit that should be nourishing and life-giving now hastens Gregor's death. A father who should be nurturing has, in fact, played a treacherous role in his son's wretched metamorphosis. Gregor has been forced to become the family savior, a role which causes him immense pain and which, almost certainly, leads to his transformation, withdrawal, and ultimate death.]

6. What is your response to Gregor? Do you find him sympathetic? To what extent does he seem responsible for his own situation?

43

7. When "The Metamorphosis" was published, Kafka urged that the cover not be illustrated with the transformed Gregor, saying, "The insect itself cannot be depicted. It cannot even be shown from a distance." Why would Kafka say this? What physical description of the insect are we given? How would the story change if an illustration were included?

8. In what ways is Gregor hero? Does he grow spiritually or emotionally during the story? Explain your response.

"The Blind Man" • *D. H. Lawrence (pp. 213–225)*

1. In what ways are the three main characters in the story "blind"?

[Maurice, of course, is physically blind, but he is also blind to what Isabel is feeling much of the time. He does not know, for example, the dread she feels about his black moods, nor does he recognize her desire for company other than his. Isabel seems to have taken on some of the characteristics of the blind; for example, she is described several times as listening carefully (see the first sentence of the story, for one instance). On p. 217, when she goes out to the stable to get her husband, she is actually blinded for a time by the lack of light. We then see her insecurity: "Whilst he [Maurice] was so utterly invisible, she was afraid of him" (p. 218). Because she feels so frightened when she is in the dark, she cannot really understand her husband's sense of peace and his newly aroused sensual consciousness. Bertie has perfect vision, yet it is clear that he cannot see in the same way that Maurice can. He is completely unable to understand the powerful sensual connection Maurice feels with him in the stable.]

2. What is the setting of "The Blind Man"? How is it related to the revelation of character?

[The Grange, which is described as "Maurice's own place" (p. 213), helps to define both Maurice and Isabel. Isabel is comfortable mainly in the rather elegant main house, while her husband has become increasingly at home on the farmstead and in the stables. His blindness has allowed him to dismiss the worries and concerns of the sighted world and to become closely related to the earthy and sensual world of animals and growing things. For Maurice, his relationship with his wife is a part of that sensual world; he feels that with her he has "a whole world, rich and real and invisible" (p. 213).]

3. How have Isabel's feelings toward her husband changed as the time to deliver her child comes closer?

[Instead of glorying in the intimacy she felt, she begins to feel indifferent and lethargic. She wants to be left alone; to her, Maurice is "like an ominous thunder-cloud" (p. 223).]

4. Isabel describes her husband as looking "cancelled" (she repeats the word twice.) How does her description relate to the feeling Maurice explains in the paragraph just before Isabel describes him this way (p. 220)?

[In the paragraph just before Isabel describes Maurice as looking "cancelled," he reveals his reactions to Bertie's arrival: He detests Bertie's Scottish accent; he dislikes intensely the way Isabel describes their marriage to Bertie; he feels left out. Maurice sums up these feelings by saying that he feels like a dependent child. He knows his hatred of Bertie comes from his own sense of being powerless. He feels weak and as though his actions and wishes counted for little. It is no surprise that his wife perceives him as looking "cancelled"—a word normally used to describe checks that no longer have any worth or stamps that have no power to enable the mailing of letters.]

5. What is the significance of the scene in the stable between Bertie and Maurice starting at the bottom of p. 223?

[In his own territory, the stable, Maurice is able to exercise power over Bertie. Maurice recognizes Bertie's inability to make any real connection with other humans, and he insists on physically touching Bertie, who is mesmerized by the action. Bertie touches Maurice, who believes the touch indicates a true desire on Bertie's part to understand Maurice and his sensual world. As they return to the house, Bertie is described as "haggard, with sunken eyes," but Maurice is a victorious giant, "a strange colossus" (p. 225). At the end, we see that Maurice is far more whole, in spite of his blindness, than Bertie, who is sighted. Bertie feels himself to have been entirely revealed, and injured by the revelation "like a mollusc whose shell is broken" (p. 225).]

6. Compare the relationship of Isabel and Maurice to the relationship of Mr. and Mrs. Ames in "Astronomer's Wife" or to that of the husband and wife in "The Yellow Wallpaper."

7. Write two different sequel sections to this story. In one section, show Maurice telling Isabel about his experience with Bertie in the stable. In the other section, show Bertie telling Isabel about the same conversation.

"The Horse Dealer's Daughter" • D.H. Lawrence (pp. 226–237)

1. Make a list of descriptive words and phrases from the first five paragraphs of the story. Then evaluate the tone established by these words and phrases.

[A typical list might include:

foolish	vaguely	callous
desolate	sullen	hot, flushed
desultory	impassive	shallow
final	confused	restless
dreary	dark	sensual
heavy	lost	glazed
critical	ineffectuality	stupor of downfall

Most readers evaluating such a list will readily identify the aura of despair and paralysis that surrounds Mabel Pervin and her brothers. The words used to describe Joe (fifth paragraph) suggest his inability to act, yet also connote an underlying sexuality. Thus the language of the opening paragraphs suggest the focus of the story—the tension between hopelessness and passion.]

2. How does the imagery of the opening section contrast with the imagery of the rest of the story to reflect the change in point of view? How does the change in point of view suggest the them?

[The opening section provides a realistic, objective view of the Pervin family. We learn that the family business has been lost and we meet the brothers and sister who must fact that loss. The brothers are described through animal imagery—they are "horsey"—or through their relationships with animals, while we see Mabel mainly through the comments of her brothers. She is "sullen" and "[t]he sulkiest bitch that ever trod." Once we are let into Mabel's mind, however, we begin to sympathize with her and to focus on her feelings and thoughts. The imagery becomes poetic and mystical as we see her in the cemetery carefully tending her mother's grave and projecting her desire to join her mother.]

3. Describe the conflicts Mabel Pervin and Jack Fergusson face.

[Both Mabel and Jack are torn by inner conflicts. Mabel can't bring herself to leave the place where she was born and brought up, yet without money to provide protection from the rough world of her brothers she sees no way to continue living. She has given structure to her life by taking care of the home she associates with her dead mother, but now even that must be sold to pay off the debts of the family business. She is already dead inside when she heads for the pond.

When Jack Fergusson intercepts her, he is saving not only Mabel but also himself. Although he has managed to keep some meaning in his life through his association with "rough, strongly-feeling people," he feels a great weariness which is relieved only by visits to taverns and to Mabel's brothers.]

4. Lawrence originally titled this story "The Miracle." Do you think this title is appropriate? Would it be a better title than "The Horse Dealer's Daughter"? Explain.

[The original title makes readers wonder whether, in fact, there was a miracle in the story and what the exact nature of that miracle might be. In a literal sense, the coincidence that brings the doctor to the pond at the moment of the attempted suicide is a miracle. The restoration of breath to the apparently lifeless body is a miracle. But, of course, the real miracle is the powerful attraction between Mabel and the doctor that causes him to overcome his rational objections and to admit that he does, in fact, love her. And Jack's recognition of love is dependent on Mabel's experiencing a miracle of her own: She is willing to give up her hopelessness and to deny the strong pull she feels toward joining her mother in death.]

5. How does Lawrence prepare us for the climactic moment and the resolution of the story? Why are we able to accept that Jack Fergusson could, in such a short space of time, discover that he loves Mabel?

[We know that Jack has been a frequent visitor to the Pervin farm and so knows Mabel reasonably well. When he calls on the Pervins at the end of their family conference, he asks her what she intends to do, and Mabel looks "at him with her steady, dangerous eyes, that always made him uncomfortable, unsettling his superficial ease." Mabel does not speak, but her stoic response clearly evokes a reaction from the young doctor, who is described as "watching her interestedly all the while." Later, when Jack sees Mabel in the cemetery, we are told that "some mystical element" touches him as he watches her. Still later, we find that her power over him has the strength of a drug. No matter how much Fergusson tells himself that he does not love Mabel or does not want to love her, his emotions lead him in a quite different direction. As he plunges into the stagnant, smelly pond water, he begins to acknowledge that love is a complicated business with a strangely compelling mixture of repellent and attractive elements.]

6. Identify elements in this story that seem to come from the tradition of fairy tales. In what way does the story differ from conventional fairy tales?

7. Compare the relationship between Mabel and Jack with the relationship between Isabel and Maurice in "The Blind Man."

8. After reading "The Blind Man" and "the Horse Dealer's Daughter," describe elements of style that you find common to both stories.

"The Short Happy Life of Francis Macomber" • Ernest Hemingway (pp. 245–265)

1. Why is Francis Macomber's happy life short? In what sense is this short part of it happy?

[Francis Macomber's happy life begins after he has faced his fear and gone hunting the buffalo. He recognizes his happiness when he is told that the buffalo, like the lion, has gone into the bush. He hears this news but feels no fear, just elation. The narrator tells us that for the first time in his life, Francis feels "wholly without fear" (p. 262). Once he faces his fear and defeats it, he can no longer be controlled by other people, particularly by his wife, Margot. The happy portion of Francis's life is short because very soon after he escapes from the control of his fear he is shot and killed.]

2. Hemingway begins the story after a significant action—Macomber's cowardly retreat from the lion—has occurred. What does Hemingway gain by doing this rather than by narrating the events in the order of their occurrence?

[By starting the story after Macomber's retreat from the lion, Hemingway lets us know that the lion-shooting episode is not the climactic event of the story. The retreat serves as a primary incident to establish the conflict, but we realize that the most important event is yet to come.]

3. What is the narrator's view of Robert Wilson? How do you think Hemingway wants us to see him? What are we to think of Francis Macomber? Of Margot?

[While Robert Wilson may seem like a comically stereotyped "great white hunter" to many students, he is presented as mostly sympathetic by the narrator. Wilson behaves according to the Hemingway code. He has made his separate peace with society and lives apart, doing what he does very well. He is embarrassed by Macomber's openness and honesty; even when he admires Francis's courage, Wilson tells him not to talk about it, not to "mouth it up too much" (p. 263). In the end, we can see that Wilson may have been right in a sense; Francis might not have been shot if he had been less forthright about his change. Wilson also adheres to the Hemingway code when he accepts sex where it is offered, particularly since Margot is a classic "bitch" stereotype and therefore fair game for the Hemingway hero. On the other hand, we do know that Wilson covers up irregularities on his safaris (chasing animals in cars), and at the end he is certainly willing to write off what might have been murder as an accident. Neither of these last actions is wholly admirable, and they temper the presentation of Wilson as a code hero.

Margot is a completely unsympathetic character. Although we may be able to create scenarios that would justify her treatment of Francis at the beginning of the story, her behavior toward him after he has faced down his fear would be extremely difficult to rationalize.]

4. The point of view of the story is such that we enter the consciousness of each character at different points. Yet we enter the minds of the characters to rather different degrees. Into whose mind do we see the most? Whose mind least? Why?

47

[We are most often in the mind of Francis Macomber, although we know a great deal of Robert Wilson's thoughts too. We know least about Margot. We see the two male characters' thoughts more often than Margot's because she is really a peripheral character, although she does have a moment in the spotlight at the end of the story. The conflict is not really between Francis and Margot, but rather between the two aspects of Francis Macomber's self. Since it is his growth we watch, we see into his mind most often. We see into Wilson's mind because Wilson represents the code Macomber is moving toward.]

5. Look over the descriptions of the buffalo and the lion. What impression do you have of each? How do these descriptions help us to understand the characters?

[The lion is described by Wilson as "marvelous" (p. 252). Macomber, however, sees the lion as looking toward them "majestically and coolly" (p. 252). Wilson seems to regard the lion as a worthy equal; Macomber sees it as superior and all-powerful. When the hunting party comes on the buffalo, Macomber sees them as huge, but Wilson describes them as "three old bulls." Once again Macomber views the animals as fierce and threatening, but this time he is able to face down the threat.]

6. Reread the opening dialogue. Explain how Hemingway has carefully controlled it to establish the rank and status of the three major characters.

[The opening dialogue establishes Wilson as the person in charge: He knows what he wants to drink and refuses Macomber's offer of lime juice or lemon squash; he also is able to communicate with the mess boy, and he knows how much to tip. Margot comes next in the power structure: She follows Wilson's lead, but refuses the suggestion of her husband. Macomber demonstrates no power at all: He does not know how to behave in his new surroundings, and his wife shows him no respect.]

7. There is some controversy among readers about exactly what happens at the end of the story. Is Margot's shooting of her husband an accident? Does Wilson think so? Do you? Why or why not? Is there any advantage to describing the scene as Hemingway has, instead of making it absolutely clear what Margot has done?

8. Comment on the following thoughts of Robert Wilson:

> The great American boy-men. Damned strange people. But he liked this Macomber now. Damned strange fellow. Probably meant the end of cuckoldry too. Well, that would be a damned good thing. Damned good thing. Beggar had probably been afraid all his life. Don't know what started it. But over now. . . . Be a damn fire eater now. He'd seen it in the war work the same way. More of a change than any loss of virginity. Fear gone like an operation. Something else grew in its place. Main thing a man had. Made him into a man. Women knew it too. No bloody fear. [p. 263]

"The Garden of Forking Paths" • Jorge Luis Borges (pp. 265–271)

1. In this story Borges puts together an amazing combination of facts and fiction. For example, Liddel-Hart's *History of World War I*, mentioned in the first paragraph, is a real book, but the incident described is not mentioned on page 22. What effect does Borges gain by combining the real with the imaginary?

[Borges is able to achieve a sense of realism and make his speculations about the nature of time seem to be plausible theorizing rather than a make-believe fairy tale.]

2. "The Garden of Forking Paths" combines elements of many different kinds of stories. What kinds can you identify?

[Detective story (discovering the mystery implied in the beginning of the second paragraph); war/spy story (Richard Madden versus Dr. Yu Tsun versus the Allies); historical fiction (the story of Yu Tsun's ancestor Ts'ui Pên); science fiction (multiple time dimensions).]

3. What is the significance of this advice Yu Tsun offers to humankind as he hurries toward Stephen Albert's garden?

The author of an atrocious undertaking ought to imagine that he has already accomplished it, ought to impose upon himself a future as irrevocable as the past [p. 267].

[This advice suggests that Yu Tsun already understands the secret of the forking paths; in one future he has already doomed Stephen Albert, and no change is possible.]

4. Why might the boys at the Ashgrove station have known that Yu Tsun was going to Stephen Albert's house?

[Perhaps they are part of the particular future Yu Tsun has set. Perhaps it is because Stephen Albert is often visited by the Chinese consul and so the boys are used to seeing Chinese people asking directions to his house. Perhaps it is because, as Yu Tsun first fears, Richard Madden has penetrated his plan (since Madden does show up in the last scene, this possibility remains open in spite of Yu Tsun's protest to the contrary).]

5. Why is the riddle of Yu Tsun's ancestor's book and garden essential to understanding the story?

[Yu Tsun's ancestor said he was going to write a book; he also said he was going to build a labyrinth. The labyrinth was never found after his death, and the book was deemed a terrible convoluted failure. Stephen Albert, however, discovered the secret. The book and the labyrinth were one. The book was written as a puzzle meant to reveal through its complex and convoluted structure Ts'ui Pên's theory of time. Unlike most scientists, philosophers, and historians, Ts'ui Pên did not believe in uniform, absolute time. "He believed in an infinite series of times, in a growing, dizzying net of divergent, convergent and parallel times" (p. 271). We have to understand this idea to recognize the ambiguity of what happens at the end of the story. The report left by Yu Tsun, we are led to believe, is only one of many possible reports about one of many possible events in one of many possible pasts.]

6. How does the first paragraph of the story relate to Dr. Yu Tsun's statement, which follows it?

[We are told that Yu Tsun's statement will throw an unsuspected light over the World War I incident. It is possible that after reading the story and learning of the theory of Ts'ui Pên, we are supposed to realize that even history—which we have supposed to be strictly linear in its chronology—could be affected by the forking paths of futures. In one time dimension the torrential rains could have been insignificant; in another, devastatingly important; in still another the rains may not have come at all and thus the attack may not have been postponed.]

7. Compare the time possibilities implied by Ts'ui Pên's theory with those implied by the magician's box in Woody Allen's "The Kugelmass Episode" (pp. 315–322).

8. Research any historical incident that interests you: John Kennedy's assassination, the hostage crisis in Iran, the Soviet nuclear-power accident at Chernobyl, the Challenger explosion. Write a paper suggesting a scenario of futures and their possible implications.

"Gimpel the Fool" • *Isaac Bashevis Singer (pp. 272–281)*

1. Why does Gimpel tell his story? Is he complaining? Explaining? Looking for sympathy? How would the story be different if it were told from an objective point of view?

[The ending suggests that Gimpel tells his story because he has recognized that in the tale of his own life is contained the story of all lives. After his dream vision of Elka, Gimpel realizes that he is not a fool after all—that he has always been true to himself. He now wanders over the land telling stories, all of which lead him closer to his true world where he will go "joyfully" and "without complication, without ridicule, without deception" (p. 281).

Told from an objective point of view, the story would present Gimpel as an infuriatingly foolish person. The objective view would not show us Gimpel's ironic inner response to the world around him, nor would we understand his dream visions or his complex and playful philosophy.]

2. Why does Gimpel continue to take the abuse which is heaped on him? What does he mean when he says, "Shoulders are from God, and burdens too"? Is his suffering pointless?

[Gimpel continues to take the abuse heaped on him because he refuses to give up on humankind. With each new deception, no matter how outrageous, he wants to give the perpetrator a chance. In addition, his suffering sometimes brings him joy. For example, he loves the first baby Elka brings to the marriage even though he is not the father. And in the end, he finds out that keeping an open mind has proved the right course.

   After many years I became old and white; I heard a great deal, many lies and false-hoods, but the longer I lived the more I understood that there were really no lies. Whatever doesn't really happen is dreamed at night. It happens to one if it doesn't happen to another, tomorrow if not today, or a century hence if not next year [p. 282].

Gimpel proves himself the wise man and the visionary; his tormentors are the short-sighted doubters and fools.

   When Gimpel says, "Shoulders are from God, and burdens too," he means that he regards his external troubles to be as much a part of him—and as much God-given—as are the parts of his own body.]

3. Of what significance are Gimpel's dreams? Of what significance are the supernatural elements of the story? Do they enhance or impede your enjoyment of it?

[Gimpel's dreams and the supernatural elements in the story provide comedy, for instance when he answers the Spirit of Evil, "What should I be doing? Eating *kreplach*?" (p. 279). But; in addition, they give power to Gimpel's story. The dream visions explain Gimpel's moral struggle and triumph and make him seem both a simple peasant and a representative, larger-than-life wise man.]

4. Why is the story arranged in four parts? How are these parts related to each other? How is the first part related to the last?

[In the first section, Gimpel begins to tell his story. We learn about his responses to the deceptions of his childhood and discover how he was led to marry his wife. The second section of Gimpel's story shows him even further deceived; not only is his wife both wid-

50

owed and divorced, but she is also pregnant with another man's child. In this section, we also see the hypocrisy and falseness of the religious authorities. In the third section, Gimpel has decided to live with his wife's deceptions; she dies leaving him nothing at all to comfort him when she reveals on her deathbed that none of the children she has borne for the past twenty years of their marriage has been his. Each time, he has believed against all odds; each time he has been—in the eyes of the world—a fool. The fourth section shows Gimpel at this lowest; he has decided to give up believing and to seek revenge on the townspeople. After his dream vision of Elka, he recognizes his own worth and sets out around the world. The parts are related because they trace Gimpel's spiritual growth in the most demeaning circumstances. The first section and the last section connect with each other because, at the end, we learn that the tale we are being told is like the tale Gimpel tells to the children when they ask him for the story. The structure is not linear, but circular, the ending and beginning clearly joined.]

5. In what sense is Gimpel foolish? In what sense is he wise?

[He is foolish in a worldly sense because he refuses to accept the evidence of his senses. Instead he relies entirely on belief. He is wise because such an openness invites the kind of strange and wonderful revelations Gimpel describes at the end of the story.]

6. What do you find funny in the story? Compare the humor of "Gimpel the Fool" with the comedy of "Good Country People."

[There are many instances of humor, most of them caused by the literalness of Gimpel's understanding and by his simple beliefs. In Section 4, however, we have the comic confrontation of Gimpel with the Spirit of Evil. It is certainly ironic that the reprisal the spirit brings to Gimpel's mind is to urinate in the people's bread. Gimpel goes through several steps of this wonderful revenge fantasy and we are certainly chuckling with him. When he throws the bread away we may feel momentarily disappointed, but the joke remains, and in addition, Gimpel shows himself once more to be the wise man and the moral superior.]

7. Explain the meaning of the final paragraph, especially the idea that the world is not real. How does this paragraph comment on the action of the story?

[The world Gimpel has had to live in is not real because it is not authentic or genuine. The people have shallow values and get their pleasure from duping and humiliating those who are simple, unsophisticated, and sensitive. Students may want to read and consider the ideas of Spinoza, whose writing Singer greatly admires, in responding to this topic.]

8. What are your responses to Gimpel's statement "I resolved that I would always believe what I was told. What's the good of *not* believing?"

"I Stand Here Ironing" • Tillie Olsen (pp. 281–286)

1. The story is cast in the form of a long, mediative monologue in which a mother reflects on the life and character of her daughter, Emily. What prompts this series of reflections? To whom are they addressed?

[The monologue is prompted by a telephone call the mother has received, probably from one of Emily's instructors, asking the mother to come in and talk about Emily so the instructor can help the daughter. The mother mentally responds to the phone call, but she is also clarifying the events of Emily's life—and their consequences—in her own mind.]

2. What circumstances of the mother's experience made it difficult for her to raise her children as she would have liked? And what is the mother's attitude toward these circumstances? How did Emily, especially, suffer from them? Did she benefit from them in any way?

[Among the circumstances are the mother's youth and inexperience, the father's desertion, the rigid rules concerning schedules for infants that mothers were expected to follow at that time, the mother's lack of family or supportive friends, the Depression, the lack of welfare funds, the war, the lack of decent daycare, Emily's illness, the high-handed negative attitude of the social workers at the clinic and at the convalescent home.

The mother regrets the circumstances deeply. She seems slightly defensive, which is certainly understandable considering that her audience is a teacher whose polite phone call may very well reflect a willingness to blame the mother for what the teacher perceives to be Emily's problems.

Emily, in particular, suffered from the difficult circumstances because she was the first child (the child of the deserting husband) who had to be shuffled back and forth from one uncaring relative to another.

Emily may also have benefited from some of the problems of her upbringing. For instance, her mother was often unable to give her much attention so, to make her laugh, Emily would imitate events or people at school. Emily developed this talent when her mother encouraged her to enter the school amateur show, which she won, and after that she gained wide recognition, being asked to perform at other schools and finally at statewide affairs.]

3. One way of looking at the story is to see it as the narrator's search for causes, the causes of her daughter's development into the young woman she has become. But it is also a search for the causes of the mother's own regret and disappointment, along with her attempt to come to terms with these feelings. Does the mother's response seem reasonable? Do her explanations seem plausible? Why or why not?

[Students will have many different ideas about this question. Some may feel that the mother is simply rationalizing her own failure and will argue that she could have done better if she had stopped blaming other people and circumstances and blamed herself instead. On the other had, some students will see the mother's testimony as completely credible. They will see her as a victim of the economic system, who did the best she could to raise Emily under extremely adverse circumstances; an admirable character who, despite great odds, raised a successful comedienne. The mother's testimony can also be taken as a statement about the role of a mother in her children's lives and the limits of a mother's responsibility for what her children become.]

4. The beginning and ending of the story contain references to ironing, as does the title. Look at these, and the two other occasions when ironing is specifically referred to, and explain their significance.

[On p. 285, the mother explains that she was always busy ironing or doing some other chore, causing Emily to begin her comic routines to get her mother's attention and make her laugh. Toward the bottom of page 285, Emily asks her mother, "Aren't you ever going to finish the ironing, Mother?" and then jokes that unlike Whistler's mother who was painted in a chair, her mother would have to be painted standing over an ironing board. Emily says this whimsically, not complainingly, but we see that she understands the ironing board as a central symbol of her mother's life. The mother has been worn down by the chores and cares of life; she is trapped by her work. The final sentence, where the mother thinks a kind of prayer that Emily will not be trapped, shows us that she too sees ironing as symbolizing her own defeat in life. She hopes that Emily will not allow herself to be run over by other people and by circumstances. And she is wise enough to know that to do this, Emily must learn to value herself: "Only help her to know . . . that she is more than this dress on the ironing board, helpless before the iron" (p. 286).]

5. What is the purpose of the next-to-last paragraph of the story? Notice that most of the sentences are short. Notice also that they begin consistently in one of three ways: "I," "She," or "There were." What is the effect of this rapid accumulation of short sentences in similar form and style?

   [This paragraph, both in style and content, seems like a summation to a jury. The mother is summarizing the events, the causes and effects, of her life and of Emily's, and is presenting them to her judges: the teacher, the voices of authority figures she has heard all her life, and, finally, to herself.]

6. Analyze the way the mother's mind moves from one detail to another. See if you can uncover any patterns underlying the shifts of direction in her thinking.

7. Imagine that you are Emily. Write a response to this story in the form of a letter to your mother.

"Battle Royal" • Ralph Ellison (pp. 286–295)

1. This story, first published independently, is the first chapter of Ellison's novel *Invisible Man* (not to be confused with either "The Invisible Man," a detective story by G. K. Chesterton, or the scientific-romance novel of the same name written by H. G. Wells). What kind of invisibility characterizes Ellison's narrator?

   [Ellison's narrator feels invisible because white people do not see him as an individual or even as a person. To the white people he knows, he is simply part of the large black mass.]

2. Ellison's story is narrated by an older (and wiser) man, who recounts an experience he had when he was younger. In a way, his position as the young man undergoing the experience is somewhat analogous to ours as we read about it—that is, we make sense of his experience in the same way he does. What do we finally understand about his experience?

   [We understand, as does the narrator, that no matter how much he tries to follow the rules or live up to the standards white people set for him, he will never earn their respect. There will always be another "Battle Royal" for him to face until he learns to be himself and to set his own standards.]

3. "Battle Royal" can be divided into six scenes. What are they, and how are they related? In particular, what is the relationship of the two grandfather scenes to one another and to the other scenes in the story?

   [Scene 1: Introduction of the main characters; the grandfather's deathbed instructions.

   Scene 2: Arrival of the narrator and the battle-royal fighters at the hotel.

   Scene 3: Dance of the blonde stripper.

   Scene 4: The battle royal.

Scene 5:   The graduation speech.

Scene 6:   Final four paragraphs, beginning "That night I dreamed . . ." (p. 295). The narrator's dream of his grandfather's response to the college scholarship.

[The scenes are all related by the narrator's growing sense of unease and anger with the white world. In the first scene, the grandfather, who has apparently been a mild and quiet man all his life, declares that his "yesses" and "grins" have been subversive. All his life he has been fighting the white world, and he wants his children to do the same. In the final scene, the grandfather comes back to taunt the narrator, who has, in fact, said "yes" and "grinned" at the white men but not for subversive reasons. The narrator still tries to please his tormentors and is ready to forgive them when he receives the college scholarship, but the grandfather of the dream pushes the boy to think about the true significance of his actions.]

4. Examine the details of dialogue and description Ellison uses in the scene of the woman dancing. What impression do we come away with of the men as they watch? Besides using this scene to reveal the nature of the men, Ellison also implies something more about the relationship between black men and white women. What does he imply and how does he do it? How is this scene analogous to the scene describing the battle royal?

[The white men behave like animals—for example, the merchant who follows the dancer "hungrily, his lips loose and drooling" (p. 289). The young black men are both terrified and fascinated, attracted and repelled, aroused and disgusted. The white men make it clear that the young black men should not respond to the woman but, paradoxically, insist that the narrator and the battle-royal fighters look at the woman. These white men clearly subscribe to the stereotyped ideas that all black men lust after white women.

What we also see in the behavior of the white men toward the woman is that they regard women very much the way they regard black people. The woman is an object to be displayed for their pleasure and amusement. And the hostility and anger they show toward her at the end of her dance parallels the way they treat the black fighters at the end of the battle royal.]

5. The description of the battle royal is a *tour de force* of controlled point of view. Explain how Ellison creates the sense of confusion the narrator experiences during the fight. Point out specific details that show Ellison keeping to the limited vision of the narrator. In this description, you might also note how the narrator is unsure how to behave. What is the source of his uncertainty? What extraneous thoughts intrude into his consciousness, and what do they reveal about him?

[One device Ellison uses is to have the young men blindfolded. Since the narrator wears a blindfold, we are given only the sounds and smells he experiences. We share his loss of equilibrium, he sense of panic. When the narrator finds himself in the ring with only one other black fighter, he is unsure whether to try to win or not. He keeps thinking of his speech, wondering what the battle royal has to do with his honors.]

6. How is the narrator's speech received? What slip of the tongue does the narrator make and what does it signify? Of what significance is his prize—a scholarship to be used at "the state college for Negroes"?

[The narrator's speech is received with less interest and attention than the blonde dancer's act or the battle royal. The men talk among themselves, laughing and seeming not to hear the narrator until he slips and shouts out "social equality" instead of "social responsibility."

The narrator has a moment of triumph before he is forced to back down and retract his brave words. At the end, he is rewarded with a scholarship to the state college for Negroes, where, we feel sure, he will receive the same kind of condescending education he has had at the Negro high school. His white instructors will encourage him to follow the paths thought proper for his race and, as his grandfather's dream suggests, will keep him running on the right treadmills.]

7. Analyze any one scene of the story, carefully explaining how the details fit together to suggest one or more ideas or attitudes. Explain what the scene contributes to the story as a whole. Consider language and tone, symbols and imagery, as well as character and action.

"A Continuity of Parks" • Julio Cortázar (pp. 296–297)

1. How would you characterize the man who reads the novel?

[Details such as signing power of attorney and "discussing a matter of joint ownership" suggest that he is concerned about making provisions in case he should become incapable of acting on his own or even die. Perhaps he is an older man, facing retirement. Possibly he has a serious illness. Or he might have an impending sense of doom and a realization of his own mortality. We know that he has attended some "urgent business conferences" and that he owns a luxurious estate so he is almost certainly a wealthy professional. He is probably a man of considerable power, as suggested both by his wealth and by his being described as someone whom "the possibility of an intrusion would have irritated . . . had he thought of it." His engagement with the novel (which focused on "the sordid dilemma of the hero and heroine") indicates that he has both a strong imagination and a purient interest in vicarious living.]

2. What do you surmise the relationship to be between the hero and heroine of the novel and the man who is described in the final sentence of this story?

[In *The Act of Reading* (1978), Wolfgang Iser describes the blanks or "gaps" readers encounter in imaginative literature. Filling in these gaps requires looking carefully at the evidence provided in the story, yet also making projections about possibilities which are neither confirmed nor denied by the details the author has provided. In this case, of course, the situation is complicated by our sense of displacement in recognizing the striking similarity between the man who is reading the novel and the man (supposedly a character in the novel) who sits, reading a novel, unaware that the hero is creeping up on him.

Looking at the details of the novel, several possibilities come to mind regarding the relationship between the three characters. The dagger that the hero carries is described as warming "itself against his chest" where "underneath liberty pounded." Where might this liberty come from? The hero might be the son of the man in the chair; perhaps the murder would allow the son to inherit money and thus give him freedom to run away with his illicit lover. Or the man in the chair might be blackmailing the hero (or the heroine—or both); the murder would eliminate that threat. I believe the mostly likely scenario to be that the woman is the wife (or daughter?) of the man in the chair. The hero will kill the man. (Quite possibly the woman has given him directions to the salon: "The woman's words reached him over the thudding of blood in his ears: first a blue chamber, then a half, then a carpeted stairway," although the words could simply be her insistence that the murder be carried out or her final declaration of love, and the directions might be a rehearsal in the hero's mind of a path he already knew well.) Once the murder is completed, the hero and the woman are freed from the control of the husband (father?), and can be together openly.

Playing with the possibilities suggests the mystery and magic of such a brief sketch. We're left with so many questions and so many ways of putting the details together.]

3. Perhaps the most fascinating theme explored by this story is the blurring between the borders of fantasy and reality. What do we accept as "real"; what as "fantasy"?

[Is the man we read of at the beginning of the story more "real" than the characters *he* reads about in his novel? Where does fiction end and truth begin. Does the man simply identify strongly with what he is reading so that, at the end, he imagines himself to be in the same situation as the potential murder victim in the novel? Or are we to read this story as completely crossing the boundaries of what we know as the traditional conventions of fiction. Has the reader actually become absorbed in the energy of the novel? We are told that he "tasted the almost perverse pleasure of disengaging himself line by line from the things around him." Why "line by line"? Why not "object by object"? Does this sentence mean that as he read each line of the novel, he became more and more part of the novel's world rather than his own world? Has he literally become "lost in a book"? The title of the story, "A Continuity of Parks," suggest that the park outside the man's own home and the park through which the hero passes to get to the estate in the novel serve as some sort of literary time/space warp. No clear break remains between the park the man sees and the park the man reads about. They meld together and, apparently, lead him into danger. Does this story, then, suggest that too great an absorption with fictional worlds can be dangerous? Or are we simply to see the final lines as a playful trick Cortázar plays on us, as readers, forcing us to think about our own roles in relationship to the characters we read about?]

4. Write a paragraph extending the action of the story beyond the current final line. In this paragraph, suggest your own view of the relationship between the man in the opening sentence and the man in the present last sentence.

5. Compare the themes and characters of this story with the themes and characters of Woody Allen's "The Kugelmass Episode" (p. 315).

"Good Country People" • *Flannery O'Connor (pp. 297–310)*

1. Consider the character's names. What do they tell us about the characters? Of what particular significance is Joy's decision to change her name to Hulga?

[Mrs. Hopewell always hopes for the best. Her ready-at-hand clichés provide a response to every occasion; she loves to give advice and urges pleasantness and nice behavior as the answer to nearly every problem. Mrs. Freeman uses her mouth freely; she says whatever she wants in spite of the fact that she is hired help. She particularly annoys Joy/Hulga by calling her Hulga. Joy/Hulga sees Hulga as her own powerful name. She had her name legally changed from Joy partly to annoy her mother and partly because it sounds ugly, but also because it reminds her of the god Vulcan to whom the goddess had to come when called (p. 299). Manley Pointer's name explains itself, and the ironic joke becomes even funnier when we realize that it is a name he gave himself, just as Joy gave Hulga to herself.]

2. Are Mrs. Freeman's daughters, Glynese and Carramae, important to the story? What would be lost if they were left out?

[When their names are first introduced, we learn that Hulga makes fun of them by changing their names to Glycerin and Caramel. By changing their names, she tries to trivialize them and make herself seem more important. In addition to Hulga's response, we see that Mrs. Hopewell envies Mrs. Freeman her "normal" daughters who attract male admirers. Mrs. Freeman talks on and on about her children, particularly Carramae, who at fifteen is already married and pregnant. The popular and fertile Freeman sisters stand in sharp contrast to Hulga, who at thirty-two has a Ph.D. in philosophy, is physically unattractive, and has no suitors.]

3. How is the title of the story ironic? How does it relate to the theme of the story?

[The title is ironic in several ways. We learn that Mrs. Hopewell will tolerate great deal from Mrs. Freeman because she recognized "that in the Freemans she had good country people and that if, in this day and age, you get good country people, you had better hang onto them." Mrs. Hopewell sees "good country people" as having a simple morality and an adherence to rural values; she contrasts "good country people" with the "trash" that worked for her in the past. But when we listen to the conversations in the Hopewell kitchen, we hear the ignorance, superstition, and prejudice that are also part of these "good country people." The ultimate irony comes at the end of the story when Hulga, who has always held herself above the "good country" values, makes the mistake of assuming that Manley Pointer subscribes to them. In his final scene with her, we see that although he is "country," he certainly is not "good." Manley represents a moral void, and Hulga, who has believed herself to be the sophisticated philosopher, knowledgeable about the existential dilemma, finds she is far more naive and ignorant than the "good country people" she has been laughing at.]

4. Mrs. Hopewell loves clichés. Make a list of as many of her favorite truisms as you can find. Then evaluate your list. What do you learn about Mrs. Hopewell? Do the clichés seem to relate to the story's theme in any way? What effect do the clichés have on Mrs. Hopewell's audience her daughter, Mrs. Freeman, Manley Pointer)?

5. One day Mrs. Hopewell picks up a book Hulga has been reading and finds a passage her daughter had underlined:

> Science, on the other hand, has to assert its soberness and seriousness afresh and declare that it is concerned solely with what-is. Nothing—how can it be for science anything but a horror and a phantasm? If science is right, then one thing stands firm: science wishes to know nothing of nothing. Such is after all the strictly scientific approach to Nothing. We know it by wishing to know nothing of Nothing. [p. 300]

What is Mrs. Hopewell's reaction to the passage? How does the passage relate to what happens between Hulga and Manley Pointer later in the story?

[Mrs. Hopewell does not understand the words, but she shivers, nevertheless, and feels that she has read an incantation of evil. Hulga sees the denial of all traditional values, the denial of any connections with the flesh, the denial of anything but the pure life of the mind as the only way an intelligent person can exist. At the end, when she is faced with Pointer—who truly lives this philosophy of nothingness and puts it into practice as a psychopath who lusts after artificial body parts—Hulga recognizes that while Mrs. Hopewell and Mrs. Freeman may be ignorant, her Ph.D. has not given her all the answers to life's complexities either. In their own way, her philosophical premises become as much clichés as her mother's aphorisms.]

6. Do you sympathize with any of the characters in this story? If not, are you unsympathetic to all of them all of the time? Explain by referring to specific episodes.

7. Compare Joy/Hulga's decision to change her name, and the consequences of the name change, with Dee/Wangero's decision to change her name in Alice Walker's "Everyday Use" (p. 346).

8. Choose one short section and analyze its humor. For example, you might look at the description of Mrs. Freeman's three expressions which opens the story. Or you might consider the conversation between Mrs. Freeman, Mrs. Hopewell, and Hulga concerning Glynese's preferences for being married by a preacher (bottom of p. 303).

CONTEMPORARY STORIES

"A Very Old Man with Enormous Wings" • Gabriel Garcia Marquez (pp. 310–314)

1. The author has subtitled the story "A Tale for Children." Do you agree with his definition of his audience? What elements suggest that it is a story for children? What elements make you doubt that children are the audience?

[The supernatural old man with enormous wings could certainly appear in a story for children. And from the beginning we have the sense that a fable is unrolling. The wise woman is consulted. The baby has a miraculous recovery. On the other hand, the scruffy feathers of the angel, the dilemma over what to do with him, the sly satirical criticism of the church and the medical profession all lead us to believe that the story is for children only in the way that Swift's *Gulliver's Travels* is for children. An adult audience is expected to see things that could not be there for younger readers.]

2. How is the old man regarded? How is he treated?

[Pelayo and Elisenda at first think the old man is a castaway from a foreign ship; they ignore his wings because they don't really want to think about them. The wise woman next door pronounces the man an angel and urges her neighbors to club him to death because she believes all angels to be survivors of a celestial conspiracy (perhaps the conspiracy described in *Paradise Lost*?). The local priest doesn't know what to do, so he writes to Rome for a definitive answer. Elisenda, in the meantime, decides to make the old man a side-show attraction and charge admission for people to see him.]

3. How does the old man react to the outside world? How is his reaction significant?

[He completely ignores the people who come to stare and to beg for miracles. He reacts only when the crowd tries to burn him, and his reaction scares them into leaving him alone. His concentration on getting comfortable and ignoring annoyances suggests a being who is not interested in killing babies, or working miracles, or acting in a sideshow. Instead we see a displaced figure, trying to gain strength.]

4. What is the Church's response to the old man? How are we supposed to regard this response?

[The Church avoids the issue and never looks at the real questions: Who is the old man? How is he affecting the people in the village? How are the people treating him? Instead, the mail from Rome poses theoretical and metaphysical conundrums that allow infinite delay. The priest and his superiors are able to respond to an extraordinary situation only in the most unimaginative and disengaged way.]

5. What is the significance of the episode of the woman who comes with the traveling show?

[The woman, who has supposedly been turned into a spider for disobeying her parents, replaces the old man in the people's interest. We are told, "A spectacle like that, full of so much human truth and with such a fearful lesson, was bound to defeat without even trying that of a haughty angel who scarcely deigned to look at mortals" (p. 313). The people don't really want to struggle with a difficult philosophical problem, either. Like the Church, they would rather turn to more sensational earthly concerns, and they are easily distracted by the spider woman's story of romance, disobedience, and punishment.]

6. What does the final section of the story mean? Come up with as many solutions as possible.

[The old man in some ways seems like a senile grandfather. He relates only to the baby; he is a terrible nuisance to the couple who take care of him; he survives under the worst circumstances, and seems to be in preparation for a journey. Perhaps the journey is death.

Of course, the old man is not an earthly grandfather; his wings suggest that he may be an angel who has had to struggle against the banality and empty forms of the society he fell into before he could find the strength within himself to regain some of his former power and fly away. On the other hand, we might ask whether angels speak in the dialect of a Norwegian seaman. Perhaps the old man represents any stranger, any new quality or possibility which average, ordinary people find in their midst. At first the newcomer is fascinating and gains much attention; but shallow people are fickle and soon desert the newcomer for the next attraction. The discarded newcomer must then find inner resources to survive and ultimately to escape. Elisenda's mixed relief and regret suggest the feelings we may have when we are relieved of a burden that was also a challenge and a rare opportunity to go beyond the confines of our ordinary existence.]

7. Write a paper explaining who the old man is, by retelling the story through his point of view. Your paper could include creative answers to the questions the story raises: Where has the old man come from? Why has he come? What motivates his reactions toward the people? Why does he leave?

"Space" • Mark Strand (pp. 314–315)

1. List the statements the man makes to the woman. After reading these statements, how do you think the man evaluates the woman's motives? What role does he see himself playing in relationship to her?

[The man makes the following statements:
"I'll take you to dinner."
"Let's go some place and talk."
"Look, if it's me you're worried about you have nothing to fear."
"I know it's depressing."
"I'll tell you what, I'll marry you"
"We'll do it immediately, and then go to Italy. We'll go to Bologna, we'll eat great food. We'll walk around all day and drink grappa at night. We'll observe the world and we'll read the books we never had time for."

While the man's actions might suggest that he is seeing the woman for the first time, his statements seem as though they are addressed to someone he knows. For instance, even

59

though he is "not sure what he [means]" when he says, "I know it's depressing," that observation sounds like a comment that would more likely come from an acquaintance or a friend rather than a complete stranger. More convincing evidence comes in his assurance that if she is worried about him, she has "nothing to fear." Since she is poised ready to jump as he comes on to the roof, she clearly is not simply fleeing from an unknown man whom she imagines to be dangerous. If he plays any role in her decision, it must be because of previous acquaintance—not this present meeting.

His statements suggest that he sees himself in the role of protector or rescuer. He tries reassurance as well as offers of things he thinks she might desire: going to dinner; going to talk; getting married; traveling to Italy. As he builds the series of offers, however, it seems as though he may be describing his own needs rather than hers. For instance, his description of the trip to Italy includes many details such as drinking grappa and reading "the books we never had time for" that suggest he is building his own fantasy rather than simply focusing on rescuing the woman.]

2. From the details in the story, what do you know about the woman. How does the point of view in the story affect the description of the woman?

[The story begins with an omniscient, objective narrator reporting that the woman is beautiful and has long, dark hair. She wears a white blouse and pale blue skirt. She has kicked off her high-heeled shoes and so stands barefoot. Then the point of view becomes mixed. While objective details are still provided ("The wind flattened her skirt against the front of her long thighs."), we begin to see into the mind of the man and to learn about his reactions and responses to the woman ("He wished he could reach out and pull her toward him."). We learn that the woman wears no wedding band (which, perhaps, implies that the man notices and finds this detail important). He sees her as a sensual and sexual being and wishes "he could touch her." Perhaps the most important detail is the space the man notes between the woman's feet and the ledge. This space, I believe, indicates that she has just begun her jump. He sees the space as a symbol of the disconnection "between herself and the world." The man seems to believe (or wants to believe) that nothing could have saved the woman—that she simply could not be part of the world as we know it. His observation, "How lovely," indicates that he now sees the suicide to be inevitable and somehow fitting. Everything about the woman's final moments have been a well-choreographed dance leading to the leap into the void.]

3. Can you speculate on the woman's reasons for jumping? Or do her motives remain a mystery?

[The man's final observation that there was "a space that would always exist now between herself and the world" as well as earlier descriptions such as her gaze being "point-blank" and the man's wondering whether she "felt anything," suggest that she may be mentally ill or suffering from depression. Other than such vague speculation, however, it's difficult to determine exactly what is going on with her. We remain as baffled as the man, and perhaps less willing than he to see the final leap as "lovely."]

4. Rewrite the story, this time beginning with these sentences:

A man suddenly stepped out of the doorway and on to the roof. He was about thirty or thirty-five and blond. He was lean, with a long upper body and short, thin legs. His black bathing suit shone like satin in the sun. I stared at him, and he finally stopped when he was no more than ten steps from where I stood near the ledge.

Continue writing. telling the story through the woman's eyes.

5. Imagine that you are the man. Write a journal entry evaluating your thoughts and actions as you look back at the strange and disturbing encounter on the roof.

"The Kugelmass Episode" • *Woody Allen (pp. 315–322)*

1. Examine the opening section of the story closely. What do we learn about Kugelmass? About his analyst? What elements suggest satire? What elements suggest the fairy tale?

[The opening scene shows us Kugelmass, who, the narrator assures us, has a soul, but who demonstrates only the most crass and stereotypical responses to life. He has married primarily for money; he thinks he can cure his malaise by having a B-grade-Hollywood-movie affair; he speculates about having an affair with one of the many "coeds" at CCNY where he teaches (he dismisses the women on the faculty as no "great shakes"). The analyst, on the other hand, gives typical analyst's responses that goad Kugelmass into coming up with a wonderfully transparent dream which he offers to the humorless analyst. Certainly these details suggest that the story will be full of satirical targets: analysts and therapy; men in midlife crisis; romantic fantasies. When the analyst says he is no magician and Kugelmass declares that he needs a magician, we recognize the opening of so many fairy tales where the main character makes a wish that is granted, and then has to live with the strange results of that wish.]

2. Identify the realistic elements throughout the story. What effect do they have when they are combined with the fantasy elements?

[The realistic elements—for instance, the detailed description of the magician's tawdry props and his reference to the canceled show for the *Knights of Pythias* (p. 316)—contrast sharply with the science-fiction literary time machine. The result is a good laugh for readers and a further clue that the entire story will be a comic satire.]

3. The story pokes fun at academics in several short scenes. Identify the scenes and explain what aspects of academics and academia are satirized.

[The first instance occurs: when students are puzzled by the appearance of a bald Jew on page 100 of *Madame Bovary*. The teacher in Sioux Falls, North Dakota, who evidently has not reread the book to prepare for class, simply assumes the students are wrong. Next, a Stanford professor discovers Kugelmass, but instead of showing disbelief or shock, the professor simply falls back on the reliable cliché of literary criticism: "I guess the mark of a classic is that you can reread it a thousand times and always find something new" (p. 320). At the end of the story, a comp lit professor uses his professional expertise (he recognizes Kugelmass in the novel) to pursue a personal vendetta.]

4. Like so many characters in fables and fairy tales who have their wishes granted, Kugelmass finds that getting his heart's desire is not all he expected. Trace the progress of his affair with Madame Bovary. How do his responses to her change? Why do they change?

[The affair with Madame Bovary goes well enough until they both get greedy. He wants to bring her back to New York, and when he does, they are both challenging the powers of Persky's box. When technical difficulties (even magicians' machines have "down time") prevent Emma from returning to France, both she and Kugelmass have to watch the changes worked on her by twentieth-century New York. As she understands her options, she becomes less and less entranced with Kugelmass. We see a classic unfolding of the Pygmalion story gone awry. Kugelmass creates the twentieth-century Emma, but she learns her lessons too well and turns on him. Of course, when Kugelmass sees that Emma is going to create difficulties and complexities for him, he rejects her and is frantic to return her to her own time and place.]

5. What is the significance of the final section? Are we supposed to find a message in the story?

[The final section suggests that Kugelmass, like many people, simply does not learn from experience. He's still hooked on the idea that romance can solve all his problems, and after a few weeks to rest up from the Madame Bovary experience, he is ready to look for an easy miracle again. The last two paragraphs are a classic fable ending: the character who refuses to learn is punished through his own foolishness and condemned to live always in the conditions resulting from the folly. The last sentence is pure Woody Allen genius— who could imagine a more horrible fate for a middle-aged hedonist than being stuck forever in a "Remedial Spanish" text? And the *coup de grâce*, of course, is that horror of all language students, the irregular verb. (Not without significance is the translation of the verb, *to have*. Kugelmass wants "*to have* it all," but in an ironic reversal he will spend eternity being relentlessly pursued by his desire "to have.")]

6. Read *Madame Bovary* and compare the title character with the Madame Bovary of "The Kugelmass Episode." Is there evidence in Flaubert's book to suggest she might, in fact, respond as Allen's story pictures her?

7. If you had free and ready access to Persky's box, what book, short story, or play would you choose to visit? Decide on a specific character you would like to meet, and in which specific page or episode in the work. Write an essay or short story describing your experience.

[Students might enjoy reading or hearing each other's papers on this topic.]

"I'm Your Horse in the Night" • *Luisa Valenzuela (pp. 322–324)*

1. What is the situation of the narrator in the story? Why must she hear a secret signal before she answers the door? When she hears the signal, she says, "[I]t could be them. . . ." To whom does "them" refer?

[The narrator is apparently the lover of a political rebel. (Note in the list of statements she makes when she first sees Beto, "I thought you were theorizing about the revolution in another country.") Students who are unfamiliar with the volatile situation in countries such as Chile and El Salvador may appreciate knowing that organized underground movements exist there, similar to those in countries such as France, Holland, and Denmark during the World War II Nazi occupation.

It is likely the narrator does not know Beto's real name as a form of protection both for her and for the movement. If she is questioned by the police, she cannot reveal what she doesn't know. The "them" she expects to hear from are probably Beto's compatriots in the rebel movement. Oddly, she later talks to someone she takes to be Andrés, apparently another movement worker, without waiting for any signal. Perhaps this is because she is so shaken by what she believes to be the visit and departure of Beto.]

2. The story is divided into three parts. Summarize what happens in each part and discuss the relationship you see among the three sections.

[The first section is the longest; we meet Beto and the woman he affectionately calls Chiquita. Tension builds as the two reunite after months apart: The narrator spills out her fears and hopes, and it becomes clear that the meeting is fraught with the danger of discovery by the forces Beto opposes. Nevertheless, the meeting is intensely romantic, filled with images of a sensuous liqueur, a soulful song, slow dancing, and love-making. As the two talk, the narrator reflects on Gal Costa's song. She sees the line "I'm your horse in the night" as meaning that the woman is a means of delivery, a mount for a spirit. Beto teases her gently. insisting that the line simply makes a sexual reference to a man riding a woman as part of intercourse.

The second section is nearly as long as the first, yet contrasts sharply with its tone of death, decay, and betrayal. The narrator hears the phone ring, just as she has heard the doorbell ring at the beginning of the first section. But rather than delivering unexpected pleasure, the phone brings a message of horror. The person she at first takes to be Beto's compatriot tells her that her lover has been dead six days. When she protests, the caller abruptly hangs up, leading her to see the call as a trap. It seems strange that since she is suspicious, she is surprised when the police show up and interrogate her. She denies seeing Beto and, through evaluating her interior monologue, the reader learns that she either truly believes or is trying to convince herself that the encounter with Beto was a dream. If the meeting happened only in her mind, she can keep her knowledge safe from Beto's enemies. She says that "dreams are none of the cop's business" and that she is "not about to tell them my dream."

The final, very short section shows the relationship between the first two sections. The narrator's comments suggest the fine line between the world of dreams and the world of nightmares (whether sleeping or waking). In addition, the concluding section shows that the woman sees herself as more than just a sexual partner. She has become her own version of Beto's "horse in the night." She says that he can inhabit her wherever she is (perhaps by appearing in her dreams). Of course, she may also have delivered him from danger by refusing to admit she saw him and thus diverting the police from discovering his hiding place.]

3. Is the first section of the story a dream? What evidence do you find to support your reading of this section?

[On an initial reading, the first section seems quite real, with details like the doorbell, the dialogue, the cachaca, and the Gal Costa record providing concrete, believable images. On a second read, with the rest of the story in mind, the reader discovers ambiguities. Note, for example, that the second section begins with the ringing telephone. Perhaps the sound at the beginning of section one was really the telephone which the sleeping narrator's mind translated into the doorbell's chimes. When Beto and the narrator look at each other, it is "out of focus." Later, they move to the bed "half-dancing. half-floating," suggesting the movement of a dream. At the beginning of the second section, the narrator awakes alone (although she does state that Beto's habit is "to [run] away while I'm asleep without a word about where he's gone").

On the other hand, the phone call in the second section almost certainly led to the arrival of the police. The caller, then, almost certainly was someone who suspected Beto of being with the narrator. So is it not unreasonable to project that she creates—consciously or subconsciously—the idea of the dream to strengthen herself for the interrogation she knows will come. She tries to convince herself that Beto's visit was a dream so that she will not betray him. Her final sentence, though, indicates that she herself is not certain whether or not the incident was real. Much as she tries to believe in the idea of the dream, she still thinks there's a "wild chance" the Gal Costa record and half-empty bottle of cachaca may be in her house. She "[wills] them out of existence" because she knows they

63

will reveal to the police that Beto has been in Brazil and then returned to her house. (You may want to mention to students that Brazilians speak Portuguese, unlike the narrator and Beto who are Spanish speakers; this accounts for her translating the title of the song.)]

4. Research the situation in a South American country where political terrorism exists. Then compare what you have learned with the details provided in this story.

5. What is your response to the narrator's vision of herself as Beto's "Horse in the Night"? Do you see role as heroic? Subservient? Misguided? Or something else? Explain.

"Rape Fantasies" • Margaret Atwood (pp. 325–330)

1. What is the narrator's attitude toward the subject? (First, of course, you'll need to determine what the story's subject *is*.)

[Is the subject of the story rape or rape fantasies? The two seem very different as described by the narrator's office friends. As she correctly points out, the other women have simply imagined sexual encounters with men they "haven't met formally." As she goes on to describe what she calls her own "rape fantasies," she seems as far adrift from the vicious crime of rape as do her office mates. The narrator, in fact, never really faces the idea of rape, but instead pictures herself in a series of bizarre encounters with severely emotionally disturbed men (all of whom she is able to placate or outwit in some way). The real subject of the story seems to be power fantasies rather than rape fantasies; none of the narrator's projections concerns the act of rape, but rather her reaction to a threatening intruder.]

2. What kind of person is the narrator? Do you find her sympathetic?

[The narrator's unsympathetic attitude toward her co-workers may be explained by their idiosyncrasies, but few readers will forgive her snooping in company records to discover confidential information which she then discusses with a casual new acquaintance she has just met at a bar. She is extremely judgmental and critical both of her co-workers and of the imaginary (pathetic) men with whom she peoples her fantasies. Although her speech suggests that she does not have a great deal of formal education, she is witty and funny. She sees the hypocrisy in the conversation of her co-workers, who first claim they never have rape fantasies and then delight in describing intimate pictures in lurid detail. The narrator's scene with the attacker and the plastic lemon is ironically witty as it undercuts the smarmy seriousness of Chrissy, Darlene, and Greta.]

3. The narrator claims to be more sophisticated and enlightened than her office mates. Do you think she is wiser than they?

[The narrator talks as though she understood more than her friends, and she certainly sees that their approach to rape is as silly and shallow as the newspaper and magazine articles she ridicules. On the other hand, she does not seem to comprehend the nature of rape herself. She does see that rape is about power rather than about sex (her fantasies suggest the need to get the upper hand), but she does not seem to grasp the extreme anger most rapists have toward women. At the end of the story she naively proclaims that she does not see how any man could rape a woman with whom he had just had a long conversation. Although she seems uncertain about this pronouncement, the mere fact that she holds out hope for such a strategy shows that she is not very far ahead of her friends in thinking through this serious issue.]

4. What do we know about the relationship between the narrator and her mother?

[The mother seems to have spent most of her time warning her daughter about the dangers of life. She didn't want the narrator to bury dead robins "because of the germs"; she urges her daughter not to "dwell on unpleasant things"; and when the narrator imagines a rapist entering through a coal chute, she thinks immediately about writing to her mother to warn her to nail up the coal chute in the family home. The narrator has clearly grown up with a sense that the world is a dangerous place, and she still thinks often of her mother as an authority figure full of cautionary advice.]

5. To whom is the narrator speaking? How does the person addressed relate to the story's theme?

[This story is, in some ways, like one of Robert Browning's dramatic monologues. The narrator addresses a specific listener who helps to create the story's theme. Early in the story we are given clues about the listener when the narrator repeatedly says that "it's different for a guy." In the final paragraphs, we discover that she is talking to someone in a bar. She is obviously a bit nervous because she tells her listener that all the waiters know her and will protect her from anyone who "bothers" her. She seems to have spent all this time describing her "rape" fantasies to a man who sits silently as she explains that she can't imagine anyone raping a woman with whom he has had a long conversation. Does she intend to go home with this man? Is she trying to ward off the possibility of rape? Is she instead challenging the man, hoping that he'll give her a chance to show how well she can take care of herself? We have no clues as the the man's responses, if in fact he shows any. But the circumstances under which the story is told are certainly significant and work discussing.]

6. To what extent can we identify the narrator with the author? What clues suggest where Atwood's beliefs and attitudes differ from those of the narrator she has created?

[Do you think this story takes a realistic attitude toward rape? Do you find the story offensive in nay way? Do you think it takes a serious subject too lightly? Or does it, in fact, address the complexities of this violent crime?

"Cathedral" • Raymond Carver (pp. 331–340)

1. What is the narrator's opinion of himself? What details does he choose to explain who he is and to justify his responses to Robert's visit?

[The narrator sees himself as a practical, down-to-earth man who gets his opinions from television and who prides himself on not liking poetry. He is uncomfortable with anything unknown, which is one reason he fears Robert's visit. He also resents his wife's close communication with Robert, particularly the fact that she and Robert had discussed (on the tapes they exchanged) whether or not the narrator and his wife should get married.]

2. The narrator describes in detail his horrified response to Robert's marriage (p. 333). What particularly disturbs him? How does his own marriage compare to the picture we are given of Robert and Beulah's marriage?

[The narrator feels sorry for Robert because he married someone whom he could never see, but he feels more pity for the wife because she could never feel that her husband knew what she was wearing or what expression she had on her face. The narrator seems to think that all understanding in marriage comes from external circumstances. He also implies that a woman dresses primarily to please her husband and that she communicates mainly through the way she looks. In his own marriage, the narrator shows himself to be insensitive to the way his wife is feeling, and we may have the sense that he should pity his own wife rather than Beulah.]

3. What does the episode about the experiences of the narrator's wife in her first marriage contribute to the story? Is the episode necessary to the plot? To characterization? To theme?

[The episode shows us a sensitive side of the narrator's wife. She is defeated by the lack of connection she feels as an Air Force wife; she feels lonely and cut off from other people. She writes poetry and sends tapes. After her suicide attempt and her divorce, her communication with Robert is her lifeline to getting well. Although the narrator dismisses the wife's tapes as "her chief means of recreation," it is clear that Robert was an extremely powerful and helpful force in her life. Through this episode, we find the suggestion of a possible theme: Emotional and moral blindness are the true handicaps to be feared; physical blindness does not affect the healing qualities of human understanding.]

4. How does Robert behave when he meets the narrator? What do we learn about both the husband and Robert from their initial exchanges?

[Robert is comfortable and warm; the husband is anxious and awkward. When the narrator blurts out a question about which side of the train Robert sat on (with the idea of explaining to Robert where he could get the best view), Robert is not defensive; he simply answers the question. Robert shows his self-confidence when he asks for scotch and tells the anecdote about Barry Fitzgerald (p. 334), The narrator's stereotyped ideas about blind people continue to be destroyed when Robert chain-smokes cigarettes, although the narrator had read that blind people didn't smoke because "they couldn't see the smoke they exhaled" (p. 334).]

5. What is the significance of the cathedral episode? Why does Carver choose a cathedral rather than some other building or object?

[Cathedrals suggest a higher power, a kind of spirituality, which the husband would normally dismiss. But he and Robert have been sharing a marijuana cigarette; the dope, the late hour, and the wife's absence promote a connection between the two men and an openness to new possibilities. When the husband first tries to describe the cathedral, he has trouble because he isn't used to really seeing carefully or to understanding another person's point of view. Robert encourages the narrator, so that, in the end, Robert is the one who is doing the showing and the narrator is the one who is learning.]

6. How has the narrator changed at the end of the story?

[The narrator has had to challenge many assumptions he had held and to change his view not only about blind people and about being blind, but also about the way sighted people see. He may have introduced Robert to marijuana, but Robert has brought a truly mind-expanding experience to the narrator. The narrator has learned how to move beyond the limits he has always known, and we have the feeling that after this experience he will be profoundly changed.]

7. Compare the treatment of the time of blindness in "Cathedral" to that of the same theme in D. H. Lawrence's "The Blind Man" (p. 213).

66

8. In "Cathedral," one incident causes the narrator to challenge old assumptions and to find a new way to approach life. Write a paper explaining how or why you changed your mind about an old assumption of your own.

"Doc's Story" • John Edgar Wideman (pp. 340–346)

1. How does the narrator describe the woman he has lost? What details in this description suggest possibilities of conflicts in their relationship? (As you consider this topic, reread the first two paragraphs and the last five paragraphs.)

[The narrator emphasizes the smallness of the woman and, while he notes that when he was with her he thought "that God made little things closer to perfect than he ever made big things," there are hints that the woman was, in significant ways, too small in spirit for him. The opening paragraph notes casually that she and he had been part of the picketing effort against Woolworth's. Since she is white (the first sentence describe her "small, white hands) and he is black, we know that the two faced the issues that are part of nearly any interracial relationship.

Throughout the story, the narrator wonders if telling the woman Doc's story might have made a difference. But in the conclusion, he admits that "to her [his stories were] folklore, superstition." He believes she would have been interested only because the story would have "revealed the psychology, the pathology of the oppressed." Unlike the narrator, the woman takes a practical, logical view of the world, taking a skeptical view of both magic and religion. She is unable to make the leap of faith required to open herself to his world and to the possibilities he sees lying before them.

2. How does the language in the story change? What significance do you see in these shifts?

[At the beginning and end of the story, the narrator's thoughts are recorded in what some call standard English. However, as he recalls the solace he found hanging out at the basketball court, shooting hoops and swapping stories, his thoughts slip into the black English of the men with whom he shared reefer, wine, and wisdom during that long, solitary summer and fall. The difference in language underlines the differences between the world of the white woman who left and the world of the narrator who finds his strength and optimism not in picketing and intellectualizing black history, but rather in immersing himself in the lore of the community that raised and nurtured him.]

3. The following paragraph introduces the narrator's response to Doc's story:

> Of all the stories, the one about Doc had bothered him most. Its orbit was unpredictable. Twice in one week, then only once more last summer. He'd only heard Doc's story three times, but that was enough to establish Doc behind and between the words of all the other stories. In a strange way, Doc presided over the court. You didn't need to mention him. He was just there. Regent Park stories began with Doc and ended with Doc and everything in between was preparation, proof the circle was unbroken.

Write an analysis of this paragraph. How does each sentence—and each image within each sentence—relate to the conflicts and themes of Wideman's story?

[The first sentence raises the question of why Doc's story "bothered" the narrator. What does he mean by "bothered"? Was he annoyed, puzzled, prompted to think? To clarify, he tells us that the story's "orbit was unpredictable." So the story is compared to a sphere (perhaps a basketball) that goes where it is not expected to go. The next two sentences tell

67

us that he heard the story three times—a magic number, familiar to fables and folk tales. Doc himself seems larger than the story; he becomes a miraculous figure who not only can do the unexpected but who can inspire others to expect the impossible. The final sentence in the paragraph suggests the cyclical, ritualistic quality of the storytelling and the ball-playing and, by extension, the lives of the tellers and players. As we discover at the end, the narrator holds on to the image of Doc and his astonishing accomplishments as proof that no reach is too far, no goal too fantastic to realize.]

4. How do the facts the narrator gives us about Doc's life relate to the story the basketball players tell about him?

[Doc is older than most of the players and acts as protector and mentor. He offers them ice water an cool spray from his lawn hose on hot days. Best of all, he defies his racist white neighbors who frown on the "bunch of loud, sweaty, half-naked niggers" he entertains. Doc has achieved success by the standards of the white world; he attended university and then became a professor. He ignores the patronizing views of whites who think he must have been an athlete to have made his way to higher education, yet he is not ashamed to show that, in fact, he does have astonished talent on the court. Doc's background, the, makes him different in some ways from the other ball players, yet he maintains a close, rooted connection with them. Perhaps it is this dichotomy in Doc's life that particularly appeals to the narrator who is in somewhat the same situation.]

5. How does Doc's blindness relate to the theme of the story?

[Doc succeeds in spite of his blindness and, even when he misses a free throw, recoups his status with the group by insisting that he will become part of a real game of basketball. The person who tells Doc's story doesn't remember who won the game—the significant thing is that he played. He did not let overwhelming odds keep him out of what he wanted to do most. The narrator tries to believe that if he had told the woman this story, she might have stayed. She might have been convinced that, as the narrator claims, "There's still a chance. There's always a chance!"]

6. Compare the experience of young black American men as depicted in this story with the experience depicted in Ralph Ellison's "Battle Royal" (p. 286).

7. Compare the narrator's response to Doc's story to the narrator's response to Robert and his story in Raymond Carver's "Cathedral" (p. 331).

8. The basketball players in "Doc's Story" have certain tales that they live by—incidents that are recounted over and over again. Most families and group of friends have their own collection of lore. Write one of the stories you live by and explain why it is so important to you.

"Everyday Use" • *Alice Walker (pp. 346–351)*

1. The story is divided into five sections. Why are the first four sections short, while the final section is long? How are the sections related to each other?

[Each of the first four sections serves to give background information that will make the episode in the final section more meaningful. For example, in the first short section we see how beautiful the yard is to the mother, and this when Dee/Wangero insists on taking pictures that include only the run-down house, we are struck by her dishonesty and manipulation. The second section begins with the mother's fantasy of what an ideal reunion with Dee might be like and a description of why such a reunion could almost certainly not happen. This fantasy prepares us for Dee's behavior in the final section.

The next section introduces Maggie, setting up the contrast between the two sisters and suggesting some of the reasons for Dee's estrangement from her family: She has gone to school and learned to read, but she has swallowed other people's ideas and tried to force them on her mother and sister. The final introductory section continues the contrast between Dee and Maggie and suggests that Dee's overbearing personality has turned away friends as well as family. The four opening sections prepare us for Dee's behavior in the long final section. We come to that section with an unsympathetic view of Dee, which is essential to the theme of the story. Since some of the things Dee says make sense, we have to understand what her mother calls Dee's "style of her own" to see how selfish and unfeeling she is in demanding her grandmother's quilts.]

2. What is the significance of the discussion between Dee/Wangero and her mother about Dee's name change?

[Dee has probably changed her name to Wangero as a radical act. She says she doesn't want to be named for her oppressors. The mother points out that she was named for an aunt who was named for a grandmother who was named for her mother. But when Dee's mother refuses to trace the name back any further than that, Dee and her friend Hakim exchange knowing looks. The mother's point seems to be that in seeking to rid herself of what she regards as the oppressor's name, Wangero is actually divesting herself of generations of real history and family connection. It is interesting to note that as the mother continues to tell the story, she uses Wangero's new name for a while—although usually with Dee as a modifier—but at the end of the story she says she snatched the quilt out of "Miss Wangero's hands," and after that she calls her daughter simply Dee.]

3. Why does Wangero want the dasher and top from the butter churn? The quilts? How do her reasons for wanting them reflect her view of her mother and Maggie?

[Wangero wants to take the churn to display on a table and the quilts to use as wall hangings. She sees them as artifacts of black culture and so as representative of black history; but she does not value the living patterns of the people who still see the objects as useful parts of daily life. Wangero seems to see her mother and Maggie in much the same way as she sees the churn top and the quilts. They are fine to display to her friends in picturesque photos, but they are not suitable to be part of Wangero's daily life.]

4. What is the significance of the ending? In what ways is the ending ironic?

[Wangero thinks she values black heritage, but in fact she sees black lives from a very narrow perspective. She tells Maggie to try to make something of herself without every recognizing Maggie's lack of opportunity and Maggie's own desires. She accuses her mother of not appreciating her heritage without seeing that her mother lives that heritage every day. When the narrator asserts herself and grabs back the quilts, she affirms both her own and Maggie's humanity and dignity.]

5. Compare the mother to Phoenix Jackson in Eudora Welty's "A Worn Path" (p. 71).

6. Describe the final incident of the quilts from the point of view of each of the following characters: Dee/Wangero, Maggie, Hakim. Try to capture their speech patterns as well as their responses to the situation and to each other.

"The View of Me From Mars" • *Lee K. Abbott (pp. 352–356)*

1. The narrator says that both the story he read at age 23 and the story he is telling now center on "illusions and the mess they make crashing down." What are the illusions and mess of the first story? Of the second?

[In the first story, the sideshow appears filled with illusions to the little girl. She sees things she cannot understand or explain. More important, she learns that her father cannot understand or explain these things and that he feels deeply distressed and inadequate because he has allowed her to see them. When he answers her question as to how the exhibits in the sideshow are possible, he replies, "Mirrors, it's done with mirrors." The mirrors, of course, suggest illusion, but the father's response itself is the biggest illusion. Unable to say what he really feels and believes to his daughter, he hides behind the smoke screen of illusory words. Realizing that her father is lying, the daughter gives up her typical child's illusion that her father is perfect. Yet she forgives him and enters into a mutual conspiracy of new illusion when she replies, "Yes, mirrors, I thought so," thus allowing her father to save face and herself to preserve some of her old relationship with him.

In the narrator's story, his whole life seems like an illusion. He is a minister, yet for four years he has been committing adultery with a woman willing to create the illusion that she is a naughty Swede or a pristine Snow White. He also seems to have remained an adolescent who preserves the importance of college status symbols. Few men in their early 40's would describe their lovers by noting what sorority they were in and where they attended college. (He also describes his wife as "a blond continental-history major.") As the narrator explains his affair, he shows over and over again how he deludes himself into thinking that he can lead two lives and somehow still be whole. At the end, he lies to his wife and hopes that his son (who knows he is lying) will accept the need to preserve the illusion of the intact family and tell a cover story that will corroborate the lie he has told his wife. The mess, of course, comes because the narrator must now admit that he cannot, with any integrity, lead two separate lives. He must also live with the knowledge that his son knows him to be a weak man and his wife suspects his duality.]

2. What is the significance of the title?

[After Ellen Kay has asked Pudge about the golf game his father supposedly watched, the narrator experiences a strange sense of alienation. He pictures himself as a Martian, observing his son as someone from another planet might look at humans. He knows that preserving the fiction he has woven depends upon his son, but he sees Pudge in highly unflattering terms. He sees Pudge as someone who "had never looked much beyond himself to see the insignificant dust ball he stood upon" and calls him "polite, fussy as a nun." He believes Pudge's only real interests to be golf and computer science. These descriptive phrases suggest that the narrator in casting himself as a Martian sees his son as an alien.

It's also significant that the story is called "The View of Me from Mars." The narrator focuses almost entirely on himself and on how he will be affected by Pudge's response to his mother's questions about the fictional golf round.]

3. The narrator claims that the story "Mirrors" has much in common with his own story and that both are about "lies and love and how forgiveness works." What similarities do you see between the two stories? What differences do you see?

[n the first story, we see only the child's point of view (or the narrator's version of the child's point of view). While the narrator claims that the story has a sad ending, in fact most readers will see it as a rather typical initiation story where the child loses a bit of innocence and sees the adult world in clearer perspective. The young girl may now know that her father does not always tell the exact truth and that he sometimes tries to cover his own mistakes, but she seems easily able to accept these relatively minor failings. The father, after all, has been trying to please her and is guilty only of bad judgment and of the human failing of wanting to appear more perfect than he is in the eyes of someone he loves.

The narrator's story is also about a father who lies. But in many other ways the story is not the same at all. This father lies to get himself out of a sticky situation with his wife. And the lie relates to a profound betrayal not only of his family, but also of the profession he follows. If Pudge does cover for his father, he is lying in a very different way than the young girl who kindly decides to accept her father's implausible explanation that the side show is "all done with mirrors." Her acceptance builds a covenant between her and her father (as suggested by the fact that the phrase "done with mirrors" becomes a standard family joke when the father is confronted with things he cannot understand). On the other hand, if Pudge lies for his father, he is betraying both himself and his mother. The narrator may rationalize that the situation is similar to the rather innocent conflict presented in "Mirrors," but this belief is simply one more illusion in a life build on deceptions, half-truths and false values.]

5. The Latin words the narrator thinks of as he tells his wife that he was at the golf course watching Pudge translate as follows: *bellum*, war; *verus*, true, real; *fatum*, fate. How do these words relate to the theme of the story and to the particular incident in the story where they occur?

6. Write two different endings for this story. One in which Pudge lies for his father and one in which he does not. Write from the narrator's point of view, depicting his response to each of these possible choices.

7. Compare the characters, conflicts, and themes in "Doc's Story" (p. 340) to the characters, conflicts, and themes in "The View of Me from Mars." Note especially the way the narrator in each story believes in the redemptive power of a story he has heard or read.

"Yellow Woman" • *Leslie Silko (pp. 359–364)*

1. Read the first two paragraphs carefully, paying special attention to the descriptive words. What pattern of imagery do you notice? How does this pattern relate to the title? What effect do these images have on the opening setting?

[The first two paragraphs have a dominant pattern of color images: "brown water birds," "brown scratches, "alkali-white crust," "green ragged moss," "red blanket, "white river sand" (repeated), "a black horse," "pale red mesas." The title too refers to color, and as we read the story we learn that Yellow Woman is a powerful legendary figure. The concentration of color images creates a vivid and dramatic opening setting which suggests the sensual and surreal qualities of the story.]

2. What do we learn about the legend of Yellow Woman and the ka'tsina in the first section What is the narrator's attitude toward the legend?

[In the first section we learn the story of Yellow Woman, who meets a spirit in the form of a man, thinks only of him, feels herself to be out of time, and goes off with the ka'tsina to the north. The narrator's grandfather used to tell stories of Yellow Woman, and in the grandfather's story the ka'tsina seems sometimes to take the form of an animal. The narrator, deeply moved by her passionate encounter with Silva, begins to wonder if she may be Yellow Woman. She tries to dismiss the idea by seeing herself as an ordinary modern woman who has been to school and has seen highways and trucks. These details twentieth-century life separate her from Yellow Woman, who is part of the past. The narrator doubts her connection with that past as she thinks of her husband Al and her family living on the reservation.]

3. How does Silva treat the narrator in Section 3? What evidence does he offer to prove that he is the ka'tsina spirit? What happens to the narrator when she sets out to go home?

[Silva insists that he is the ka'tsina. He points out to the narrator that someday, in the distant future, people will talk about them and say, "Those two lived long ago when things like that happened" (p. 360). He tries to convince the narrator that they are both a continuing part of the legend of her grandfather's tales. His description of himself as outside all the tribes and societies at the bottom of his mountain and his stealing of cattle also suggest the spirits of traditional legends.

When Yellow Woman objects to Silva's laughing at her, he physically overpowers her and she seems mesmerized by him. When she sets out to return home the next day, she finds herself ending up not at her reservation at the foot of the mountain, but back at Silva's stone house.]

4. How does Silva's image in Section 3 contrast with his image in the earlier sections?

[In the first two sections we see Silva only through the narrator's eyes; in the third section we see the white rancher denouncing him as a dangerous, despicable thief. During the confrontation, Silva sends the narrator away. He pulls his gun and looks at the rancher with an "ancient and dark" look in his eyes. In this section, Silva is not the ka'tsina lover spirit, but the ka'tsina avenging spirit. He alone, among all the tribes he has named, seems to stand proud and free, still living in the woods and not on territory assigned to him by the white government.]

5. Plan an argument either refuting or defending this premise: Silva really is the ka'tsina spirit and the narrator is Yellow Woman.

[Certainly the original ka'tsina legend could have grown in much the same way as this story seems to have. A woman, weary of her daily life, wanders away and meets a strong, independent man who, by choice, lives apart from others. She goes off with him, and her family relates what has happened in terms of the supernatural. In this sense, Silva is the modern ka'tsina and the narrator is (as she speculates in this first section) a modern Yellow Woman.]

6. Write a fifth section to the story, showing the narrator telling her story to her family.

7. Compare the narrator and Silva's experience with the experience of Calixta and Alcée in Kate Chopin's "The Storm" (p. 141).

"Girl" • *Jamaica Kincaid (pp. 356–357)*

1. Who are the two characters whose voices we hear in this brief story? What do you learn about each one? (Try highlighting the lines from one voice in one color and the other voice in another color.)

[One voice, the advice-giver, clearly dominates. This voice is almost certainly female since the topics she addresses are those considered traditionally women's concerns. She is probably the mother of the young girl to whom she is speaking, although she could be the grandmother, aunt, or much older sister. She cares about the girl and lets her in on secrets such as "how to love a man" and "how to make good medicine to throw away a child before it even becomes a child." On the other hand, she also cares a great deal what other people think and much of her advice is aimed at controlling the girl's behavior so she will be thought well of. For example, "always eat your food in such a way that it won't turn someone else's stomach," and "don't sing benna in Sunday school." She is particularly concerned with the girl's sexual behavior and continually warns her against becoming a "slut." The girl must "walk like a lady" and she must not "squat down to play marbles." The second voice is barely heard. The girls speaks only twice (her speeches appear in italics), and each time the mother either ignores or treats her comment with contempt. The first time the girl speaks, she denies singing benna (Calypso music) in Sunday School. The mother makes no appropriate response and instead continues with her relentless list of do's and don'ts. The second time the girl speaks, she expresses a worry—a concern that she might not be able to carry out the order her mother has given her. "[B]ut what if the baker won't let me feel the bread?" she asks. Rather than stopping to listen or to respond with sympathy, the mother takes the opportunity to chastise he daughter and, once again, to suggest her fear of what others may think of her child: "[Y]ou mean to say that after all you are really going to be the kind of woman who the baker won't let near the bread?]

2. Make a list of words and phrases that are frequently repeated. Note also the punctuation between sentences. What is the effect of the repetition and unusual punctuation? How do these devices relate to the theme of the story?

[Repeated words include "don't," "and," and "slut"; the most commonly repeated phrase is "this is how." Sentences are connected by semi-colons rather than being separated by periods. One effect of both the repetition and the semi-colons is to create a breathless, hurried, relentless tone that suggests how the daughter must feel as she listens to the endless advice with which her mother constantly assaults her. We also get the sense of urgency that the mother feels. She has so little time to provide her daughter with the practical information she needs to stay safe and respected in her world.]

3. Do you feel more sympathetic or empathetic toward one of the characters? Explain.

[Many students will feel immediate sympathy for the daughter. Most of us can remember being on the receiving end of such advice and can relate to being ignored as we tried to question or challenge the advice. One the other hand, while the mother may be annoying, her deep concern for her daughter is obvious in nearly every category of advice. She tells her how to do chores, offers patterns for social behavior, gives her medical secrets, informs her of ways to grow the food needed for survival, and passes on what she knows of the psychology and sociology of the culture in which her daughter will live. Most readers will deplore her negative tone—particularly her repeated accusation that her daughter will become a "slut," but most will recognize that this meanness is motivated by a deep seated fear and a wish to keep her daughter safe and respected.]

4. Write a short story called "Boy" or "Girl" and in it give the advice you, as a parent, would give to your son or daughter. Use the style and format of Jamaica Kincaid's "Girl."

5. Compare the mother-daughter relationship in "Girl" with the mother-daughter relationship in "I Stand Here Ironing."

"Eleven" • *Sandra Cisneros (pp. 364–366)*

1. What is the central metaphor of the story? How does it suggest the story's theme?

   [The central metaphor is the concept that each person is a series of selves, all nested one inside the other "like an onion or like the rings inside a tree trunk or like . . . little wooden dolls that fit one inside the other, each year inside the next one." As Rachel tells about her eleventh birthday, she recognizes that numbers of years mean very little; a person responds to varying circumstances with varying patterns of behavior. Events that surprise or sadden or embarrass us may strip away the defenses we've been building up and reduce us to a reaction that comes from the two- or three- or four-year-old within.]

2. In addition to the nested-ages metaphor, Rachel uses many other figurative descriptions that indicate the consciousness of an eleven-year old. List some of these descriptions and comment on what they tell you about Rachel and her encounter with Mrs. Price.

   [Rachel describes her eleven years as "rattling inside me like pennies in a tin Band-aid box" and says the red sweater is "all stretched out like you could use it for a jump rope." Both saving pennies in a Band-aid box and jumping rope are activities typical to childhood; these are not comparisons an adult would normally make. She also describes the red sweater as looking like a mountain and a waterfall. While these images are not unique to childhood speech, they sound natural and plausible. Everything she says sounds like a young child speaking and thus gives us a sense of immediacy and of presence in the classroom. Unlike, for instance, the experiences of the boy in James Joyce's "Araby," the incidents in this story are not filtered through the eyes of an adult narrator. The words Rachel chooses show the extent of the child's distress, her sense of powerlessness, and her humiliation at the hands of the insensitive Mrs. Price.]

3. Why is Rachel so upset by this experience? After all, Phyllis Lopez calmly acknowledges owning the sweater. If it were really so terrible, would anyone admit to that?

   [Rachel characterizes Phyllis Lopez as "even dumber than Sylvia Saldivar." Possibly Phyllis does not recognize that admitting to owning the sweater will in some way cause her to lose face with her classmates. On the other hand, it is also possible that to others the sweater does not appear as bad as it does to Rachel. The real tragedy here is the behavior of Mrs. Price. Unfortunately, she is one of a legion of mediocre, narrow, limited individuals who have, for a variety of not very noble, idealistic, or even clear reasons, chosen teaching as a profession. She does not seem intentionally cruel; she is merely insensitive and self-concerned. Encountering the minor irritation of the abandoned sweater, Mrs. Price persists in trying to get rid of it.

   She pays no attention to Rachel's denial but takes the word of another student (probably because finding an owner quickly will solve the immediate problem of the sweater). As Rachel's discomfort grows, Mrs. Price fails to defuse the misery she sees and instead adds to it by insisting that Rachel put the sweater on. Worst of all, after Rachel is reduced to humiliating sobbing and Phyllis Lopez has admitted owning the sweater, "Mrs. Price pretends like everything's okay." On her eleventh birthday, Rachel has learned the lesson of far too many classrooms: she is at the mercy of an insensitive, probably insecure teacher. Rachel knows that for at least the rest of this year she'll have to spend her school days enduring the fact that "because she's older and the teacher, she's right and I'm not."]

4. Write a sequel to this story in which an older Rachel confronts Mrs. Price with her feelings about the sweater incident.

5. Compare Rachel's experience in "Eleven" with the experience of the narrator in "Battle Royal."

"Snow" • *Julia Alvarex (pp. 366-367)*

1. How does Yolanda develop her image of nuclear holocaust? What relationships can you see between this image and the falling snow?

   [Yolanda, as well as the other students, knows nothing about nuclear war except what she hears in school and sees on the television at home. From these descriptions. she knows that such an event would be filled with horror. Sister Zoe, apparently with the best intentions, illustrates her idea of nuclear fallout by drawing large marks on the blackboard. Being drawn in the white chalk that was almost universally used in schools in the 1950s and early 60s, those marks look something like the snowflakes Yolanda later sees. Unlike the other students in the class, she is unfamiliar with snow and so her mind jumps to the conclusion that these flakes are the same as Sister Zoe's drawing. The final line of the story gently underlines the profound tragedy that nuclear attack would bring. The snowflakes, Sister Zoe says, are each different, "like a person, irreplaceable and beautiful." The snowflakes embody beauty and individuality while the ashes of nuclear holocaust would destroy it. We have the sense that Yolanda must sort out from the host of new experiences she encounters as an immigrant those things that are good and positive from those that are harmful and threatening.]

2. What is your evaluation of Sister Zoe's teaching style?

   [Most readers will respond positively to this "grandmotherly fourth grade teacher." She admires Yolanda's name and helps her become part of the class by asking her to teach the other students to pronounce it correctly. Sister Zoe also spends extra time tutoring Yolanda, helping her to learn English. And when Yolanda mistakenly believes snowflakes to be nuclear fallout, the teacher does not scold or humiliate her but rather explains gently what the white crystals are. She offers the lovely image of individuality and beauty to comfort and reassure Yolanda.

   On the other hand, some readers may object to Sister Zoe's isolating Yolanda in a "special seat in the first row by the window" so that the other students are not disturbed by the tutoring. In addition, many of us would prefer that the lessons on nuclear attack be less graphic, although those of us old enough to remember the Cuban missile crisis and the air raid drills nearly all schools held regularly will be less likely to condemn Sister Zoe.]

3. Compare Yolanda's experience, and the response of her teacher, to Rachel's experience and the response of her teacher (in "Eleven," p. 364). What does each story suggest about the relationship between authority figures and those over whom they hold power?

4. Choose an incident from your own school years when a teacher responded in a positive way to a mistake made by you (or someone you know). Write about this incident in a narrative form similar to Julia Alvarez's "Snow." That is, begin with a description of the teacher, go on to describe the events that precede the mistake, explain the mistake, and then show the teacher's response.

5. Jamaica Kincaid's "Girl" (p. 356), Sandra Cisnero's "Eleven" (p. 364), and "Snow" all show pre-adolescent or adolescent girls who are in the process of learning lessons from older women. Compare these three stories, including in your comparison an evaluation of the learners, the teachers, and the lessons learned (both intentionally and unintentionally).

Additional Topics for Writing—Fiction

1. Choose a description or explanation of war from any nonfiction source outside this text (for example, a history book, a newspaper or journal article, an armed forces manual). Focus on one aspect of war (preparing for a battle, or identifying casualties, for instance). Then compare what you have read to the same aspect of war as treated in any of the following stories:

   War 88
   The Garden of Forking Paths 265
   Guests of the Nation 29

2. Compare the theme of friendship as presented in any of the following stories with your own experiences of friendship:

   The Open Boat 163
   The Blind Man 669
   Cathedral 331

3. Evaluate the concept of progress or change as it is treated in the following stories:

   Shiloh 45
   A Rose for Emily 57
   The Metamorphosis 183

4. What do you consider to be the most serious difficulty facing parents and children who want to establish good relationships? Explain your ideas by referring to examples from any of the following stories:

   Shiloh 45
   The Boarding House 179
   I Stand Here Ironing 281
   Everyday Use 346
   Girl 336

5. Read a nonfiction account of any part of the minority experience in the United States from a source outside of this text. You might read, for example, accounts of voter registration in the South, or government treaties with Native Americans. Focusing on this one aspect of the minority experience, compare what you read to the way this same aspect is reflected in any of the following stories:

   A Worn Path 71
   Battle Royal 286
   Everyday Use 346
   Yellow Woman 356

6. Several of the stories in the fiction section present characters whom society might call handicapped. Consider this theme and its implications for the characters' lives, choices, and behavior in any of the following stories:

7. Consider the theme of how men combine and balance the various aspects of their personal and professional lives in the following stories:

8. Examine the theme of women's roles in any of the stories listed below. How do you think women's roles today vary from those described? How are they the same?

9. Compare the attitudes toward religion and spirituality of the characters in the following stories:

10. What are the most significant issues for young people as they grow toward adulthood? Explain your ideas by referring to examples from any of the following stories:

PART TWO

Poetry

CHAPTER SIX

Reading Poems

Like the initial chapter in the Fiction section, this chapter describes and illustrates the process of reading. The commentaries are not meant to include every possible aspect of the poems, nor are they intended to suggest one correct or final interpretation. Instead, the annotations and explanations demonstrate how active, critical readers bring their own experiences and knowledge to a text.

Students often bring to poetry reading a resistance born of the belief that poems are puzzles to which only a gifted few hold the key. "The Experience of Poetry" urges them to abandon that view and to see the similarities between reading poetry and reading fiction, drama, or the essay. In addition, and more important, this section encourages students to value their own responses to poems—to note what feelings and memories the poems evoke. The section following Robert Hayden's "Those Winter Sundays" (p. 372) reinforces the importance of personal responses to poetry as the beginning point for any further consideration. After students have read and responded to Hayden's poem, you may wish to assign several selections from the anthology so that they may practice responding freely to poems. Lively discussions often result when students exchange the feelings and memories prompted by the following works:

"The Interpretation of Poetry" and "The Evaluation of Poetry" sections help students put their responses to work. After they have read these sections, students should recognize that one of the most important approaches to reading poetry well is learning to ask significant and useful questions. As an in-class exercise, you might have students read one or two poems from the anthology and then ask them to reread them, and to write down their comments and questions. To begin asking questions, students may focus on the speaker Who is he/she? What do we learn about him/her? What is the speaker's point of view? What is the poet's attitude toward the speaker?). After formulating questions about the speaker, students may move on to questions about the subject and the situation.

You may want to remind students that reading is a recursive process. Their questions will not necessarily occur in neat, linear sequence: speaker, subject, situation. Any one question may prompt a rethinking about, or a relooking at, a previous question; and the rethinking often leads to new questions. An exercise like this should generate a certain amount of "mess," and it's helpful if students realize that all they have to do at this point is to ask questions, not find answers or arrange their thoughts in logical sequence.

After students have completed writing their questions, they might meet in groups or pairs to compare questions and to discover what new queries can be prompted by collaborative brainstorming. When the groups have finished, bringing the class together and listing as many questions as possible on the chalkboard helps to suggest the many different directions that the

81

consideration of a poem can take. You might then want to take three or four representative questions and ask students to write brief, paragraph-long responses to each. If you ask them to bring their responses to the next class, you might open by asking several students to read their papers. After they have read, other students may want to ask further questions or add their own comments. In addition, an exercise like this is an excellent opportunity to point out ideas that might fruitfully be explored as paper topics. Or, if a student is having a particularly difficult time with a question, you could point out a different approach. With writing exercises like these, the students get a great deal of practice, and they also get valuable suggestions from the instructor and other students. In addition, informal writing has the practical advantage of not requiring extensive correction or conference time.

As students work on evaluating "Aunt Jennifer's Tigers," their commentaries will vary. Certainly they will see that the speaker is probably a woman (she seems closely associated with the poet herself) who values her aunt's embroidered tigers greatly. We may or may not think much about the nameless uncle whose wedding ring weighs down his wife's hand (and apparently her heart as well). Certainly all readers will be impressed with the celebration of the tigers.

The poem begins and ends with the tigers, and they appear with Aunt Jennifer in the title. The tigers thus are associated with her; they somehow belong to her. The tigers are said to "prance"; they also "pace," and they are not afraid of "the men" (possibly hunters) whom Aunt Jennifer has depicted under the tree. These tigers are both beautiful and strong—far more powerful than the men in the poem. As the poem progresses, we see Aunt Jennifer nervously working her stitches; she finds it hard to create her tigers because her hand is made heavy by her wedding ring. Since even the most ornate ring would not weigh enough to impede a woman's sewing, we can see that Rich probably means the wedding band to represent a psychological rather than a physical oppression. Aunt Jennifer's struggle to create something beautiful and powerful, something that belongs only to her, suggests that she feels stifled and constrained in her marriage.

In the final stanza, we find the narrator projecting Aunt Jennifer's death and imagining that she will still lie "ringed" with ordeals that oppressed her in life. Aunt Jennifer herself has never stepped out of the roles dictated by society, and the poem implies that even death cannot remove these strictures from her. On the other hand, her tigers continue to prance. They go on living, a product of her handiwork, representing an aspect of Aunt Jennifer that she could not herself display. Vibrant, strong, certain, and very much alive, the tigers symbolize a power and vitality Aunt Jennifer could possess only in imagination. Ironically, Aunt Jennifer truly lives only through the projected energy of the needlepoint tigers that survive her earthly existence.

While students are generating questions or working on their responses to the poems you have assigned, they will note the importance of paying attention to word choice. For example, the analysis of Hayden's "Those Winter Sundays" in "The Interpretation of Poetry" emphasizes the connotations of "austere" and "lonely." In addition, the analysis contrasts the highly abstract language of the conclusion with the concrete details of the preceding stanzas. When students consider the poet's word choice and use of language, they should, of course, also consider these aspects of their own writing. No other genre demonstrates so clearly the impact of the right word, the power of the exact image.

Additional Topics for Writing and Discussion

"Those Winter Sundays" • Robert Hayden (p. 372)
"My Papa's Waltz" • Theodore Roethke (p. 383)

1. Compare the fathers in these poems. Is one a more sympathetic character than the other? Why?

2. Each of these poems is written by a man looking back on his boyhood. How is this point of view significant to the picture we get of the fathers and to the theme of each poem?

3. The narrator in each poem presents a loving but honest picture of his father. Write a similar description of someone you know well. Be sure to pick someone who has qualities you admire as well as qualities you do not admire. Try to balance the details in your description so that the reader is given a fair picture—not bitter but not overly sentimental either.

4. Both poems, but particularly "My Papa's Waltz," suggest that the father had conflicts with other people in the family. Write a narrative describing the incident in either poem from the point of view of someone else in the family. For example, tell about the Sunday mornings from an older sister's point of view, or describe the father and son's waltz as experienced by the mother.

"Stopping by Woods on a Snowy Evening" • Robert Frost (p. 376)

1. What contrasts are suggested between the man who owns the woods and the speaker in the poem?

2. What is your feeling toward the speaker? Are you sympathetic to the speaker's response to the snowy woods and to his final decision? Consider the final stanza carefully. Try substituting other words for "promises to keep" to see how your feelings might change (for example, "But I have business deals to make. . .").

3. Consider the experience of the speaker in the poem; then think of a similar situation in your own life. Describe in detail the place you found so attractive; then explain why you left.

"Aunt Jennifer's Tigers" • Adrienne Rich (p. 381)

1. Can an argument be made that Uncle is indeed the villain of the poem? Or is he simply a decent fellow who unthinkingly follows the customs of his time?

2. Would Aunt Jennifer and Uncle ever see themselves the way the speaker does? Might it be that Aunt Jennifer is not unnaturally submissive, but simply following an accepted social pattern?

3. Do you see Aunt Jennifer's embroidery as truly a form of art (and an implicit rebellion), or do you instead see simply another example of how she (and women in general) perform only socially sanctioned acts in socially acceptable ways?

CHAPTER SEVEN

Types of Poetry

Chapter Seven briefly explains the different poetic genres. Under the major categories of *narrative* and *lyric*, numerous subdivisions are described. Brief excerpts of the *epic* are included in the chapter; other types of poetry are defined; and references to examples in the anthology are provided. If you like to teach poetic form in detail, this chapter provides the basis. To accompany Chapter Seven, you may also want to teach the Structure: Closed Form and Open Form section (pp. 452–461, in Chapter Eight), which provides a close study of the sonnet form. For an interesting exercise that encourages both appreciation and understanding of various types of poetry, ask students to select one type and write their own example.

CHAPTER EIGHT

Elements of Poetry

This chapter of the text explains the traditional approach to the study of poetry by defining and illustrating critical terms. Each poetic element is discussed through reference to the poems included in Chapter Six, encouraging students to become aware of how repeated readings and reconsideration of a work can reveal new aspects and meanings. The references to the poems from Chapter Six are direct and concise. More detailed analyses follow new examples introduced at various points in the discussion. (See, for example, the commentary on pp. 392–393 that follows Browning's "My Last Duchess.")

Each element of poetry is discussed to emphasize its most important aspects. The explanation of each element is followed by several poems, as well as questions about the poems that focus on the element under consideration. Throughout Chapter Eight, the study of the elements of poetry is always integrated with the concerns of Chapter Six—reading poems. In addition, with the discussion of each element, this manual will suggest ways of addressing students' own writing processes while they learn to read actively and to evaluate the writing of others.

VOICE: SPEAKER AND TONE

The discussion of speaker and tone focuses attention on the way readers come to understand the attitude a poem expresses toward its subject. To supplement the commentary in the text, you may want to discuss the difference between poet and speaker. In some poems, such as Hayden's "Those Winter Sundays," it is difficult to distinguish between poet and speaker. We can certainly discuss the tone of the poem simply by talking about the words the speaker uses. When we consider "My Last Duchess," however, the problem becomes more complex. Here we have a speaker, the duke, who conveys a particular tone about his subject—the duchess. Looking further, however, we realize that we are not to take the duke at his word; the tone of the poet toward *his* subject (the relationship of the duke and duchess) provides a whole new phase of the discussion. You might ask students what episodes from the duchess's life Browning chooses to have the duke reveal and how he chooses to have the duke discuss these episodes. How do these rhetorical decisions let us know that we are to question the duke's motives?

In discussing speaker and tone, students might think about the way they establish their own persona in their essays, reports, and letters. How can they avoid becoming a "duke"? How can they speak honestly but persuasively to their audiences? How does the duke think of his audience? Has he been convincing? Does evaluating an audience and addressing its members' needs and concerns necessarily indicate a manipulative speaker?

Additional Topics for Writing and Discussion

"War Is Kind" • Stephen Crane (pp. 390–391)

1. In addition to the contrast of images and rhythm in stanzas 1, 3, and 5 to those in stanzas 2 and 4, what other device does Crane use to emphasize the irony in his poem?

[The visual layout of the poem immediately notifies the reader that stanzas 2 and 4 will in some way serve as a counterpoint to stanzas 1, 3, and 5.]

2. Analyze carefully the impact of phrases like "hoarse, booming drums," "unexplained glory," "swift blazing flag," and "the excellence of killing." Consider both the connotation and denotation of individual words as well as phrases. In addition, note how these particular words and phrases contribute to the ironic meaning of the poem.

3. Why does the speaker address a maiden, a babe, and a mother rather than an employer, a neighbor, or a colleague? How do his choices suggest his view of war and its effects?

4. Compare Crane's view of war and its effects to Thomas Hardy's view in "The Man He Killed" (p. 430).

"My Last Duchess" • Robert Browning (pp. 392–393)

1. Why do you think the duke chooses to tell the ambassador about his last duchess? What effect do you think his story will have on the ambassador?

2. We do not learn until the end of the poem the occasion for the duke's speech, nor do we learn who is hearing the speech until the final lines. Would your reading of the poem have been different if you had known the occasion and the listener from the beginning? Why do you think Browning chooses to withhold this information until the end of the poem?

3. Write the report of this meeting that the ambassador will send back to the count.

4. Compare the duke and duchess in the poem with Professor Ames and Mrs. Ames in "Astronomer's Wife" (p. 00).

Possible Responses to Questions following the Poems

"In the Orchard" • Muriel Stuart (pp. 394–395)

1. The man's dialogue is full of romantic, lighthearted, sensuous images: the shining harvest moon, "the quiet . . . that sang like the drum," the rose that "smelt all warm." On the other hand, the woman's dialogue is darker, with many references to pain and cruelty: the blackbird being stoned, the kitten being drowned. The speakers' language characterizes their attitude toward the subject they are discussing—their love affair. To the woman, the love relationship was serious and important; breaking it off is painful, almost like a death. For the man, the relationship was simply a passing fancy, a thing of the senses, not of the soul.

2. The questions, ellipses, and repeated words contribute a sense of realistic dialogue. They represent the hesitations and uncertainties of an actual conversation.

"Thou art indeed just, Lord" • Gerard Manley Hopkins (pp. 395–396)

1. The speaker uses many words with legal connotations; he seems like a lawyer pleading before a judge. His tone is respectful but argumentative.

2. Words such as "thwart," "sots and thralls of lust," and "defeat" suggest an angry and deeply disappointed tone. Lines 9-13 reflect weariness and frustration, while the tone of the final line becomes supplicating, yet hopeful.

"Western Wind" • Anonymous (p. 396)

The final couplet expresses desperation and despair, while the alternate lines merely express wistfulness and longing.

"Naming of Parts" • Henry Reed (pp. 396–397)

1. In each of the first four stanzas, the first voice ends at the sentence break in the fourth line. The first voice explains the use of weapons in a direct, literal way. We hear the tones of the first sergeant or drill instructor. The second speaker seems to be the inner voice of the young soldier who is listening to these dry, matter-of-fact pronouncements which consider only the parts of the weapons and not their potential use as killing instruments. The second speaker contrasts the parts of the weapons to the parts of nearby gardens he can see. His language is sensuous and filled with vivid imagery.

2. The two voices converge in the final stanza, where the juxtaposition of the sergeant's droning instructions and the young soldier's lively gardens underlines the irony implied in the contrasts of each stanza. The bees which "fumble" and fertilize the flowers, enabling them to bring forth new life, stand out defiantly against the weaponry instruction, which can bring forth only death.

"Family Portrait" • Jacques Prévert (pp. 397–398)

The first three lines have a literal, matter-of-fact tone. There are no startling images, no descriptive language. Everything is business as usual. The tone alters at line 10, where the statements end and a question intrudes. The son has neither the daily chores of the household nor the mundane business deals to hold his life together. The length of line 13 suggests both the monotony and the all-encompassing nature of the war which finally kills the son. Even when the son is killed, the monotony and predictability, both of the lines and of the parents' responses, continue.

Additional Topics for Writing and Discussion

1. In the final lines of "In the Orchard," the man indicates that the woman was going to tell him something. She, however, says, "It wasn't anything really." What do you think she was going to tell him? What details in the poem prompted your response?

2. Compare the relationship of the couple in "In the Orchard" to the relationship of the couple in "The Horse Dealer's Daughter (pp. 226–237).

3. How does the tone of the man's dialogue in "In the Orchard" contrast with the tone of the speaker in "Western Wind"? How does this contrast in tone suggest their different feelings about their lovers?

4. The first three lines of Hopkins's "Thou art indeed just, Lord" ask an interesting philosophical question. Prepare an argument to answer the speaker. Avoid clichés and use concrete examples to support your point of view.

5. Compare the attitude toward God of the speaker in "Thou art indeed just, Lord" with that of Gimpel in Singer's "Gimpel the Fool" (pp. 272–281).

6. In "Thou art indeed just, Lord" the images of sinners in lines 7-8 contrast sharply with the images of nature in lines 9-12. How does Hopkins use both kinds of images to build his case? What does the phrase "Time's eunuch" mean? How does the connotation of "eunuch" reinforce Hopkins's argument?

7. What connection do the first two lines in "Western Wind" have with the final two lines? Do they set the scene? Why would the speaker want rain and wind?

8. Compare the view of war given by O'Connor's speaker in "Guests of the Nation" (pp. 29–37) with the view of the second speaker (the young soldier) in "Naming of Parts."

9. How does the speaker in "Family Portrait" view the three people he describes? Does he seem to be sympathetic with any of them?

10. Compare the responses of the parents in "Family Portrait" with the responses of the parents in "War" by Pirandello (p. 88).

11. Choose one stanza or set of lines from any of the poems in the Voice: Speaker and Tone section. Make revisions which will change the tone of the stanza or set of lines. You may add words, change words, or delete words. Explain how the changes you have made alter the tone. Reread the poem with your revised lines. Has its meaning been changed? How?

DICTION

The discussion of diction on pp. 398–405 emphasizes the important distinction between the denotation and connotation of a word. Students are encouraged to use the dictionary to discover differences in connotation which they may not have previously known. When they discover how greatly a poet's meaning can be affected by his or her choice of words, students also become more aware of the power of finding the right word in their own writing. The issues addressed in this section provide the opportunity for discussing expansion of vocabulary and variety of word choice. Many students consult a thesaurus to find synonyms, but they are not always aware of the connotations of the new words they use. Looking at the importance of shades of meaning in the words poets choose should convince students that understanding connotation is essential to clear, precise communication.

Additional Topics for Writing and Discussion

"I wandered lonely as a cloud" • *William Wordsworth (p. 400)*

1. As the speaker describes his experience in the poem, we realize that it was not until some time after he saw the scene with the daffodils that he understood its full significance. Explain a similar experience you have had. Be sure to describe what you saw in detail so

that readers can picture the scene just as clearly as they can picture Wordsworth's lake and daffodils. Then discuss your later response to the scene.

2. Compare Wordsworth's description of the daffodils to Stuart's description of the orchard (p. 394). How does each poet's description serve a different purpose? Do you prefer one description to the other? Why?

3. What is the tone of the Wordsworth poem? Is the tone of the final stanza different from the tone of the first three? Consider the poet's word choice carefully as you explain whether you do or do not find differences.

"Miniver Cheevy" • Edwin Arlington Robinson (pp. 402–403)

1. Some of the words suggesting that "Miniver loved the days of old" are "swords," "steeds," "warrior," "Thebes," "Camelot," "Priam's neighbors," "Romance," "Medici," "medieval grace," "iron clothing."

   Verbs suggesting inaction: "grew lean," "sighed," "dreamed," "rested," "thought." Verbs suggesting action: "wept," "loved," "set him dancing," "mourned," "would have sinned," "cursed," "eyed," "scorned," "scratched," "coughed," "kept on drinking." These words suggest that Miniver was a complainer who never acted to change his lot, but merely existed in order to long for the bygone days. The only positive action suggested by any of the verbs is "dancing" (line 8), and there is certainly a strong overtone of irony even there.

   Miniver's final act, habitual drinking, underlines his hopeless approach to life.

2. Although "ripe" and "fragrant" often suggest positive interpretations of fruit and flowers at their peak of perfection, here they seem to suggest that fame and nobility flourished in the past, but are now faded and decayed. Art and Romance are no longer noble; Romance is readily available to any casual street celebrant, while Art has become a low-life to be found in the gutter without visible means of support.

"It is a beauteous evening" • William Wordsworth (p. 404)

These words all relate to religion and therefore support the poet's idea that a quiet and beautiful part of nature can arouse feelings that are just as holy as those evoked by being in a church or by formal ritual. In the final four lines, the words "divine," "Abraham," "worship'st," "Temple," "shrine," and "God" are congruent with the religious imagery in the first ten lines.

"Delight in Disorder" • Robert Herrick (pp. 404–405)

1. These words suggest a sprightly, spontaneous, unplanned disorder. "Err" comes from the Latin errare (to wander, to go astray); "tempestuous" comes from the Latin tempestas (a calamity, storm, tempest). Both words suggest sensuality and sexual adventure.

2. The connotation of these words suggests that the speaker's physical passion and sense of playfulness are aroused by the disorder of women's clothing.

"Rape" • Adrienne Rich (pp. 405–406)

The words "prowler and father" suggest that the policeman has qualities of both a dangerous criminal and the authoritative male parent. Because the words are used together, they also suggest that the father may be a "prowler" in the life of a woman—someone who constantly threatens and lurks in the shadows. The word "confessor" suggests a priest and thus links the policeman with another authority figure. In addition, since the policeman is identified with the rapist, both the father and the priest are also tied to the image of the violator. In line 8, the policeman is pictured as riding on a male horse, behaving like a warlord (another male violator figure). The "trash" is both the literal garbage and debris on the street and also the people, particularly the women, who do not have the power of the mounted policeman.

Additional Topics for Writing and Discussion

1. The speaker in "Miniver Cheevy" clearly demonstrates disdain for Miniver Cheevy and his philosophy. Is there any way you can defend Miniver? Can you imagine someone who might defend him? Explain.

2. Compare Miniver Cheevy and what you know about his life to Iván Ilych and what you know about his life ("The Death of Iván Ilych," p. 105).

3. Compare Wordsworth's use of setting in "I wandered lonely as a cloud" with his use of setting in "It is a beauteous evening."

4. Compare the attitudes toward women expressed in Herrick's poem "Delight in Disorder" and in Rich's "Rape." Consider the attitude of the speaker in the first poem and that of the policeman described by the speaker in the second poem.

5. Are there any ideas expressed in the poem "Rape" that cause you to react strongly? Identify the ideas and explain your reactions.

6. Compare the treatment of rape in Rich's poem with Atwood's treatment of the same subject in "Rape Fantasies" (p. 325).

IMAGERY

Beginning writers often do too much *telling* in their writing and not enough *showing*. The discussion of imagery on pp. 406–412 suggests ways of finding words that convey to the reader an exact picture and not just a vague general discussion. As a class exercise introducing imagery, you might ask students to come up with as many specific sensory images as possible to describe a common experience: a day at the beach, a ride on the subway, a holiday celebration. Urging them to address all the senses demonstrates how full and alive such a description can be.

Additional Topics for Writing and Discussion

"First Death in Nova Scotia" • Elizabeth Bishop (pp. 407–408)

1. Point of view is essential to the meaning of this poem. How would the poem be changed if it were seen through the eyes of the child's mother or through the eyes of Uncle Arthur?

Which images do you think would not appear? Which would be changed? How? Can you think of other images that might be added?

2. What is the significance of the title of the poem? How does the title connect both to the imagery of the poem and to its meaning?

3. Compare the attitude of the speaker toward the images of cold—such as the frozen lake (line 30)—to that of the speaker toward similar images in Frost's "Stopping by Woods on a Snowy Evening." Consider the words each speaker chooses to describe the cold.

4. Compare the image of royalty in "First Death" to those in "Miniver Cheevy" (p. 402).

"The Lake Isle of Innisfree" • William Butler Yeats (p. 410)

Images of sound include "bee-loud glade," "cricket sings," "evening full of the linnet's wings," "lake water lapping with low sounds."

Sight images include "small cabin . . . of clay and wattles," "nine bean-rows," "a hive," "peace . . . dropping from the veils of the morning," "midnight's all a glimmer," "noon a purple glow," "roadway," "pavements gray."

The images in the first ten lines contribute to the sense of solitude, peace, beauty, and quiet of Innisfree. The images in line 11 contrast sharply, showing the harshness and barrenness of life away from the small cabin.

"Meeting at Night" • Robert Browning (p. 410)

"Gray sea," "long black land," "yellow half-moon," "startled little waves," "fiery ringlets," "three fields," "farm," "blue spurt" are images appealing to the visual senses.

"Pushing prow," "quench its speed," "two hearts beating" appeal to the sense of touch.

"A tap," "a voice," "two hearts beating" appeal to the sense of sound.

"Warm, sea-scented beach," "blue spurt" appeal to the sense of smell.

The images all contribute to the sensual feelings of the lover going to the beloved. The reader has a sense of warmth, power, and energy.

"Heat" • H. D. (p. 411)

The wind is pictured as a plowman who is able to cut through the unbearable heat just as a farmer is able to cut through fields of hardened sod. Stanza 2 suggests that the heat must be turned aside before any living things can flourish, just as the hard sod must be turned aside before crops can grow.

"Neutral Tones" • Thomas Hardy (p. 412)

1. The images in stanza 1 suggest coldness and barrenness: the white winter sun, the gray leaves on the "starving sod." In stanzas 2 and 3, the images of barrenness become images of death and decay, for example the "ominous bird a-wing."

2. The final two lines sum up and juxtapose the images that come earlier, thus making explicit the comparison of the deceptive lover with the God-curst sun and the dead leaves.

93

Additional Topics for Writing and Discussion

1. Compare the experience and attitude of the speaker in "The Lake Isle of Innisfree" to the experience and attitude of the speaker in "I wandered lonely as a cloud" by Wordsworth (p. 400). Consider particularly the contrast in each poem between the first sections and the final lines.

2. What does the speaker in "The Lake Isle of Innisfree" seem to get from the lake isle? Describe briefly how he gets it.

3. Compare "Meeting at Night" to its sequel poem, "Parting at Morning."

   > Parting at Morning
   >
   > Round the cape of a sudden came the sea,
   > And the sun looked over the mountain's rim:
   > And straight was a path of gold for him,
   > And the need of a world of men for me.

   A. Identify the images in "Parting at Morning." What senses are stimulated? How does the imagery compare with that of "Meeting at Night"?

   B. Does your reading of "Meeting at Night" change after you have read "Parting at Morning"? Does the speaker seem different in the two poems? In what ways?

   C. When read together, what do the two poems suggest about the experience described?

4. In H. D.'s poem "Heat," the wind is urged to take violent action: "rend open," "cut apart," "rend it to tatters." Discuss the apparent contradiction implied here: violent action must be taken to produce positive, desirable results.

5. Compare the relationship suggested by the imagery in "Neutral Tones" to the relationship described by Hemingway in "The Short Happy Life of Francis Macomber" (p. 245).

6. What do you think has happened to the couple described in "Neutral Tones"? What has occurred between the time of the first three stanzas and the time of the final stanza?

FIGURES OF SPEECH: SIMILE AND METAPHOR

This section further explains the power of poetic language. By recognizing the difference between literal and figurative language and by seeing how poets can say a great deal with a few words when they use figurative language, students discover possibilities for their own writing.

You may want to warn against the use (at least in writing) of the dead, clichéd metaphor such as the "Go jump in the lake" example given in the first paragraph. Students often enjoy making lists of such worn-out metaphors and similes, evaluating what they might have meant when they were fresh and original and then coming up with new figures of speech to replace the old ones.

You may also want to discuss the problem of mixed metaphors and reasons for avoiding them. The following examples (reprinted in the *New Yorker*) demonstrate the fuzzy thinking of the mixed metaphor:

"He took a chance. He took a shot, and, after the dice stopped rolling, he hit a home run." Mr. Ackerman said.

From the *Washington Times*
[reprinted in *The New Yorker*,
March 31, 1986, p. 68]

In suggesting that Lilco be taken out of the political arena, Mr. Purcell said that the public-power issue needed to be thoroughly studied. "We shouldn't jump into something that will be an Achilles' heel down the road," he warned.

from the *Times*
[reprinted in *The New Yorker*,
March 3, 1986, p. 107]

Possible Responses to Questions following the Poems (pp. 416–417)

"That time of year thou may'st in me behold" • *William Shakespeare (p. 414)*

"Hymn to God the Father" • *John Donne (pp. 415–416)*

1. In stanza 2, Donne describes one kind of sin he has committed by comparing it to a door. By sinning he has created an opportunity for someone else to enter into sinning, just as a door provides the opportunity for entering into a room or building. Wallowing in sin suggests that the sins are like the mud and dirt in a pigsty, where we think of pigs enjoying what humans might consider disgusting.

2. In line 15, there is a play on "son"—comparing God's son to the sun that shines—and in line 17 is a play on Donne's name. "Thou has done" can mean both that God has provided all the forgiveness the speaker asks for and also that God now has the poet (Donne) with him. The puns contribute to the affirming and positive tone of the poem.

"The Double-Play" • *Robert Wallace (pp. 416–417)*

1. Words and phrases that connect the double-play to the dance include: "bounds like a vanishing string," "shortstop magically scoops," "whirling above his invisible shadows," "poised," "pirouettes leaping." The precise and stylized movements required to complete the double-play make it like a ballet.

2. In the first stanza, the pitcher's mound is compared to a distant place which can be seen only as one might see something that was illuminated under the sea. The pitcher's preparation to throw is compared to the winding of a clock which will soon strike. In the second stanza, the ball in flight is compared to a string that we can see when it is close but not when it is stretched into the distance.

3. The double-play has occurred and made its effect felt just as a poem does. In addition, this particular poem has been created through the description of the double-play.

"The Battle" • *Louis Simpson (p. 417)*

The helmet rifle, pack, and overcoat are synecdoches. By mentioning only parts of the soldiers' gear and uniforms, the poem emphasizes the impersonality of war. The final two lines of the first stanza offer a simile comparing the night to a throat that has been cut, suggesting the mutilation and death in combat. The first two lines of the second stanza compare the soldiers to moles, indicating the dehumanizing effect of war. The mood of ugliness and fear is reinforced by the images of despair and hopelessness in the final stanza.

"Woman to Child" • *Judith Wright (p. 418)*

"All a world I made in me" suggests that by nurturing a new life within her, the speaker created an individual who will have a world all his or her own. The phrase also suggests that all children are created in this way and thus the speaker's pregnancy reflects the birth process of the entire world.

"All time lay rolled in me" indicates that the speaker feels the connection of the embryo both to generations past and generations to come.

"I hold you deep within that well" conveys the idea that even after the baby has been born, the mother still feels attached to the child and still protects the child just as she did when the embryo was protected by her uterus.

"I am the earth, I am the root" reflects the mother's feelings that she is the source of nurture and of beginning for the child.

"I am the stem that fed the fruit" again suggests that the mother is the source of support for the growing child.

Additional Topics for Writing and Discussion

1. Shakespeare presents many images which represent the passing of youth ("That time of year thou may'st in me behold"). Do you agree with his picture of aging? If so, explain why you think his images are particularly appropriate. If not, explain why, and in addition, suggest your own comparisons for the aging process.

2. Donne gives a catalogue of various kinds of sins in his "Hymn to God the Father." Explain what these categories are and then construct a argument describing what type of sin you consider to be the most serious and most difficult to forgive.

3. In "The Double-Play," Robert Wallace describes part of a baseball game by comparing it to a dance. Think of an activity with which you are familiar and write a description of one part of it by using a metaphorical comparison.

4. Compare the view toward motherhood of the speaker in "Woman to Child" with that of the speaker in "I Stand Here Ironing" by Tillie Olsen (p. 281).

SYMBOLISM AND ALLEGORY

You may want to discuss with your students the difference between fixed symbols—such as an eagle symbolizing the United States—and a symbol that takes on a particular meaning within the context of a poem, work of fiction, or drama. Some symbols, of course, bring their outside or fixed associations to poems, thus creating yet another layer of meaning. In "A Poison Tree" (pp. 422–423), Blake uses the garden and the apple, biblical symbols of deceit and death, as similar symbols for the speaker. We can note important differences, however. For example, the creator of the tree in the poem is someone who hates an enemy. God, the creator of the tree in Eden, did not view Adam and Eve as enemies.

Some students may want to insist on personal associations for symbols. For example, a student who is adamantly opposed to the use of alcohol may resist seeing the wine in the final lines of "Advice to My Son" as a positive symbol. Understanding the validity of personal symbols, yet recognizing the danger of applying those associations to the context of the poem, is an important part of the active reading process.

Possible Responses to Questions following the Poems

"A Poison Tree" • William Blake (pp. 422–423)

1. The story tells of the power of hidden anger. Anger that is hidden behind smiles and soft words can grow and appear to one's foe to be a safe, vulnerable attitude. When the enemy comes to take advantage of the apparently safe attitude, the hidden anger erupts and destroys the enemy.

2. The apple in the garden represents temptation. The foe is tempted by what seems to be appealing and attractive but is really death-dealing. The apple and garden are, of course, associated with the garden and apple in Genesis: the biblical fruit, too, seems attractive and desirable but also carries death.

"The Road Not Taken" • Robert Frost (p. 423)

1. The final stanza suggests that we should see the poem on more than a literal level. Why would someone be telling about a walk in the woods "ages and ages hence," and why would the speaker tell of the walk with a sigh? The choice is clearly more than just which of the two woodland paths the speaker should explore that morning. Frost suggests life's choices, although he does not clearly indicate one choice as bad and one as good. Line 6 tells us that both paths were equally "fair"; the paths differ very little, in fact, since we learn (line 10) that the road "less traveled by" was "worn . . . really about the same" as the other road. Frost seems to concentrate on the consequences of choices ("knowing how way leads on the way") rather than on making an absolutely right or wrong choice.

2. In answering this question, students should be encouraged to recognize, as suggested in the responses to question 1, that the two choices are not vastly different. It is the consequences of the choices that are really significant.

"Virtue" • George Herbert (pp. 424–425)

Symbols of transience include a beautiful day, a rose, springtime, and finally the world itself. Students might note that comparing the soul with seasoned timber to explain its permanence presents some problems. Surely the timber will eventually break or rot or be burned. If the world is likely to turn to coal, the timber will not outlast it.

97

"Because I could not stop for Death" • *Emily Dickinson (p. 425)*

The poem is generally allegorical because Death is pictured as a person and remains personified consistently. Each stanza shows one part of the journey taken by the speaker and Death as they move toward the grave. Lines 9-13 suggest passing childhood by, as well as passing the growing fields that represent the labor of adults, and eventually passing the sun, which represents earthly time. The details in lines 17-20 suggest a grave or tomb, particularly a nineteenth-century grave where slabs of stone ("The Roof," "the Cornice") were often laid flat across the burial site.

Additional Topics for Writing and Discussion

1. Do you agree with the speaker's advice to his son in "Advice to My Son" (p. 420)? If so, plan an argument defending this thoughts. Try to imagine what a critic of his ideas would say as you are developing your defense. If you do not agree with the speaker's advice, explain why and then describe your own advice to a son or daughter. Try to come up with new symbols to make your explanation lively and original.

2. Compare the speaker's view of the journey toward death in Christina Rossetti's "Up-Hill" (p. 422) with the speaker's view in "Because I could not stop for Death." Do either of the speakers reflect what you see as the current attitude toward death? If not, how do their views differ from those held by you and the people you know?

3. "A Poison Tree" describes an action and tells a story. The story shows the consequences of letting anger grow. Describe a time in your own life when you let your anger grow. Be sure to make clear the consequences of this growing anger.

4. Describe a choice in your own life similar to the one suggested by Frost's "The Road Not Taken." Explain how that choice expanded or limited your own paths. Be sure to give specific examples to demonstrate the points you are making.

5. George Herbert explains the immortality of a virtuous soul by comparing it to things that are not immortal. Develop your own definition of an abstract concept (love, loyalty, anger, despair) by identifying one of its qualities and then comparing it to things that do not share that quality.

SYNTAX

The discussion of syntax emphasizes the relationship between the arrangement of words and the meaning conveyed. You might point out to students that poetry demonstrates a wider range of syntax variation than does prose. Nevertheless, as they become aware of how the poet can change emphasis, tone, and pace by careful planning of syntax, they should also consider the possibilities varied syntax can bring to their own writing. You might mention that in prose writing, syntax variety is often achieved through the use of parallel structure, contrasting sentence lengths, or the inversion of the standard subject-verb pattern.

"The Man He Killed" • *Thomas Hardy (p. 430)*

1. The first two stanzas are parallel in structure. Each is a single sentence that suggests a conversational tone. The reader gets the feeling of an informal commentary rather than a dramatic pronouncement.

2. The dashes suggest the hesitation and confusion the speaker feels as he grapples with the contradictions and bitter ironies of war.

3. The final stanza does not necessarily suggest that the speaker has worked through the confusion of the middle stanzas. He has not found any answers. Instead, what we find is a tone of understated bitterness and resignation.

"An Irish Airman Foresees His Death" • *William Butler Yeats (p. 431)*

1. Each pair of lines is balanced in structure and contrasted in meaning. Note especially the last four lines, which are two parallel pairs that connect ("balanced" in line 13 relating to "balance" in line 16). These carefully controlled pairs of lines reflect the airman's sense of being locked into a fated pattern.

2. The parallel structure calls attention to the contrasts in the paired lines and emphasizes the lack of traditional motivation the airman feels as he goes to war. The pairs in lines 1-10 cover most of the standard reasons for going to war and reject them. The poet's revelation of his real motivation, in lines 10-16, is thus emphasized and dramatized.

"The Silken Tent" • *Robert Frost (p. 432)*

The "She" of the poem is compared to a tent that is connected to earth by many ties of which one is almost not aware. The conjunctions have the effect of uniting all the details of the poem, making sense of each image, and keeping the reader almost unaware that the entire poem is one connected sentence. The woman and the poem have something important in common: their connections are essential, but the observer must look closely to notice them.

"Me up at does" • *e. e. cummings (p. 432)*

1. A possible rearrangement: "I am up and quietly staring at a poisoned mouse who is still alive on the floor, asking, 'What have I done that you wouldn't have?'"

2. The situation emphasizes the relation of the speaker to the mouse. By giving us the speaker's point of view first, the ironic comparison of the speaker and the mouse is emphasized.

"Mother, Among the Dustbins" • *Stevie Smith (p. 433)*

The balanced phrases and repetitive word groups suggest the cadence of the King James Bible. The meaning of the words contrasts with the ponderous rhythm. The speaker discusses theology in terms of dustbins and manure. In the third stanza, the argument turns around and playfully suggests that all this "pronouncing" is frivolous. Line 18 presents the reversal that has been suggested by the contrasting long and short sentences when the speaker describes God as a "folly" created by man. The final short sentence underlines the irony through its direct and surprising accusation/question.

Additional Topics for Writing and Discussion

1. In Donne's "The Sun Rising," the speaker addresses the sun as "Busy old fool." The speaker is making an argument to the sun, trying to persuade the "old fool" to take certain actions. Trace the progress of the argument in each stanza. How does the action requested in the second stanza contrast with those requested in the first?

2. Compare the analysis of the motivations for fighting in a war made by the speaker in "The Man He Killed" with that in "An Irish Airman Foresees His Death."

3. The speaker in "An Irish Airman Foresees His Death" balances a number of things one against another. Describe a situation in which your primary purpose was to balance one thing or set of things against another. Your description might be a description of a dilemma or an account of an attempt to achieve an equilibrium.

4. "The Silken Tent" is a poem in which meanings exist and coincide. Examine the imagery and figures of speech carefully. Then explain the multiple possibilities.

5. Compare the speaker's response to finding a dead animal in "Me up at does" to the speaker's response in "Traveling through the dark" by William Stafford (p. 686).

6. Imagine the response of the mother addressed in "Mother, Among the Dustbins." How do you think she would answer each of the speaker's statements and questions?

SOUND: RHYME, ALLITERATION, ASSONANCE

This section discusses and defines various sound devices used by poets to enhance the meaning of their poems. The concepts introduced here will come alive and be reinforced by reading the poems in the chapter aloud. As you or your students read the poems, you might point out the different nuances of meaning that come from experimenting with several possible ways of reading a poem aloud. In addition, this section provides an ideal opportunity to bring in a recording of a poet reading his or her work. One particularly impressive example is the Caedmon recording of Yeats reading "The Lake Isle of Innisfree."

"During Wind and Rain" • Thomas Hardy (p. 438)

1. The rhyme scheme is *a b c b c d e*: in the first and third stanzas the d line has internal rhyme. The repetitions give the poem the feeling of a ballad and emphasize the universality of the experiences described. The beauty and joy of the world give way, inevitably, to decay.

2. Some examples of alliteration include line 3, "treble and tenor"; line 12, "shady seat"; line 15, "blithely breakfasting"; line 16, "men and maidens"; line 21, "rotten rose"; line 24, "Clocks and carpets, and chairs." The alliterations provide a strong, insistent rhythm, almost like a chant or a dirge, which accompanies the relentless sense of progression toward decay.

"Sound and Sense" • Alexander Pope (p. 439)

1. Each line that follows the advice-giving line 4 serves as an example to reinforce its message. See, for example, the explanations to question 2 below.

2. Lines 5-6 use the soft *s* sound which is introduced in line 5 and emphasized by the alliterative line 6 to suggest the soft sound of the gentle wind and the smoothly flowing brook. By contrast, lines 7-8 use a series of harsh-sounding words—"surges," "lashes," "hoarse," "rough," and "roar"—to reflect the rhythms of a storm. In lines 9 and 10, the reader is slowed down by words that require individual and careful pronunciation, suggesting the ponderous and difficult labor of Ajax striving to throw a rock. These lines contrast to lines 11-12, where the words may be read quickly, just as Camilla would skim along the plains.

"Adams Song" • Bob McKenty (p. 440)

McKenty's rhyme scheme is extremely clever and witty. The poem is written in couplets, each of which ends with eye rhymes (but not ear rhymes). The frustration the reader might feel at the "failed" rhyme resolves into ironic laughter with the final couplet which provides the ultimate example of the horrors caused by the Fall from Grace: "poets who are surely deaf." A deaf poet would not need to hear a rhyme so his/her poetry could be written with sounds that were pleasing only to the eye. These poems would tease and taunt the reader who could hear, thus providing a taste here on earth of what had been lost.

"The Universe" • May Swenson (p. 440)

While there are witty puns in each section of the poem, each also moves the reader to hear as well as understand the expanding and circular nature of the universe. The lines urge us to feel the questions of the universe as both external and internal, both intellectual ("about us" meaning "concerning us") and sensual ("about us" meaning "surrounding us"). The repetitions emphasize the cyclical aspects of the ever-changing, ever-the-same universe.

"The Word Plum" • Helen Chasin (p. 441)

1. The initial sounds of several words in lines 2-3 spell out "plum." By embedding the letters of *plum* in sensuous words like "pout," "push," "luxury," and "murmur," the poet connects sound and sense.

2. Examples of alliteration include line 2, "pout and push"; line 3, "self-love, and savoring"; lines 2 and 3, "luxury of self-love'" lines 4-5, "full . . . falling . . . fruit"; lines 6-8, "taut . . . tart." Examples of assonance include "plum" (line 1) with "luxury" (line 2); "skin" (line 7) with "bitter" (line 8) and "lip" (line 10).

Additional Topics for Writing and Discussion

1. In Hopkins's "In the Valley of the Elwy" (p. 436), how do the image of the house and the image of the mothering wing relate? How do these two images together contribute to the theme suggested by the final two stanzas?

2. What do the final lines in each stanza of "During Wind and Rain" contribute to the meaning of the poem? consider carefully the connotation and denotation of each image in those lines.

3. In "Sound and Sense," Pope suggests that Dryden's poetry recognizes the "pow'r of music." Choose any of Dryden's poems—in this text or elsewhere—then analyze your selection, showing that you either agree or disagree with Pope. Does Dryden's poetry, in fact, demonstrate the vital connection between sound and meaning?

4. What are the questions May Swenson asks in "The Universe"? How many different ways can you think of approaching those questions? (Consider various fields of study—for example, philosophy, theology, astronomy.) Can you suggest any answers to the questions? Can you find in your research any possible answers?

5. Write a short paragraph describing a fruit or vegetable. Use Helen Chasin's "The Word Plum" as a source of inspiration for connecting the sound of the word to a description of its qualities.

RHYTHM AND METER

This section explains and defines different patterns of poetic meter. A relaxed and enjoyable way to begin teaching about rhythm is to bring recordings of several different kinds of music to class. Ask students to identify the varying rhythms of classical, country, hard rock, and jazz, or to imagine how the music would be changed if a different rhythm were imposed on it.

"The Destruction of Sennacherib" • George Gordon, Lord Byron (p. 448)

1. The meter of the poem is anapestic tetrameter. The rising, rapidly moving rhythm suggests the swift, bold movements of the Assyrians.

2. The regular, insistent movement of the two unaccented beats and one accented beat stresses the inevitable destruction of the Assyrians. The biblical rhythms of the lines are particularly appropriate to the story of Gentiles triumphing over unbelievers through divine intervention.

"Her Kind" • Anne Sexton (pp. 449–450)

1. Sexton keeps the poem moving by varying the metric pattern and by using enjambment to carry the sense of the poem swiftly from one line to the next. Many lines have extra accented beats which help to emphasize the power and energy of the theme.

2. Examples of enjambment include lines 3-4 and lines 17-18. These lines cause the reader to pause after the last word of line 3 and the last word of line 17 and to consider the implications of those words before moving into the lines that complete their meaning. The caesurae in lines 2, 4, and 15 also cause the reader to pause briefly. By interrupting the rhythm of the line, the caesura emphasizes the importance of the word immediately preceding or following it.

"Junk" • Richard Wilbur (p. 450)

As is suggested by the epigraph from "Waldere," this poem follows the ancient pattern of Old English verse: the standard line contains four stressed syllables along with a varying number of unstressed syllables. The line is broken into two half-lines by a break in the middle. The half-lines are tied together by alliteration, the third stressed syllable in a line alliterating with either the first or second stressed syllable and sometimes with both.

"The Red Wheelbarrow" • William Carlos Williams (p. 452)

1. Lines 1 and 7 match each other, as do lines 2, 4, 6, and 8.

2. The breaks cause the reader to pause and consider each of the images carefully.

Additional Topics for Writing and Discussion

1. Summarize the events of each stanza in "The Destruction of Sennacherib." What do all the events considered together suggest about the meaning of the poem? How are we supposed to regard the Assyrian? The Gentile?

2. In the poem "Her Kind," what is happening to the woman in the final stanza? What has caused her fate (look at the details in lines 7-13)? Is the woman described a historic figure or do you think she could live today? Write a character description of a modern woman who could be considered "Her Kind."

3. In the final two lines of "Junk," Richard Wilbur refers to Hephaestus, the Greek god of fire and the forge, and to Wayland, an invisible smith in Germanic and English folklore. What do these references contribute to the meaning of the poem? How do classical allusions relate to the details in the first part of the poem?

4. To suggest the many possible factors that can affect the reading of a poem, ask students whether their response to "The Red Wheelbarrow" would be any different if they knew this poem's background: Williams was a doctor and he got the idea for this poem while sitting by the bedside of a seriously ill child. As he gazed out her window, he saw the images described in the poem.

STRUCTURE: CLOSED FORM AND OPEN FORM

Studying closed form and open form in poetry provides a fine opportunity to talk about the importance of structure in the students' own writing. You might, for example, call their attention to the way two parts of a Petrarchan sonnet work together, the first part often presenting details or explanations that lead to the statement of the poem's theme in the final six lines. Seeing the logic and precision of a sonnet leads to understanding the strength a carefully planned structure can give to any piece of writing. In addition, you might point out the contrast between open forms that permit experimentation and closed forms that require strict attention to standard arrangement as in some ways parallel to the contrast between their own informal writing (journals, letters) that allows experimentation and their formal writing that demands fairly traditional organization.

Possible Responses to Questions following the Poems (pp. 459–461)

"The Dance" • William Carlos Williams (p. 459)

1. The poem describes a country dance, one that probably includes much stomping and swinging. The first long sentence imitates the lively peasant rhythms of the people as they move in time to the music of fiddles and bagpipes.

2. The first and last lines of the poem are the same, suggesting that the dance takes the dancers around in a large, informal circle so that they end where they began. The two parallel lines also serve as a frame to the poem, just as the picture itself would be contained in a frame.

"O Taste and See" • Denise Levertov (p. 459)

Because the stanzas are separated, the central image of each is delineated and emphasized. In addition, the reader gets a little surprise as he or she moves from the last line of one stanza to the first line of the next. For example, if the stanzas all ran in together, the apparently secular opening lines would not contrast so sharply with the subway Bible poster introduced in the second stanza.

"The Waking" • Theodore Roethke (p. 460)

Lines 1, 6, 12, and 18 are the same—"I wake to sleep, and take my waking slow." Because of the repetition, we realize that the poet wants to emphasize the paradox of these lines. How does the narrator sleep by waking? Perhaps he achieves rest and peace only through waking to some new truth. In any case, he moves slowly through life's changes, and the repetitive lines suggest that life is a recursive, rather than a linear, progress. The parallel structure in lines 3, 9, 15, and 18 is interesting because lines 9 and 15 change slightly. Line 9 begins with "And," which replaces "I" and which connects the rest of the sentence more clearly to the previous line. Line 15 retains the "And" but adds the word "lovely" which suggests that the speaker is asking his lover to share his gentle way of facing life. The return to the "I" in the final line shows the speaker once more by himself. The rhymes, particularly the *a* rhyme lines, are intermingled throughout the poem, paralleling the connected images of the poet's life.

"The City" • C. P. Cavafy (p. 461)

The poem can be divided into two parts: lines 1-8, where the first voice—the "you" mentioned by the speaker in the first line—speaks, and lines 9-16, where the second voice, that of the speaker, replies. The first voice delivers its angry, embittered message, and the second voice makes an observation about that message.

Additional Topics for Writing and Discussion

1. Keats describes his experience reading a work that greatly affected his life ("On First Looking into Chapman's Homer," p. 454). Explain how a particular book, play, poem, or film affected you. Try to make your response to this work just as clear and vivid to your reader as Keats makes his response to Chapman's translation of Homer.

2. Compare the astronomer in Whitman's poem "When I heard the learn'd astronomer" (p. 455) to the astronomer in Kay Boyle's "Astronomer's Wife" (pp. 40–43). What kind of person and view of life does each astronomer represent? How are the speaker in the poem and the plumber in the story contrasted with the astronomers? Why do you think Boyle and Whitman chose astronomers to represent the views suggested by these characters in their works?

3. Find a print of Breughel's painting *The Kermess* and compare what you see in the painting to what you read in William Carlos Williams's "The Dance." What has Williams omitted? Has he described the central figures accurately? What would you add to Williams's description? Does the poem convey the same mood that the painting does?

4. Explain the philosophy of life suggested by Denise Levertov's "O Taste and See." Plan an argument either defending or attacking such an approach to life. Be specific and give details as vivid as Levertov's to support your ideas.

5. The first line of Theodore Roethke's "The Waking," which is repeated in lines 6, 12, and 18, contains a paradox (an apparent contradiction). What solutions to the paradox can you suggest? How can one wake in order to sleep?

6. In "The City" by C. P. Cavafy, what advice does the speaker, in the final eight lines, give to the speaker of the first seven lines? Do you agree with the second speaker's observation? How do you respond to the thoughts expressed by the first speaker?

THEME

This section helps students to see the difference between the topic of a poem and its significance. Students often feel relieved to know that there are many possible ways of stating the theme of a poem and to learn that poems can have multiple themes. It is essential, however, to emphasize the danger of oversimplifying, distorting the meaning, or insisting on a personal response when stating the theme of a poem. For example, Frost"s "Stopping by Woods" may remind some students of experiences they have had while cross-country skiing, but the theme of the poem could not be stated as "People should get out into the country and enjoy winter sports which will bring them into the snowy wilderness." Students needs to understand the difference between a response—which is a great place to begin thinking about a poem—and a demonstrable statement of theme.

Additional Topics for Writing and Discussion

"Crumbling is not an instant's Act" • Emily Dickinson (p. 463)

1. In this poem Dickinson argues that ruin or decay of any kind—but particularly spiritual decay—does not take place in a short period of time. Change this profound, according to Dickinson, requires a long process of "organized Decays." Do you agree with her idea? Explain.

2. Compare Dickinson's use of the Borer (line 7) to support her theme to Blake's use of the worm in "The Sick Rose" (p. 503).

3. What are the effects of the long dashes in Dickinson's final stanza? How do they support the ideas expressed in the concluding lines?

CHAPTER NINE

Approaching a Poem: Guidelines for Reading and Writing

This chapter summarizes and applies the approaches to reading poetry explained in detail in Chapters Six through Eight. You may want to work through various stages of the response and analysis process with your class, asking students to respond—either in writing or through discussion—to Hopkins's "Spring and Fall: to a Young Child" before they read the commentary that follows the poem.

Additional Topics for Writing and Discussion

"Spring and Fall: to a Young Child" • *Gerard Manley Hopkins (p. 466)*

1. In this poem, an adult speaks to a child, explaining a particular aspect of life. Margaret is apparently mourning the loss of her innocent childhood. In addition, she grieves because she has recognized the inevitability of death. If you were to give advice to a child in a similar situation, would you take the approach of the speaker? Explain why you would or would not. If you would take a different approach, defend your choice.

2. Compare the experience of the child in this poem to the experience of the child in Elizabeth Bishop's "First Death in Nova Scotia" (p. 407).

3. The last six lines of the poem imply that the sorrows of children and of adults are similar. Do you agree? Explain.

4. In the poem, autumn is used as a symbol for inevitable death and the process of dying. Do you see autumn in that way? What other symbolic interpretations of autumn are you familiar with? (Consider other stories, poems, and plays as well as experiences outside of literature, such as autumn holidays.)

CHAPTER TEN

Transformations

This chapter discusses and demonstrates the effects of change on creative work. The first section concentrates on revisions, showing why poets seek exactly the right word or why they move a line from one place to another or why they eliminate whole sections of poems. The Parodies section shows how one poet can playfully or ironically twist the words and lines of another poet to change a serious poem into a comic imitation. In the Translations section, students have the opportunity to see again how greatly the meaning and tone of a poem can be changed through each translator's choice of slightly different words or phrases. Poems and Paintings shows the most dramatic changes: how visual images have been translated into words. The Adaptations section indicates the rich possibilities poets may find as they recognize in the work of another poet the beginnings of their own poems. And the final section, Responses (Point-Counterpoint), illustrates the fine points of argument.

REVISIONS

The Revisions section offers a fine chance for students to think about their own revision processes. As you discuss the changes each poet has made in his or her work, you might ask students to consider how that kind of change might also be used in revising an essay or report. Of course, poetic revision is different from prose revision in some ways, and you may want to start off with a discussion of these contrasts, then move to consideration of the similarities: changes in word choice, sentence structure, organization; addition of details; elimination of details. The close analysis of the revision of Blake's "London" (pp. 473–476) suggests a pattern for considering the other revisions in the chapter.

Possible Responses to Questions following the Poems

"A Dream of Death" • *William Butler Yeats (p. 476)*

1. The first version is much more romantic and sentimental. "Mournful stars" makes the stars sound pathetic and concerned with the lady, while "indifferent stars" reflects the real tragedy of the situation: this death would have gone unmourned and unmarked if the speaker had not come along to carve an epitaph. The final lines of the revision are stronger than the corresponding lines of the original because they force the reader to see the lady buried "under boards" rather than simply lying beside trees.

2. In the second version, Yeats has kept the cypress trees but dropped the yew, which is a traditional and almost clichéd symbol of death. The lady's cross in the first version seems to simply appear conveniently above the grave so that the speaker will have something to write on. In the revision, the cross is made by the peasants from "two bits of wood," The trees, the mournful stars, and the mournful breeze of the first version are replaced simply

109

by indifferent stars. The poet carves—rather than writes—the epitaph in the revision. The changes give a much harsher and more realistic tone to the revision. The original seems like an almost pleasant, dreamy fantasy, while the revision emphasizes the speaker's pain as he sees the indifference of the world (and the universe) to the beautiful lady's death.

"The Wind begun to knead the Grass" • Emily Dickinson (p. 477)

1. The second version is much easier to read because each of the stanzas now contains a set of unified and related images. The first version is more difficult to understand because the images run into one another for no apparent reason. In addition, in the revision the one image that *does* run over into the next stanza is the appropriate picture of the hands parting and thus letting the rain water flow from the sky.

2. The tone in the revision is much more ominous and consistent with the storm being described. In the first version, the women kneading dough suggest peaceful domesticity— quite the opposite of a wild thunderstorm. In the revision, the wind "rocks" and "threatens" the grass instead of "kneading" it.

3. In the first version, we cannot really be sure what the image is supposed to be, but the revision clearly pictures the lightning as a scrappy, threatening bird with a "Yellow Beak" and a "livid Claw."

"The Piano" • D. H. Lawrence (p. 479)

Questions 1 and 2 are dealt with together in the following response.

The entire first and fourth stanzas have been eliminated. The revision is about the speaker's relationship to his mother; thus the poem need not begin with the description of the contrasting pianos (original stanza 1) or wander off to discuss the speaker's sister (original stanza 4). In addition, line 2 of the first revised stanza has the speaker being carried by his mother's voice rather than creeping on his own. The first two lines of the revised stanza 2 are completely changed; the new version focuses on the sad longing which the music arouses in the speaker. In the third line of the new stanza 2, "darkness" becomes "winter," providing a stronger contrast between the coldness outside and the warmth in the house.

The final stanzas both recount the same incident, but the revision take a very different point of view. In the first version, the mother's tunes are "devoured" by the passion of the woman who is signing to the speaker. In the revision, the speaker is overcome by the memories of his mother and cannot respond to the woman's passionate singing. The tone of the revision is much more serious and solemn than is the tone of the first version.

Additional Topics for Writing and Discussion

1. Compare Blake's view of London (in the revised version of "London") with Wordsworth's view (written during the same time period) in "Composed upon Westminster Bridge, September 3, 1802" (p. 568).

2. Discuss the possible associations and symbolic meanings of the cross as it is described in both the original and revised versions of "A Dream of Death."

3. Trace the image of hands (kinds of hands, actions of hands) throughout the revised version of Dickinson's poem "The Wind begun to rock the Grass." How do these references to hands affect the tone of the poem?

4. The two versions of "The Piano" give greatly differing views of the speaker's reaction to the conflict between the memory of his mother and the appeal of his passionate woman companion. Which version do you find to be more convincing? Do you empathize with the speaker more in one version than in the other? Why?

PARODIES

Students usually enjoy parodies and are more likely to have had experience with writing this form of poetry than any other. You might want to invite class members to choose a poem from the text, write a parody, and present it to the class. If you can stand some silliness, it's a relaxed and humorous way to complete the formal study of poetry in the course.

Possible Responses to Questions with the Poems (pp. 481–484)

William Carlos Williams • "This Is Just to Say" (p. 480)
Kenneth Koch • "Variations on a Theme by William Carlos Williams" (p. 481)

1. Koch's title puns on the musical "variations on a theme." Here Koch picks up William's poetic theme—rather than a musical signature—and weaves it into a poem of his own.

2. Koch probably made his lines long and included more stanzas both to emphasize that he was doing as his title suggests—writing a variation—and also to poke fun at Williams's cryptically short lines by writing extraordinarily long lines in contrast.

3. Each variation takes up Williams's theme, which might be stated as "I did something thoughtless and now I am explaining by giving you a personal, idiosyncratic reason for my behavior."

4. While Koch's poem certainly exaggerates, presenting truly outrageous acts and truly pathetic explanations, it addresses a valid question about William's theme: is the speaker's selfishness really balanced by his ability to turn the action into a vivid sensual image?

   Koch's poem might not be easily understood if it were read without knowledge of "This Is Just to Say," but read in the context of Williams's poem, it is coherent and certainly worth reading.

"Breakfast with Gerard Manley Hopkins" • Anthony Brode (p. 482)

Brode pokes fun at the way Hopkins used words to suggest patterns he discerned in natural phenomena. The hyphenated adjective phrases suggest Hopkins's complex descriptions of these designs, for which he coined the term "inscape." Hopkins also experimented with rhythms which intriguingly combined the cadence of Old English verse with the most modern, experimental sounds. Hopkins called his new syntax "sprung rhythm." Brode's poem imitates and exaggerates Hopkins's unique sound patterns.

111

William Shakespeare • "Shall I compare thee to a summer's day" (p. 482)
Howard Moss • "Shall I Compare Thee to a Summer's Day?" (p. 483)

Shakespeare's tone is formal and elegant; the poem is developed with graceful images that build to the heroic declaration in the final stanza. Moss, on the other hand, turns Shakespeare's "summer day" into a "dog day" and thus establishes early on his informal, conversational tone. The short sentences and lines, as contrasted with Shakespeare's longer, more even structure, reinforce Moss's informality. The parody does make sense on its own; besides poking fun at Shakespeare's formal approach to love, Moss's version also laments and criticizes the modern reader's inability to understand anything other than an abridged and watered-down version of a poem.

Robert Frost • "Dust of Snow" (p. 483)
Bob McKenty • "Snow on Frost" (p. 484)

McKenty's poem uses the same stanza form as Frost's two four-line stanzas, each rhymed *a b a b,* and each written in iambic dimeter. Both Frost and McKenty begin with the image of a crow, but McKenty's transformation of Frost's "way" to "wayward" suggest right away that "Snow on Frost" will be comic rather than quietly thoughtful. The biggest change, of course, comes in the final stanza. Whereas Frost pauses to comment on the charm of the moment and on the hopeful emotion it evokes, McKenty cynically leads us to consider baser matters. He jokingly suggests that Frost's improved mood comes from his happiness in escaping a dropping of something other than snow from the black bird. Possibly this is McKenty's way of undercutting and challenging what he sees as Frost's romanticized view of nature. Frost sees a brief moment of beauty and hope; McKenty points out the ugly (or perhaps realistic and even comic) side of nature by urging us to envision the bird defecating on Frost's head.

TRANSLATIONS

Studying translations allows students yet another opportunity to consider the importance of word choice. Contrasting the translators' decisions concerning diction, imagery, line length, rhythm, syntax, and rhyme encourages active, thoughtful reading. Students learn how writers can create engaging work on the same topic, yet in very different ways.

Der Panther • Rainer Maria Rilke (p. 485)
   "The Panther" • translated by Stephen Mitchell (p. 485)
   "The Panther" • translated by C. F. MacIntyre (p. 486)

Mitchell's translation provides images that demonstrate the pain of the caged tiger: "the constantly passing bars," "behind the bars, no world," "paces in cramped circles," "tensed, arrested muscles," "plunges into the heart." The corresponding phrases in MacIntyre's poem are softer and more passive: the bars are "before him," "behind them nothing merely," "easy motion of his supple stride," "quiet tension of the limbs," "glides . . . into the heart." MacIntyre's poem emphasizes the panther's helplessness and torpor, Mitchell's the suppressed power and rage.

   Neither poem uses rhyme, unlike the original, which has a regular *a b a b (c d c d, e f e f)* pattern in each stanza. The repeated rhyme scheme in the German emphasizes the ritual pacing and turning of the caged panther. That aspect of the poem is lost in the translation. If you or any of your students reads German, you might have all three versions read aloud to see exactly what is lost—and perhaps to consider what might be gained in the unrhymed versions.

Le Pont Mirabeau • Guillaume Apollinaire (p. 486)
"Mirabeau Bridge" • translated by Richard Wilber (p. 487)
"The Mirabeau Bridge" • translated by W. S. Merwin (p. 488)

Wilbur's translation maintains the same rhyme scheme as the original, while Merwin's rhyme patterns are much looser. The sentence patterns in Wilbur's version are not as close to the patterns of conventional speech as Merwin's are. See, for example, the first stanza of each translation. Wilbur's repeats "recall," which creates emphasis but causes the sentence to pause unnaturally. There are minor differences, also, in the images. In stanza 3, for instance, Wilbur says, "All love goes by as water to the sea," while Merwin says, "Love slips away like this water flowing." The latter translation focuses the reader's attention more clearly on the Seine ("this water flowing") and is closer to Apollinaire's original (*cette eau courante*), but Wilbur's simile connects the individual experience with a greater universal ("to the sea"). Of the two versions, Wilbur's seems more formal, both in tone and in form, while Merwin's is more conversational and informal.

Nocturno Soñado • Juan Ramón Jiménez (p. 489)
"Dream Nocturne" • translated by Eleanor L. Turnbull (p. 489)
"Dream Nocturne" • translated by Thomas McGreevy (p. 490)

Turnbull's translation is closer to the original in its stanza patterns and line patterns. Her version conveys a mystical tone with biblical echoes ("the way of the flesh"). McGreevy's translation changes the stanza pattern, making the poem one long stanza, and the varied, frequently enjambed lines of the original become shorter and starker. Turnbull's version is lyrical, close to a song. McGreevy's brief lines and cleanly unified single stanza suggest a sharper, more startling view of the journey to death.

You might ask students to evaluate the differences in meaning conveyed by Turnbull's use of "through" in lines 1 and 3 and by McGreevy's use of "by" in the same lines. Prepositions are not usually given much attention, but here they change the sense of the line considerably. "Through" suggests an intermingling and connection, while "by" implies passing (or perhaps standing beside).

Activity

If students know another language, they might try a translation; if they do not, they could gain some sense of the problems of the translator by trying to put part of Chaucer's "Pardoner's Tale" (p. 529) into modern English.

POEMS AND PAINTINGS

Comparing visual art with verbal art helps students to learn a great deal about what words can and cannot do. Studying poems in the context of related paintings brings new meaning to both works. You may find, however, that students need some help in learning how to look at paintings with the same analytic, active view they now bring to their reading. The following suggestions should encourage thoughtful responses:

1. What is the setting of the painting? Indoors? A city street? A quiet country hill? If there are people in the picture, what is their relationship to the setting? Do they seem at ease or uncomfortable? Does the setting seem to be more important than the people? Or do the human figures dominate?

2. Is there more than one person in the painting? How do the people relate to each other? Does one person seem to be more prominent than another? Do the people seem to be opposed to one another? (What do their postures suggest? tension? anger? cooperation? curiosity?)

3. Does the painting tell a story? If so, what is happening? Why is one figure standing in a particular place? Why is one part of the painting brightly lit while another part is in shadow? What events might have led up to the incident depicted in the painting? What might happen after the incident?

Most important, students should ask themselves: What is my response to this painting? Am I amused, horrified, surprised? As I look at the painting, do I feel angry, peaceful, discouraged?

After looking at and analyzing the paintings, students should feel comfortable moving to the poems inspired by them. And, as always, the process is recursive; students will want to move from the poem to the painting, back to the poem, and then again to the painting, and so on.

Possible Responses to Questions preceding the Paintings and Poems (pp. 491–493)

Vincent Van Gogh • The Starry Night *(p. 494)*
Robert Fagles • *"The Starry Night" (p. 494)*
Anne Sexton • *"The Starry Night" (p. 495)*

1. Fagles captures the sense of swirling, upward motion with phrases like "ride the lightning up," "up / with the cypress," "lifts me up the nightfall," and "stars of heaven wheeling in its wake / wheels in wheels around the moon. . . ." He also brings Van Gogh's remarkable use of color and light to his poem: "black is burning green," and "conflagration blazing down." The images in Fagles's stanzas take us past the cypress in the foreground to concentrate on the mountains and stars. Just as in the painting, these parts of nature are emphasized, while the village lies lost in the shadows.

2. The poem makes clear the feeling of madness in the painting as well as the idea that the humans in the village need some kind of protection (stanza 4). The final stanza calls attention to the artist's need for the painting to purge him of his madness and to feel at one with God through the vision he has created.

3. Because the poem is written in the first person with the artist as speaker, attention is certainly focused on the artist and his process. On the other hand, the images in each stanza which explain the poet's state of mind are clearly related to the details of the painting. The description is certainly not neutral. Words like "benighted," "execute," "coiling," "conflagration," "claustrophobic," and "frenzy" all suggest the tension and turmoil both of the starry night and of the artist.

4. A comparison with Sexton's poem is particularly interesting because she sees the painting as filled with female images. She sees the night as powerful and tumultuous, but not as threatening or mad. Like Fagles, she sees a dragon, but hers is not coiling up in a threatening way. Instead her dragon would deliver her to a safe, painless, and entirely beautiful death. She would become part of the starry night which dominates both her poem and the painting.

Francisco de Goya y Lucientes • **The Third of May** *(p. 495)*
and The Disasters of War *(p. 497)*
Lawrence Ferlinghetti • *"In Goya's greatest scenes we seem to see" (p. 496)*
Audrey Voznesensky • *"I Am Goya" (p. 497)*

1. In line 21, Ferlinghetti turns from Goya's paintings to make a comparison of his scenes with scenes of modern life. By juxtaposing the image of the freeways and billboards with Goya's blasted trees and screaming monsters, he suggests that the horrors of war can also be part of everyday life without our ever recognizing and acknowledging it.

2. Ferlinghetti wants to make a political statement and a satirical criticism of American society. He uses Goya's painting to deliver his message. Voznesensky, on the other hand, identifies with Goya's version of the devastation of war. The poet creates his statement by becoming part of the scene, instead of standing outside and commenting on it. Robert Fagles treats the theme of madness by describing the images of Van Gogh's painting with words that connote a violent internal struggle of the mind with itself.

3. Because each poet provides us with vivid images and examples from the paintings, the poems could certainly be appreciated even by someone who was not familiar with Goya. Voznesensky's poem presents Goya's scenes in a somewhat more objective way than does Ferlinghetti's, yet each poet uses the paintings for his own purpose.

Pieter Breughel the Elder • **Landscape with the Fall of Icarus** *(p. 498)*
William Carlos Williams • *"Landscape with the Fall of Icarus" (p. 498)*
W. H. Auden • *"Musée des Beaux Arts" (p. 499)*

1. Williams ends with Icarus to remind us that all of the more dominant details in the painting, the ones we would notice first, are overshadowing the truly significant event of Icarus's fall and death. Auden mentions Icarus only at the beginning of the second stanza. The Icarus of Breughel's painting demonstrates the thesis of the first stanza: that the Old Masters were never wrong about suffering. Auden ends with the ship sailing on, its sailors paying no attention to the amazing event they must have seen. What the Old Masters understood about suffering, Auden tells us, is that each of us must endure our own pain alone; the world does not care or even take note of our tragedies and disasters.

2. Williams's first stanza and his use of the past tense suggest that he is putting the poem into the context of the legend, a story told for our contemplation, If he used the present tense, the poem might seem simply to report what a viewer of the painting was seeing. We would not look so carefully at the relationship between what we know about the Icarus legend and what the picture tells us about the world's response. Auden's first two lines set up his intention: to demonstrate that the Old Masters understood the human position. The rest of the poem shows exactly what they understood.

3. See the discussion of the relationship between the first and second stanzas of "Musée des Beaux Arts" in response 1 above. If the stanzas were reversed, we would not understand that Breughel's Icarus is intended to serve as a developed example of a larger generality. We might read the fate of Icarus as an isolated instance. If the commentary on the Old Masters and on the less fully developed examples from their other paintings followed the more powerful and extended example of Icarus, they would seem anticlimactic.

4. Williams imitates the painting in words, while Auden advances an idea. Surely, however, Williams's poem also has meaning beyond the description (see 2 above), and Auden's final stanza provides a fine description intertwined with the idea that he is advancing.

5. Williams, whose poem is closer to a poetic imitation, indicates his intention by using the same title as Breughel, while Auden, who sees Breughel's *Landscape with the Fall of Icarus* as representative of the Old Masters, names his poem after a museum rather than one particular painting or artist.

Pieter Breughel the Elder • Hunters in the Snow *(p. 500)*
Joseph Langland • *"Hunters in the Snow: Breughel" (p. 500)*
John Berryman • *"Winter Landscape" (p. 502)*

1. Berryman's poem suggests the symbolic importance of the hunters. (Stanza 3 focuses on their apparent ability to be part of a time, yet also stand outside of time.) Langland's poem, on the other hand, draws the eye of the reader to details in the painting that might otherwise have been overlooked: the hunched dame with her bundled sticks (line 17), the half-unhitched sign of the inn (line 23), the night-black raven (line 35), for example.

2. Langland sticks close to the details of the painting. Only in the final stanza does he suggest his own interpretation of its meaning: the hunters (and of course all that lies before and around them) are stalked by darkness and ultimately by death. Berryman leaves the painting—particularly in stanzas 3, 4, and 5—to speculate on what the three hunters might signify both for their own world and for the larger world beyond their time and space.

3. Langland opens by naming the figures as hunters; Berryman calls them simply "men." Langland's tone is descriptive, almost neutral (as suggested by his calling the evening "neutral" and "indeterminate"). Berryman's first stanza, on the other hand, establishes a cold and isolate tone. The hunters, "cold and silent," return "past the five figures at the burning straw." The ending of Langland's poem suggests that the hunters themselves are stalked by death, while Berryman's final stanza sees the hunters as eternal figures, part of the continuing process of life and death.

4. In Langland's poem the birds are harbingers of death who weave "a net of slumber" over the village and from whose wings shadows stream down, encircling the neighboring hills. Berryman, on the other hand, sees the birds as witnesses to the ever-recurring scene. They are not threatening figures, but rather impartial observers.

5. Langland uses a three-part organization: a relatively short exposition, a longer middle section which develops the details he sees as important, and finally a brief ending section that emphasizes his vision of the hunters being the hunted. Berryman's structure is much more regular. He has five five-line stanzas, and his lines are all of similar length. The recurring patterns underline his theme, as suggested in responses 3 and 4 above.

William Blake • **The Sick Rose** *(p. 503)*
William Blake • **"The Sick Rose"** *(p. 503)*

1. In the picture, the roses are female and the worm, by invading them, is destroying them. We can speculate that the worm represents some perverted form of sexuality (perhaps rape) and that love, represented by the female rose, is destroyed through this brutal and cruel act.

2. The picture suggests one reading but should not be limiting. It seems likely that the picture was drawn to illustrate the poem.

Botticelli • **Adoration of the Magi** *(p. 504)*
Giotto • **Adoration of the Magi** *(p. 504)*
T. S. Eliot • **"The Journey of the Magi"** *(p. 504)*
William Butler Yeats • **"The Magi"** *(p. 505)*

1. Botticelli depicts the Magi as part of a large crowd of richly dressed people who have been attracted to the birthplace of Jesus. The emphasis is on the crowd; the holy family is in the background. Many people seem to be curiosity seekers rather than true worshipers; they talk among themselves and look away from the child rather than toward him. In addition, the event takes place during the bright light of day and thus seems more like a street festival, in some ways, than a holy event. Giotto shows the adoration as a private event between the holy family and the wise men, whose attention is clearly focused on Christ. The stylized halos and the prominent figures of the angel also stress the sacred nature of the meeting. Behind the figures, the sky is the dark blue of night; this meeting takes place during the quiet of a silent evening, appropriate to a spiritual epiphany.

2. Yeats sees the Magi as mystical, stylized figures, much like those in Giotto's painting. He emphasizes their mythical quality and their search for significance in the child at Bethlehem. Eliot offers a far more realistic picture. His wise men seem like fallible, even prosaic, individuals who observe and respond to the rather trivial pleasures and pains of earthly life and who return to their own country, after seeing the newborn Jesus, with questions and doubts rather than a sense of revelation. We can imagine these Magi among the crowd in Botticelli's painting.

3. Yeats's rhythms, diction, and structure are formal, suggesting dignity, grandeur, and mystery. He focuses on the external features of the wise men; they stand as symbols for those who see meaning in the birth of Christ. In contrast, Eliot's rhythms and diction are close to those of ordinary speech. The speaker is not an omniscient observer—as is Yeats's—but rather one of the Magi himself. He describes the journey to Bethlehem in detail, emphasizing the physical difficulty of the quest, and reveals in the final stanza the interior scene of the mind as it seeks to grapple with a disturbing and unresolved experience.

Henri Matisse • **"The Dance"** *(p. 506)*
Natalie Safir • **"Matisse's Dance** *(p. 506)*

1. Elation, connection, and joy are all reflected in the painting. The women's arms arch high, suggesting lifted spirits, perhaps even a sense of triumph. The joined hands, and the hand that reaches toward the temporarily disengaged sister emphasize the unity and sense of

117

mutual support among these women. The position of the legs suggests lively movement; because the legs are in various poses—rather than a single, common pose—the painting also brings to mind spontaneity and improvisation.

2. The ring of dancers suggest unit and continuity; because the figures are female, perhaps the cycle of birth and renewal is suggested. The break may indicate an individual who is currently separated from the support of the group, yet she reaches out to the others, and they to her. There is a sense that she will rejoin the circle and that her arms, too, will raise in triumph and connection.

3. Safir sees the disconnected figure as frightened and somewhat lost. The imagery of her poem captures in words the richly and joyously feminine aspects of the painting. She notes, for example, the "spirals of glee" and the "grass mounds" that "curve ripely." Safir's poem also celebrates the beauty of the female body as does Matisse's painting. She invites us to see the breasts that "swell and multiply" as the dancers "rhythms rise to a gallop." She urges the figure who has lost her grip to hurry so that she may once again find the support of the group and, perhaps, also discover what it is that the tallest woman knows and that keeps "her torso a green-burning torch," celebrating her own victory and leading the others on to recognize their strengths and possibilities.

Pablo Picasso • **Girl with Mandolin** *(p. 507)*
Still Life With Pitcher *(p. 508)*
Vinnie-Marie d'Ambrosio • *"If I Were a Maker"* *(p. 507)*

Girl with Mandolin

1 and 2.   d'Ambrosio does with words and verbal images with Picasso does with paint and visual images. She combines the unexpected to create pictures that tease the mind. For example, she asks the reader to imagine her as a "maker" who can take an orange-yellow melon and turn it from an ordinary fruit (which would please the eye and tongue) into a musical instrument (which would please the ear). The boundaries of what we know as reality do not apply to the "maker" whose vision can go as far as imagination will travel.

Students might be asked to describe the sounds of the "mooncurled" song that would come from this playful, delicious instrument.

3. Most readers will notice immediately the delightful alliteration in such lines as "pick/from a suppleplump pit" and "bunches of grapes and/the ghosts in motley/no-shaped and graced/would pin the grapes." In addition, she uses onomatopoeia in the phrase "and ring-a-ling them." Throughout the poem, both the short and long "o" sounds dominate, thus suggesting the plaintiff beauty that might characterize the "mooncurled song."

Still Life With Pitcher

1. The painting is filled with circles, globes, curved handles and other gently sloping shapes that suggest the magical melons and grapes that role and leap in D'Ambrosio's poem. The colors and shadows in Picasso's work provide a sense of mystery and wonder that D'Ambrosio offers through her image of "ghosts in motley" and the final provocative promise of a "mooncurled song."

2. D'Ambrosio's poem piles rounded image upon rounded image just as does Picasso's painting. The circles and curves accumulate in the mind of the reader or viewer to create an impact which D'Ambrosio describes as song and which the viewer may experience as a unified beauty much like that one hears in a particularly fortunate combination of musical instruments.

Gustave Klimt • "The Kiss" (p. 509)
Lawrence Ferlinghetti • "Short Story on a Painting of Gustav Klimt" (p. 509)

1. Responses will vary, of course, but students will almost certainly note that the figures are each composed of small patterns, the woman is primarily created through the use of circles, while the man is comprised mainly of oblongs. The emphasis is on the couple, and it is interesting that while the man dominates the woman, it is her face that we see. In addition, her pale arm and hand stand out against the background and against the darker hands of the man.

2. Ferlinghetti's poem offers an interpretation of the poem that places sympathy primarily with the man. Her hand is "like a languid claw" while he "holds her still/so passionately/ holds her head to his so gently." He is depicted as the caring, kind, yet deeply committed lover, while she is seen as the rejecting mistress. She is the person who holds all the power. Note that Ferlinghetti states that "the summer couch . . . must be hers." By placing her in the relative safety of her own home, the poet leads the reader away from interpreting the closed eyes as fearful and the pale hand as attempting an unheeded refusal of agressive and unwelcome advances.

ADAPTATIONS

Like parodies and translations, adaptations demonstrate the great changes that can be made in a work by revising it. If you have a recording of Seeger's "Turn! Turn! Turn!" or Simon's "Richard Cory," you might play it to see how the added dimension of music changes the original just as much as do the altered line structures and word choices.

From Ecclesiastes 3:1-8 (p. 511)
Pete Seeger • "Turn! Turn! Turn!" (p. 511)

Pete Seeger's song picks up the biblical repetitions and emphasizes them not only by repeating the phrase "a time to . . . ," as does Ecclesiastes, but also by inserting the "Turn, turn, turn" lines in the refrain. The final line of the song is the most changed from the biblical verse. Seeger does not mention "a time for war," but rather stresses his final theme by adding "I swear it's not too late" to the phrase "a time for peace."

Edwin Arlington Robinson • "Richard Cory" (p. 512)
Paul Simon • "Richard Cory" (p. 513)

Simon's song has a personal, rather than a universal, narrator who refers to him/herself as "I" rather than as "we." The dissatisfaction of the narrator with the life of poverty is emphasized by the song's repeated refrain, whereas the lives of the people in Robinson's poem are detailed only in lines 13-14 and merely mentioned in other lines. The effect of the repeated refrain is

119

that the listener focuses on the discontent of the narrator as much as on the actions of Cory. In the poem, on the other hand, Cory is clearly the central focus. Simon also gives details of Cory's life that are quite different from Robinson's details. We can hardly imagine Robinson's "imperially slim" Cory, who was "admirably schooled in every grace," holding "orgies on his yacht" as does Simon's Cory. Simon's Cory seems a rich but vulgar and spoiled only child of a banker. This is a Cory who gives to charity, but is primarily concerned with seeking pleasure and power. Robinson's Cory is much more aristocratic and mysterious. We have no glimpses behind the door of the home where, one calm summer night, he puts a bullet through his head.

Langston Hughes • "Dream Deferred" (p. 514)
Langston Hughes • "Same in Blues" (p. 514)

These are two variations on a theme. The only line that is repeated in "Same in Blues" is "a dream deferred." The second poem is an expansion of the first, with Hughes giving specific illustrations of exactly what does happen with a dream deferred. He is answering the final question of his first poem with the jarring, repetitive images and refrains of this second poem. "Same in Blues" is much more informal than "Dream Deferred." The conversational rhythms and slang diction make "Same in Blues" the practical application of the philosophical theory in "Dream Deferred."

Activity

Students may enjoy adapting one of the poems in the text to song lyrics. Those who play an instrument and/or sing may be willing to share their adaptations with the class. Or, if "in person" presentation is too threatening, some students may instead agree to make a tape of their creations.

Woody Guthrie • "This Land Is Your Land" (p. 516)
Don McClean • "Vincent" (p. 517)
John Lennon and Paul McCartney • "Yesterday" (p. 518)

Here are three pieces students (or at least some students) will know as songs rather than as poems. As a class activity, ask someone to read each of these selections aloud. Then discuss how they work as poems—apart from the familiar music we associate with them. Some students will note that Guthrie's piece uses many of the poetic devices of the ballad. Note, for instance, the repetition, particularly in the refrain, and then the reversal in the final stanza where the poet introduces his doubt, rather than his assertion that "This land was made for you and me."

"Vincent" may be considered both as a song that can function as poem and as a response to Van Gogh's "Starry Night" (p. 494). You may want students to compare this piece with Robert Fagles's and Anne Sexton's versions of "The Starry Night" (pp. 494–495). Note that Fagles, like MacClean, focuses on the artist, while Sexton focuses on the painting. Students may note that MacClean's piece uses and insistent rhyme and rhythm which catches the reader up in the dual forces of beauty and despair the song writer sees in Van Gogh's work and in his life.

Readers' responses to "Yesterday" will vary widely, of course, but to me the "Oh's" in stanzas one, two, and three come across as overly-dramatic when read as poetry. In song, there's a blended sound that conveys a gentle sense of loss and regret.

After reading these pieces aloud and discussing them as poems, you might play tapes of the songs and ask students to comment on how their responses change with this added element.

RESPONSES (POINT-COUNTERPOINT) (P. 519)

The Responses section offers a good opportunity to teach the finer points of argument. In each of these pairs, one poet or speaker critiques the tone, style or view point of another poet or speaker. Students will see immediately the opposing views of the speakers in Raleigh's and Marlow's poems and may decide for themselves which is more persuasive. You may want to look closely at MacLeish's and Hecht's poems, which use irony rather than direct statement to counter the views of earlier poets.

Christopher Marlowe • "The Passionate Shepherd to His Love" (p. 519)
Sir Walter Raleigh • "The Nymph's Reply to the Shepherd" (p. 520)

Responses to these poems will vary, but the nymph seems in many ways to outclass the shepherd. His pleas are gallant and extravagant but ultimately frivolous and not much different from the playful wooing of swains throughout the ages. The nymph, on the other hand, makes a rather philosophical and thoughtful reply. She is not about to be moved by the material gifts of a moment. Rather, she thinks about larger and more significant concerns. She is not against love and pleasure, but because she recognizes that romantic fantasies cannot last, she is not willing to become involved in a relationship based only on fleeting joy.

William Shakespeare • "Not marble, nor the gilded monuments" (p. 521)
Archibald MacLeish • "Not Marble, Nor the Gilded Monuments" (p. 521)

Shakespeare's sonnet stands as a tribute to the lover praised in the poem. The poet exults in having outwitted the ravages of time and the forces of both humans and gods. If his words are passionately conceived and carefully crafted, they will have the power granted to few: to create an undying paean that assures his love immortality. MacLeish uses the first two stanzas of his poem to establish his argument: the poets who boast that women live on in their poetry lie; only the words endure, not the flesh-and-blood lover. MacLeish, therefore, proposes to describe his mistress in great detail while always acknowledging the inevitability of death. MacLeish offers specific images of his lover rather than abstract praise and, in the poem's final lines, seems to hold out a hope that in fact the specific picture he captures may live on. With the words "Till the world ends and the eyes are out and the mouths broken/Look! It is there!" he shows himself just as hopeful as Shakespeare that he can, in fact, stay the hand of obscurity.

Matthew Arnold • "Dover Beach" (p. 523)
Anthony Hecht • "The Dover bitch: A Criticism of Life" (p. 524)

Arnold's speaker faces the challenges to traditional values, patriotism, and religious faith that were part of Victorian culture. As he counts the losses of his modern world, he turns to his mistress and urges that they take comfort in one another. By remaining steadfast, perhaps they can create an island of security in an otherwise violent and frighteningly uncertain world. Hecht's bitter satire undercuts Arnold's hope and suggests that his speaker's longing is both hypocritical and hopelessly romantic. Hecht's speaker shows the mistress as a shallow opportunist simply out for a good time. The speaker claims he knew this "girl" and implies that they still have occasional casual sexual encounters. Certainly she is not the answer to Arnold's hope for steadfastness, and Hecht implies that Arnold was a fool to imagine that there was any answer to the growing nihilism he saw around him.

CHAPTER ELEVEN

Topics for Writing and Discussion for a Collection of Poems

"To me he seems like a god" • *Sappho (p. 525)*

1. Describe the experience of the speaker in the poem. What is her relationship with the man she describes?

2. Imagine that you are the person sitting and talking to the godlike man. How might you respond to the speaker's words and feelings?

Ballads
"Barbara Allan" (p. 526)
"Edward, Edward" (p. 527)

1. Ballads concentrate on a single episode, usually the climactic episode of a particular story. We usually find ourselves in the middle of a dramatic situation, and it is up to us to infer the background from the details we are given as we go along. Sometimes we are not even given that much help; we must create the events leading up to the ballad's central episode entirely from imagination. Choose any one of these ballads and explain what you infer its background to be. What has happened to the characters before we hear about them? What decisions have they made? What are their motives?

2. Ballads emphasize dialogue. Choose one of the ballads and consider what effect the use of dialogue has on the poem. Consider the speaker(s), the tone, and the word choice. How would the poem be changed if it were done without dialogue?

3. Ballads make use of repetition in many different ways. Study any one of these ballads and explain how repetition is used and what effect it has on the tone and meaning of the poem.

4. Read these two ballads. What generalizations can you make about the topics? About the characters/speakers? About the outcomes?

5. Choose any ballad and tell its story from the point of view of someone other than the speaker.

"The Pardoner's Tale" • *Geoffrey Chaucer (pp. 529–543)*

You may want to introduce this selection by explaining the structure of the *Canterbury Tales* and noting that the Pardoner was one of a motley group making a springtime pilgrimage to Canterbury Cathedral. The Pardoner, a rascally clergyman, presents his tale as his contribution to the story each pilgrim promises to tell to make the time pass more pleasantly on the journey.

1. From the details in the prologue, what can you tell about the Pardoner's character? Do you agree with the scholar who called him a "lost soul"?

2. The Pardoner's Tale, a sermon really, uses an illustrative anecdote to teach a lesson. Summarize this anecdote and explain what you think it is intended to teach.

3. Compare the lesson the Pardoner purports to teach with this character as suggested by the prologue. What ironies do you detect?

4. In the final lines of his tale, the Pardoner pronounces: "O cursed sin! O blackguardly excess! O treacherous homicide!" and follows with some questions addressed to the pilgrims. How does he want them to apply the lesson of his sermon? How does this application relate to his liturgy of sins in the prologue?

"They flee from me" • Thomas Wyatt (p. 544)

The title of "They flee from me" is sometimes given as "The Lover Showeth How He Is Forsaken of Such as He Sometimes Enjoyed." Does this title suggest any relationship between the first and second stanzas? Why does the speaker think he has been forsaken both by his old supplicants and by his mistress?

"One day I wrote her name upon the strand" • Edmund Spenser (p. 545)

1. Try reading this poem as three units of four lines each and one final couplet. Who is the speaker in each section? What point is made in each section? How convincing do you think the final speaker's argument would be to his love? To modern readers?

2. Characterize the tone of the poem. Note especially the use of hyperbole (exaggeration for emphasis).

From "Astrophel and Stella" • Sir Philip Sidney (p. 545)

1. Explain the cause-and-effect relationship described in lines 1-4 in "Astrophel and Stella." What series of events does the speaker hope will happen? What is the incident that will set off this series of events? What would the desired outcome be?

2. In lines 6-14 in "Astrophel and Stella" the speaker describes his writing process. How many different aspects of this process can be identified? What approach did not work? Why? What approach finally worked for him?

3. In Astrophel and Stella," what does the speaker mean in line 12 when he is "great with child to speak"? How does this comparison contribute to the point he is making to his lover?

"Since there's no help, come let us kiss and part" • Michael Drayton (p. 546)

1. How is love pictured in the final six lines? What effect does this personification have on the tone and meaning of the poem?

2. This poem presents some clever persuasive devices. What does the speaker appear to be asking for at the beginning of the poem? What does he, in fact, ask for at the end of the poem? How does the dual nature of these pleas reinforce the meaning of the poem?

3. Compare this poem's treatment of the death of love with Hardy's treatment of the same subject in "Neutral Tones" (p. 412).

William Shakespeare
"When in disgrace with fortune and men's eyes" (p. 546)
"Let me not to the marriage of true minds" (p. 547)
"Th' expense of spirit in a waste of shame" (p. 547)
"My mistress' eyes are nothing like the sun" (p. 548)

1. Summarize the idea of any of these poems in twenty-five words or less.

2. Paraphrase any of these poems either line by line or sentence by sentence.

3. Try writing an imitation of the first twelve lines of "When in disgrace . . ." but without worrying about rhyme or metrical regularity. Try, that is, to imitate the sentence structure of lines 1-12 by writing your own sentence that imitates the form of Shakespeare's sentence. Use the following pattern, and fill in your own words to replace the dots.

```
1       When . . .
2           I . . .
3               And . . .
4               And . . . and . . .
5                   Wishing me like . . .
6                   Featured like . . .
7                   Desiring . . . and . . .
8                   With what I most enjoy . . .
9       Yet in these thoughts . . .
10          I think of . . . and then . . .
11              Like . . .
12              . . . sings hymns at heaven's gate.
```

4. Take an abstract word such as "justice," "courage," "truth," "honesty," "integrity," "hate," "democracy," "chutzpah," and make a list of four or five characteristics that define it. Or think of one essential defining characteristic and compare it with three or four other things. Keep in mind Shakespeare's process of defining "love" in "Let me not to the marriage of true minds" as you plan your definition.

5. The "Th' expense of spirit in a waste of shame," the speaker argues against lust. What is the tone of the poem? Do you find the argument convincing?

6. The speaker in "My mistress' eyes are nothing like the sun" seems to be speaking negatively about his lover, yet in the final lines he offers her praise. Do the negative comparisons work effectively to support the point of the final lines? Explain your response.

John Donne
  "Song" (p. 548)
  "The Canonization (p. 549)
  "A Valediction: Forbidding Mourning" (p. 550)
  "The Flea" (p. 551)
  "Death, be not proud" (p. 552)
  "Batter my heart, three-personed God" (p. 552)

1. The major characteristic of Donne's poetry is the metaphysical conceit, an extended metaphor that compares and links two apparently unrelated subjects in a surprising combination. Careful consideration of the implications of the conceits yields rich readings of the poetry. Choose any one of the poems anthologized here; identify a conceit which you find particularly puzzling, intriguing, or thought-provoking, and analyze exactly what it contributes to the meaning of the poem. For example, you might take the conceit of the "stiff twin compasses" (lines 26ff. in "A Valediction: Forbidding Mourning"), or you might take the conceit of the flea and the fleabite in "The Flea."

2. In the first stanza of "Song" the speaker lists a series of impossible tasks. How does he use this list to make his argument? Do you agree with the point he makes at the end of stanzas 2 and 3? How might a woman respond to the speaker's arguments?

3. What can you tell about the speaker's audience in "The Canonization"? Whom is he addressing in the first line? What clues do you get to the listener's character by reading the middle stanzas and especially the last stanza, where the speaker addresses his listener directly?

4. Both "A Valediction: Forbidding Mourning" and "The Flea "are love poems addressed by the speaker to a woman. How are the two poems different? How are they the same? Are the relationships in each at different stages? How do the comparisons used to make the arguments in each poem differ? What do their differences indicate about the speaker's attitude toward the importance of the two arguments?

5. Imagine yourself to be the woman addressed in "The Flea." Do you find the argument convincing? How would you counter each of the points made by the speaker if you wanted to disagree with him? As you plan your response, try to maintain the same tone as the speaker—you do not want to alienate him completely, but you do want to refuse his plea.

6. Evaluate the language in "Batter my heart, three-personed God." What is the tone of the poem? Consider especially words like "Knock, breathe, shine," and "break, blow, burn." Would you expect to find words like these in a supplication to God? How does the speaker characterize God?

Ben Jonson
  "On My First Daughter" (p. 553)
  "Son My First Son" (p. 553)
  "Still to be neat, still to be dressed" (p. 554)
  "Song: To Celia" (p. 554)

1. Compare "On My First Daughter" with "On My First Son." How does Jonson try to reconcile himself to the deaths of his children? How convincing do you find his arguments for reconciliation?

2. The poems "Still to be neat, still to be dressed" demonstrate Jonson's penchant for witty, biting satire. What does he criticize in this poem? What particular words and images tell you that he is making fun of the lady described?

3. Compare the tone of "Song: To Celia" to Donne's "The Flea" (p. 551) and Marvell's "To His Coy Mistress" (p. 558). Do you find one speaker more convincing than the others? Why? How are the images in the three poems related?

Robert Herrick
"Upon Julia's Clothes" (p. 555)
"To the Virgins, to Make Much of Time" (p. 555)

1. Consider the words Herrick chose to use in "Upon Julia's Clothes" along with the words he chose to use in "Upon Julia's Voice" (printed below). How does he use sound devices to echo the sense of his poems?

> Upon Julia's Voice
>
> So smooth, so sweet, so silv'ry is thy voice,
> As, could they hear, the Damned would make no noise,
> But listen to thee (walking in thy chamber)
> Melting melodious words, to Lutes of Amber.

2. In the first stanza of "To the Virgins," we could interpret the rosebuds literally. What clues in the final two stanzas indicate that we should also give them symbolic importance? How do both the literal and symbolic meanings of the rosebuds contribute to the meaning of the poem?

3. "To the Virgins" was written in 1648. Are the subject matter and the advice given by the speaker hopelessly outdated or are they still of interest to modern audiences?

George Herbert
"The Altar" (p. 556)
"Easter Wings" (p. 556)

1. What is the central metaphor in "The Altar"? How does the form of the poem reflect the metaphor? How do both format and metaphor contribute to the meaning?

2. Some critics and scholars have dismissed "Easter Wings" as a mere exercise in cleverness. What do you think? Does the intricately planned structure reflect and support the sense of the poem, or does it distract you?

3. What form does each stanza of "Easter Wings" take? How is the form particularly appropriate for Easter and the theme of resurrection?

John Milton
 "When I consider how my light is spent" (p. 557)
 "On the Late Massacre in Piedmont" (p. 557)

1. Explain how the two meanings of "talent," along with the biblical allusion to Matthew 25:14-30, contribute to the meaning of "When I consider how my light is spent." What is Milton's "one talent"?

2. What is the relationship between the first eight lines of "When I consider . . ." and the final six lines?

3. Do you agree with the point made in the final three lines of "When I consider . . ."? Explain.

4. The background for "On the Late Massacre in Piedmont" is the battle between Protestants and Roman Catholics during the Reformation. Milton, a Protestant Puritan poet, wrote this sonnet after the soldiers of an Italian Catholic duke had massacred a group of Protestants in northern Italy. Find images and allusions in the poem that indicate the religious nature of the struggle.

5. How do the sound devices contribute to the tone and relate to the meaning of "On the Late Massacre . . ."? Consider the rhythm, the alliteration, and the onomatopoeia.

"To My Dear and Loving Husband" • *Anne Bradstreet (p. 558)*

Can you resolve the paradox of the last two lines of "To My Dear and Loving Husband"? How do those lines relate to the extravagant comparisons of the first nine lines?

"To His Coy Mistress" • *Andrew Marvell (p. 558)*

1. Is "To His Coy Mistress" primarily about love or primarily about time? Or are the two subjects intertwined? How do the images of space and distance relate to the two subjects and thus define the speaker's theme?

2. Trace the parts of the speaker's argument in "To His Coy Mistress." Identify the central point in each of the three sections of the poem.

3. Analyze the following images from "To His Coy Mistress" and explain what they contribute to the poem: "vegetable love" (line 11); "Time's winged chariot" (line 22); "slow-chapped power" (line 40); "iron gates of life" (line 44).

"An Essay on Man" • *Alexander Pope (p. 560)*

Explain how the details in the first seventeen lines of "An Essay on Man" supports the conclusion of its eighteenth line.

"Elegy Written in a Country Churchyard" • *Thomas Gray (p. 560)*

1. Compare the views of the speaker in this poem with those of Miniver Cheevy ("Miniver Cheevy" p. 402). Do you have more sympathy for one than for the other? Do you take one more seriously than the other? Why?

2. The speaker in "Elegy" defends the quiet and simple village life as opposed to the encroaching changes brought on by progress and modernization. Could the same kind of arguments be made today about life in small towns? How valid would you find such arguments?

3. What does the Epitaph (lines 117-128) add to the poem? How would the poem be changed if it were omitted?

William Blake
"The Clod & the Pebble" (p. 564)
"The Lamb" (p. 564)
"The Tyger" (p. 565)
"The Garden of Love" (p. 566)

1. Blake regarded the world of the senses as an ever-abundant source of symbols and metaphors. Every object, animal, or event pointed beyond itself to a greater, transcendental meaning. The following poem suggests his beliefs and feelings:

   To See a World in a Grain of Sand

   To see a world in a grain of sand
   And heaven in a wild flower
   Hold infinity in the palm of your hand
   And eternity in an hour.

   Choose any of Blake's poems in the text and show how he uses a central symbol or metaphor to "see a world in a grain of sand."

2. Read "The Clod & the Pebble," and then write a dialogue between two objects of your choice. The dialogue should present contrasting views of the same subject (love, death, war, work, sexuality, power, television—whatever). If you like, you can keep Blake's clod and pebble but have them talk about something other than love.

3. Characterize the speaker and the listener in "The Lamb." How are the two related?

4. What are your responses to Blake's tiger ("Tyger, Tyger")? Is the tiger supposed to arouse fear? Awe? Respect? Do your responses to the tiger help to answer the questions the speaker poses throughout the poem? Are the questions supposed to lead to answers?

5. What criticism of organized religion does the speaker make in "The Garden of Love"? Plan an argument attacking or supporting the speaker's criticism.

"A Red, Red Rose" • Robert Burns (p. 566)

1. Identify the figures of speech in "A Red, Red Rose" and explain how they contribute to the poem's meaning. How do the figures of speech in the first stanza differ from those in the final three stanzas?

2. Try to write a few lines of this poem following Burns's basic style but updating the images.

William Wordsworth
"The world is too much with us" (p. 567)
"The Solitary Reaper" (p. 567)
"Composed upon Westminster Bridge, September 3, 1802" (p. 568)
"Lines Composed a Few Miles Above Tintern Abbey" (p. 568)

1. Wordsworth was concerned with the relation between the inner life of humans and the outer life of nature. He was convinced that human happiness was to be found only when the intellect recognized and affirmed its essential connection to the world of nature. After reading the selections here, choose one or two poems to demonstrate how Wordsworth expressed these convictions.

2. What is the situation about which the speaker is complaining in "The world is too much with us"? How does the speaker feel he and other members of this society have been affected by this situation? Wordsworth wrote this poem in 1807; are the ideas expressed in it still applicable to our society today?

3. In "The Solitary Reaper," what do the solitary reaper and her song symbolize for the speaker? Consider especially the final stanza for suggestions of what the experience of hearing the reaper means to the speaker.

4. How does the setting of "Composed upon Westminster Bridge" affect the meaning of the poem? Consider both the place and the time of day in which the poem was written. How might the images—and thus the meaning of the poem—differ if the speaker were looking at the city at a different time of day?

5. In "Lines," the speaker describes how his relationship with nature has changed from his youth to his maturity. Describe what the changes are by referring to specific images in the poem. Has your own response to nature changed since you were a child? Explain.

Kubla Khan" • Samuel Taylor Coleridge (p. 572)

1. What is your response to Xanadu? Is it a place you would want to experience? Or does it suggest dark and dangerous events?

2. How do the sound images in particular contribute to the tone of the poem? Do they convey a unified picture, or are they contradictory and fragmented?

"She walks in beauty" • *George Gordon, Lord Byron (p. 574)*

1.   What qualities does the woman described in this poem share with the night?

2.   What does the speaker value most in the woman he describes?

Percy Bysshe Shelley
   "Ozymandias" (p. 574)
   "Ode to the West Wind" (p. 575)

1.   Write a character descriptions of "Ozymandias." How do you think he treated his subjects? Can you compare him with any twentieth-century leaders?

2.   What is added to the poem by the speaker's reporting that he heard about Ozymandias from a "traveler from an antique land"?

3.   How are the images of the West Wind contradictory? What do these contradictions contribute to the meaning of the poem?

4.   What does the speaker see as his relationship to the West Wind? See the fifth stanza particularly.

John Keats
   "When I have fears" (p. 577)
   "La Belle Dame sans Merci" (p. 578)
   "Ode to a Nightingale" (p. 579)
   "Ode on a Grecian Urn" (p. 581)

1.   In "When I have fears," the speaker seems to give love and fame equal weight. Why then, at the end of the poem, does he say that he stands alone and thinks "Till Love and Fame to nothingness do sink"? How does this action represent a solution to the dilemma he explains in the first twelve lines of the poem?

2.   Compare Keats's use of a speaker who reports the words of another speaker ("La Belle Dame sans Merci") to Shelley's use of the same device in "Ozymandias" (p. 574).

3.   What exactly does the speaker yearn for in "Ode to a Nightingale"? Does he want to escape reality entirely? Does he place any value on the real world, or does he long only for a fantasy world?

4.   Read the biblical Book of Ruth. How does knowing the story of Ruth affect your reading of the seventh stanza of "Ode to a Nightingale?"

5.   What is the speaker in "Ode on a Grecian Urn" doing as he speaks" What does he see in each stanza, and how does each new image contribute to what he is saying?

6.   In the final stanza of "Ode on a Grecian Urn," the speaker tells us that the turn has a message to deliver. The lines that follow "thou say'st" can be read in two ways. Either the urn is delivering the final two lines as its message, or the urn is saying "beauty is truth, truth beauty," with the last line and a half being the speaker's commentary. How would the meaning of the poem change with a change from one of these readings to the other?

"How Do I Live Thee" • Elizabeth Barrett Browning (p. 583)

1. Compare the view of the lover and the beloved in this poem with the view in Robert Browning's "Meeting At Night" (p. 410) and "Parting At Morning" [not listed].

2. Ask students what they know about E. B. Browning's life. Then fill in any gaps to let them know about her overbearing father who tried to keep his talented daughter a recluse by emphasizing and overdramatizing her somewhat frail health. Although he reluctantly allowed her to write and publish poetry, he tried to keep her shut away from the world. Robert Browning, however, admired her poetry so much that he insisted on a meeting which she finally granted. Over a series of visits the relationship flourished and R. Browning finally convinced Elizabeth Barrett to marry him. Together, they left England and lived together in Italy until her death fifteen years later.

   After hearing this story, students may reread the poem and see how their responses to it change.

Edgar Allan Poe
"To Helen" (p. 583)
"The Raven" (p. 584)

1. What do each of the classical references (Nicean barks, hyacinth hair, Naiad airs, Psyche) add to the characterization of Helen? How do these pagan references relate to the final line?

2. Compare Helen with the woman described in "She walks in beauty" (p. 574). How does Poe's vision of the ideal woman contrast with Byron's ideal woman?

3. Comment on the effect of repetition in "The Raven."

4. What does the raven represent? How can you account for the speaker's intense response to this bird?

5. Read "The Black Cat" (p. 80). How does Poe's use of the cat as a symbol compare to his use of the raven as symbol?

Alfred, Lord Tennyson
"Ulysses" (p. 587)
"Tithonus" (p. 588)
"The Eagle" (p. 590)
from "In Memoriam A. H. H." (p. 591)

1. Write a character sketch of Ulysses. What way of life does he symbolize? How does his way of life contrast with his son's? Does the poet seem to favor the life choices of Ulysses over those of Telemachus?

2. How does Ulysses' old age contrast with the old age of Tithonus? How does each character view death? Why does Tithonus see immortality as cruel? Ulysses plans to sail west and Tithonus begs, "Hold me hot for ever in thine East" (line 64). What are the connotations of "east" and "west"? How do these directions symbolize the lives of the two men?

3. Write a brief description of a bird or animal, capturing one minute of its life. Use "The Eagle" as an example of describing such a moment. Try to use vivid images and comparisons to make your subject come to life.

4. Compare the speaker's view of death in "In Memoriam" to the speaker's view of death in Donne's "Death, be not proud" (p. 552). What is the tone of each poem? Is one poem more optimistic than the other?

"Soliloquy of the Spanish Cloister" • Robert Browning (p. 594)

1. Contrast the speaker in the poem with Brother Lawrence. Which character is more appealing? Is either one totally sympathetic or totally unsympathetic? Explain.

2. Describe this morning in the garden as Brother Lawrence might. What does he think of the speaker? Of the flowers? Of religious ritual? Of "brown Dolores" and "Sanchicha"? What about that "scrofulous French novel"?

"Remembrance" • Emily Brontë (p. 594)

1. Compare the speaker's view of the lost love to the speaker's view of the lost friend in Tennyson's "In Memoriam A. H. H." (p. 591)

2. If you are familiar with Emily Brontë's novel *Wuthering Heights*, compare the actions and feelings of Heathcliff in the final chapters to the actions and feelings of the speaker in the final stanza of "Remembrance."

Walt Whitman
"A noiseless patient spider" (p. 595)
"Crossing Brooklyn Ferry" (p. 595)

1. Explain the relationship between the two stanzas of "A noiseless patient spider." Consider the rhythm, syntax, and imagery as well as the meaning.

2. What is accomplished in each section of "Crossing Brooklyn Ferry"? How are the sections of the poem connected and related to each other? Notice the combination of logical and rhythmic progressions. Consider the carefully wrought changes of pace. Try to identify the continuous thematic development.

3. Whitman had great faith in democracy. He believed it to be the universal law, the order of nature. What evidence of his optimistic faith in America and in the American way of life do you find in "Crossing Brooklyn Ferry"? What does he particularly value and praise?

Emily Dickinson
  "I like a look of Agony" (p. 600)
  "Some keep the Sabbath going to Church" (p. 600)
  "Wild Nights—Wild Nights" (p. 600)
  "After great pain, a formal feelings comes" (p. 601)
  "Much Madness is divinest Sense" (p. 601)
  "I died for Beauty—but was scarce" (p. 601)
  "I heard a Fly buss—when I died" (p. 602)
  "The Bustle in a House" (p. 602)
  "Tell all the Truth but tell it slant" (p. 603)
  "Pain—has an Element of Blank" (p. 603)
  "A narrow Fellow in the Grass" (p. 603)
  "I taste a liquor never brewed" (p. 604)
  "I dreaded that first Robin, so" (p. 604)
  "I like to see it lap the Miles" (p. 605)
  "Further in Summer than the Birds" (p. 606)
  "A Route of Evanescence" (p. 606)
  "Apparently with no surprise" (p. 606)

1. Read all the poems by Emily Dickinson in this text. What generalizations can you make about her voice, diction, syntax, use of rhythm and rhyme, choice of imagery? Can you identify any predominant themes and subjects?

2. In "I like a look of Agony" Dickinson explains why she takes this view. Do you find her explanation convincing? Do you think she implies that she would really like to spend her life seeing only people who are in horrible pain or close to death? If not, what is the central idea she expresses through her rather shocking statements?

3. In "Some keep the Sabbath going to Church" what does the speaker mean when she says that she wears "Wings" (line 6) and that "Our little Sexton—sings" (line 8)?

4. How do the images of stanzas 2 and 3 relate to the Wild Nights described in the first stanza of "Wild Nights—Wild Nights"?

5. If you read "He" in line 3 of "After great pain" as referring to Christ, how does that affect your understanding of the poem?

6. What comment does Dickinson make on nonconformity in "Much Madness is divinest Sense"? Can you think of historical examples that would prove or disprove her view?

7. Compare Dickinson's treatment of the relationship between truth and beauty ("I died for Beauty—but was scarce") with Keats's view in "Ode on a Grecian Urn" (p. 581).

8. "I heard a Fly buzz—when I died" captures the last moments of life. What are the images the dying person perceives? Who is the King referred to in stanza 2? After considering these questions, compare the speaker's final moments with the final hours of Iván Ilych's life in Tolstoy's "The Death of Iván Ilych" (p. 105).

9. Contrast the view of death in "I heard a Fly buzz—when I died" with that in "The Bustle in a House."

10. Compare the main idea of Plato's "Allegory of the Cave" (widely anthologized) with the thought of "Tell all the Truth but tell it slant."

11. In "Pain—has an Element of Blank" why does Dickinson use the plural verb "contain" rather than the singular "contains" in line 6? How would the meaning of the line change if the verb were singular?

12. Although the speaker in "A Narrow Fellow in the Grass" does not identify her subject, we have no doubt that she is describing a snake. How do the poem's images clearly indicate its topic?

13. How does the speaker in "I taste a liquor never brewed" picture herself? What sort of creature might drink dew and seem "drunk" with the summer air as it appears high enough and far enough away to seem to lean against the sun?

14. What is the situation of the speaker in "I dreaded the first Robin, so"? What do all the things she mentions in the poem symbolize? How do they contrast with her circumstances?

15. In "I like to see it lap the Miles" what is the sustained metaphor Dickinson uses to describe the engine of a train?

16. List every word that has a religious connotation in "Further in Summer than the Birds." How do these words suggest the poem's theme?

17. In "A Route of Evanescence," what has happened to the blossoms? Who or what has "tumbled" their heads?

18. What is the relationship between the action in the poem and the final line of "Apparently with no surprise"?

"Jabberwocky" • Lewis Carroll (Charles Lutwidge Dodgson) (p. 607)

1. Can you make any sense of this nonsense poem? Is Carroll trying to convey any point, or is he just being playful?

2. Read "Jabberwocky" in its original context, the first chapter of *Through the Looking Glass* and *What Alice Found* There. Does your response to the poem change at all when you reread it as part of Alice's story?

Thomas Hardy
"The Ruined Maid" (p. 608)
"Channel Firing" (p. 608)
"Ah, are you digging on my grave" (p. 610)

1. What view is represented by each of the speakers in "The Ruined Maid"? Does the poem seem to recommend being "ruined," or is there some other main thought conveyed by the ironies in the dialogue?

2. How is God portrayed in "Channel Firing"? What does this characterization of God contribute to the meaning of the poem?

3. How would the meaning and tone of "Ah, are you digging on my grave" be changed if the final stanza were omitted?

Gerald Manley Hopkins
   "God's Grandeur" (p. 611)
   "The Windhover" (p. 611)
   "Pied Beauty" (p. 612)

1. Explain the meaning of the following images, then discuss what they contribute to the central idea of "God's Grandeur": "shining from shook foil," "reck his rod," "bent World."

2. What is the relationship between the first ten lines of "The Windhover" and the final six lines? Consider, for example, the way the speaker refers to the bird ("morning's minion," line 1; "dapple-dawn-drawn Falcon," line 2; "my chevalier," line 11; "my dear," line 13).

3. How does the subtitle of "The Windhover" ("To Christ Our Lord") relate to the meaning of the poem? In what sense is the poem religious or about religion?

4. Write a series of sentences using parallel structure, as Hopkins does in "Pied Beauty," to explain a category of things you are thankful for.

A. E. Housman
   "When I was one-and twenty" (p. 612)
   "To an Athlete Dying Young" (p. 613)

1. What exactly is the advice that the wise man gives in each of the stanzas of "When I was one-and-twenty"? How does the attitude of the speaker change toward the advice? What can we assume are the reasons for the change?

2. In "To an Athlete Dying Young," does Housman imply that most people would be better off if they died at the moment of their greatest success? Plan an argument explaining, first, why you do or do not think this is what Housman is saying and, second, why you agree or disagree with his idea.

William Butler Yeats
   "Adam's Curse" (p. 613)
   "The Second Coming" (p. 615)
   "The Wild Swans at Coole" (p. 615)
   "Leda and the Swan" (p. 616)
   "Sailing to Byzantium" (p. 617)
   "A Prayer for My Daughter" (p. 618)

1. In the first stanza of "Adam's Curse," the speaker discusses the difficulty of writing; in the fourth stanza he speaks of the difficulty of loving well. How does he get from one topic to the other? What provides the bridge? How are the two ideas related?

2. What kind of a second coming does Yeats expect in "The Second Coming"? Does his imagery suggest the traditional view of the second coming as a rebirth of Christ? How does his imagery contrast with established Christian imagery? Does your reading of this

poem change if you know that Yeats wrote it in 1919 when his country, Ireland, was in the midst of bitter rebellions and bloody confrontations between opposing forces?

3. In "The Wild Swans at Coole," Yeats carefully gives the exact number of swans: fifty-nine. Later in the poem he describes them swimming "lover by lover" (line 19), yet if there are fifty-nine swans they cannot be equally paired off. Can you account for this apparent discrepancy?

4. What question is raised by the last two lines of "Leda and the Swan"? Do the images of the earlier lines suggest any answers? Consider how the description of Leda contrasts with the description of the swan/Zeus.

5. Byzantium, the capital of the eastern Roman Empire, was an important cultural center. In Yeats's private mythology, Byzantium stands for art and eternal forms as opposed to the natural world and mortality. How does Yeats express and develop this contrast through the images of "Sailing to Byzantium"?

6. In a complete collection of Yeats's poetry, you will find "A Prayer for My Son." Contrast this poem with "A Prayer for My Daughter." How do you feel about the way the speaker defines the world he wants for his daughter? How is it the same or different from the world you would want for your daughter? For yourself?

"Mr. Flood's Party" • Edwin Arlington Robinson (p. 620)

Characterize the two voices in "Mr. Flood's Party." What do we learn about Eden Flood from the dialogue? What observations on human nature can be abstracted from the dialogue?

"We wear the mask" • Paul Laurence Dunbar (p. 621)

1. What does the mask symbolize? What is the speaker's attitude toward the mask?

2. Do you find wearing "the mask that grins and lies" an accurate description of most people you know? Of some people? Of yourself? Explain.

"Patterns" • Amy Lowell (p. 622)

1. This poem presents the narrative of a grieving woman. Unlike traditional narrative poems, however, "Patterns" does not present the events in straight chronological order. How has Lowell varied the chronology? How do her choices contribute to the meaning of the poem?

2. What does the title of the poem mean? How many kinds of patterns are identified in the poem? What is the speaker's attitude toward patterns? How do the language and form of the poem reflect the subject?

Robert Frost
  "Mending Wall" (p. 624)
  "Fire and Ice" (p. 626)
  "Birches" (p. 626)
  "Design" (p. 627)
  "Desert Places" (p. 628)
  "Tree at my window" (p. 628)
  "Acquainted with the night" (p. 629)
  "Putting in the Seed" (p. 629)

1. Robert Frost is known for his deep concern with nature and rural life. Read the examples provided here to find the generalizations you can make about the way he presents nature and uses images and symbols derived both from nature and from rural life.

2. What is the relationship of the two neighbors in "Mending Wall"? What does each of them think about walls? Does the poem seem to value one view over the other? Note that the two most famous lines of the poem, the first and the last, express exactly opposite views.

3. Who are the "some" who say the world will end in fire? Who are the "some" who say ice? Consider who makes prophecies of the world's end as you think of these lines in "Fire and Ice." Do the speaker's observations on the end of the world (lines 3-8) conform literally to the prophecies suggested by the first two lines? How exactly do the speaker's observations relate to the opening lines?

4. What do you think the speaker in "Birches" means when he says in the final line of the poem, "One could do worse than be a swinger of birches"? Do you agree with his observation? Explain your answer.

5. In line 2 of "Design," the speaker reports finding a "white heal-all" (this flower is usually blue). How does this white image work with the other white images in the poem? White is often a symbol of innocence and purity, although anyone who has read *Moby Dick* knows that it can also symbolize evil. Does Frost's poem suggest innocence or evil? Or maybe a combination?

6. In "Desert Places," Frost describes a landscape filled up with snow. Compare this poem with the view of its speaker, with "Stopping by Woods on a Snowy Evening" (p. 376).

7. What does the speaker of the poem in "Tree at my window" mean by "inner weather" (line 16)" how do inner and outer weather relate in the poem? Who is the "she" referred to in line 13? How does "she" relate both to the speaker and to the tree?

8. Unlike many of Frost's poems, "Acquainted with the night" uses city images. Compare this poem with any of the poems that use rural images. Does Frost present the city in a more negative light than he does the country? Are any of his images of rural life and nature pessimistic or negative?

9. Why does Frost capitalize the words "Love" and "Putting in the Seed" in line 10 of "Putting in the Seed"? How does this variation on the standard use of capital letters tell readers something about the meaning of the poem?

"Portrait of My Father as a Young Man" • *Rainer Maria Riike (p. 630)*

What do the last two lines of "Portrait of My Father as a Young Man" mean? Why is the speaker's hand disappearing more slowly than the photograph? What does the disappearance of both the photograph and the hand imply about the relationship between the speaker and his father?

Wallace Stevens
  "The Snow Man" (p. 630)
  "Thirteen Ways of Looking at a Blackbird" (p. 631)

1. Who is the snow man referred to in the title of "The Snow Man"? Are the images in the poem primarily concrete or abstract? List examples of each kind of image. How do these images lead to the final line of the poem? What does the speaker mean by "Nothing that is not there and the nothing that is"?

2. What *are* the thirteen ways of looking at a blackbird? What does each way of looking suggest? Consider each image and see whether it represents a different emotion or frame of mind.

William Carlos Williams
  "The Widow's Lament in Springtime" (p. 633)
  "Spring and All" (p. 633)
  "To a Poor Old Woman" (p. 634)
  "The Young Housewife" (p. 635)
  "Danse Russe" (p. 635)

1. Like Walt Whitman, Williams believed that American poets should use the patterns and vocabulary of American speech. He favored vital, lively language which conveyed direct, honest images. Read the examples of his poetry provided here and note which poems are particularly strong illustrations of the characteristics just described.

2. What is the opening metaphor of "The Widow's Lament in Springtime? How does this metaphor lead to the description of the change that has taken place in the speaker's life?

3. Spring is usually seen as a season of hope and rebirth. How does Williams turn that traditional view around in "Spring and All"? Is the poem ultimately optimistic or pessimistic?

4. What effect does the repetition of "They taste good to her," in stanza 2 and again in line 15, have in "To a Poor Old Woman"?

5. How does the speaker's image of the poor old woman as a fallen leaf relate to the last three lines of "The Young Housewife"? What do these images, considered together, suggest about the speaker's view of woman's life?

6. What do the last two lines of "Danse Russe" suggest abut the speaker's view of being lonely? How do the earlier images in the poem explain his rather unorthodox view?

"Snake" • D. H. Lawrence (p. 636)

Compare the experience of the speaker in "snake" with the experience of Macomber in Hemingway's "The Short Happy Life of Francis Macomber" (p. 245). How are their motivations, actions, and emotions similar? How are they different? Do you have more empathy or sympathy for one than the other? Why?

"The River-Merchant's Wife: A Letter" • Ezra Pound (p. 638)

After reading "The River-Merchant's Wife: A Letter," compose the letter that the River-Merchant might have sent to this wife.

"Poetry" • Marianne Moore (p. 639)

1. What does Marianne Moore mean in the first line when she says she dislikes "it"? Doe she dislike all poetry? What kind of poetry does she admire?

2. After reading Marianne Moore's poetic creed, write your own. What kind of poetry do you admire? Why? Give concrete examples to explain your taste.

"The Love Song of J. Alfred Prufrock" • T. S. Eliot (p. 640)

1. In "The Love Song of J. Alfred Prufrock," Eliot clearly demonstrates his break from traditional poetry and his experimental approach to language. The poem may be difficult to understand because the logic is different from what one usually expects. Instead of providing links that connect aspects of external reality, Eliot offers a series of scenes that are flashing through the mind of the speaker. You might begin work on this poem by trying to identify the various scenes and also by thinking about the possible mental connections the speaker makes between the scenes. Remember that the relationships between the scenes are psychological; they represent a "stream of consciousness" from the speaker's mind.

2. What relationship does the epigraph to "Prufrock" have to the rest of the poem?

3. What kind of person is J. Alfred Prufrock? What are his hopes? His fears? What do you know about his past? What do you predict for his future? How old is he? How does he dress?

4. Who are the "you and I" in the first line of "Prufrock"?

5. Find two or three particularly interesting figures of speech and analyze them. What do they contribute to your understanding of J. Alfred Prufrock?

6. "Prufrock" is filled with allusions. While you can certainly understand and appreciate the poem without recognizing every reference, try researching two or three of the classical, biblical, or literary images to see whether knowing what they mean changes your response to the poem.

7. What is your response to the final stanza of "Prufrock"? Does it help you to identify a central thought in the poem?

"Piazza Piece" • John Crowe Ransom (p. 644)

Who are the two speakers in "Piazza Piece"? What is the irony in line 14? For whom doe the "young lady" think she is waiting for? For whom do you think she is waiting?

"Requiem" • Anna Akhmatova (p. 644)

1. Paraphrase each part and each section of this poem. How are the parts related to each other? What purpose, for example, does the opening stanza serve? Why doesn't the poem simply begin with the "By Way of a Preface" section? Why the elaborate structure of a "Dedication," a "Prelude," and a two-part Epilogue?

2. Some parts of the poem are titled and some are not. What effect do the titles have? Would the other sections be more effective if they were titled? Can you suggest titles for those sections?

"Winter Night" • Boris Pasternak (p. 651)

1. What is the effect of the repeated phrase "the candle burned"? What other repetition do you find? how are the repeated phrases related?

2. What situation is suggested in stanzas 4 through 7? What is the speaker's attitude toward this situation?

"The Tropics in New York" • Claude McKay (p. 652)

Compare the image of the city in "The Tropics in New York" with that in Frost's "Acquainted with the night" (p. 629) and with Whitman's "Crossing Brooklyn Ferry" (p. 595)

"The Stalin Epigram" • Osip Mandelstam (p. 652)

The extended metaphor of this poem pictures the Russian dictator Stalin as a mountaineer (line 4). We usually think of a mountaineer as someone who is brave, adventurous, an admirable. how does Mandelstam use the image of the mountaineer in his poem? Why is the poem called an "epigram"?

Maria Tsvetayeva
"No one has taken anything away" (p. 653)
"Yesterday he still looked in my eyes" (p. 654)

1. In "No one has taken anything away," whom is the speaker addressing? What do we know about him? How does the speaker view her relationship to him?

2. Consider the figurative language of "Yesterday he still looked in my eyes." For example, "today all those larks are ravens (line 4); "my life fell out like a rusty kopeck" (line 21); "A child-murdered before some court / I stand" (lines 22-23); "He taught me to live in fire" (line 29). What does each of these images contribute to the meaning of the poem?

"Ars Poetica" • *Vicente Huidobro (p. 655)*

1. Compare Huidobro's "Ars Poetica" with MacLeish's "Ars Poetica" (p. 656).

2. Huidobro was writing during the first part of the twentieth century. What do you think he meant by "We are in the age of nerves" (line 8)? Could his description be accurately applied to the 1990s?

"Ars Poetica" • *Archibald MacLeish (p. 656)*

What does stanza 4 mean? How can a poem be "wordless"? How does this image relate to the poetic philosophy suggested by the final lines: "A poem should not mean/But be"?

"Our Daily Bread" • *César Vallejo (p. 658)*

In "Our Daily Bread," to whom do lines 10-13 refer? How is the speaker to the poem related to the image conveyed by those lines? How do the final lines relate to lines 10-13.

"Dulce et Decorum Est" • *Wilfred Owen (p. 658)*

1. Wilfred Owen, a British soldier, died in battle one week before the World War I armistice. Does this biographical information affect your response to the poem in any way? Explain.

2. What is Owen opposing in the poem? Is he arguing that one should never fight for one's country? Read the final lines carefully as you plan your response.

e. e. cummings
  "anyone lived in a pretty how town" (p. 659)
  "my father moved through dooms of love" (p. 660)
  "i thank You God" (p. 662)

1. e. e. cummings challenged traditional poetic forms with his unconventional word order and his use of one part of speech as though it were another. Locate examples of these devices in "anyone lived in a pretty how town." How do these devices affect your reading of the poem?

2. Try to summarize "anyone lived in a pretty how town." What are the people who live here like? What do they do? How do they think? Who is "anyone"? What is the speaker's attitude toward "anyone" and his fellow residents of the "pretty how town"?

3. Are most of the images of "my father moved through dooms of love" positive or negative? How do those images relate to the concept of doom? Is this poem primarily about the speaker's father? How do lines 53-64 relate to the father's actions and character?

4. Compare cumming's "i thank You God" with Gerald Manley Hopkins's "Pied Beauty" (p. 612). Notice not only the meanings of the two poems but also the way the poets use rhythm, rhyme, and other sound devices.

"Reapers" • Jean Toomer (p. 662)

What is the significance of the title "Reapers"? How does it relate to the death of the field rat and to the workers' continued activity after the rat is sliced by the mower?

"Women" • Louise Bogan (p. 663)

1. What is the speaker's view of women? Do you agree? How would you respond to this speaker?

2. Compare this poem with May Swenson's "Women" (p. 685). Is either poem ironic? Are both poems ironic? Or is neither ironic? Explain.

"Lament for Ignacio Sanchez Mejias" • Federico Garcia Lorca (p. 663)

1. Summarize the meaning of each of the four sections of the poem. What is lost in the prose summary? How does your response change when you hear the events described in prose an then in Garcia Lorca's poetry?

2. What effect does the insistent repetition of the time of death have on the first section of the poem? Can you explain all the images? For example, "the oxide scattered crystal and nickel" (line 12); "a thigh with a desolate horn" (line 15); "Death laid eggs in the wound" (line 29).

3. How do the sections of the poem suggest the stages of the speaker's recognition and response to Mejias's death?

"The Blind Man" • Jorge Luis Borges (p. 669)

Compare Borges's poem on blindness "The Blind Man" to Milton's "When I consider how my light is spent" (p. 557).

"Pitcher" • Robert Francis (p. 670)

Can the sports images in this poem be applied to any situation outside a baseball game? What kind of person might the batter represent? The pitcher? What kind of situation (other than a game) might they be involved in?

"Incident" • Countee Cullen (p. 671)

1. What effect to the regular rhythm and rhyme scheme create? How do the rhythm and rhyme relate to the fact that the incident was a childhood event?

2. Compare the experience of the speaker with that of the narrator in Ellison's "Battle Royal" (p. 286).

"The Groundhog" • Richard Eberhart (p. 671)

How do the changing images of the groundhog—and the speaker's responses to the groundhog at the varying stages—lead and relate to the final lines of the poem? How is the groundhog like China, Greece, Alexander, Montaigne, Saint Teresa?

"The Word" • Pablo Neruda (p. 673)

According to the speaker in "The Word," what are the unique and essential qualities of words? What do words give to human life?

"True Love" • Robert Penn Warren (p. 675)

Compare the experience of the speaker in "True Love" to that of the narrator in James Joyce's "Araby" (p. 66).

W. H. Auden
"The Unknown Citizen" (p. 676)
"In Memory of W. B. Yeats" (p. 677)

1. In "The Unknown Citizen," the testimonial to citizen JS/07/M/378 has apparently been written by a public official. Why does this official praise the citizen? What do we learn about the citizen's life? How do we know that the speaker s view of the citizen's life differs from Auden's view?

2. Compare the Unknown Citizen to Willy Loman in Arthur Miller's *Death of a Salesman* (p. 323).

3. "In Memory of W. B. Yeats," written to honor the poet Yeats, also explains Auden's poetic philosophy. Find lines that particularly relate to his definition of poetry and explain their meaning. For example, consider, in line 36, "poetry makes nothing happen."

"Elegy for Jane" • Theodore Roethke (p. 679)

In "Elegy for Jane" find as many images as you can that compare Jane to a bird. Why is this comparison particularly apt, given the subject of the poem?

"A Song on the End of the World" • Czeslaw Milosz (p. 680)

1. Contrast the images in the first two stanzas with the images commonly associated with the end of the world. Why are the people in stanza 3 described as "disappointed"?

2. Why does the old man repeat the final line? How is the action of tying up the tomatoes while he chants this line significant?

Elizabeth Bishop
  "The Fish" (p. 681)
  "Sestina" (p. 683)

1. How do the lines "until everything / was rainbow, rainbow, rainbow! / And I let the fish go" (lines 74-76) relate to the rest of the poem? What connotative meanings does the word "rainbow" have?

2. What is the situation in "Sestina"? How are the Little Marvel Stove and the almanac related to the situation? How are tears related to the stove, the almanac, and the two characters in the poem?

"Myth" • Muriel Rukeyser (p. 684)

1. What is the point of the Sphinx's reply? Why does she imply Oedipus was punished?

2. What is the tone of this poem? Playful? Serious? Ironic? Humorous? Or a combination? Something else entirely? Explain.

"Women" • May Swenson (p. 685)

1. Does the speaker in "Women" think that women indeed "should be pedestals to men"? Consider carefully line 12 before you plan your response.

2. How does the form of the poem relate to its meaning?

CONTEMPORARY POEMS

"Wind, Water, Stone" • Octavio Paz (p. 686)

1. Ask students if they know the child's game "Paper covers rock/Rock breaks scissors/Scissors cut paper which is echoed in the way the elements are described in this poem. How might the children's verse relate to the meaning of the poem?

2. This poem mentions three of the elements we commonly associate with our world. Why is the fourth (fire) omitted? How would the poem be changed if it were introduced?

"Traveling through the dark" • William Stafford (p. 686)

Compare the speaker's view of the dead doe with the speaker's view of the dead groundhog in Eberhart's "The Groundhog" (p. 671).

"The Melting Pot" • Dudley Randall (p. 687)

What are the ironies on which the meaning of "The Melting Pot" is based? Who is the speaker? Why is he rejected from the pot?

Dylan Thomas
"Fern Hill (p. 688)
"Do not go gentle into that good night" (p. 689)

1. Find all the references to time in "Fern Hill." How does he say, in the next-to-the-last line, that time held him "green and dying"?

2. What is the speaker's argument in "Do not go gentle . . ."? To whom does he direct his argument? Plan a response, either disagreeing or agreeing with each point the speaker makes.

"Lineage" • Margaret Walker (p. 690)

Compare Margaret Walker's view of her foremothers with Alice Walker's view of hers ("In Search of Our Mothers' Gardens" (p. 1644).

Robert Lowell
"Skunk Hour" (p. 690)
"The Drinker" (p. 692)

1. How does the title of "Skunk Hour" suggest the poem's central meaning? Consider the connotations of "skunk"; then try to relate those connotations not only to the final two stanzas but also to the people and their lives as they are described in stanzas 1-6.

2. What is the situation in "The Drinker"? What is the immediate scene? What has happened before this scene? What might happen in the future?

3. Why does the man think this woman has left him? Can you think of any other possible reasons? How do you think this woman might respond to the man's charges in stanzas 6-8?

Gwendolyn Brooks
"the mother" (p. 693)
"First fight. Then fiddle" (p. 694)

1. In "the mother," what is the speaker's attitude toward abortion? Do the images and the language in the poem convince you that the final lines reflect the speaker's true feelings?

2. Compare the images—especially lines 9 and 10—of "First fight. Then fiddle" with the final section of Baldwin's "Notes of a Native Son" (p. 1612).

"Constantly Risking Absurdity" • Lawrence Ferlinghetti (p. 694)

Describe the role of the artist in society as suggested by the images of this poem.

"Juggler" • *Richard Wilbur (p. 695)*

What kind of triumph is suggested, both literally and figuratively, by the final line of "Juggler"? How does each image in the previous stanzas relate to both levels of meaning?

"Summer Sestina" • *Marie Ponsot (p. 696)*

Compare the gardening experience as described in "Summer Sestina" with the gardening experience described in "In Search of Our Mothers' Gardens" (p. 1523). How is the gardener in Ponsot's poem like the mother Alice Walker shows us?

"A Study of Reading Habits" • *Philip Larkin (p. 697)*

The speaker in the poem traces his changing reading tastes and his responses to the popular reading choices. How would you explain your own changing reading tastes, beginning with the earliest books you remember reading or having had read to you?

"Love Song: I and Thou" • *Alan Dugan (p. 698)*

1. Why does Dugan title his poem "I and Thou" rather than "You and I"? How would a change to the more conventional form alter the meaning of the poem for you?

2. If Dugan's strange house stands for his life, how does the attempted self-crucifixion at the end fit into the picture?

"You Can Rely on Him" • *Yehuda Amichai (p. 699)*

What does the speaker in "You Can Rely on Him" say that he learned from his father and mother? How do these lessons relate to his view of himself in the final stanza? Why does he say that those who really love him know that he is not someone you can rely on?

"Intimacy" • *Eva Feiler and Nina Cassian (p. 700)*

1. Describe what you picture the "tacit understanding" described in stanza two to be. What is the implied relationship between the speaker's pencils and "the trees outside" and between the rain and her "luminous hair."

2. Does the poem provide evidence to support the speaker's claim that she knows "how to be alone"? Do you see being alone as a special skill? What is your own view of being alone—do you like it, or would you prefer to be with others, most of the time? Explain.

"How It Is" • *Maxine Kumin (p. 700)*

Why does the speaker call her dead friend's blazer "dumb" (line 28)? In what ways is the blazer "dumb"? In what ways is it not "dumb"?

"I Know a Man" • *Robert Creeley (p. 701)*

Identify examples of nonstandard use of language in "I Know a Man." How does the language relate to the meaning of the poem?

"The Other House" • *David Wagoner (p. 702)*

Compare the images describing the abandoned house and the speaker's "proper house" (line 9). What do the differences between the two suggest about the speaker's childhood and about the role played by the abandoned house?

"A Supermarket in California" • *Allen Ginsberg (p. 703)*

1. Read the selections by Walt Whitman in this text, then explain how Ginsberg uses Whitman's style to pose his questions in the final stanza. Does Ginsberg's imagery in the earlier stanzas suggest answers to these questions?

2. Compare Ginsberg's responses to the images of a market with Claude McKay's response to similar images in "The Tropics in New York" (p. 652).

"April Inventory" • *W. D. Snodgrass* [not listed]

What kind of a teacher is the speaker in "April Inventory"? What is his attitude toward his students? Toward his colleagues" Toward teaching? Toward learning? What has he learned? What has he taught? Would you like to be in one of his classes? Explain.

"Jocasta" • *Ruth Eisenberg (p. 704)*

1. Read *Oedipus Rex* (p. 806), then list as many ways as possible that Eisenberg's protagonist differs from the Iocastê of Sophocles.

2. Rewrite one scene of *Oedipus Rex* (or add a scene not already there) using Eisenberg's "Jocasta" as your source.

Galway Kinnell
   "To Christ Our Lord" (p. 712)
   "Saint Francis and the Sow" (p. 713)

1. How does the scene outside the window in "To Christ Our Lord" relate to the scene inside"

2. How does Kinnell use the extended description of the sow to illustrate the point he is making in the first eleven lines of "Saint Francis and the Sow"? What is the point? How could this philosophy be applied to human lives and relationships?

James Wright
  "Lying in a Hammock at William Duffy's Farm in Pine Island, Minnesota" (p. 714)
  "A Blessing" (p. 714)

1. Why does the speaker in the final line of "Lying in a Hammock" say that he has wasted his life? Do the images in the earlier lines suggest waste? How does the title give a clue about why the speaker might have this response to the images of the farm at sunset?

2. Why does the poet put the stanza break in "A Blessing" after line 13? How would the meaning of the poem change if the break came after line 14 instead? What if there we no break?

"My son, my executioner" • Donald Hall (p. 715)

Compare Hall's view of parenthood suggested by "My son, my executioner" to Yeats's view of parenthood suggested by "A Prayer for My Daughter" (p. 618).

"Two Hands" • Anne Sexton (p. 715)

Compare this creation story with the version in Genesis.

X. J. Kennedy
  "In a prominent bar in Secaucus one day" (p. 716)
  "First Confession" (p. 718)

1. What kind of advice does the lady "in a prominent bar . . ." give to young girls (lines 29ff)? Can we take her advice seriously? Does she really seem to regret her life? What do you think the poet's attitude is toward the lady? Does the poem make fun of her?

2. What do the final two lines of "First Confession" suggest about the speaker's attitude toward the priest and communion?

"Innocence" • Thom Gunn (p. 718)

How does the character in "Innocence" respond to military execution? Compare this character's response to those of the Irish soldiers in O'Connor's "Guests of the Nation" (p. 29).

John Hollander
  "Adams" Task (p. 719)
  "Swan and Shadow" (p. 721)

1. Rewrite the fourth stanza of "Adam's Task" in standard grammatical order. What does this stanza tell you about the meaning of the poem and the list of unfamiliar names that makes up the earlier stanzas?

2. Does the sense of "Swan and Shadow" become apparent to you from the poet's arrangement of the words to depict its title? What would be lost if you read the poem aloud to someone who could not see the printed page? Would the poem make any sense?

"Diving into the Wreck" • Adrienne Rich (p. 722)

Critics have interpreted "Diving into the Wreck" in various ways. Some see the poem as a metaphorical description of Rich's separation from her husband (who died in 1970, before she wrote the poem). Other scholars read the poem more broadly and consider the wreck to represent the demise of patriarchal society in which males hold most of the power. What do you think of these ideas? What other interpretations can you suggest?

"Marriage" • Gregory Corso (p. 724)

Which clichés about courtship, engagement, weddings, and married life does "Marriage" challenge? How does Corso twist the standard expectations to create his own vision of the experience?

"Ethics" • Linda Pastan (p. 727)

1. Identify the two sections of the poem and discuss their relationship to each other. [The first section of the poem, ll.1-16, sets up a long-ago classroom situation and shows the speaker as a child or adolescent; the second section of the poem, ll 17-25, shows the adult speaker in a museum, reflecting on the question she once challenged in the classroom.]

2. What does the speaker suggest as the relationship between fine art and human life? Do you agree with her view?

Sylvia Plath
 "Mirror" (p. 728)
 "The Applicant" (p. 728)

1. Write a conversation between the mirror and the woman described in the second stanza of "Mirror." Choose a particular part of a particular day in the woman's life as the focus of the dialogue.

2. Is the applicant male or female? For what is he or she applying? What does the poem suggest about marriage?

"The Mosquito" • John Updike (p. 730)

Compare Updike's "The Mosquito" with Donne's "The Flea" (p. 551). How are fleas and mosquitoes alike? What relationship do the insects have to the people in the poems? What do the insects represent?

"People" • Yevgeny Yevtushenko (p. 730)

In this poem, Yevtushenko mourns the human tendency not to notice the special qualities in the people we see every day. Write an essay describing the unique qualities you now recognize in someone you once considered to be quite ordinary.

"Eating Poetry" • *Mark Strand (p. 732)*

What effect does poetry have on the speaker? Why is the librarian upset? Whom or what does the speaker represent? The librarian? The dogs on the basement steps? Poetry?

"Music Lessons" • *Mary Oliver (p. 732)*

1. What is the situation in the poem? What is the narrator doing? The woman she describes?

2. Why was there death in the metronome which the piano teacher tried to forget?

Lucille Clifton
"Homage to My Hips" (p. 733)
"The Lost Baby Poem" (p. 733)

1. In "Homage to My Hips," how does the speaker regard her hips? How is her attitude different from what might be expected?

2. How would you describe the tone of "The Lost Baby Poem"? How, apparently, was the baby "lost"? What is the effect of the extra spaces in the final two lines of the poem?

Marge Piercy
"A Work of Artifice" (p. 734)
"To Be of Use" (p. 735)

1. What is your response to "A Work of Artifice"? Note especially the figure of the gardener. He stunts the growth of the bonsai not only physically but also psychologically as he encourages it to appreciate and accept its limitations. Does the gardener figure accurately reflect the way men have treated women historically? Are there still men who are "gardeners" and women who are their "bonsai trees"?

2. In "To Be of Use" what kind of work does the speaker admire? What relationship does the work described bear to the work of being a writer?

"The Bride" • *Bella Akhmadulina (p. 735)*

Compare Akhmadulina's view of a wedding and marriage with Corso's view of his "Marriage" (p. 724).

Seamus Heaney
"Digging" (p. 737)
"Mid-Term Break" (p. 738)

1. What specific words and phrases in "digging" express the speaker's feelings for his father and grandfather? How are the speaker and his progenitors connected? How does the speaker feel about himself and his father and grandfather at the end of the poem?

2. What are the possible meanings for the title "Mid-Term Break"?

"This Is a Photograph of Me" • Margaret Atwood (p. 738)

Are we supposed to believe that the speaker in the poem has literally drowned and speaks to us from beyond the grave? What other possibilities are suggested by the images of the poem?

"Photograph of My Father in His Twenty-Second Year" • Raymond Carver (p. 739)

Choose a photo taken at least five years ago and write an essay describing the people, the place, the occasion, your memories and reflections relating to the photo.

"In Baseball" • Baron Wormsler (p. 740)

1. Compare this poem with Robert Francis's poem "Pitcher" (p. 670).

2. Identify the stanza and rhyme patterns and suggest how they relate to the meaning of the poem. Consider especially the final stanza as you think about this topic.

"Eve Names the Animals" • Susan Donnelly (p. 741)

1. Compare this poem with John Hollander's "Adam's Task" (p. 719).

2. What significance do you see in the names Eve chooses for animals? For herself? How do those names differ from those Adam chooses?

"Driving Lessons" • Neal Bowers

1. What is the central image in each stanza? How does each stanza relate to the other parts of the poem? How do all the parts in some way relate to the title?

2. What lessons do you think the speaker learned from his father? From his mother? How would you evaluate those lessons? Which do you see as positive? Which are negative?

Nikki Giovanni
"Dreams" (p. 743)
"Ego Tripping" (p. 744)

1. How do the sleeping dreams of the speaker in "Dreams" contrast with her waking dreams? What was her fantasy of revolution like? What did she recognize her real revolution was going to be?

2. Create your own poem of fantasies and dreams following the pattern of "Ego Tripping." End with the image you find most wonderful and fantastic of all.

"Size and Sheer Will" • Sharon Olds (p. 745)

1. List the images the speaker uses to describe Gabriel. What picture of him do you get from these images?

2. How do you think the speaker feels about Gabriel? What do you think her relationship is to him? Explain your reasons.

"Anorexic" • Eavan Boland (p. 746)

1. What has happened to the poem's narrator? Why is she starving herself?

2. Compare the connotation of the words Boland's narrator uses to describe her body to the words choices made by the narrator in Clifton's "Homage to My Hips" (p. 733).

"Mother's Revenge" • Kathleen Iddings (p. 747)

1. Why is the poem called "Mother's Revenge"? Why does she have a simpering smile when she serves the rooster?

2. People eat chicken much more often than rooster. Would the poem be the same if the fowl killed were a chicken rather than a rooster? Explain.

"Cruel Teeth of the Trap" • Sheryl Noethe (p. 751)

1. Make two separate lists, noting in one what the speaker gave and in the other what she received. In your opinion, did one person benefit more than the other from this relationship? Explain.

2. Write a paragraph or two responding to the final stanza. What might be the speaker's "dangerous edges"? What do you think of when she says she showed "Just the bare bond of it./ Just the foot of the animal"?

"Waiting Table" • Kraft Rompf (p. 748)

1. Identify examples of repetition and explain how Rompf uses this device to emphasize the theme of this poem.

2. Note the images the speaker uses to describe his customers. How do these images suggest his feelings about the people he must serve?

"Soccer Match" • James Zoller (p. 749)

1. What is the relationship between the epigraph by Theodore Roethke and the poem that follows? What danger might "the small" be facing?

2. Comment on the following lines: "These blue and red figures/ become men as I draw near,/ covered with dirt and sweat." What does the speaker mean by this? In what ways do the boys become men"?

"Wanting to Strip" • Marti Hohmann (p. 752)

1. How does the epigraph from Colette's novel *Claudine at School* relate to the poem that follows?

2. Both stanzas are about breasts. Who is the speaker in each stanza? How do the stanzas relate to each other?

Additional Topics for Writing—Poetry

1. Read the following poems that show a character moving from innocence to experience:

   Those Winter Sundays 372
   In the Orchard 394
   Incident 671
   Fern Hill 688
   Innocence 718

   What kinds of lessons are being learned? What do the characters gain or lose through their new knowledge? How do they react?

   After thinking about these questions, write a paper either defending or attacking the following statement:

   Most of the lessons we learn from experience are harsh and embittering. We would be better off if we never had to face such situations.

2. Read the following poems about fathers, then write a paper explaining what qualities these fathers seem to have in common. In addition, comment on their differences. Conclude your paper by suggesting which father you think would make the best role models for their children and explain why.

   Those Winter Sundays 372
   My Papa's Waltz 383
   Advice to My Son 420
   Ulysses 587
   A Prayer for My Daughter 618
   my father moved through dooms of love 660
   Photograph of My Father in His Twenty-second Year 739

3. Red the following poems about mothers, then write a paper explaining what qualities these mothers seem to have in common. In addition, comment on their differences. Conclude your paper by suggesting which mothers you think would make the best role models for their children and explain why.

   Woman to Child 418
   Mother, Among the Dustbins 433
   Edward, Edward 527
   the mother 693
   The Lost Baby Poem 733
   Mother's Revenge 747

4. Read any ten poems listed under "Men and Women" in the Thematic Table of Contents—Poetry. What is the picture you get of male-female relationships? Do you think this picture is accurate?

5. Read any of the following poems describing men, women, and love. Do you find some of the views more accurate than others? Explain.

6. Read the following poems describing the plight of the individual in society, then write an essay explaining how your own view agrees or disagrees with the views given by these poets.

7. Do human lives and relationships depend mainly on finding and playing roles? Is playing a role—wearing a mask—always a negative thing? Read the following poems, then write an essay explaining the views suggested by the poems. In addition, include your own ideas on the subject.

8. Read any ten poems listed in the Thematic Table of Contents—Poetry under "Religion and Spirituality." What are the various views of religion and spirituality suggested by these poems? Do the poems you have read have any points of agreement? Disagreement? How do their views compare with your own spiritual/religious philosophy?

9. Read any ten poems listed under "Women's Roles" in the Thematic Table of Contents—Poetry. Which roles are emphasized? Do you find any roles missing entirely? What picture of woman would a reader get if he or she had only these poems on which to base an evaluation?

10. Read any five poems listed in the Thematic Table of Content—Poetry under "War." Compare the images of war in these poems with descriptions of war in a history textbook or other nonfiction report of war.

PART THREE

Drama

CHAPTER TWELVE

Reading Plays

The opening section defines drama, emphasizing style and purpose. Students, many of whom frequently refer to anything written in prose form as a "story," need to be reminded that genres differ in both purpose and style. You may want to compare, for example, the opening scene of *A Doll House* with Chopin's "The Story of an Hour" (pp. 14–15). In each we see evidence of a marriage that is not as perfect as it appears to be, but the authors choose to present their material in different ways. The first scene of a drama is usually designed with exposition as its primary purpose; the audience must become acquainted quickly with the major characters and the dramatic situation. Chopin's story, given its length, is devoted almost entirely to exposition—as we learn who Mrs. Mallard is and what her marriage has been like, she learns how stifling it has been. Each writer, however, has chosen to provide exposition within a particular genre: Chopin is ever-present in her story, providing commentary on every one of Mrs. Mallard's actions. Ibsen, on the other hand, writes in a genre that denies him that luxury. Students may be asked to imagine how that first scene would be written if it were the first chapter of a short novel, for instance. Small-group exercises in which students collaborate to produce a prose version of the scene can provide students with invaluable experience in making choices about how to present material to an audience. A slightly more difficult task would be to translate Chopin's story into a short play (difficult because of the lack of dialogue; intriguing, nevertheless, because of the possibilities for stage directions).

As students attempt to write a prose version of *A Doll House*, they will begin to understand how to read drama. If they provide their own commentary after sections of the first scene, using "The Interpretation of Drama" as their guide, they will recognize the importance of dialogue to the playwright (and, of course, to the reader of drama). Clues about character, situation, theme, and purpose are provided in both *what* the characters say to one another and *how* they say it. Annotations will focus the general comments so that students will begin to discover just where authorial commentary might be made in a prose version. Annotating the first scene may be the final step before students actually write their translation. The exercise will not only teach students to read actively, but will also introduce them to various purposes for writing: they write to learn as they provide commentary; they write to express what they have already learned as they compose the story.

Drama is meant to be performed; therefore, any classroom study is significantly removed from what the playwright intended. The oral and visual nature of drama, unlike other literary genres, adds a dimension beyond the printed text of a play. Acting out scenes and even oral sight-readings can enliven and enrich classroom study.

Students' reluctance to participate in oral sight-readings can be reduced in several ways. Students respond to an instructor's assumption that producing portions of a play is more valuable than merely reading the text. Through their class readings, they more easily recognize the dynamic relationships between characters. The reading brings the dramatist's vision of the play to life by letting the students hear the dialogue and respond to stage directions—the pacing and inflection that transform printed lines into human voices.

CHAPTER THIRTEEN
Types of Drama

This brief chapter summarizes *tragedy, comedy,* and *tragicomedy*—a useful review that balances the practical suggestions in Chapter Twelve, Reading Plays, and Chapter Fifteen, Approaching a Play: Guide for Reading and Writing, with the structural elements in Chapter Fourteen, Elements of Drama.

During an initial discussion, you can introduce the three terms and ask students to suggest definitions. Student responses during this brainstorming can generate a list that will help them distinguish between the common meanings they already know and the literary meanings of tragedy, comedy, and tragicomedy they learn through reading, lectures, and research.

Chapter Fourteen

Elements of Drama

If drama is taken up after fiction, students should not have much of a problem understanding plot and character. What will look different to them, however, is the dramatist's method. Without the authorial presence, dialogue and staging become the primary vehicles for advancing plot and establishing character. They will have practiced gleaning information from dialogue in Chapter Twelve; staging will present them with something new to consider. It's easy to overlook stage directions, for we often subconsciously consider them important only to a director. But a glance at the elaborate directions in the opening of *A Doll House*, coupled with a review of the notes taken from dialogue in the first scene, should reveal the importance of staging. In drama, more than in any other genre, readers must actively imagine the scene before them.

If students are keeping journals, it should be helpful for them to practice identifying various elements of drama. For each play they read, students can outline plot and describe characters, referring to dialogue and staging for guidance. They'll soon be able to differentiate between Renaissance theater and realistic drama, for example, as they see themselves relying far more on dialogue in the former and making use of elaborate stage directions in the latter. Since the key word in this chapter is *synthesis*, however, the exercise should not stop here. As students try to identify themes in each of the plays, they are engaged in synthesizing material in order to make a coherent statement about it. If students regularly read from their journals to the rest of the class, they should become aware of the various themes present in a work of literature, the innumerable methods of reaching conclusions, and the infinite number of ways of expressing those conclusions.

CHAPTER FIFTEEN

Approaching a Play:
Guides for Reading and Writing

The chapter works well as the basis for an in-class activity. Students can paraphrase the guidelines for reading a play, then sight-read Lady Gregory's one-act play, *The Rising of the Moon* (p. 790), before discussing the brief analysis that follows (p. 797). Because of the simple plot and tight structure in this play, students can easily identify the elements of drama introduced in Chapter Fourteen.

Additional Topics for Writing and Discussion

1. What hints show that the sergeant might have been a criminal as easily as a police officer? What might have turned him to uphold, rather than break, the law?

2. In what ways is this one-act play an example of satiric comedy?

3. Imagine that you're the sergeant reflecting on your actions. Record your ideas in a journal entry a few days after the incident on the quay.

4. Create a dialogue between Policeman A and Policeman B as they return to the station.

5. Rewrite the end of the play, beginning with the entrance of Policeman X and Policeman B after they've put up all the placards. Change the situation slightly so that these two stay with the sergeant rather than return to the station.

CHAPTER SIXTEEN

The Greek Theater

Chapter Sixteen takes students to the birthplace of drama: ancient Greece. Because Greek drama is so different from what students are used to, they need to understand the religious ritual that evolved into drama. Several excellent films and slide-tapes are available that show students the structure of Greek amphitheaters and the formal and rigid nature of the costumes and masks. Students need to visualize the physical location and the appearance of the actors in order to appreciate that this physical formality is balanced by equally formal and structured language.

Students often have difficulty understanding the structure of Greek drama because they are so accustomed to the acts and scenes of contemporary drama. They may find it helpful to review the structure before reading the plays. Sophocles's tragedies open with a *prologue* that establishes the conflict, followed by a *párodos*, a song the chorus sings as it enters the stage. The play progresses in a series of *scenes*, each of which builds, or later resolves, the conflict. Each scene is followed by an *ode* that presents the communal voice of the chorus. The play ends with an *exodos* that concludes the action.

Students may also have difficulty relating to the characters in Greek tragedy, for the characters are playing stylized roles, not individual people. This distance is reinforced in part because the characters and plots are derived from myths well known to the Greek audiences and also because the masks and costumes help to create universal characters.

What students can understand in Sophocles's tragedies is the conflict. Although the situations Sophocles presents are centuries away from us, the issues are still relevant. Sophocles sees human beings in conflict with the world around them. His characters experience not only internal conflicts but also conflicts with society, government, laws and customs, nature, gods, and a sense of justice.

Greek drama has strongly influenced Western theater. Modern tragic characters are still examined for characteristics that fall into the patterns established in Aristotle's *Poetics*, based on his firsthand observations of drama. Students who understand Greek drama not only know more about our heritage—the myths and the rituals, the poetry and the music—but they also are better able to appreciate the evolution of drama presented in this text, from the seventeenth through the twentieth century.

Oedipus Rex • *Sophocles (p. 806)*

The stage directions for *Oedipus Rex*, like those for any Greek drama, are simple, in keeping with the outdoor amphitheaters in which the plays were originally performed. The opening scene, the Prologue, establishes the conflict, which Oedipus swears to investigate.

The values and relationships of the main characters are presented in dialogue, as emphasized in the introduction on p. 803. The play can be seen as a kind of moral lesson, reinforcing the values that would have been important in Athens in the fifth century B.C.

Students often need to review the brief definition of tragedy in Chapter Thirteen (p. 777), examining the ways in which *Oedipus Rex* fulfills Aristotle's definition. The tragedy of Oedipus's experiences forces audiences to recognize that people are less powerful than the gods, that even in the search for self-knowledge, a person must exert caution and self-control.

Possible Responses to Questions (pp. 846–847)

1. Students can review the characteristics of a tragic hero on text p. 778. Following Aristotle's criteria, Oedipus is a tragic hero because the catastrophe that befalls him and his family results in part from a flaw in his character—his pride. He is unwilling to concede that he cannot rid Thebes of the murderer or Laïos. Oedipus fulfills the prophecy that he has spent his life trying to avoid, his fall destroying his life and those related to him. When Oedipus, as a tragic hero, recognizes what has happened to him, the immensity of his crime so horrifies him that he blinds himself and has himself banished from Thebes.

   Audiences continue to be intrigued by *Oedipus Rex* because we understand Oedipus's quest. We see parts of ourselves in him and share with him the horror of his deeds. The *catharsis* Aristotle speaks of engages the audience in the emotional conflicts of the play, vicariously creating anxiety and then relief, what is sometimes called "empathic identification."

2. Oedipus contributes to his own downfall. Several times during the play he has the opportunity to stop seeking; however, despite desperate urging from Iocastê, the shepherd, and Teiresias, Oedipus persists. The irony, of course, is that Oedipus is seeking the truth, freely choosing to pursue it rather than leave his questions unanswered; yet his search leads to his ruin. His courage to investigate regardless of the outcome, his loyalty to the citizens of Thebes, his desire for truth—these are major factors in Oedipus's downfall.

   Students' opinions will vary about the change in Oedipus's attitude and manner. Oedipus's total control at the beginning seems reasonable, given his position of power. In the Prologue of the play, Oedipus demonstrates concern for the citizens of Thebes—while still looking out for himself: "By avenging the murdered king I protect myself" (line 143). In the Exodos, when Iocastê dies and Oedipus blinds himself, realizing that he will be banished, he still has a difficult time relinquishing control. Now, however, he is in a powerless position, and his concern is for his children.

3. *Irony of circumstance or situation* occurs when a discrepancy exists between what seems to be and what is, or when an individual expects one thing to occur only to discover that the opposite happens. Here are two examples of irony of situation:

   > When Oedipus leaves Corinth and arrives in Thebes, he believes he has escaped the risk of the prophecy.

   > When Oedipus hears that Polydoros is dead, he mistakenly thinks that the prophecy was wrong.

   Dramatic irony occurs when a discrepancy exists between what the characters know and what the audience or readers know. Two important examples of dramatic irony follow:

   > In Scene I, Oedipus says, "I take the son's part, just as though I were his son, to press the fight for him and see it won!" (lines 48-50)

   > In Scene II, Oedipus says, "I think that I myself may be accurst by my own ignorant edict" (lines 216-217), little realizing the ironic accuracy of his statement.

4. The imagery of light and darkness throughout the play serves to reinforce Oedipus's search for truth. The ultimate irony, of course, is that he does not recognize the truth when he has sight; the truth is clear to him only when he is blind.

The play contains many allusions to light and darkness, some of which refer to natural phenomena, particularly references to the sun, lightning, flaring light, and so on in Odes I, II, III, and IV. Other allusions follow:

Prologue   Thebes is "all darkened" (line 33).

            Oedipus "must bring what is dark to light" (line 134).

Párodos   The chorus tells of the "nightfall of the past" (line 7).

Scene I   Teiresias warns Oedipus that "the double lash of your parents' curse will whip you out of this land some day, with only night upon your precious eyes" (lines 202-204).

Scene II   Oedipus tells Iocastê that "a shadowy memory crossed my mind" (line 201).

5. The chorus represents the elders of Thebes, leading citizens of the city. The chorus acts as an actual character in the play, commenting on the events, reciting strophes and antistrophes that rhythmically reflect the action. The chorus also marks the progression of the action, with lyric odes separating scenes.

Párodos   The chorus generalizes about the plague afflicting Thebes, supplicating the gods to end the torment.

Ode I   The chorus recalls the murder of Laïos, telling us that the murderer will be hunted down. But the chorus also calls Teiresias's accusation of Oedipus' lies.

Ode II   The chorus stresses the importance of keeping the laws of the gods, warns against pride, and questions whether the oracle is reliable.

Ode III   The chorus invokes the help of the gods to solve Oedipus's problem.

Ode IV   The chorus tells us that Oedipus has fallen to a pitiful fate because he "understood too late."

Unlike the chorus, the Choragos interacts with the other characters in the play. The Choragos functions as the leader of the chorus, voicing the conscience of the community and provoking Oedipus to examine issues and implications.

Scene I   The Choragos suggests that Oedipus might learn the truth of the murder from Teiresias and then urges Oedipus to listen to the seer.

Scene II   The Choragos defends Oedipus when speaking to Creon. Then the Choragos advises Oedipus to listen to Creon and to Iocastê. Later, the Choragos reports events to Iocastê, then swears loyalty to Oedipus. Near the end of Scene II, the Choragos expresses dismay when the identity of Laïos's murderer becomes known.

Scene III   At the end of this scene, the Choragos worries that Iocastê has returned to the palace in a "passion of sorrow."

Scene IV   The Choragos verifies the identity of the shepherd.

Exodos   The Choragos grieves for Iocastê and worries about Oedipus. When Oedipus is led in, blinded, the Choragos laments and wishes that Oedipus had never discovered the truth. The play ends with the Choragos's comment about human frailty.

6. Some of the horrible events occur before the start of the play: piercing the ankles of the infant Oedipus; the murder of Laïos. Because of the chronology, these events are reported rather than seen. *Oedipus Rex* also contains other reports of horrible events such as the death of Iocastê and the blinding of Oedipus. Staging these events would have presented technical difficulties on the ancient Greek stage, so Sophocles took advantage of the audience's imagination. Because of the building tension in the play, the audience imagines the horror of these events, reinforced by seeing Iocastê's body and Oedipus's bloody and blinded face.

7. Iocastê recognizes the truth of the situation long before Oedipus does. Even though she begs Oedipus to put off his search, he moves ahead to his ultimate destruction—and hers. Although the audience can project their own feelings and understand the anguish Iocastê feels, Sophocles's character provides little indication of her thoughts and feelings, largely because such revelations are not in the nature of Greek drama.

    Students will like comparing Iocastê in Sophocles's *Oedipus Rex* with the Jocasta in Ruth Eisenberg's poem (p. 704). The poem provides a window into the individual, explaining feelings and motivations. Study of the poem can be further developed through Writing and Discussion topics 1 and 2, below.

Additional Topics for Writing and Discussion

1. Create another view of Iocastê, consistent with the character in Sophocles's play yet with feelings and motivations quite different from those expressed in Eisenberg's "Jocasta." Present this alternative Iocastê in a scene extending the play, a poem modeled after the Eisenberg poem, or a character sketch.

2. In a formal essay, compare and contrast the Iocastê in Sophocles's *Oedipus Rex* with the Jocasta in Eisenberg's poem "Jocasta."

3. Read Aristotle's *Poetics*, then discuss Oedipus as a character who fulfills Aristotle's definition of a tragic hero or the play as one that fulfills the definition of a tragedy.

4. Investigate the moral precepts and laws of fifth-century B.C. Greece. Discuss the ways in which *Oedipus Rex* serves to illustrate and model social standards and expectations.

5. Agree or disagree with the following comment by Sigmund Freud about the play *Oedipus Rex*:

    > For at the bottom it is an immoral play; it sets aside the individual's responsibility to social law, and displays divine forces ordaining the crime and rendering powerless the moral instincts of the human being which would guard him against the crime. [Sigmund Freud, in Michael J. O'Brien, ed., *Twentieth Century Interpretations of Oedipus*]

Antigonê • *Sophocles (p. 847)*

If students have not read *Oedipus Rex*, they need to pay special attention to the footnote on p. 848 to prepare them for the tragedy of the family history Ismenê summarizes in lines 36-42 of the Prologue.

As in *Oedipus Rex*, the stage directions for *Antigonê* are simple, stating that the play begins at dawn in front of the palace in Thebes. Antigonê and Ismenê enter from the palace, engaged in a conversation that clearly establishes their relationship and the conflicts between them: Antigonê and Ismenê disagree about burying their brother, Polyneicês, and about the necessity to uphold Creon's edict.

The tension builds slowly; not until Scene II do Antigonê and Creon come face to face. The clash between law (as defined by Creon) and justice (as advocated by Antigonê) forms the theme for the play. As with other Greek tragedies, each scene focuses on a specific theme-related issue that emerges through the confrontation of the two characters (with a third actor often commenting or interjecting additional information).

Possible Responses to Questions (p. 877)

1. Students will argue vehemently about whether Creon or Antigonê has the stronger case. Both have a legitimate position: Creon has social and political laws to uphold; Antigonê has honor and religious obligations to fulfill. But both also step beyond their roles: Creon oversteps his authority in his lack of reverence for the gods, and Antigonê is perhaps too willing to be a martyr.

   As discussion evolves, students will probably move toward the position taken by Charles Paul Segal in his essay "Sophocles' Praise of Man and the Conflicts of the *Antigonê*:"

   > We must avoid seeing the protagonists as one-dimensional representatives of simple oppositions: right and wrong, reason and emotion, state and individual, or the like. Such oppositions have some validity, but a validity purchased at the price of oversimplification and ultimately a misunderstanding of Sophocles' sense of the tragic.

   Segal goes on to say that the characters and their issues require a more complex response than simply deciding who is right:

   > Recent critics, abandoning the simple thesis-antithesis opposition and looking at the play in terms of the action itself, have made it clear that it is hart to find much pure "right" on Creon's side, though this is not to say that his fate entirely lacks a tragic dimension or that the conflict is settled merely by a kind of moral default. Antigonê, on the other hand, is vindicated by the end of the play, but only at the cost of tremendous suffering, her own and that of those closest to her.

2. Both Creon and Antigonê are strong, stubborn, and constant in their positions, although Creon is more concerned with his public image and Antigonê with upholding her values.
   From the beginning, Creon maintains that his position as king gives him the right to determine what is just. Even when presented with convincing arguments from his son, the chorus, and Teiresias, Creon only changes his mind when he is reminded of two things by the Choragos: Teiresias has never been wrong, and the will of the people will oppose him.
   Antigonê is equally stubborn. Claiming her defiance of Creon's order results from her respect for the "immortal unrecorded laws of God," she demonstrates uncompromising values.

3. Haimon parallels Antigonê's decision to demonstrate that beliefs are worth dying for. Of all the characters, Haimon comes closest to understanding Antigonê decision.

171

Despite Haimon's youth (Creon refers to him as an "adolescent fool"), he demonstrates insight into his father's nature and a clear sense of justice that would have made him a fine ruler. He knows that Creon will be pleased if he "subordinate[s] everything . . . to your father's will," so he begins gently. He suggests that "reason is God's crowning gift to man," urging Creon to consider that other men's "opinions might be helpful." When Creon is not persuaded, Haimon strengthens his argument:

> They say no woman has ever, so unreasonably
> Died so shameful a death for a generous act:

Creon apparently remains unmoved, so Haimon reminds Creon that he has "no right to trample on God's right." Haimon and Creon clearly disagree about what is "just." Haimon's sense of justice is beyond what Creon understands—until the end of the play.

4. Ismenê acts as a foil for Antigonê by providing a vivid contrast: Antigonê is decisive; Ismenê is indecisive. Antigonê is single-minded; Ismenê wavers. Antigonê has a strong sense of justice; Ismenê is more concerned with propriety. Antigonê is absolute in her sense of right; Ismenê is swayed by people and circumstance.

Eurydicê, by her suicide, emphasizes the impact of Creon's decision, his unwillingness to listen to reason. She contributes to the play by partially fulfilling Teiresias's prophecy.

5. The structure of *Antigonê* follows the traditional format of a Greek tragedy:

Prologue	Antigonê informs Ismenê of Creon's edict not to bury Polyneicês and of her decision to bury him despite the threat of death. Ismenê refuses to help, citing women's roles, defiance of the law, and concern for public good as reasons. Antigonê is determined to bury her brother, regardless of the consequences.
Párodos	The chorus and the Choragos tell of the great battle in which Polyneicês, leader of the attacking army, and his brother Eteoclês, loyal defender of Thebes, kill each other "face to face in matchless rage."
Scene I	Creon, as the new king of Thebes, announces his values to the chorus, followed by his public proclamation not to bury Polyneicês. A sentry who had been guarding the body of Polyneicês enters, terrified to tell Creon that someone had mounded "new dust on the slimy flesh!" Creon is irate, perhaps even paranoid, first questioning the guard and then arguing with the Choragos. The bold sentry leaves, swearing never to return.
Ode I	The chorus offers a philosophical comment in Strophe 1: "Numberless are the world's wonders, but none/More wonderful than man . . . "; Antistrophe 1 comments that man is more powerful than wild animals. Strophe 2 notes that man "has made himself secure—from all but . . . death . . . "; Antistrophe 2 praises intelligence that works to keep the law.
Scene II	The sentry brings in Antigonê, accusing her of burying Polyneicês. When he tells Creon the story, Antigonê says, "I deny nothing." She prefers death to living in a corrupt society. After the Choragos reminds us of her father (Oedipus), Creon and Antigonê argue about the honoring of the dead. Creon decides to involve Ismenê, who now want some credit for the burial; Antigonê refuses. Creon orders both Antigonê and Ismenê taken away.

Ode II	Strophe 1 alludes to the tragedy of Oedipus, while Antistrophe 1 comments on its impact on Oedipus's children. Strophe 2 refers to the arrogance of Creon: "No pride on earth is free of the curse of heaven"; Antistrophe 2 warns the audience that "Man's little pleasure is the spring of sorrow."
Scene III	Haimon vows love and support for Creon, who says Haimon will be better off without Antigonê. Haimon suggests that Creon be flexible and seek the opinions of others. Creon argues that "the State is the King!" Once Haimon realizes that Creon is blind to reason, he leaves. Despite a warning from the Choragos, Creon orders Antigonê's death.
Ode III	The strophe warns of the power of love; the antistrophe warns that no one benefits from the love we see here.
Scene IV	The Choragos mourns Antigonê's impending death. In Strophe 1, Antigonê says good-bye; the chorus speaks of her honor. In Antistrophe 1, Antigonê recalls the story of Niobê; the chorus responds that Antigonê is mortal. In Strophe 2, Antigonê worries that she is laughed at and "unjustly judged"; the chorus wonders what role Oedipus's fate plays in Antigonê's death. In Antistrophe 2, Antigonê castigates "father and brother" for the "blasphemy of my birth"; the chorus responds, "Your death is the doing of your conscious hand." In the Epode, Antigonê pleads for death. When Creon orders her taken away Antigonê welcomes her death.
Ode IV	The chorus comments that "no power . . . /Can prevail against untiring Destiny," recalling gruesome tales of those who have angered and defied the gods.
Scene V	Teiresias tells Creon that he himself has "brought/This new calamity upon us." Even when Teiresias warns that "the only crime is pride," Creon responds that "no man can defile the gods" and refuses to change his sentence upon Antigonê. Only when the Choragos reminds Creon that Teiresias has never been wrong does Creon decide to free Antigonê.
Paean	The interplay between the chorus and the Choragos calls upon Iacchos (Bacchos or Dionysos).
Exodos	A messenger recalls the change in Creon, from "once happy" to a "walking dead man." The messenger reports to the Choragos the deaths of Haimon and Antigonê. Eurydicê, wife of Creon and mother of Haimon, enters the scene for the first time. The messenger tells her of going with Creon to give honorable burial to the body of Polyneicês and their finding the bodies of Haimon and Antigonê. Eurydicê enters the palace and commits suicide. Creon realizes, too late, that "my own blind heart has brought me/From darkness to final darkness." The Choragos concludes the play saying that "proud men in old age learn to be wise."

6. The chorus comments on the action, both with philosophical observations and attempts to sway the actors. Students might select any of the following comments:

Ode I honors the power of man, safe from everything but death.

Ode II reminds the audience of the fate of Oedipus and his children and of the imminent downfall of Creon because of pride.

Scene IV, Antistrophe 2, reminds Antigonê that her death is directly the result of her "conscious hand."

The Choragos, considered as a separate voice from the chorus, is even more important to the play:

> In Scene I, the Choragos agrees to support Creon (line 51). Later in the scene, the Choragos questions whether the gods might have buried Polyneicês (line 99).

> In Scene III, the Choragos notes that Haimon makes good sense (lines 49-50). Later in the same scene, the Choragos warns Creon that Haimon's rage is dangerous (line 135).

> In Scene V, the Choragos convinces Creon to set Antigonê free and to honor Polyneicês (lines 96-97, 99-100,103).

7. This subject can be extended to an effective writing assignment. Responses will vary as students explain Creon's suffering as a ruler trying to uphold civil laws for the common good and Antigonê's suffering as one individual fighting for human rights based on universal laws.

8. Until the end of the play, Creon stubbornly resists the opinions and advice of everyone—city elders, his son, the seer. Creon does not change until the Choragos convinces him that the will of the gods and the sentiment of the citizens will be against him if he doesn't save Antigonê. Unfortunately, he is too late to save her life or the lives of his son and his wife. At the very end of the play, Creon recognizes that his pride has caused needless deaths.

Additional Topics for Writing and Discussion

1. Decide whether Antigonê is a fanatic, desperate to martyr herself, or a rational person whose beliefs are so strong that she is willing to risk civil disobedience.

2. Who is the tragic hero of *Antigonê*—Creon or Antigonê? Use Aristotle's definition of a tragic hero summarized in the text on p. 778, or examine the detailed definition in Aristotle's *Poetics*.

3. Considering the emphasis in the play on Creon, why isn't the play titled Creon instead of *Antigonê*?

   [This question is an extension of question 2 above. However, even students who identify Creon as the tragic hero usually say that the play is correctly titled *Antigonê*. Antigonê is the one who sacrifices her life for her principles, her values. Although she is obsessed and becomes a martyr for her beliefs, she exposes human flaws and social injustice, showing that people extend themselves beyond normal limits.]

4. Investigate the beliefs and attitudes of Greek citizens in the Athens of the fifth century B.C. Would the original audience have been more in sympathy with Creon or Antigonê?

5. "Oedipus is the good ruler in spite of his defects, and Creon is the bad ruler in spite of his virtues" (O'Brien, p. 74). Discuss the similarities and differences between Oedipus and Creon as rulers of Thebes.

6. Read Jean Anouilh's *Antigonê*, comparing the differences between Anouilh's and Sophocles's versions. Explain whether you agree or disagree with the changes that Anouilh has made. Has he tampered with the story? Has he legitimately updated it for twentieth-century audiences?

174

CHAPTER SEVENTEEN

The Elizabethan Theater

Although students often find the drama of ancient Greece unfamiliar in style and structure, most have read at least one or two Shakespearean plays. Yet despite their previous experience—or perhaps because of it—they are filled with apprehension about their ability to understand Elizabethan language.

Classroom discussion that opens with an examination of common ground puts students at ease. Many of them have a background that includes some knowledge of the Globe theater and the social and political realities of sixteenth- and seventeenth-century England, so this may be an effective place to start. Discussion can begin with a review of Elizabethan attitudes toward drama, followed with the limitations imposed by an Elizabethan stage.

Elizabethan drama shares similarities with the Greek theater beyond those pointed out in the chapter introduction. For example, the heroes in Shakespearean tragedies often display the characteristics outlined in Aristotle's *Poetics*, and the plays present universal themes.

Shakespeare's plays also share a great deal with twentieth-century drama—not only the tremendous amount of action (often violent) and the humor (both subtle and bawdy) but also the character development and the complex plots.

Many students will enter college having studied several Shakespearean plays—commonly *Romeo and Juliet, Julius Caesar, Macbeth,* and *Hamlet*; less commonly *A Midsummer Night's Dream, The Merchant of Venice,* and *The Taming of the Shrew*. Their experience with Shakespeare can serve as a point to begin discussions about language, character development, plot complexities, and themes, using examples from the Shakespearean plays commonly taught in secondary schools.

The Tragedy of Othello • *William Shakespeare (pp. 880–965)*

An introductory discussion of *Othello* could focus on thematic issues: racial prejudice, appearance versus reality, friendship and loyalty, envy, love and jealousy, justice. You might ask students to define these concepts and suggest examples of their abuse in contemporary society.

For another introductory activity, you could identify the characters in the play and summarize the initial conflicts (white woman marries an older black soldier against her father's wishes; a subordinate of the black man swears revenge because he has been passed over for a promotion).

When students begin reading the play, they discover that the stage directions for the opening scene aren't much more detailed than those for Greek drama; clues about the setting come from the dialogue. Conflicts also appear nearly as quickly as in Greek tragedy. The characters, however, are presented more realistically; for example, although Iago is an archetype, he is also a believable character.

The characters in *Othello* appear in complex relationships, some real and some imagined or promoted by Iago. For example, an Othello-Cassio-Iago relationship exists; the Othello-Desdemona-Cassio relationship exists only in Iago's envious mind and later, of course, in Othello's jealous mind. The play also balances the nature of one character against another: hating Iago/loving Desdemona, sexually pure Desdemona/practical Emilia/sensual Bianca, loyal Cassio/treacherous Iago, and so on.

The play provides rich opposites for in-class activities: performing sections of the play, role-playing extensions of the action, examining the changes in the emotional, social, and political issues during the nearly four hundred years since Shakespeare wrote *Othello*.

Possible Responses to Questions (pp. 965–966)

1. Kirschbaum, in "The Modern Othello," says:

   Shakespeare has shown us that his hero is not as strong or as good a man as he thinks he is, that the hero's flaw is his refusal to face the reality of his own nature. This Othello . . . is rather different from the modern Othello, who is always thoroughly noble—before, during, and after his downfall. [Leo Kirschbaum, "The Modern Othello," in Leonard F. Dean, ed., *A Casebook on Othello*, New York: Thomas Y. Crowell Company, 1961, p. 165]

   The Elizabethans believed people were responsible for their own lives. Although Iago is deceitful and manipulative, Othello had the free will to doubt, or even reject, Iago's accusations of Desdemona. The play contains examples of characters doubting Iago; for example, as Kirschbaum points out:

   Iago tells four of the characters [Roderigo, Cassio, Emilia, and Othello] that Desdemona is unchaste—and the only one who believes this accusation is Othello! . . . Shakespeare has underlined the premise that Othello need not have believed Iago's imputations. [Kirschbaum, p. 158]

   Othello is not a careful observer of human nature. He is unrealistic in that he ignores the human qualities that make everyone—including himself, Cassio, and Desdemona—less than perfect. Kirschbaum calls Othello "a romantic idealist. . . . He considers human nature superior to what it really is."

2. A. C. Bradley's classic essay "The Noble Othello" clearly and simply traces Othello's decline (in Leonard F. Dean, ed., *A Casebook on Othello*). In Act I, Othello is self-confident, open, enthusiastic. He expects the respect people give because of his position and reputation. His soliloquy in Act Ill, scene iii, shows the beginning of his jealous passion. Later in the same act and scene, he exhibits unbearable agony, but demands proof of Desdemona's infidelity; he is suspicious and at the same time indecisive. Act V shows Othello willing to sacrifice Desdemona; he believes he is justified in his decision to kill her.

3. Iago appeals to Roderigo's desire for Desdemona, easily done since Roderigo is so gullible. Roderigo persists, despite the fact that we know Roderigo's intentions from the beginning of Brabantio's rejection:

   In honest plainness thou hast heard me say
   My daughter is not for thee; . . .
   (I. i. 94-95)

   Cassio and Othello both trust Iago; his trust allows Iago to build his plot to destroy them both. Iago persuades Cassio to drink, knowing that Cassio prefers not to. Cassio's drunkenness cause Othello to dismiss him. Iago gradually poisons Othello's mind against Desdemona and Cassio by manipulating Othello's perception of reality, causing him to doubt what he already knows, and also feeding his jealousy.

4. Iago wanted to be Othello's lieutenant:

   > . . . Three great ones of the city,
   > In personal suit to make me his lieutenant,
   > Off-capped to him, . . .
   > But he, as loving his own pride and purpose,
   > Evades them with a bombast circumstance [and says] . . .
   > "I have already chose my officer."
   > (I. i. 7-15)

   Iago says Cassio is a theorist with no field experience, "Mere prattle without practice," a bookkeeper. Iago believed himself to be more than qualified for lieutenant because of his battle experience at Rhodes and Cyprus. Although Iago's motive is clear, it hardly seems adequate or credible for destroying Cassio, Othello, and, ultimately, Desdemona.

5. Emilia goes along with Iago's plans until she recognizes his lies and manipulation; her indignant response to accusations against Desdemona and her open defense of Desdemona's innocence heighten the evil of Iago's manipulations.

   Emilia acts as a foil to Desdemona by contrasting sexual awareness with sexual purity, by contrasting willingness to do a small favor with political naiveté.

6. Bianca continues the sexual spectrum that started with the contrast of Emilia with Desdemona. While Desdemona is innocent and Emilia is practical, earthy, and sometimes crude, Bianca sees sex as a commodity.

   Brabantio is easily riled and rises to Iago's taunts about the virtue of the fair Desdemona. His reaction adds to the general uproar that Iago continually creates.

7. The dual setting of Venice and Cyprus provides the contrast between the civilized and the barbaric. Shakespeare "makes Venice over into a form of *The City*, the ageless image of government, of reason, of law, and of social concord" (Alvin Kernan, "*Othello*: An Introduction," in Alfred Harbage, ed., *Shakespeare, the Tragedies: A Collection of Critical Essays,* Englewood Cliffs, NJ: Prentice-Hall, 1964, p. 77). One example of the rational control in Venice occurs when Brabantio's passions and complaints are examined with reasoned judgment by the Senate. Cyprus is an outpost where "passions are more explosive and closer to the surface than in Venice" (Kernan, p. 78).

   The dual settings show "a movement expressed in geographical and social symbols from Venice to a Cyprus exposed to attack, from *The City* to barbarism, from Christendom to the domain of the Turks, from order to riot, from justice to wild revenge and murder, from truth to falsehood" (Kernan, pp. 79-80).

8. Othello loves Desdemona, but perhaps he loves her image more than the individual woman. The images of love expressed by Othello and Desdemona are pure, unsullied by base instincts. In contrast, the speeches of Roderigo, Iago, Emilia, and Bianca convey their assumption that love is a base physical act, not an intellectual or spiritual union. For example, Iago tells Roderigo that when Desdemona "is sated with his [Othello's] body, she will find the errors of her choice" (I. iii. 332-333).

9. The handkerchief, which symbolizes the love and trust Othello has given to Desdemona, has a critical role in the play. The following list summarizes the scenes that depend on the handkerchief:

III. iii. 287-326	Emilia finds the handkerchief Desdemona has dropped and gives it to Iago, who plans to place it in Cassio's room.
III. iv. 46-101	Othello demands that Desdemona produce the handkerchief, which she cannot do.
III. iv. 170-185	Cassio gives Desdemona's handkerchief to Bianca.
IV. i. 1-42, 160-164	Iago poisons Othello's mind about the scene they witnessed in which Cassio gave Bianca Desdemona's handkerchief.
V. ii. 210-233	Othello learns the truth about the handkerchief from Emilia.

10. Othello sees himself as completing an honorable act. His murder of Desdemona is the only way he can see of atoning for what he believes is her guilt. Many critics believe that Othello views Desdemona's murder as a sacrifice that saves her from dishonor. Othello expresses sorrow, not anger; reasons, not rantings. However, at this moment he does not see the enormity of his misjudgment.

11. Iago's manipulation of Othello includes three specific techniques:

    (1) Iago plants an idea. Othello repeats the idea a few moments later in his own words. Iago then agrees with, and reinforces, the idea.

    (2) Iago begins a leading statement that he does not complete. Othello finishes the statement, and Iago agrees.

    (3) Iago uses words that can be interpreted in more than one way. By using these techniques, Iago leads Othello without ever having to make the initial damning statements.

12. Student responses will vary. They need to consider the lighting of the individual actors and the scene as a whole. Students might be interested to know how lighting can not only create the mood or atmosphere of the scene but also influence the audience's perception of the characters.

13. Student responses will vary. Students may find tracing the changes throughout the play a useful exercise that could precede any analysis of characters, plot, or theme.

14. Nearly every instance of prose in *Othello* involves discussion of negative images of love, suspicions of dishonor, plans for manipulation of others, corruption, and so on. Also, nearly all of the prose lines are spoken by Iago. Some of the major prose passages occur in the following places: I. iii, II. i, II. iii, IV. i, and V. i.

Additional Topics for Writing and Discussion

1. Why was Desdemona attracted to Othello?

[Students will identify a range of possibilities from her being intrigued with his exotic and exciting career to true love.]

2. What contradictions appear between what Othello says and what he does?

[The most obvious contradiction occurs in his protestations that he is not jealous as he displays increasingly irrational jealousy.]

3. Explain whether you believe in the rapidity with which Othello accepts Desdemona's guilt. Is Othello's jealousy consistent with his character? How much does the age difference between Othello and Desdemona feed his jealousy? How much can be attributed to the differences in race and culture?

   [One of the least believable elements of the play is the speed with which Othello accepts Desdemona's guilt. In analyzing the situation, Othello displays none of the insight that made him a brilliant soldier. Some critics attribute his behavior to a presumed ignorance about European women. Others say the difference in their ages leads him to a natural insecurity. The play does not provide much support for either of these views.]

4. After reviewing the characteristics of a tragic hero, discuss whether the character Othello fits the definition of a tragic hero, and whether the play *Othello* fits the definition of a tragedy.

5. How does Shakespeare's use of opposites in language reflect the themes in *Othello*?

   [The following are only two of the many examples in *Othello*:

   EMILIA: . . . O, the more angel she,
      And you the blacker devil!
   (V. ii. 133-130)

   OTHELLO: She was false as water.

   EMILIA: Thou art rash as fire to say
      That she was false.
   (V. II. 133-134)]

6. G. B. Shaw criticized *Othello* by saying

   Othello . . . is pure melodrama. There is not a touch of character in it that goes below the skin. [G. B. Shaw, "*Othello*: Pure Melodrama," in Leonard F. Dean, ed., *A Casebook on Othello*, p., 135].

   Agree or disagree with this statement, and support your position with specific textual references and quotations.

7. Assume you are directing a performance of *Othello*. How would you direct Othello in Act V?

As You Like It • *William Shakespeare (pp. 966–1030)*

As the title implies, *As You Like* It is a play meant to please and to entertain. Students enjoy the humorous, light-hearted banter as well as the intricate, playful treatment of the love theme. As a prereading exercise, you might ask students to define romantic love and discuss their varied answers.

Other prereading discussion might introduce the contrast between the corrupt court and the natural forest. Invite your students to consider links between this theme and modern society. In addition, you might invite the members of your class to imagine what modern women might be able to do if they disguised themselves as a man, as Rosalind will in the play, and encourage discussion of gender issues that arise. (Conversely, what might men be able to do if they disguised themselves as women?}

179

Contrast between the natural and harmonious and the artificial and calculated creates a central theme in this play. As students begin reading the play, encourage them to envision each scene on the stage. How could the scenery, the costumes, the casting, and the blocking on stage emphasize the many contrasts Shakespeare introduces? Challenge them, for example, to see the different kinds of violence in Act I as they would play out on stage. Ask them to picture the Forest of Arden and its inhabitants and consider how the contrast between court and country might be emphasized on stage.

After they are finished reading the play, ask your students to apply their definitions of romantic love to the different couples Shakespeare presents. Discussion might center around each couple's pattern of courtship, the reasons they are attracted to each other, and their motivations for marriage.

Possible Responses to Questions (p. 1030)

1. As a major theme, *As You Like* It explores the varied aspects of romantic love. Shakespeare presents four pairs of lovers who each define love in different ways. Rosalind and Orlando represent mature, intelligent lovers. Orlando, the more romantic of the two, hangs his love poems on the trees, professes that he will love Rosalind "for ever and a day" (IV. i. 138), and claims that he will die if she will not have him. Rosalind, more realistic and practical, responds, "Men have died from time to time, and worms have eaten them, but not from love" (IV. i. 101-102). Though she loves Orlando deeply, Rosalind keeps her sense of humor and reason about the state of romantic love and sets out, in her guise as Ganymede, to teach Orlando the same balance. When they marry, they are profoundly in love, but they also understand that this romantic love is only one part of a full and complete life. They respect and admire each other and together enter, with open eyes, a marriage of equals.

    To Touchstone, the fool, and Audrey, the dim-witted country wench, love is a much less lofty pursuit: their relationship is based primarily on physical desire and, in Touchstone's case, a sense of control. To Touchstone, Audrey is a woman who can satisfy his physical needs, and to whom he will always be superior. As Ralph Berry puts it, "In the context of Touchstone's other relationships, it is a likely guess that the certainty that he will remain the dominant partner is uppermost in his mind" when he weds Audrey. ("No Exit From Arden, *Shakespeare's Comedies: Exploration in Form*, Princeton, NJ: Princeton University Press, 1972, p. 191.) Audrey has trouble expressing her thoughts and does not begin to grasp Touchstone's wit, but her lusty desire for Touchstone and her wish to be a "woman of the world" is enough to convince her to marry him.

    The shepherd Silvius represents a lover so filled with ardor for an unrequited love that he has lost all sense of reason and pride. To Silvius, love is "to be all made of sighs and tears" (V. ii. 81) and "all adoration, duty and observance" (V. ii. 94). The self-centered Phebe has little interest in him, but puts up with him because it suits her vanity. She tells Silvius,

    > But since that thou canst talk of love so well,
    > They company, which erst was irksome to me,
    > I will endure . . . (III. v. 94-96)

    Phebe finally weds Silvius, but only after Rosalind, as Ganymede, tricks her into it. Silvius agrees to marry Phebe, saying, "Though to have her and death were both one thing." The romancing between Phebe and Silvius, the natural inhabitants of the forest, is, ironically, the most artificial love match in this play. The reader has no doubt that the reluctant bride will be able to manipulate her doting husband into doing almost anything for her once they are married.

The relationship of the final pair, Celia and the reformed Oliver, is a case of love at first sight. Even Orlando remarks at the swiftness of their courtship; "Is't possible," he asks Oliver, "that on so little acquaintance you should like her . . . and, wooing, she should grant?" (V. ii. 1-3). Oliver asks him not to question the "giddiness" of his proposal, but to consent so that he and Celia "who he still thinks is the servant girl, Aliena) "may enjoy each other." Romantic convention requires all eligible couples in Arden to wed, as such, Oliver and Celia's marriage represents the marriages of so many couples who wed without knowing much about each other.

While it is clear that Shakespeare lifts up the relationship between Orlando and Rosalind as the ideal love match, his attitude toward all the romantic couplings in this play is one of lighthearted humor at the perplexities of love. Although he represents each variety of romantic love with unfeigned honesty, Shakespeare is neither sentimental nor cynical.

Other themes in *As Your Like It* include: (a) the contrast between the natural life in the Forest of Arden and the civilized world of the court, (b) Shakespeare's exploration of gender differences symbolized by Rosalind's use of disguise, (c) the definition of true friendship as shown through the relationship between Celia and Rosalind, and (d) the resolution of familial strife that sets brother against brother and parent against child.

2. Helen Gardner, in her essay "As You Like It," comments:

    In *As You Like It* the plot is handled in the most perfunctory way. Shakespeare crams his first act with incident in order to get everyone to the forest as soon as he possibly can and, when he is ready, he ends it all as quickly as possible. [Helen Gardner, "As You Like It," in Kenneth Muir, ed., *Shakespeare: The Comedies*, Englewood Cliffs, NJ: Prentice Hall, 1965, p. 61.]

    Certainly plot does not drive this play; rather, the play relies primarily on complex dialogue, well drawn setting, and contrasting relationships to develop its themes.

    It should be a fairly straightforward exercise for students to trace the main lines of action in this play. Act I contains an explosion of activity, animosity surfaces, murders are attempted, ribs are cracked, romantic attraction blooms, and several major characters set off for the Forest of Arden. In Acts II through IV, Shakespeare slows down the pace and allows the major themes of his play to unravel as different pairs of characters wander through the Forest of Arden to debate matters of love, society, and family; they sing, laugh, and fall in love. In Act V, the action picks up again. The two villains, Oliver and Duke Frederick, are reformed; Oliver and Celia fall instantly in love; Rosalind casts off her disguise; and the four pairs of lovers line up to be wed. The play ends in a final dance, an image of harmony. With the exception of Jaques, who refuses to take part, and Adam, who is too old, everyone—dukes, fools, shepherds, princesses, noblemen, servants, and country people—joins together in the dance which symbolizes the new order and draws *As You Like It* to a close.

3. *As You Like It* begins with a glimpse into the disordered and corrupt court of the tyrannical Duke Frederick. The court is a morally bankrupt and violent place where broken ribs are considered entertaining, and a nobleman can brutishly treat his servants and his brother as animals simply because he is the eldest son. To the members of Duke Frederick's court, the Forest of Arden is a place where the banished Duke Senior lives like Robin Hood, where "many young gentlemen flock to him every day and fleet the time carelessly, as they did in the golden world" (I.i. 112-114). Indeed, the Forest of Arden is a place set apart, a place of natural beauty and peace where one can live a pastoral life in simple

harmony with Nature. Duke Senior finds "books in the running brooks" and "sermons in the stones." Aimens sings sweetly of lovers lying under the greenwood trees. Worldly assets and political successes do not matter in Arden. As Robert Ornstein suggests, " When the exiles reach its borders, they leave all sense of urgency and crisis far behind" (*Shakespeare's Comedies: From Roman Farce to Romantic Mystery*, London: Associated University Press, 1986, p. 142). In Arden, people are free to find their own happiness and fulfillment. When Duke Frederick and Oliver arrive in Arden, its restorative powers reform them. Oliver is reformed by Orlando's generosity in saving his life; Frederick is reformed by contact with an old religious man.

Arden is not, however, paradise. The winters bring bitter cold weather, the ground is hard, deers must be killed to feed the Duke and his man, and some of its native inhabitants are uncouth and stupid. Touchstone remains untouched by the beauty of Arden and remarks, "When I was at home I was in a better place, but travelers must be content" (II. iv. 14-16). Indeed, the majority of Arden's inhabitants are travelers. Arden cannot serve as a permanent residence for people who are not farmers or shepherds. As Ornstein says of Arden's many visitors, "They play at pastorality while they wait for the opportunity to return to the court, which is their natural milieu. . . . Those bred at court do not adapt to forest ways; they adapt life in the forest to their courtly tastes" (p. 142, 145). At the end, most return joyfully to the court, which, thanks to what they have learned and how they have changed in Arden, they plan to transform.

4. Rosalind is certainly one of Shakespeare's most fully drawn female characters. She is brave, intelligent, witty, loyal, and full of the joy of life. She calmly endures misfortune, always maintains her sense of integrity, and is admired for her virtues" (I. iii. 284). Although Shakespeare allows Rosalind to outshine everyone else with her bright intelligence, she is very human as well. When she falls in love with Orlando, she does so thoroughly and impulsively. She tells Celia, "My affection hath an unknown bottom" (IV. i. 199). This love makes her vulnerable. When Orlando arrives late for their meeting in Act III, scene iv, Rosalind becomes distressed and sullen, and she confesses later that she "cannot be out of the sight of Orlando: (IV. i.208). Her love for Orlando will not, however, define her life. When she weds Orlando, she will become an equal partner in marriage and she will remain a strong individual, a loving daughter, and a loyal friend.

Celia resembles Rosalind in many ways. The two young women have almost identical backgrounds: both are physically attractive, both are intelligent, both have a good sense of humor. Nevertheless, Celia plays a role subordinate to Rosalind; she doesn't emerge as a strong woman in her own right. Although she easily partakes in witty conversations with Rosalind and Touchstone, Celia is generally reserved in public. In important scenes where both princesses are present, Rosalind dominates. Celia's disguise as a servant to Rosalind's Ganymede provides a symbolic representation of their actual relationship. Throughout this play, Celia acts as companion to Rosalind and serves as a foil who brings out the main character's strengths. When Celia finally falls in love, she is won over by Oliver immediately; the audience doesn't take part in her courtship as they do in Rosalind's. The character of Celia does shine powerfully as a devoted and loyal friend. Celia does not hesitate to stand up to her father in defense of her friend, nor does she waver in her decision to leave the comforts of court to go into exile with Rosalind. Although her romance with Oliver is sudden and undeveloped, the depth of her ability to love her friend is a strong indication that she will be a loyal and loving wife. The fact that Oliver falls instantly in love with Celia in her disguise as Aliena implies that his betrothal is based on true emotion and not ambition.

The other two female characters in *As You Like It* are rather stereotypical. Audrey is a simple country woman who lacks intelligence but dreams of becoming a "woman of the world" when she marries Touchstone. She will never become Touchstone's equal, and that is part of her attraction to him. Phebe is a pastoral figure who, nonetheless, rejects the advances of love-sick Silvius. She feels no compassion or pity for him and only allows him near her because he speaks to her so prettily. Comically, Shakespeare induces Phebe to fall wildly in love with Rosalind in her disguise as Ganymede. Only after realizing Ganymede's true identity does she keep her promise to marry Silvius. Phebe is a reluctant bride, and will most likely maintain control in her marriage to the devoted and adoring Silvius.

[For extended discussion on gender issues see Barbara Bono's "Mixed Gender, Mixed Genre in Shakespeare's *As You Like It*." In *Renaissance Genres: Essays on Theory, History, and Interpretation*, ed. Barbara K. Lewalski. Cambridge: Harvard University Press, 1986, and Clara Claiborne Park's "As We Like It: How a Girl Can Be Smart and Still Popular." *The American Scholar* 42 (1973): 262-278.]

5. Several of the minor characters in *As You Like It* serve as what Ralph Berry calls "anti-romantic elements . . . who provide a running fire (within the spectrum realism-satire) on the posturing of the romantics" ("No Exit From Arden." *Shakespeare's Comedies: Explorations in Form*, Princeton, NJ: Princeton University Press, 1972, p. 175). Jaques certainly serves this function. His melancholy and jaded view of the world acts as a measure of sanity in situations where expressions of love, optimism about human nature, and faith in mankind might otherwise get carried away. Jaques ridicules human ideals and stands apart from others; he alone refuses to join in the celebratory dance at the end of the play. Indeed, he decides to stay at Arden with Frederick; he cannot be part of the harmonious circle returning to change the court. Although Shakespeare hints at Jaques's darker side, this comic misanthrope's verbal attacks and pessimistic speeches are not hurtful to others, nor are they taken too seriously. While others do not deny that love cannot be absurd, that life can be disappointing, and that old age and death is inevitable, they do reject Jaques's hopelessness and his notion that life is without purpose or meaning.

    Touchstone is just as skeptical as Jaques, but he sees the absurdities and follies of life as occasion for parody and wit, not cynicism and pessimism. As a professional fool, he observes the games people play and humorously points out the foolishness of those around him. Berry notes, "His realism . . . is a touchstone to keep the balance of the play. We can agree that Touchstone supplies an essential ingredient in the play's composition, and that his comments—pungent, witty, realistic—on the Court, Arden, and love provide a welcome leavening." Touchstone's view of the world doesn't change while he is in Arden; he is immune to the forest's charms. Although he does marry, his marriage is a parody of the institution and not a serious attempt at commitment.

    These two minor characters, along with others your students may decide to explore, allow Shakespeare to flesh out more fully the two major contrasts in *As You Like It:* that between court and forest and that between romantic harmony and pessimistic discord.

6. Students' selections will vary. This exercise will encourage students to consider the visual elements of the many poetic images Shakespeare creates in this play.

7. Students' selections will vary. Many may choose Jaques's "Seven Stages of Man" speech at the end of Act II; this extended philosophical statement is certainly one of Shakespeare's most famous. Others may opt to discuss one of Orlando's romantic speeches, one of Touchstone's humorous orations, or one of Rosalind's intelligent and witty speeches.

8. In Act I, Rosalind and Celia discuss the relationship between Nature and Fortune. Celia complains about the blind goddess Fortune randomly bestowing her favors, but Rosalind reminds her, "Fortune reigns in gifts of the world, not in the lineaments of Nature" (I. ii. 40-41). To Rosalind, a person's nature, or integrity, is more important than wealth or power. Rosalind speaks for Shakespeare here, and the rest of the play sets out to realign the forces of Fortune and Nature.

   At the beginning of *As You Like It*, it is clear that Fortune has unjustly distributed her gifts. Duke Frederick, a villianous usurper, rules the throne while the evil-spirited Oliver reaps the advantages of society and treats others cruelly simply because he is the eldest brother. These characters thrive while the more noble characters, Rosalind, Duke Senior, and Orlando, suffer. By the end of the play, this imbalance has been resolved, not by violence or punishment, but by the miraculous reformation of the evil characters. Their natures changed, Duke Frederick and Oliver become the agents who restore the rightful fortunes of Duke Senior, Rosalind, Orlando, and Celia. Fortune and Nature are now realigned.

9. Songs, music, and dance are an integral part of the pastoral atmosphere in the Forest of Arden. Beyond that, the songs act as a kind of Greek chorus to the action surrounding it. They often restate the theme of the dismal and corrupt court life versus life in the clean and fair forest. Occasionally, the songs smooth out the movements between scenes between the court and the forest. In addition, dance, music, and songs make up part of the masque elements in this play. (You might explain to students that masques are short allegorical dramatic entertainments which were popular in the 16th and 17th centuries.) Shakespeare uses these masque elements to emphasize different thematic strands or to help delineate character.

   For example, in Act II, scene v, Aimens sings of the beauty and ease of life in the forest, where lovers rest under greenwood trees and listen to the "merry note" from a "sweet bird's throat," where "ambition: is not important and a man is "pleased with what he gets (3-4, 41). Jaques, who has insisted that Aimens sing, adds his own verse to Aimens's which rebukes the pastoral sentiments that Aimens has expressed. According to Jaques, a man who would leave his "wealth and ease" to live in such a place as Arden is "an ass" and a "fool." Song has served two purposes in this scene. It emphasizes Shakespeare's recurring theme of the contrast between court and forest, and it also establishes Jaques's role as an opposing, argumentative, and pessimistic voice which will be heard throughout this play.

10. Students' choices will vary. The following questions may help students envision staging:

   A. Use the design of your set to emphasize the central meaning or contrast of the scene you are staging. What sort of atmosphere will your set evoke? How will the action of the scene fill the space? How will the actors use the set? What props might you use?

   B. Consider carefully how you will cast your actors. What, specifically, will they look like and why? What images will their presence on stage project? How will you costume them?

   C. How can you use blocking to emphasize the meaning of your scene? Where will the actors be placed on stage and why? How will they move around?

   D. How will you direct your actors to deliver their lines? Imagine how key lines might sound, what words or phrases might delivered in a certain tone or manner. What words or phrases should be emphasized? How can body language or motion be used? Try to picture how the actors interact on stage; include both those who are speaking and those who are not.

Additional Topics for Writing and Discussion

1. Discuss the significance of the title *As You Like It*.

   [Students should be able to identify Shakespeare's desire to write a play his audience would enjoy expressed in this title and relate it to Rosalind's plea in the Epilogue for the women "to like as much of the play as please you" and to the men "that between you and the women the play may please" (V. iv. 13, 16).]

2. Trace the development of two of the four couples who marry in *As You Like It*. Characterize each couple and discuss the concept of love they represent.

   [Student responses will vary; see the extended discussion on pages 179–184 of this guide for possibilities.]

3. What purpose does Rosalind's disguise serve in the play?

   [Literally, Rosalind's disguise helps her escape to Arden unnoticed and unmolested. Once she is in Arden and disguise is unnecessary, however, she maintains her Ganymede identity. Students will identify many reasons for this including the freedom the disguise gives her to speak her mind, the way it allows her to play the game which tests Orlando's love for her, and the power it gives her to move about the forest and affect conversations and events. In addition, students should be urged to consider *Shakespeare*'s motivations for maintaining the disguise: mainly, to provide an excuse for Rosalind to express her more unromantic, realistic views of love and present her as a more complete, intelligent character.]

4. Harold Jenkins claims,

   "It is a mark of Shakespeare's mature comedy that he permits criticism of his ideal world in the very center of it." (Harold Jenkins, "As You Like It," in Leonard F. Dean, ed., *Shakespeare: Modern Essays in Criticism*. London: Oxford University Press, 1967, p. 122.)

   Explain what you think Jenkins means and support your position with specific textual references and quotations.

   [Students will draw primarily from the characters of Jaques and Touchstone and the less than idealistic attitudes they express in many scenes.]

5. How do you think the court will change after all the travelers return? Be specific.

   [Most students should agree that the court will most certainly be a more humane, moral, and joyful place to live.]

CHAPTER EIGHTEEN

The Neoclassical French Theater

Many student will find Richard Wilbur's fine translation of Molière's *Tartuffe* much more accessible than Greek or Elizabethan drama. Molière's adherence to precise conventions (discussed briefly in the introduction) does not detract from the play's appeal. In fact, students find the number of classical elements present in seventeenth-century drama interesting.

Students can discuss the artistic and practical merits of using satire instead of persuasive essays (or any other genre) as a means of identifying problems and provoking social or political change They can point to political cartoonists such as Paul Szep and columnists such as Art Buchwald as effective contemporary satirists. (Some modern drama has moved into theater of the absurd, which contains satiric elements but does not depend on the unities that are part of classical, neoclassical, and even some contemporary realistic theater.) Most students will agree that satire, including satiric drama, can be a powerful and provocative influence in society.

Students can extend their understanding of satire by noting the techniques writers use to achieve it, such as irony, sarcasm, innuendo, and so on. Students can create satiric skits of campus or community life, ridiculing aspects of their own world. They quickly discover that preparing even very short satiric skits is extremely difficult, thus increasing their appreciation for Molière's skill.

Tartuffe • Molière (Jean-Baptiste Poquelin) (pp. 1033–1085)

As with Greek and Elizabethan drama, the set description and stage directions are minimal. However, students will perceive that the dialogue is different—understandable, believable, and fast-paced. Beyond this, students are attracted by the humor in *Tartuffe*, but they also understand and appreciate the underlying commentary on individual and social power.

The central conflict of the play is established as soon as Tartuffe's name is brought into the conversation (Act I, Scene 1, line 41). The plot centers around Tartuffe, but he could not be successful in his duplicity without Orgon's cooperation. In *Men and Masks: A Study of Molière*, Lionel Gossman writes, " . . . in Tartuffe, those who are duped by imposters are themselves imposters in their own way" (Baltimore: The Johns Hopkins Press, 1963, p. 101). This quotation can be adapted to a question that can serve as a focus for students as they read the play: In what ways are Tartuffe and Orgon imposters?

Possible Responses to Question (p. 1086)

1. Students' responses will vary, with most criticizing Tartuffe's behavior while admiring his cleverness. Some students will raise the point that the play revolves around Orgon, not Tartuffe.

2. By delaying Tartuffe's appearance, Molière gives the other character a chance to describe and react to Tartuffe, so that the audience has formed a strong image and opinion. By Act III, the sides of the conflict are clearly drawn.

3. While Orgon, Madame Pernelle, and Tartuffe represent an unhealthy, distorted, dark side of society, Elmire, Cléante, and Dorine represent the positive side. Students will argue whether it is Elmire or Cléante who more closely represents Molière's view. Students can support their opinions by reading background information about Molière and the court of the Sun King, Louis XIV.

Elmire remains somewhat of a mystery despite her influence in persuading Orgon of Tartuffe's false piety. She creates the impression of having more depth than her character reveals, as if in portraying the faithful wife, she assumed a role that forced her to hide some of her true nature. This view, however, is a matter of interpretation. One critical view says, "Elmire represents a way of life, which Molière seems to have considered the most decent and honest open to human beings in the modern world" (Gossman, p. 141).

Cléante, Orgon's social equal, discerns the falseness of Tartuffe's piety; he sees behind the mask that deceives Orgon, recognizing that Tartuffe's actions conflict with his avowed beliefs. Cléante bases his opinions on observations, unlike Orgon, who ignores what is patently obvious to everyone else.

Dorine, the entertaining and observant stock servant character, easily recognizes Tartuffe's true nature, seeing through his affectations. She is also impatient with Orgon's cruel and selfish decision to force Mariane to marry Tartuffe. Readers/viewers recognize her common sense and compassion; unfortunately, she has no real influence.

4. Students can begin by referring to the definitions in the glossary.

Comedy: A type of drama in which the characters experience reversals of fortune, usually for the better. In comedy things work out happily in the end. Comic drama may be either romantic—characterized by a tone of tolerance and geniality—or satiric. Satiric plays offer a darker vision of human nature, one that ridicules human folly [p. 1744].

Romance: A type of narrative fiction or poem in which adventure is a central feature and in which an idealized vision of reality is presented [p. 1747].

Satire: A literary work that criticizes human misconduct and ridicules vices, stupidities, and follies [p. 1747].

Tartuffe is satiric because the action exposes human weaknesses. Tartuffe willingly, even eagerly, accepts every opportunity that Orgon presents for worming his way into emotional and financial control. Orgon is duped, but he is a partner in the deception, deliberately ignoring warnings from his family and allowing himself to be victimized. By the time Orgon recognizes what is happening, his ability to control his finances, his family, or Tartuffe is gone. The happy ending is the result of intervening outside forces, not the insight of a dynamic character.

Molière clearly feels that Orgon's devotion to Tartuffe is misplaced; thus the tone is critical of Orgon's behavior. Overriding the many very funny scenes in *Tartuffe* is the constant tension caused by Orgon's refusal to recognize reality. This counterpoint of humor and tension heightens the audience's involvement in the play.

5. Students' responses will vary depending on their interpretation of the play and their experience in staging. Students can work effectively in groups for this activity, first deciding on the scene and then developing the staging. If students photocopy the scene they're staging and place these pages in a three-ring binder along with blank paper, they'll have the beginning of a play book for their staging.

You might suggest that blocking a scene is most easily accomplished if students draw a diagram of the stage, indicating the placement of furniture and props. A series of such diagrams placed on pages facing the script can conveniently be used to indicate the movement of characters. Annotations indicating gestures and facial expressions can be placed in the margins next to the appropriate place in the script.

6. Here also students responses will vary depending on their interpretation of the play. Most students, however, will recognize that Molière is not ridiculing religion and piety, but excesses and abuses.

Additional Topics for Writing and Discussion

1. Respond to this quotation from an essay about *Tartuffe*:

   The idols of the modern world have become progressively more base, more empty, more dangerous, and more like Tartuffe as time has gone on. They even resemble Tartuffe in being so taken up by the roles they play for their worshipers that they are no longer aware of playing them. Tartuffe feels strong indignation when he accuses Orgon of imposture and calls for justice, and in the same way the fanatical dictators of our own times have really believed the monstrous fabrications of their deranged minds. [Gossman, pp. 121-122]

2. Assume the role of Elmire writing a letter to a close friend just after the events in Act III, Scene 3, in which Tartuffe makes his unwelcome advances. What do you say about the upheaval in your household because of Tartuffe? What are you going to do about his advances to you?

   [Having students assume the role of a character requires the same close reading necessary for a critical essay, but students often enjoy the assignment more.]

3. Create a dialogue in which Orgon tries to explain and justify to Madame Pernelle his change of opinion about Tartuffe as a result of the events in the final act.

4. Compare and contrast the female characters in *Tartuffe*. Do they represent types or caricatures of women? Do they depict believable women?

5. Investigate the social and political conditions of seventeenth-century France. In what ways does *Tartuffe* reflect French society? French politics?

CHAPTER NINETEEN
The Modern Realistic Theater

Chapter Nineteen introduces one of the most powerful movements in the history of drama: realism. The plays in this chapter differ from those in the previous three chapters in a number of ways, perhaps the most obvious being setting. The introduction of the invisible "fourth wall" in the late nineteenth century revolutionized drama: audiences suddenly because eavesdroppers, bring them much closer to the action of the play. They also saw onstage characters with whom they could readily identify, rather than the archetypal royalty and heros. And these new characters used language that approximated everyday speech.

Realism was a natural outgrowth of the social and philosophical changes of the nineteenth century, notably those precipitated by the theories of Darwin and Freud. *A Doll House* and *The Cherry Orchard* are perhaps the plays most closely associated with the social change that swept Europe during the nineteenth century; Ibsen shows us the consequences for the individual, Chekhov for established society. Shaw's *Arms and the Man* playfully illustrates the folly of traditional romanticism. These plays can be taught in various combinations; see discussions of individual plays for further suggestions.

A Doll House • Henrik Ibsen (pp. 1088–1139)

The opening scene of *A Doll House* establishes the conflict and tension in the Helmer home. The audience immediately senses that Nora is more complex than her superficial behavior indicates. Ibsen also establishes Torvald's attitude toward Nora; affectionate and condescending. Nora readily responds to, and even encourages, his attitude; therefore, both contribute equally to the facade of their marriage.

The opening scene introduces symbols that appear throughout the play. Some of the symbols are material objects—the Christmas tree, the stove, Nora's clothing. Perhaps more important, however, are the characters who represent aspects of Nora's growing awareness of the world: Mrs. Linde (pragmatic survival), Dr. Rank (physical deterioration), and Krogstad (moral corruption).

In this play characters represent certain social attitudes. Ibsen's characters sound like real people, however, thus differentiating this realistic play from earlier drama. Rolf Fjelde's translation accurately reproduces the natural speech patterns Ibsen used to create the impression that the characters onstage are responding spontaneously to one another. If you like to have students sight-read scenes in class, this play works particularly well because of the believable dialogue.

Ibsen originally gave *A Doll House* the subtitle *A Modern Tragedy*. However, this nineteenth-century tragedy is significantly different from the Aristotelian tragedy of ancient Greece or the Shakespearean tragedy of the seventeenth century. Ibsen's characters are ordinary people with whom students can identify. This is a middle-class family complete with money problems, and yet the sentiments expressed by Nora at the end are among the noblest in literature. The nature of tragedy has shifted: you don't have to be a king to solve great problems.

In "Ibsen's Search for the Hero" (in Rolf Fjelde, ed., Ibsen: *A Collection of Critical Essays*, Englewood Cliffs, NJ: Prentice-Hall, 1965, pp. 91-108), John Northam reinforces Ibsen's position:

> Ibsen suggests, through devices similar to those that we have observed in the earlier plays, a tragic struggle that lies behind the trivial anxieties of a housewife, a struggle involving an heroic figure in conflict with the secret, powerful and ineluctable forces of society. [p. 100]

Using Rank's illness as a metaphor for the deterioration of Nora's world, Northam says that "society works upon Nora like some dreadful, hidden, and inexorable disease" (p. 108), that the symbols in the play "help to create the sense of fatality; and Nora's consistent fight against that, a fight in which she will sacrifice no basic principles however desperate her situation, makes her into a heroine" (p. 108).

As students begin to recognize the tragic elements of the play, they should come to understand that the characters and their situation represent a universal struggle of human beings to define themselves and their relationships. In his foreword to *Ibsen: Four Major Plays* (New York: Hirmont, 1966), Fjelde says:

> . . . the crux of the play is not primarily an individual, but a relationship—the modern middle-class conception of marriage. . . . Ibsen's] interest centers on Nora because, in her own terms, she internalizes the conflict, which Ibsen designates in his notes as "natural feeling on the one hand and belief in authority on the other' "
> (pp. xxvi-xxvii).

Possible Responses to Questions (pp. 1139–1140)

1. Torvald most obviously displays the following characteristics, although students may identify others:

   - Egocentric
   - Status-conscious
   - Oblivious to his surroundings: he believes Nora when she denies munching macaroons, the bag bulging in her pocket and crumbs around her mouth as she eats.
   - Presumptuous and pompous
   - Moralistic: Torvald calls Krogstad "morally lost," creating an "atmosphere of lies [that] infects the whole life of a home."
   - Rigid
   - Controlling: he regulates the amount of money given to Nora for household and personal use.
   - Cautious about money: he tells Nora she can have anything—"within reason."
   - Caring: he urges Nora to spend more money on things for herself rather than just household needs.

   Torvald does not change, but by the end of the play he does realize that Nora is actually leaving. He doe snot seem to understand Nora's need to "have a true marriage." The egocentric and status-conscious behavior exhibited at the beginning of the play is still evident in his response to Krogstad's letter, showing concern only for the social implications and damage to his reputation rather than Nora's well-being. He still seems incapable of sustaining the kind of relationship that Nora wants.

2. Responses will vary. Whether the decision is "right" depends on who is affected. Some will argue that Torvald is right; obviously Nora should stay because she is incapable of surviving on her own. Some will argue that Nora should stay for the sake of the children; however, the play clearly shows that Nora has minimal contact with them and that their primary caretaker is the nurse, Anne-Marie. Some will see Nora's decision to leave as the first important indication that she is, in fact, capable of functioning independently. Students should also be aware that Nora will not find independence easy; her society has not changed, and she has few personal or professional skills for surviving.

3. Every person deserves the opportunity to function fully and independently, but that opportunity cannot simply be given to an individual. Human rights can only exist when an individual recognizes the need to be independent and assumes responsibility for exercising these rights. Nora shares equal responsibility for her oppression with Torvald, who represents societal expectations. Nora can exercise her independence only after she recognizes that she alone controls the direction of her life. However, Nora's predicament is not unique to women; all people sometimes find themselves blocking their own development.

4. While students will obviously differ in their initial answers to this question, it might be useful to start by asking why they think an alternative ending was provided. Discussion may involve reference to currently popular books, movies, or television programs, all of which usually end happily. Audiences want to be reassured that all's right with the world; they generally do not like to see their values and expectations shattered.

   Ibsen provided an alternative ending for *A Doll House* because he worried that some directors would rewrite his play. In the alternative, which Ibsen hoped would not be used Nora does not leave Torvald. The play ends with Nora looking at her sleeping children and saying, "This is a crime against myself, but I cannot leave them." In the original ending, Torvald sits crushed and defeated; in the alternative ending, Nora crumples to the floor, her hopes defeated.

   If a work is to be *artistically* effective, it must remain true to its theme. To unite Nora and Torvald in the end is to negate Nora's awakening. The play emphasizes not only the need for independence but its cost as well. If students focus on the discrepancy between Nora's newfound values and the traditional values of society, they should be able to recognize that while an audience might initially be relieved at the alternative ending, the play would suffer artistically. Theatrically, the alternative ending makes the entire last scene anticlimactic. Students may need assistance in recognizing just what this scene is leading toward; you may want to ask them why Ibsen should have bothered opening Nora's eyes like this if she weren't going to do anything about it.

5. Most students have little problem recognizing the function of Krogstad: not only does he provide the necessary conflict between Nora and Torvald, but his downfall stems from precisely the "crime" of which Nora is guilty.

   Nora is acutely aware of Krogstad's relationship to her when Torvald describes how a crime like Krogstad's "infects the whole life of a home" (p. 1108), endangering the moral lives of the children. Of course, Torvald doesn't realize that he's prophetically casting judgment on his own character when he later proposes to "cover up" Nora's forgery in much the same way as Krogstad did his own.

   Mrs. Linde's function is also clear. The contrast between her life and Nora's is drawn starkly in the first act. In addition, she provides us with the first hint that Nora is more than what she seems: in response to Mrs. Linde's comment that she is "just a child" (p. 1095), Nora reveals that it was she who saved Torvald's life. But perhaps the most important function of Mrs. Linde is to give us a glimpse of what lies ahead for Nora after she leaves. The life Mrs. Linde has lived has changed her so that Nora hardly recognizes her old friend when she arrives in Act I. This is what Nora has to look forward to after the curtain falls.

Dr. Rank's function is more complex. Students should have no trouble recognizing his function in the plot: he reveals both Torvald's myopia (as Torvald fails to recognize Rank's feeling for Nora) and Nora's reluctance to defy societal constraints. When Rank, dying, finally admits his love for her, she is shocked, offended—even though she has played upon his feelings all along. It is fine for him to be in love with her, but not for him to say so openly. Here we get the chance to see just how drastically Nora's view of society changes in the end. Rank's illness may be difficult for students to understand, however. They may need to be told that Ibsen is referring to venereal disease here; that's why Rank says that he's paying for the sins of his father. It may be interesting to acquaint them with nineteenth-century misconceptions about VD: In Ibsen's time, it was thought that the disease could be *inherited*; even medical professionals didn't realize that a child could contract the disease only if the mother had been infected. This might engender an interesting discussion: while themes may sometimes be based on "facts" that later turn out to be untrue, the revelation doesn't diminish the power of the theme. The point remains the same in the 1990s as in 1879: Rank has been innocently infected by his father in the same way that Nora thinks she will infect her innocent children.

6. Ibsen gradually builds the plot by adding small bits of information that mesh with what the audience has already learned. The pace of the play changes with nearly every entrance or exit of a character, as the following example shows:

   Act I: • frivolous conversation between Nora and Torvald
          • serious conversation between Nora and Kristine
          • increase in tension with brief entrance of Dr. Rank

   Students could select any section of the play and list the changes that occur with character entrances and exits. Students will note that the pace shifts often, stimulating audience attention and reflecting the uncertain nature of Nora's emotions and confidence.

7. If students have read the introductory material in text Chapter Nineteen, they should be able to recognize the Christmas tree, in its various states of adornment and disarray, as a indicator of the state of the Helmers's marriage. They also may recall that Nora dons a costume for her "last dance," the last time she will be able to live in her fantasy world. She moves to the stove, the warm heart of the house, whenever anything seems to shake her fantasy world. When Dr. Rank confesses his love for her, she calls for a lamp, the light symbolizing the truth that has come out. There is also Dr. Rank's card with the black cross which signals not only his death, but that of the Helmers's marriage. Again, if students are encouraged to read the stage directions, they should be able to offer many examples here.

8. Because students will select difference scenes, a lively class discussion can result from their justifications of one scene instead of another as particularly revealing. Regardless of the scenes selected, similar elements are used to reveal character. However, students may need to review the standard techniques dramatists use to establish character:

   • dialogue—from the character and about the character
   • vocal clues and delivery (indicated in stage directions)
   • actions and reactions—of the character and toward the character
   • clothing worn by the character
   • props used by the character
   • setting in which the character performs

Additional Topics for Writing and Discussion

1. Imagine that it is one year after the final curtain. Assume the role of Nora and write a letter to Torvald in which you try to explain what has happened. You may find yourself repeating a few of the things you told him on that last night, but now you are both distanced from the event. Explain just what you were before your revelation, who you think was to blame, and how you have changed. You may want to use one of the other characters to help explain to Torvald what you are becoming.

2. Imagine that it is several weeks after the final curtain. Assume the role of Torvald, and write a letter to Nora in which you try to explain why you acted the way you did. Think about the character of Torvald as he is revealed to us throughout the play. Is he sincere in believing that he truly loves Nora? Does he believe that he is a compassionate man? Is he capable of the introspection necessary to analyze his situation objectively?

3. Some critics have called *A Doll House* a tragedy, and Nora a tragic heroine. Consider the description of tragedy on pp. 777-778, and discuss whether or not you agree. You may find yourself redefining some of the elements of tragedy in order to adapt it to the realistic theater.

   [Perhaps the strongest evidence in favor of the play's being called a tragedy is the aura of *fate* that surrounds the action. Torvald hints at the capriciousness of fate early in Act I when Nora asks if they can't borrow money until his raise comes through: "What if today I borrowed a thousand crowns, and you squandered them over Christmas week, and then on New Year's Eve a roof tile fell on my head, and I lay there—" (p. 1090).

   But fate also entails an inexorable chain of events. In this play we have an intricate interweaving of seeming coincidences, all precipitated by one event, worthy of Shakespeare: Torvald's promotion sets into motion a series of incidents, ranging from Mrs. Linde's appearance in search of a job, to Krogstad's blackmail in order to save his job, to Nora's hope that at last she can pay off the loan.

   Irony, another element of tragedy, is abundant: Mrs. Linde, once the love of Krogstad's life, reenters it only to unsuspectingly take his job; Nora, viewing the promotion as her financial and emotional salvation, soon discovers that it threatens her and her husband's reputation; additionally when the blackmail letter arrives and she thinks the miracle that will solidify her marriage is about to occur, Torvald's self-serving reaction signals instead the emptiness of the marriage.

   This, of course, reveals another element of tragedy—namely, the errors in judgment that seal Nora's fate. She carelessly believes that the date of a document is of no consequence; she believes that she can convince Torvald to keep Krogstad on; and finally, she thoroughly misjudges her husband's character.

   Perhaps the stickiest point in this discussion will be viewing Nora as a tragic heroine; here students may need to redefine the terms *grand* and *noble*. If we consider those qualities to come from within, then it is entirely possible to consider a middle-class housewife as a heroine. And if we consider the implications of her action to women and oppressed people everywhere, then we can also believe that her downfall will send out ripples throughout her world.]

4. We tend to applaud Nora's actions in this play and view Torvald as a villain. But Torvald represents society itself, the norms and values that create the fabric of a community. Consider what Nora is saying at the end: that her forgery was justified, indeed heroic; that she is doing a noble thing by leaving her husband and children; that society and religion

are bankrupt. She says that her most sacred duties are not to her husband and children, but to herself. If we carry this view to its extreme, we risk total anarchy. Is this what Ibsen is advocating? How can we justify our response?

[In responding to this, students may need a little encouragement. To question society is not to advocate its destruction; many of our own heroes preached radical change—the founders of this country, reformers like Martin Luther King, Jr., Gandhi, Jesus Christ. The key lies in recognizing just what the enemy is—not the idea of society itself, but rather what a particular society has become.

Nora does not condemn her society; she merely says that she has to educate herself in order to discover whether or not society is right. She does question, however, the right of society to deprive a woman of the means to save her husband"s life. Here she's discovering the notion of unjust laws. She begins to recognize that, as King said, any law that does not uplift humanity is invalid. She is discovering that the laws of society should be based on a higher, moral law and that society is not infallible.

In addition, students may need to be reminded that Nora is not the Meryl Streep character in *Kramer vs. Kramer*, running off to sunny California and a top job on a national magazine. Nora will have to struggle; her decision is not frivolous. We have seen through Kristine Linde how hard it is for a woman alone in this society, and Kristine does not suffer the stigma of a woman who has abandoned her family. Nora will pay dearly for her newfound wisdom. Ibsen, then, does not imply that society can be defied without pain or punishment.]

5. As Nora, write a series of five journal entries that reflect your emotions, thoughts, and plans as they evolve during the play. The journal entries should reflect your confusion and concern as well as your growing awareness and insight about your life and marriage.

6. Support or refute Ibsen"s contention (presented in the text's introduction of *A Doll House*, p. 1087) that the play is "less about the rights of women than about human rights generally, less about the particular social conditions responsible for the position of women in nineteenth-century Norway than about the need for individuals of both sexes to treat each other with mutual respect."

7. Create the dialogue of a frank and open conversation between a contemporary woman and Nora, after Nora has decided she must leave Torvald. What issues would each bring up? How would each view the other's position?

8. Ibsen believed that men and women each had a different kind of conscience and that they did not understand the view of the other:

> The superstructure of Torvald's conscience, his sense of right and wrong, is founded on the formulation: "the most important thing is that *I* be a success; all else will follow from that." Nora's moral sense, on the other hand, tells her than "the most important thing is that *we* live in, and out of, the truth of our feelings; all else will follow from that." (Fjelde, p. xxvi)

Do you agree that there are differences is the way men and women approach relationships? Explain.

The Cherry Orchard • *Anton Chekhov (pp. 1141–1177)*

Students will need to become acclimated to the context of this play; they probably have little or no knowledge of prerevolutionary Russia. Questions about the society depicted in the play may elicit sufficient response to piece together a view of the society in which these characters act out their drama. For example, it is easy to see that Russia is only a generation away from the feudal society in which serfs were slaves to the landowners. Both Firs and Lopahin continually refer to the time when their people were not free. Their respective reactions to emancipation should give students a clue to how emancipation was accepted—or not accepted—even by the freed serfs. While Lopahin revels in his freedom and buys the home that once housed his ancestors as slaves, Firs rejects his freedom and laments the passing of the old ways. Emancipation is fresh in the memory of these people; like the American South of the same era, this society is trying to adjust to radical change.

Some students of history may also recognize that the play takes place just prior to the first Russian revolution. Trofimov's aspirations for his country indicate the ardor of those who wish to usher Russia into a new era. This is a society in flux; the old values have been shattered, but have yet to be replaced by new values. Thus the characters are left without a basis for their action—this is one of the reasons why nobody but Lopahin *does* anything in the play; the rest simply react as things happen to them. And Lopahin acts only as a businessman, not as a friend or patriot.

The opening stage directions do not provide a great deal of information, but they do introduce the central symbol of the play, the cherry orchard itself. They also establish one of the motifs used to indicate mood in the play: the weather. It is spring, but the frost reminds us that winter still holds its grip on this land. As the scene progresses, we are not only introduced to the main characters, but we begin to see the various relationships among them. The central conflict is also introduced in the form of Lopahin's paradoxical solution to Mme. Ranevskaya's money problems: she can save the cherry orchard by cutting it down and putting up cottages on the land.

Chekhov is more difficult to deal with than a playwright like Ibsen, since his introduction of various conflicts does not lead to an ultimate resolution. Students may also find themselves uncomfortable trying to deal with a play that has no real climax. A more profitable approach than focusing on plot and structure might be to ask students about the various ironies in the play. For example, Mme. Ranevskaya comments that "nothing has changed" in the cherry orchard since she was a child—that "the heavenly angles have not left" either the orchard or its owners—when we already know that if she cannot raise enough money, the orchard will be sold at auction. And Gayev, after affirming that he will never let the orchard be sold, says excitedly, "I swear by my whole being!" We, of course, have already begun to form an opinion of just what constitutes his whole being. Even Trofimov, the student who pontificates on the subject of the failings of the Russian intelligentsia, cannot recognize what's going on in front of him. He is convinced that he and Anya are "above love" and that the "goal and meaning of their life" is to "avoid the petty and illusory, everything that prevents us from being free and happy." What he fails to recognize is that Anya is quite obviously in love with him. Thus we begin to see why nobody is capable of moving the action forward in this play; none but Lopahin are even remotely aware of what is really happening around them.

You may wish to divide students into groups, assigning each group several scenes and asking them to write a description of the action. Doing so may reveal to them that it is the reactions of the characters, and not the action itself, which forms the center of the play.

Possible Responses to Questions (p. 1177)

1. In the eighty years since *The Cherry Orchard* was first performed, critics have argued for both the comic and the tragic elements of the play. It obviously seems tragic at first, simply because of the unhappy ending. Furthermore, many of the characters seemed doomed by forces beyond their control. While students may need a little help in understanding the history of the play, once they realize that Firs was once the equivalent of the Southern slave in pre-Civil War America, they may be able to make the connection between the collapse of the plantation economy as a result of the Civil War and the downfall of the Russian aristocracy as a result (in part) of the emancipation of the serf. The characters in the play did not initiate either serfdom or emancipation; they are at the mercy of history here. The idea of fate, then, does suggest tragic elements in the play. Furthermore, the once-noble characters reflect the highborn heroes of classical tragedy—we suspect that the loss of the cherry orchard will have vast ramifications (even if only symbolic) for Russia itself. Trofimov articulates this sentiment in Act II:

   > All Russia is our orchard.. . . . Your orchard is a fearful place, and when you pass through it in the evening or at night, the old bark on the trees gleams faintly, and the cherry trees seem to be dreaming of things that happened a hundred, two hundred years ago and to be tormented by painful visions. . . . It's all so clear: in order to live in the present, we should first redeem our past, finish with it, and we can expiate it only by suffering. . . . (pp. 1160–1161).

   There is more than an echo of Aristotle in Trofimov's speech.

   It will probably be more difficult for students to envision the play as a comedy. They should recognize the humorous elements in Gayev's lofty speeches juxtaposed to his billiards talk, as well as in Yepihodov's many misfortunes, from squeaking boots to tripping over tables. But there are other comic elements here, too—elements of hope. Mme. Ranevskaya has seen many a calamity before this, and yet she retains her love of life, even after having lost a husband, a child, a lover, and all of her money We can expect that she will survive when she returns to Paris. Gayev, as well, will be taken care of. While he may not hang on to his new job, he is remaining among people who will look out for him. Even old Firs, forgotten at the doorstep of the locked-up house, will find in death the comfort he has been seeking since the "calamity" of emancipation. At the close of the play, his last speech, in fact, indicates a view of the events that contradicts Trofimov's: "Life has gone by as if I had never lived" (p. 1177). He who has seen it all recognizes the insignificance of everyday human problems—Russia will not be destroyed for the loss of a cherry orchard.

   You may find some students labeling the play tragicomic, probably the most reasonable response. Since it includes so many of the elements of tragedy and comedy and since it reflects the complexities of postindustrial living, it may well exemplify the tragicomic mode best.

2. Chekhov does not revere his characters as Ibsen does. He seems to pity these sad people.

   In Yepihodov, he presents us with the ultimate incompetent; the man cannot even walk across a room without some calamity befalling him. But the rest of the characters are genuinely fond of Yepihodov, as well they should be, for he is simply an exaggerated version of themselves: Mme. Ranevskaya throws gold away even though her servants are starving and she is about to lose her home; Anya is so caught up in her romantic notions about Trofimov that she is oblivious to his disdain for love; Trofimov himself entertains illusions of being a great spokesman for Russia; Gayev fancies himself a poet; Varya cannot decide between the spiritual life of a convent and a crassly materialistic life as Lopahin's wife; Lopahin's aggressiveness in business is of no use to him when it comes to proposing to Varya; and the minor characters' foibles help point out the human ineffectuality that permeates the play.

Chekhov treats these characters the way they treat Yepihodov, with fond amusement. When Mme. Ranevskaya weeps at the loss of the cherry orchard, Chekhov is kind to her. Lopahin, the very man who will destroy the orchard, comments, "Why, why didn't you listen to m? My dear friend, my poor friend, you can't bring it back now. . . . Oh, if only our wretched, disordered life were changed!" (p. 1169). His attitude is indicative of Chekhov's attitude toward his characters.

3. Of the many such passages in the play, perhaps the first is the most indicative of the purpose of disjointed dialogue. In Act I (pp. 1142–1143), we find a series of lines which don't seem to belong together. Mme Ranevskaya reminisces about her home, Gayev comments on the late train, Charlotta tells Pishchik that her dog eats nuts, Anya complains of the cold, Dunyasha announces that Yepihodov has proposed to her—all in the same scene. Nobody in this play ever really communicates with others; characters are more often than not talking to themselves. This impression of each character's being lost in his or her own world emphasizes Chekhov's theory that no action creates a unified reaction, that individuals respond to an event in vastly different ways. Other such conversations can be found throughout the play (i.e., p. 1153).

4. Students should take great pleasure in answering this question, since to the modern reader, nothing *does* happen in the play. It might be useful to ask students specifically what they disliked about the lack of action. This discussion frequently elicits the complaint that the whole play is leading up to the attempt to raise the money to save the orchard and the subsequent auction of the property, and yet both actions occur offstage.

Some students may also point out that expectations we have—about the Yepihodov-Dunyasha-Yasha triangle, or about Varya and Lopahin, or Anya and Trofimov, about Yasha and his mother, about Pishchik's financial woes—simply never are satisfied. We respond to a number of conflicts according to Chekhov's clues, but we are not rewarded in the normal way. There are no real climaxes in the play. A little prod may help students reach a conclusion about why Chekhov does this. The simple question "Why?" may help them to formulate possible reasons for this aberration from traditional dramatic form. Chekhov, of course, is more interested in the various reactions of the characters than he is in the culmination of one great action. His purpose is not to expose injustice (as in *A Doll House*) or to ridicule people's romantic notions (as in *Arms and the Man*), but instead to explore the ramifications of changes over which his characters have little control. If we were to become caught up in the action of *The Cherry Orchard*, we would lose sight of Chekhov's real focus, his characters' ability, or lack of ability, to cope with a changing social order.

5. Of course we expect Lopahin to propose to Varya in this scene; whether or not she'll accept is our only question. But Chekhov turns the tables on us: Varya is willing here—her distracted searching hides her discomfort as she anticipates his proposal—but Lopahin himself avoids the question. Part of the reasoning may lie in his ineffectuality when it comes to personal, rather than financial, dealings. He cannot convince Mme. Ranevskaya to subdivide the orchard in order to save herself from financial ruin; nor can he convince himself to marry Varya in order to save himself from a lonely future.

A deeper reason may be found in an examination of the couple's comments on the weather (so frequently used symbolically in this play). Lopahin offers that it was snowing last year at this time, while it's sunny now, but cold. Varya, on the other hand, hasn't noticed the weather, and adds, "And besides, our thermometer's broken." The two are worlds apart here: he is anticipating the profits from the destruction of the cherry orchard and facing the loss of his friends; she is aimlessly searching for something she's lost in the house. Varya's kind are on their way out in Russia—the aristocracy is crumbling—while Lopahin and his fellow businessmen are just beginning to realize both the rewards and the costs of their new financial status. These two represent the extremes of Russian society, its past and its future. They can never be united.

6. At the end of Act I, a shepherd's piping is heard as the stage empties. It is a soothing sound, reflecting a pleasant pastoral scene. However, the irony is that there is nothing pleasant about the situation, nor will the cherry orchard be pastoral much longer. The characters are fooling themselves into thinking that life can be the same as it was before financial ruin hit them.

Then, in Act II, we have the guitar playing and singing of Yepihodov and Yasha. It is apparently unpleasant, as Charlotta comments that their singing is "abominable." This singing emphasizes the discord in the household—the pleasant and pastoral will not last much longer. Later, Yepihodov's playing is described as "mournful," heightening the sense of impending doom.

In another scene, the Jewish orchestra is heard in the background, as the conversation turns from the problem at hand to the larger issues of the changes Russia has undergone in the past fifty years. According to Francis Fergusson, "when Chekhov wishes us to raise our eyes from the people in the foreground to the wider setting he often uses music as a signal and an inducement" (*"The Cherry Orchard*: A Theater-Poem of the Suffering of Change," *Chekhov: A Collection of Critical Essays*, Twentieth Century Views, Englewood Cliffs, NJ: Prentice-Hall, 1967, pp. 147-160). (Students may need assistance in recognizing this; if they are asked what happens to their attention when they and the characters hear music in the distance, they may understand Chekhov's technique better.)

Later in the scene, as the characters sit "plunged in thought" (p. 1159), we hear the sound of a string snapping, sending the characters onstage into speculation. Firs compares it to the sound of the owl screeching before "the calamity," emancipation. The sound hints of the calamity to come.

In Act III, in the midst of the new calamity, we have the ironic sounds of a billiards game and the orchestra at Mme. Ranevskaya's party. These sounds stand in stark contrast to what is happening in town, the auction of the property.

Finally, in Act IV, we hear the constant sound of the axes chopping down the cherry trees. No more music now; there can be no more pretending. The axes signal the end of an era for these people. We do not see them leaving the estate; we only hear the sound of doors locking and the carriages driving away—this emphasizes the emptiness of the stage. The final sounds, the repeated string snapping and the ax chopping, operate as does the door closing at the end of *A Doll House*. We recognize that these people have witnessed the end of life as they once knew it. A new era is emerging, destroying the old as the axes destroy the cherry trees.

7. While we never see the cherry orchard, the characters consistently refer to it. The orchard represents to Mme. Ranevskaya and her family their glorious past. In Act I, as she looks out into the orchard, Mme. Ranevskaya says, "Oh, my childhood, my innocent childhood" (p. 1150), and imagines that a white tree is her mother walking in the garden.

But the orchard, like their way of life, is doomed: In the beginning of Act II, the orchard is obscured by a row of poplars which "loom darkly" (p. 1153), and is overshadowed by telegraph poles and the outline of the city. All of these visual images symbolize the forces encroaching on the cherry orchard—the poplars indicating doom, the poles and the city indicating industrialization, the source of the doom.

That the orchard represents the old Russia is indicated in Trofimov's speech which begins, "All Russia is our orchard," when he calls it "a fearful place." He goes on to imagine that at night, "the cherry trees seem to be dreaming of things that happened a hundred, two hundred years ago and to be tormented by painful visions" (p. 1161). Thus what happens to the orchard is symbolic of what is happening to Russia: it signals the end of the old order.

Among other symbols is the concrete symbol of Varya's keys, which represent the family's continued ownership of the estate. When Lopahin announces that he has bought the property, she throws the keys on the floor before him.

The weather is also used as a symbol. Anya and Mme. Ranevskaya left in winter and return in spring with the hopes of a new life. But this spring is cold, like winter, and at the end of the play it is still cold. In the beginning of Act II, we are confronted with the visual symbols of the decline of the old order in the form of the abandoned church and the graveyard. There is irony in the concrete symbol of the telegrams from Paris. Mme. Ranevskaya keeps tearing them up, wishing to escape from her recent past, but she will ultimately return to Paris when she has nowhere else to go.

Characters function symbolically as well. The tramp in Act II, on his way to the railroad station, provides an ominous hint of what will happen to the family at the end as they, too head for the train station, penniless. Firs is a living symbol of the old order: Clinging to the old ways, he wanders about aimlessly, muttering to himself about the changes he's seen. His decline parallels the decline of life as these characters have known it.

The play is rich in symbols; students will probably find many more in addition to these.

Additional Topics for Writing and Discussion

1. Dreams are mentioned frequently in the play. What do they signify?

[From the opening scene, characters refer to sleep and dreams. The weary Anya longs for sleep when she arrives home, and when she asks Varya about her relationship to Lopahin, Varya replies, "it's all like a dream" (p. 1145). Mme Ranevskaya mistrusts her senses when she arrives home, exclaiming, "Can it really be I sitting here? . . . But maybe I am dreaming" (p. 1146). Other, less direct, references to dreams include Lopahin's lament "One tells you in plain language that your estate is up for sale, and you don't seem to take it in" (p. 1156), and Trofimov's accusation that "the only purpose of all our fine talk is to hoodwink ourselves and others" (p. 1159). These, and the many other references to dreams, underscore the fact that the central characters in this play act as though they were in a dream; they exercise no control over events happening around them; they are like sleepwalkers. Their hope that somehow everything will turn out all right is a dream, as is their clinging to a past that no longer exists. They are living in a dream world. Firs's lien at the end of the play, "Life has gone by as if I had never lived" (p. 1177), is a fitting description of the way these people have let their lives pass them by.]

2. What is the purpose of Charlotta's magic tricks?

[Like the dreams, Charlotta's antics emphasize what is happening to the central characters. Her tricks are based on illusion, just as the behavior of Gayev, Mme. Ranevskaya, and their family is based on the illusion that somehow, someone will save the cherry orchard.]

3. Of what significance are Anya and Trofimov to the play, both individually and as a couple?

[Regardless of students' various perceptions of these characters, what will probably emerge from responses is the notion of Anya and Trofimov's youth—they are Russia's future. Anya is lost in romanticism, Trofimov in philosophy; both are rather ineffectual. Their relationship isn't very promising either—neither can see the other for what he or she truly is.]

4. Based on what we know of them from the play, what do you suppose will happen to Mme. Ranevskaya, Gayev, and Lopahin after the play is over?

[This question should work well as a journal or small-group assignment. There are no absolutely right or wrong answers; as long as students use evidence from the play to support their speculations, their responses will be valid. In fact, the more varied the valid responses, the better.]

5. How does Firs's line at the end, "Life has gone by as if I had never lived" (p. 1177), appropriately sum up the play?

[As noted in the suggested response to question 1, this line describes the actions of someone in a dream. It also emphasizes, however, the fact that almost all the people in the play never *do* anything. Perhaps the reason why they do not act to save the orchard is that they subconsciously recognize the inevitability of change—anything they do will prove ineffectual in the face of history. In a larger sense, Firs's line suggests that *all* history progresses as if the individual had nothing to do with it. According to this play, change is inevitable.]

6. This play was written at the beginning of the modern era; the forces that influenced change at the turn of the century are still in effect today. Write several journal entries in which you explore the themes of *The Cherry Orchard* as being appropriate to contemporary society.

7. What does the party in Act III tell us about the central characters and the society in which they live?

[We see in this party just how out of touch wit reality Mme. Ranevskaya and her family are. The auction which will signal her eviction and the destruction of her way of life is taking place in town, and she hosts a party. The dancing and music emphasize the unreality of the scene. That an era has passed can be seen in the guests: no longer is the hall filled with nobility; instead we find the post-office clerk and the stationmaster. Charlotta entertains the crowd with her tricks, suggesting the illusion in which the central characters live. But throughout the act we are reminded of the reality of the situation, as Varya moves among the revelers, in tears, the keys on her belt symbolizing the soon-to-be lost possession of the estate.]

Arms and the Man • *Bernard Shaw (pp. 1178–1223)*

Students should have little trouble identifying with characters in this play; while it takes place around roughly the same time as the others in Chapter Nineteen, its romantic flavor can be found in many contemporary works. Students might enjoy imagining how the play would be presented to a contemporary television audience, for example. It seems to fit quite comfortably into the soap-opera genre, given its melodramatic quality. The Sergius-and-Raina story, as the two lovers perceive it in the beginning, would also be appropriate to the Harlequin Romance formula. If students are able to see these similarities, they should be better equipped to deal with Shaw's tongue-in-cheek attitude toward his characters.

The majesty of the Balkans described in the opening stage directions contributes to the romanticism, but then we also see the pretentiousness of the house; Shaw is offering us his commentary on the Petkoff "estate." With his character descriptions Shaw is far less subtle, however. We're not used to seeing so much editorial commentary. It might prove instructive for students to sight-read several of the early scenes after having closely read the character descriptions. Ask different students to interpret Raina's romanticism, or Sergius's self-importance, and the class can comment on similarities and differences among the performances.

There is little sustained suspense in the play; most conflicts are brought into the open shortly after having arisen. In fact, the only character in the play who remains in the dark throughout is Petkoff. Students may find this plot device difficult, especially if they have recently read *A Doll House*, in which the suspense remains until the end of the play. Shaw seems to undermine his climaxes here, to promote anticlimax instead. Rather than build everything up to fever pitch before resolving things, Shaw seems to slowly deflate his plot, until the climax unfolds precisely as we expect it to. Eric Bentley, in "The Making of a Dramatist (1892-1903)" (in G.B. *Shaw: A Collection of Critical Essays*, Englewood Cliffs, NJ: Prentice-Hall, 1965, pp. 57-75), asserts that Shaw revels in anticlimax:

> Where, in a well-made play, Bluntschli and Louka would have to soar to the heights of Raina and Sergius, in the Shaw play Raina and Sergius drop with a bump to the level of Bluntschli and Louka. Such is resolution by anticlimax. [p. 63]

To make up for the lack of suspense, Shaw offers us irony, a commodity found in abundance in the play. The characters constantly provide us with verbal irony, heightening our sense that appearance and reality are separated by a wide gulf in the Petkoff household. But the conflicts that produce this irony are not serious—even when Bluntschli finds himself pursued by enemy soldiers, or when Sergius challenges him to a duel, we never take the matter seriously. Why? This might be a good question for students to try to answer. How do playwrights convey their attitudes toward their characters and situations? If students were to compare several scenes from *A Doll House* and *Arms and the Man*, scenes in which characters confront one another with accusations, they might recognize how stage directions, tone, and diction reveal the intentions of the playwright. Such an exercise is useful in determining the more subtle differences between tragedy and comedy, but it should also help student writers to become more aware of how *they* can establish tone in their own writing.

As students discuss Shaw's attitude toward his characters, the question of the theme of the play should arise. Again, a comparison with Ibsen is informative. We have little trouble deciphering Ibsen's message at the end of *A doll House*, but what of the end of *Arms*? Has there been any movement? Has Shaw developed a statement about relationships between men and women? Here the notion of anticlimax might be reintroduced. Many scholars have trouble figuring out just what this man is trying to say; students are not alone in their confusion. His use of anticlimax may well go hand in hand with his trick of appearing to have tied things up neatly at the end, only to leave us wondering why we're a bit dissatisfied. The final lines of the play refer us right back to the title, and we're not much clearer on the definition of "man" at the end than we were in the beginning.

Possible Responses to Questions (p. 1223)

1. Before answering this, students should be sure to look up the terms *romance* and *satire* in the glossary. The romantic elements of the play have less to do with the love stories than they do with the idealistic portrayal of adventure.

   When we hear the story of Sergius's cavalry charge and when we see Raina's reaction to the news, we find ourselves in the firm grip of romance. But Shaw never provides us with a romantic moment without undermining it with satire. Shortly after Catherine relates the romantic version of the cavalry charge, for example, the fugitive deflates the tale. He does the same thing when Raina attempts to show her bravery when he threatens to shoot her if she cries out. She may be willing to die, but as he reminds her, she could never receive the cavalry in her bedroom, wearing only a nightgown.

   Shaw continually creates stories of romance, only to usher in satire. From the fugitive's ammunition bag filled with chocolates instead of bullets, to the much-touted "library" that turns out to be a single shelf half full of books, Shaw undermines romantic and idealistic notions of love, war, and social position. (If you wish to use this question for small groups, individuals within groups can choose one of these three categories.) But in the last scene, everything turns out as it should be. The realistic Bluntschli is revealed to be a hopeless romantic, and Shaw thus undermines his own satire with romance.

2. Shaw is second only to Ibsen in his careful use of stage directions; the sheer volume alone reveals how important they are to the play. Shaw's directions differ from Ibsen's, however, in that he includes a great deal of editorial commentary, particularly in his character descriptions. Raina is "intensely conscious of the romantic beauty of the night, and of the fact that her own youth and beauty are part of it" (p. 1179), Sergius is characterized by a "jejune credulity as to the absolute validity of his concepts and the unworthiness of the world in disregarding them" (p. 1195), and Petkoff is "naturally unambitious except a to his income and his importance in local society" (p. 1192).

   The setting, with its depiction of the Petkoff's shabby attempts at gentility against the majestic backdrop of the Balkans, underscores the play's theme of shattering illusions. These people are products of a magnificent natural setting, but they can see beauty only in prestige and wealth. Their ignorance of the social conventions that should accompany wealth and position is indicated in Shaw's descriptions of such things as the poor excuse for a library and the washing hung over the bushes.

   Finally, Shaw uses stage directions to emphasize characters' responses to various situations. The speed with which people move, their tone of voice, the facial expressions—all contribute to characterization and movement of plot. In his use of stage directions, Shaw acts more as a novelist or short-story writer than as a playwright.

3. Love and war are the classic subjects of literature, especially of drama, and Shaw underscores that point with his title. *Arms* refers quite literally to weapons of war, but various other weapons are used here as well, including innuendo (Louka's suggestions to Sergius about his lady), cruel words (Sergius's handling of Louka), coquettishness (Raina's flirtation with Bluntschli), and feigned subservience (Nicola's handling of his employers).

   Early in the play we become aware of the different connotations of "*man*" as well. The description of Sergius's cavalry charge defines "*man*" in terms of bravery in war, but then the fugitive Bluntschli undermines that image with his talk of fear, weariness, and survival by any means. Later Louka calls into question the manhood of Nicola because he has the "soul of a servant" (p. 1192). But Nicola proves to be a wise man, capable of manipulating his employers in order to realize his own goals. Sergius, Raina's "ideal man," confesses to Louka that there are a "half dozen Sergiuses who keep popping in and out of this handsome figure of mine" (p. 1198). And then when we and the entire cast think we have finally determined what a real man is—realized in the image of the realist Bluntschli—he confesses to a hopeless streak of romanticism, and we are all back where we started.

4. If this play is read after reading *A Doll House*, students may want to recall the strategies they used to determine the function of the secondary characters in that play.

Here, of course, Louka is more central to the play than Nicola, but the two reveal to us that love and war are not the sole properties of the aristocracy. Nicola uses strategies worthy of a general in outwitting his employers; Louka acts with the dignity and hauteur of a countess, even though she is a servant. Nicola, the realist, is closest in attitude to Bluntschli, as he too harbors a dream (opening his own shop in town).

Louka, on the other hand, reveals Raina's character through contrast. What Raina tries to achieve through coquettishness and manipulation, Louka attacks head on. For example, when Sergius will not let go of her in the garden, she pragmatically suggests that they move to a less conspicuous spot. Raina, although she finds herself attracted to Bluntschli, denies it and feigns haughty indifference. As a couple, they may reveal that a relationship based entirely on convenience is as lacking as one based on a false notion of romantic love. Their relationship is founded on an entirely different basis from that of Sergius and Raina: while the latter revel in idealistic superlatives, Louka and Nicola talk about helping each out socially and financially. Neither foundation provides a lasting bond.

5. Sight-reading may help students to tackle this one. As they read various passages, they can imagine how the characters are being portrayed.

Perhaps the most fruitful scene occurs in Act III, when Sergius challenges Bluntschli to a duel. Here we see the difference between their two definitions of "man." While Sergius is concerned with the appearance of nobility and fairness, Bluntschli's main concern is avoiding injury—to either party. Thus he mocks Sergius by choosing a machine gun as his weapon, and then by refusing to fight on horseback because "I don't want to kill you if I can help it" (p. 1215). Another possibility is a comparison of Sergius's account of the effect of war on men on p. 1197, and Bluntschli's on pp. 1208–1209.

In the end, of course, Sergius has learned the value of realistic assessment of a situation from Bluntschli, and Bluntschli has admitted his romantic temperament. So while the two appear throughout the play to be opposites, one the romantic and one the realist, Shaw doesn't let us off that easily. In the last scene, when Sergius says of Bluntschli, "What a man! Is he a man!" we can't be quite sure any more of what a man really *is*. At this point, the two actors may well appear interchangeable, whereas during the rest of the play we probably see a very proud, self-important Sergius and a hard, simple Bluntschli.

6. As responses to other questions indicate, Shaw turns the tables on us in the end. Throughout the play he pokes fun at romantic notions, shattering almost every illusion held by these characters. But in the end, we find the grand illusion intact: the two couples are finally united, and we expect them to live happily ever after.

While Raina and Sergius have seen the folly of their romanticized notions of one another, the new relationships are based on equally romantic foundations. Louka wins Sergius by reminding him of his promise that the next time he touches her she will be his fiancee, and Bluntschli wins Raina by confessing to his sense of romance and adventure.

It may take a little prodding for students to realize what Shaw has done here, but once they do they should enjoy the play all the more. Shaw is a true iconoclast: nothing, not even the belief in pragmatic realism, is sacred. Whether or not the characters have truly changed, their attitudes will never be known; to Shaw, that is not as important as having shattered any illusions they may have harbored in the past.

Additional Topics for Writing and Discussion

1. Find several instances of irony in this play, and discuss their purpose.

   [We find dramatic irony in several places: Sergius's apology to the women for telling the story of the soldier in the young lady's bedroom, not knowing that the story is about Raina; Catherine's account of Sergius's brave cavalry charge, when in fact he succeeded because of an accident; and (a more subtle instance) Sergius's welcoming Bluntschli as "our friend the enemy," thinking he is being ironic about the war, when in fact Bluntschli is his enemy in love. Shaw uses these incidents to heighten our awareness that appearance does not always coincide with reality in this play. Each instance of irony underscores the satire inherent in the play's theme.]

2. In *A Doll House*, Ibsen also shatters illusions about romantic love. But the two plays differ significantly in tone. Compare Ibsen's treatment of the subject to Shaw's, noting particularly the authors' attitudes toward their characters, as well as the implications of the plays.

   [This would make a good assignment for a standard critical essay. Students might note that Ibsen, while taking his characters more seriously than does Shaw, doesn't always *like* them as much as Shaw likes his. Ibsen shows hardly any sympathy for Torvald, and he simply uses Kristine, Rank and Krogstad to illustrate Nora's situation, offering little compassion for the characters themselves. Shaw, on the other hand, reveals sympathy for all his characters, even when he's laughing at them. There's no doubt that we want Sergius and Raina to be happy, silly as they may be.

   Another difference between the two dramatists lies in their tone. It's obvious that Shaw does not consider the situation in *Arms and the Man* to be of great significance. He treats war casually, never allowing us to think of the misery it creates. Love receives the same treatment here: nowhere do any of the characters seem devastated by losses in love. Ibsen, however, presents us with a situation in which a woman must leave her children in order to assert her dignity, knowing that she will face a life of hardship and ostracism.

   These comparisons point to the central difference between the two play: Shaw is writing about foibles; he likes his characters precisely because he doesn't take them seriously. By contrast, Ibsen is writing human rights; he cannot like characters who threaten the dignity of the individual.]

3. Imagine that you are Raina writing in your dairy after the "chocolate cream soldier" has left. Describe your adventure of the night before, and speculate on how this affects your relationship to your hero, Sergius. Remember that you are outrageously romantic, as well as quite taken by your own charms.

4. Nobody pays much attention to poor Petkoff in this play. Why do you suppose that is so? How does his character function in the play?

[Petkoff's description in the stage directions gives us our first clue as to why he seems so ineffectual: he is unambitious. And his scene with his wife reveals that he has long since given up arguing with her. When she haughtily tells him what peace terms she would have demanded, he humors her. The scene also hows his innocence, or ignorance, or social customs. His dissertation on the perils of washing prompts his wife to call him a "barbarian at heart." Later, when he is baffled by the mysteries surrounding his favorite coat, we seem him in the role of buffoon.

Answers will probably vary with respect to his purpose, but Shaw seems to have drawn this character with considerable affection: he represents, perhaps, the only way to handle a household caught up in hopelessly romantic pursuits. He simply doesn't pay too much attention, and lets things happen as they will, always confident that eventually he'll understand what's going on.]

5. Imagine the scene several months, or perhaps a year, after the curtain has come down. Choose either couple, Raina and Bluntschli or Louka and Sergius, and describe their relationship. Have the characters remained true to what they learned during the play? Who is the boss in each marriage? How does the boss exert his or her power?

[You may want to use this assignment to encourage practice of the entire writing process, from journal entries to final draft. In journal entries students can jot down the changes that take place within the characters during the play, and the bases for those changes. As they write in their journals, they should begin to recognize which pair would provide more information for a paper. Then they can engage in speculation, perhaps by composing a series about their characters. Once the questions are answered, students can decide how to write the description. It might make the assignment more exciting for students and more interesting for instructors if students are given the option of writing a straightforward description, a narrative, or a drama. If enough students choose different genres, the class can compare treatments in order to further their knowledge of the differences between genres.]

6. On the basis of this play, write a description of Bernard Shaw. If it helps to make up a few particulars, go ahead. But concentrate primarily on his world view, on his attitude toward life's problems, and on his romantic and/or realistic tendencies. Then find an actual biographical sketch of the man and compare it to yours. If there are discrepancies, how do you account for them? Is your sketch valid, even though it may not be true facts?

[The important part of this assignment lies the final question. Students may well stray far from the truth in characterizing Shaw, but if their responses are consistent with his character as revealed by his art, then they have shown insight into the playwright's character.]

The Stronger • *August Strindberg (pp. 1224–1228)*

August Strindberg's life was as intense and anguished as his drama. He has attracted droves of biographers over the years and during his own lifetime wrote nine autobiographical books. Born the fourth in a family of twelve children in Stockholm, Sweden, Strindberg was four years old when his father declared bankruptcy and thirteen when his mother died. The playwright sums up his childhood by claiming that he "was afraid of his brothers' fists, of the girls' hairpulling, of his grandmother's snubs, of his mother's birch, of his father's cane" (quoted by F.L. Lucas in *Ibsen and Strindberg*, Cassell, 1962). How much this tortured early life affected him can only be speculated, but certainly he grew to be a strange and haunted (although certainly gifted) adult.

He adopted (and discarded) a series of religious beliefs and was by turn Buddhist, Roman Catholic, and atheist (among others). Strindberg's relationships with women were distinctly strange. We can perhaps best understand the perplexity and frustration of his three wives and many lovers by considering this anecdote from Lucas's book concerning his second wife. Strindberg had left Frida behind while he took a vacation with friends. After a few days, he complained that he had had no mail from his wife. When six days passed with no letter, he declared the circumstance grounds for divorce. His friends, trying to comfort him, suggested that Frida might not know their exact location and asked if he were sure he had given her the address. His response suggests both both his eccentricity and his need to dominate: I did *not!*" Am I bound to render account to my wife of where I go to stay!"

In addition to his domineering qualities, he also entertained mad fantasies. For example when his first child, a daughter, died shortly after birth, he tortured himself by insisting that his wish for her death had killed her. Even before this mental breakdown in the 1890s, he had been deeply superstitious, imagining that advertising signs or initials written on walls contained hidden messages predicting and dictating his future actions.

If any theme runs through these bizarre adventures, it is Strindberg's problems with women. Whether he was fearing his mother's birch, railing against her death (or against the stepmother who replaced her in one year's time), or abusing one of his wives or mistresses, he showed his misogyny. This quality runs through many of his plays. The mean-spirited and domineering Mrs. X in *The Stronger* serves as a prototype for the way Strindberg viewed what the nineteenth century called "the new woman."

The Stronger demonstrates Strindberg's experimental approach to drama. The two characters are named symbolically rather than realistically, the set is starkly simple and the action comprises entirely the monologues of one character who "talks at" the other for the duration of the drama.

Possible Responses to Questions (p. 1228)

1. It is difficult to assess Mr. X accurately since we know only what Mrs. X tells us about him. We must base our judgment on a unreliable narrator and highly contradictory pictures. For instance, in the early part of her monologue, Mrs. X pictures Mr. X as a comic bombast who imagines he controls his household by insulting the servants behind their backs. He seems a blustery coward. In the next breath, Mrs. X assures Miss Y (and herself) that her husband has never cheated on her. Since we later come to suspect strongly that he has, in fact, has an affair with Miss Y, we can hardly find this characterization entirely credible. Still, we are left to wonder. Was the affair with Miss Y an unusual event, a truly loving relationship that Mr. X allowed himself to feel only when she was apparently "safely" engaged? Or are we to believe that it is just as likely that he had an affair with the would-be actress Frédérique? Miss Y's lack of success in the theater and Mrs. X's implication that the "violent friendship" between her and Mr. X is over suggest that he may be simply a cold-hearted user who welcomes unencumbered relationships and that he may promise roles he has to deliver to lure unwitting young actresses. In her final speech of the play, Mrs. X proclaims her husband to be a wonderful lover (taught "how to love": by Miss Y) to whom she now wishes to return. The saccharine portrait is extremely hard to believe and is almost certainly a bitter rationalization aimed partly at convincing herself that she has won out over Miss Y and partly at providing a final, killing shot to any shred of self-esteem Miss Y may have left.

2. Although we are never entirely sure what the "truth" is, Mrs. X's mode seems to be primarily rationalization. Certainly the early speech about Mr. X rationalizes his relationships with women. Note the speech that begins, "And when he gets angry . . ." and the long speech after that beginning, "And when he come, he goes hunting for his slippers. . . ." Here she first makes Mr. X (Bob) sound foolish, and then she goes one to describe how he admits honestly to the temptations he faces from young actresses. If Bob does make such admissions, the chances are that he does so to avert his wife's growing suspicions. Mrs. X, however, rationalizes his ploy as simple frankness, with the explanations offered to prevent the sting of any gossip Mrs. X may hear. At the end of the play, her rationalization is quite different. She then acknowledges that Bob has cheated on her, but she puts the best possible face on the affair, taunting Miss Y with the idea that the illicit relationship is over and that she, Mrs. X, will benefit after all because Miss Y has taught her husband "how to love."

   Only in the speech beginning "Our relationship was such a strange one . . ." and in the first part of the speech beginning "Don't Speak! You Needn't say a word!" does Mrs. X appear to understand and acknowledge the truth both to herself and to Miss Y. She admits that when she first met Miss Y she "was so frightened that I didn't dare let you out of my sight." Certainly that fear indicated a foreshadowing of the danger Miss Y proved to be. In addition to her relationship with Mr. X, we learn that Miss Y also seduced (in the emotional sense) Mrs. X. The betrayal of the affair, then, was a double treachery that Mrs. X finds painfully difficult to admit.

3. Most students will see Miss Y as the stronger. Her silence is eloquent and powerful, and one imagines an extremely talented actress with a wide range of pantomime skills playing the role. A shrug, a lifted eyebrow, or a series of increasingly loud laughs allow Miss Y to express her responses more intensely than she might have with words. Mrs. X, of course, claims to have won the battle because Miss Y is no longer involved with Mr. X. What Mrs. X does not acknowledge is her own painful recognition of weakness that results from her having been disillusioned both by her husband and by Miss Y, whom she has both feared and admired. By remaining silent, Miss Y neither agrees to nor denies Mrs. X's charges. Miss Y seems to put herself above the emotional ranting of Mrs. X and to suggest that she has made peace with herself.

   On the other hand, some students may see Miss Y's silence as a kind of defeat. After all, she no longer has a relationship with Mr. X, and there is evidence to suggest that she may have been just one of many to him. If Mr. X is viewed as a "prize," Miss Y certainly does not win the confrontation. She is left with her career ruined and her engagement broken, alone on Christmas Eve. Her silence may indicate an emotional death that permits only outward ironic gestures and has left no life within. In this alternative (and somewhat less plausible) reading, Mrs. X would been seen as the stronger because she has managed to endure in the relationship she desires. Unlike Miss Y, she has a career, a husband, and children.

4. Calling the characters "X" and "Y" makes them seem like examples in a case study. They are the classic spurned wife and "other woman" in some senses. We do, in fact, know that Miss Y is named "Amelie," so the labels clearly have symbolic intent, suggesting that the characters' situations have a universal quality. Miss Y never speaks for herself, so we have only Mrs. X's analysis of the situation; we are left to infer how (or if) Miss Y would have defended herself. Mr. X remains a mystery; if we saw him, we would be able to tell how accurately his wife's analysis of the triangle really is. With Bob's remaining offstage, the audience if left with a wide range of speculations.

5. The play is set in a cafe on Christmas Eve. a traditionally lonely time for the "other woman" in an affair. The setting emphasizes Miss Y's isolation and Mrs. X's cruelty in pursuing her relentless monologue about Miss Y and Mr. X. In a social situation with others present, we would have many points of view rather than the one point of view offered in this stark, lonely setting.

6. When Mrs. X enters, Miss Y simply looks up, nods, and resumes reading, indicating, perhaps, that she does not really want to engage in conversation. Very soon, Miss Y expresses disdain, then makes a gesture of fright (when the toy gun appears); and when Mrs. X discusses tulips, Miss Y "looks up from her magazine with an expression of irony mixed with curiosity." For a lively exercise, ask several groups of students to rehearse just these opening gestures and expressions (with two students playing the roles and at least one other in each group serving as director). Then have the groups present their interpretations, with the audience evaluating the different meanings suggested by the various interpretations of those playing Mrs. X and Miss Y.

Additional Topics for Writing and Discussion

1. Discuss the significance of the toy gun.

[Beginning with Mrs. X's earliest speeches, she seems the stereotyped bitch who pushes every emotional button she can find in her verbal envelopment of Miss Y. Mrs. X taunts her companion by reminding her that she has has been dismissed from her acting position and that she has missed the chance to be married and have children (unlike Mrs. X, who brags about the gifts she has purchased for her offspring). The violence of this outwardly civilized meeting is underscored by the toy gun Mrs. X pulls from her bag. Her comments indicate that Miss Y has feared a real gun, a foreshadowing that alerts us to watch for motivations for Miss Y's defensive reaction.]

2. What do you think Mrs. X means when she says at the end of her second speech, ". . . you mean to say? . . . Ah but there is a certain difference, don't you think?" What might Miss Y have implied by her look that would make Mrs. X respond in this way?

[As Mrs. X speculates on the dreary future of a bridge who reads the comics at the wedding reception while her groom plays billiards with her friends, Miss Y might have given her a look that says, "Who are you to talk. Communication in your own marriage is nonexistent. You both go your separate ways." Mrs. X might then defensively respond that the situation in her relationship with Bob is different—perhaps because she see their separate lives as socially above what she considers the tawdry and "lower-class" actions of the bridge and groom she has described."]

3. Note the many references to slippers (along with the stage business). What is suggested about the husband's character by these references?

[A particularly representative segment begins with Mrs. X's eighth speech when she shows Miss Y the pair of slippers she has embroidered for the person she ironically calls her "better half." While she claims to do everything to please Bob—such as embroidering tulips on the slippers, she manages to suggest that he is finicky and childishly emotional. She uses the slippers as puppets to suggest Bob's actions when he becomes angry with the maids and Miss Y joins her in meanspirited laughter as they both contemplate his foibles and idiosyncrasies.]

5. Imagine this play with Mrs. X as the silent character. Write several speeches for Miss Y, with stage directions indicating the gestures and reaction of Mrs. X.

CHAPTER TWENTY

The Theater of the Absurd

This chapter introduces perhaps the most difficult form of drama for students to grasp. Absurdist conventions—including lack of plot, disconnected and sometimes incoherent dialogue, dimensionless characters, and bizarre sets—provide the audience with an extremely disorienting experience. Of course, disorientation is precisely the purpose of these conventions. The dramatist, viewing life as meaningless and disconnected, asks the audience to actually experience that feeling. Perhaps students can understand absurdist drama better if they make the connection to abstract art. In each case we are presented with the artist's own perception of reality, rather than with a generally agreed-upon objective view. The audience must see the world through the eyes of the artist.

In absurdist drama, the key word is *alienation*. Absurdist dramatists consider humans to be alienated, divorced from any context previously provided by history, religion, or philosophy. The existential view of the human being facing the cosmos alone is illustrated in these plays by the inability of characters to communicate with one another. When the audience feels that lack of communication and is disturbed by it, then the dramatist has achieved his or her purpose.

The Lesson is an appropriate introduction to the theater of the absurd, given its central image of the destructive power of language.

The Lesson • *Eugène Ionesco (pp. 1231–1252)*

For students, the first unsettling thing about this play is that there is no social context in which to place the action. We can think about the political climate of Ibsen's Norway or the social upheaval of Chekhov's Russia, but this play simply has no climate: it is of no particular time or place. The apartment is innocuous; all we know of the surroundings is that there is a small town below. The country is unimportant, as is the era.

Equally unsettling is the fact that these characters are not real people with personality traits or values. The lines they speak have virtually nothing to do with the action, and thus the action seems to take place entirely without motivation.

None of the techniques we normally use to read drama seem to apply to this play. It is necessary, then, for students to try to develop an alternative method for approaching it. Perhaps the most nonthreatening way to begin discussion is to ask students to articulate the difficulties they encounter in reading the play. The ensuing list will certainly touch upon some of the problems mentioned above.

If students simply ask "Why?" they may begin to grasp the concept of Theater of the Absurd. For example, when they ask why the Professor keeps talking about language, they may begin to see that language is precisely what he is using to gain power over the Pupil. When they ask why the characters have no personalities, they may consider that Ionesco wants us to think more about the idea of power than its effect upon particular individuals. Such questions should make students feel more comfortable with the play, and lead them to a sufficient understanding of its central theme.

Martin Esslin comments on the theme of *The Lesson* in his *The Theater of the Absurd* (New York: Anchor, 1961):

> This is a demonstration of the basic impossibility of communication—words cannot convey meanings because they leave out of account the personal associations they carry for each individual. . . . Here language is . . . shown to be an instrument of power. [p. 95]

Esslin interprets the sexual imagery in the play as reflecting the sexual nature of all power, and he responds to questions about Ionesco's choice of a tutorial as his vehicle with the following explanation:

> What Ionesco is saying is that even behind so apparently harmless an exercise of authority as the teacher-pupil relationship, all the violence and domination, all the aggressiveness, the cruelty and lust are present that make up any manifestation of power. (p. 96)

If the theme of the play is the exercise of power, pure and simple, what better way to portray it than in an unspecified place, using undeveloped characters? Once students come to terms with the fact that Ionesco has adapted the genre to fit his needs, they should enjoy an ever greater understanding of the relationship between form and content.

Possible Responses to Questions (p. 1252)

1. It may be difficult for students to respond emotionally to much of this play, simply because the characters are difficult to identify with. They should be able to recognize their sympathy for the Professor early in the play, perhaps mixed with some pity for this timid little man. But as the play progresses, the most likely emotion for students to feel will be fear. As the Professor becomes more and more frenzied, as his sadistic tendencies begin to take shape, a sense of uneasiness arises. Now and then the tension is alleviated by humor, but even the humor becomes grim as the toothache develops from the cause of a girl's distraction from her lessons into a pain searing through her whole body. Obviously, the ending elicits horror. Not only do the Professor and the Maid treat murder as a minor annoyance, but the audience realizes that this play represents one element in a long pattern.

2. The comedy in the play is true to the title given this genre; it is absurd. From the first halting lessons in naming seasons and adding numbers through the elaborate "translation" sessions, we are presented with situations so bizarre that our only response can be laughter.

   A pupil cannot subtract 1 from 3, but she can rattle off the answer to a question involving billions at the drop of a hat. The notion that the Professor can teach her "fundamental principles of . . . linguistic and comparative philology" in fifteen minutes is an absurd parody of education. His contention that the word for "France" in Italian is "Italy"—since when the Italian says "My country is Italy," he or she means the same thing as does the French person who says "My country is France" — is so absurd, and yet so naggingly logical, that we have to laugh.

   What students should begin to realize as they compare responses to this question is that all of the comedy revolves around *communication*. Language, as well as its power, lies at the center of this play. The play says two things at the same time: it is absurd to think that language really fosters communication, but at the same time it is the power of language that allows us to dominate others.

212

3. Of course, students will recognize the parody of rote learning here. Nothing that the Pupil already knows is of any real use to her, and what the Professor imparts is gibberish. But students may need help in recognizing the underlying satire. They should readily see that the Professor and the Pupil do not communicate with one another: she cannot understand his explanation of subtraction, and he ignores her pain when she develops the toothache. And yet, on pp. 1242–1245, they actually complete each other's sentences, even words. The play ridicules our belief that language is what binds us together, what allows us to share our feelings and ideas. In fact, Ionesco implies that language is what forever separates us, what allows one person (or political entity) to dominate another. The "lesson" ultimately kills the Pupil, as it has killed forty before her and will kill an infinite number of new pupils after her.

4. If students pay close attention to the interchanges between the Maid and the Professor, they should recognize the mother-son relationship. Her warnings that "philology leads to calamity" are words of a rather ineffectual mother trying to keep her strong-willed son out of trouble. And when she returns after he has killed the Pupil, she sounds like a scolding mother. As he tries to deny responsibility for the murder, she retorts, "And who was it? Who was it then? Me? . . . Or the cat?" She tells him that he should be ashamed of himself, and even throws in her own version of an "I told you so." Later she relents, assuring him that he's "a good boy in spite of everything." What they may miss on first reading is that the Professor tries to stab her when her back is turned, but she is far too quick for him. Her reaction, "You wanted to do that to me? I'm not one of your pupils, not me!" indicates that she is aware of his desire to escape from her domination. Since he cannot dominate her, he dominates his pupils. Her role is central to the theme of power and control.

5. Ionesco is telling us that language divides and conquers rather than unites, that attempts to understand knowledge are fruitless, since those who lay claim to knowledge have all the power over those who seek to learn. What students may be reluctant to acknowledge are the sexual "lessons" of the play. As they read the initial stage directions, however, they should recognize that the Professor feels his power as a sexual dominance; his lewd glances at the Pupil become more frequent and pronounced as the play proceeds. And the murder scene itself is described in such a way that it suggests rape as well: the weapon, the positions of the characters, the sounds, and the aftermath all carry heavy sexual overtones. So Ionesco is also talking about the sexual nature of power, and the relationship between lust and cruelty.

6. Responses will vary. Students may want to actually stage several scenes of the play in order to get the feel of its direction. The play can be produced very seriously, with characters acting as though they were actually communicating, or comically, almost slapstick, with characters acutely aware of the absurdity of their dialogue. Pacing will be important, since a performance of *The Lesson* has to be permitted enough time for viewers to perceive the subtle changes that overtake the characters.

Additional Topics for Writing and Discussion

1. At what point in reading the play did you begin to realize that the nature of the lesson has little to do with the plot? How did you adjust your reading of the play as a result?

[This question is ideal for journal responses. To many students, theater of the absurd is an entirely new genre; they are used to following realistic characters through a discernible series of actions that lead to a climax. Thus they need to reassess how they approach a play. Students should be encouraged to share their responses with the class, thereby generating a discussion just what this type of theater intends to accomplish, and how playwrights like Ionesco view the theater.]

2. Write a short prose version of *The Lesson*. What is lost in the translation? Why do you suppose the material cannot be related in another genre?

[Like the previous question, this one should help students understand both the difference between two genres and the unique nature of theater of the absurd. The class will probably get more than a few laughs out of the prose versions, most of which will be no more than a paragraph. That response is healthy; after their initial recognition that this play simply cannot be translated into prose, students should begin to recognize why. The discrepancy between the dialogue and the action is the problem; in this play we have almost pure drama, a form in which the meaning is carried not by words, but by action. While Ionesco provides us with an extreme here, all drama depends on action to convey meaning.]

3. The murder scene is described as if it were really a rape scene. How does Ionesco prepare us for this vision? What is the purpose of the sexual imagery?

[In the character description of the Professor, Ionesco tells us that "occasionally a lewd gleam comes into his eyes and is quickly repressed," and that by the end of the play, "the lewd gleams in his eyes will become a steady devouring flame." We see the repressed gleam in several instances, and then, as the Professor begins his lecture on linguistics, he uses the most sensual terms, describing air passing over vocal chords "delicately, caressingly," as they "agitate, vibrate . . . or uvulate . . . or sibilate. . . ." But in this same speech he includes hints of violence as well. After his first violent physical gesture, he calls the Pupil "my pet," thus reinforcing the connection between sexuality and violence and domination. Just as language, which purports to unify us, is used for domination here, so too is sexuality. Instead of unifying and creating life, it divides and destroys life.]

4. On p. 1244, the Professor recounts a story of a comrade who had a serious pronunciation problem. According to the Professor, the man "pronounced filly instead of filly, Firmin instead of Firmin, French bean instead of French bean. . . ." How do you react to this speech initially? Does your reaction change as you continue with the play?

[While, on first reading, the story is comical in its absurdity, it becomes frightening later, as we realize that this man can tell his Pupil anything and she will believe it. The notion of domination through language is beginning to take hold here. Even though what the Professor says is pure gibberish, it is feeding his sense of power and further weakening the Pupil.]

5. Ionesco tells us that as the Pupil grows weaker, the Professor becomes stronger, and he reveals that process throughout the play. Through what devices does he indicate that the Professor is actually draining the strength from the Pupil in order to increase his own strength?

[Several instances of this appear in the play. At first the two are seated across the table from one another, but as the Pupil begins to encounter difficulty, the Professor draws away from her. Her immediate response is a hesitancy in her answers to him. During that same scene, as he tries to explain subtraction to her, he uses removing her fingers and nose and eating her ear as examples. As he walks back and forth on the stage, he seem to gain strength in direct proportion to her loss of it as she twists around to keep him in sight. Perhaps the clearest indication of the transfusion taking place occurs when he begins completing her sentences, and she his on p. 1245. There is no lifeline between the two, but he is drawing the life out of her. By the end of the play she is little more than a shell. When he finally kills her, he draws the last life out of her and shudders with a violent convulsion, as if the act has physically affected him as well.]

6. Imagine that you are Ionesco responding to a traditionalist who cannot understand how you can call this thing a play. The traditionalist points to such problems as lack of social context, characters who really do not represent people, and incoherent dialogue. How do you explain your play?

[If students have recognized that Ionesco is taking liberties with the genre in order to better convey his meaning, they should enjoy answering the critic. They can use many of the responses to the questions above to explain to the traditionalist that the lack of characterization, for example, emphasizes the fact that the play is about the *idea* of power, that the incoherent lectures on language illustrate the fact that language does *not* communicate, and that the lack of a social context underscores the notion that power itself is destructive, regardless of the context.]

CHAPTER TWENTY-ONE

A Collection of Twentieth-Century Plays

Riders to the Sea • *John Millington Synge (pp. 1255–1262)*

Although John Millington Synge wrote mainly about the rural Irish Catholic Peasantry, he was born into a wealthy, Protestant landholding family outside of Dublin. Synge made the connection with a world very different from his own through a series of circumstances and interests. First, because of his poor health, he was kept from school and grew up relatively isolated from peers who would have reinforced the values of the Protestant aristocracy. Separated from others his own age, he became an avid observer of the people and country side around him. He learned to listen carefully and watch intently, often recording what he saw and heard in a journal. His isolation also led him to study on his own and he became fascinated with science. At 16, led by this interest, he read Darwin and then began to doubt and challenge the accepted religious beliefs of his family, taking a skeptical view toward dogmatic, organized religion. Another interest, also developed to fill the space left empty by his lack of companions, was music. Music provided the final bridge between Synge and the broad world that lay outside the narrow village in which he lived. He traveled to Germany, France, and Italy, learning and playing music with whomever he met. Yeats described him as "playing his fiddle to Italian sailors and listening to stories in the Bavarian mountains" (quoted by J. F. Lydon in his essay "John Millington Synge: The Man and His Background" in *Mosaic*, Spring 1971). When Synge returned from the continent, he became deeply interested in Irish politics and in the plight of Irish peasants. He, William Butler Yeats, and Lady Gregory (among others) founded the Abbey Theatre in Dublin, and he spent the rest of his short life (he died at 38) gathering material for and writing his plays. He thought nothing of becoming a tramp, sleeping in ditches, and eating half-rotten food if it afforded him a chance to talk to the Irish men and women whose stories of the past mesmerized him and whose current living conditions moved him deeply. His plays, perhaps more than any others, bring the Irish peasantry—with all its virtues, flaws, foibles, strengths, and weaknesses—to the eyes of the world.

Although *Riders to the Sea* concerns rural Irish peasants in the nineteenth century, its theme is universal. Most students will know people whose lives are stunted by futilely repeated efforts. These people are caught in a cycle from which they could escape, yet they refuse to make the decisions necessary to free themselves from their self-defeating actions.

Possible Responses to Questions (p. 1263)

1. Certainly if we are using the standards of Aristotelian tragedy, *Riders* does not qualify completely. There is no character of high estate who falls from a position of power and happiness because of a tragic flaw. Still, the play has tragic elements. Certainly fate plays an important role. The young priest has assured Maurya that God will not take Bartley and leave her without a son to care for her. The sea, however, operates outside the Christian framework. Steadily, inexorably, it has claimed every one of Maurya's male protectors. She cannot protect Bartley with her prayers and her worrying. The play's climax comes

with Maurya sees the vision of Michael and recognizes her lack of control over the power of the sea. Once she admits this, she is able to reconcile herself to Bartley's death and to Michael's. As Thomas Kilroy suggests in his essay "Synge the Dramatist," she "attains tragic stature because [she] finds a freedom in isolation within [herself] . . . [she] attains a splendid isolation, self-containment, rising above the community of the play . . . with a contempt for the values that are left behind" (*Mosaic*, Spring 1971).

2. The characters speak in the dialect of Irish peasants. For example, Nora and Cathleen call Maurya "herself," giving her both affection and the respect due the oldest woman in the household. All the characters sprinkle their speech liberally with "God help us," or "The Son of God forgive us," or "The blessing of God on you." Still the Christian speech seems to be merely an external trapping, automatic phrases used superstitiously to ward off disaster. At the end of the play, Maurya acknowledges that her trips for holy water and her prayers have been for naught. She has been unable to win out against darker forces. We see hints of the supernatural in her vision of Michael, which portends both the news of his death and Bartley's drowning accident. The sea (and perhaps, by implication, the old wrathful gods of natural forces) overpower the young priest's feeble assurances that "Almighty God won't leave her destitute with no son living."

3. Both daughters are concerned about their mother, but Cathleen, the elder, is sharper and takes her mother to task. For instance, when Maurya allows Bartley to go off to market without her blessing, it is Cathleen who scolds her and urges her to catch up with him. Cathleen also takes charge more than Nora does. The older sister hides the bundle of clothes and later directs the examination of the garments and then urges that the sad evidence be hidden from Maurya until Bartley returns from his voyage. When Maurya returns and tells of her astonishing vision, Cathleen gently insists that she could not have seen Michael because he is dead. As the play closes, Cathleen is once again taking charge of the family concerns. She asks the men to make a coffin and explains to Nora (who thinks her mother's lack of tears at Bartley's death means she loved Michael better) that Maurya is old and that she has exhausted herself with the depth of her weeping for the nine days since Michael was reported drowned.

4. Maurya is the play's protagonist, an old woman who has suffered greatly and who comes to a epiphany of grief at the end of the play. She recognizes that she can now let go of all her worrying and fearing. She has experienced her worst nightmare and nothing else can touch her. The actress who plays Maurya must be able to depict a simple peasant woman convincingly for the earlier scenes with Nora and Cathleen when she scolds and goads them and for her scene with Bartley when she tries to convince him not to go to sea. But she must also be able to project an existential transcendence in her moving final speech. Students may enjoy naming actresses who might be recruited for the role.

5. The nets and oilskins that hang on the kitchen walls suggest that the sea and its related occupations are an integral part not only of the men who work at sea, but also of the women who wait for them in the cottage. Cathleen sits at the spinning wheel as the play opens, suggesting the spinning wheel of fate that pulls together, inevitably, the threads of human lives. The boards, we learn, have been purchased for Michael's coffin. The sea, fate, and death, then, are the central residents of the cottage kitchen. Other props include Michael's clothes, the rope (intended to lower Michael into his grave, but taken by Bartley to lead his horse), the shawl Maurya puts over her head, and the bread Maurya takes to Bartley (an intended communion that ends as last rites).

218

6. Bartley is, of course, a literal "rider to the sea," but the title clearly implies a great deal more. All the men in Maurya's life have been drawn to (or forced to) the sea to make a living. In spite of the terrible dancers and the losses they face, these men move (ride) through their lives knowing that, at the end, the sea will claim them. As is discussed in question 5, the props of the play show the domination of the sea, as do the dialogue and actions of the characters as they ask each other about the condition of the sea, go to the window to watch the approach of the shops, and so on.

Additional Topics for Writing and Discussion

1. Why is the information concerning the deaths of Maurya's husband, father-in-law, and first four sons withheld until near the end of the play? How would the play be changed if the audience knew about these losses from the beginning?

[If the catalogue of deaths were given at the beginning, the reader would almost certainly know that Maurya's prayers for her last son would be in vain. As it is, we hold some of the same hopes she does as she listens fearfully to the reassurances of the priest. Then when the enormity of the past deaths is revealed, we feel the profound emptiness in Maurya's life and shudder with the recognition that she is doomed once again to be bereaved.]

2. What are we to make of Maurya's vision of Michael? Does she really see a ghost? Does she imagine him? Why is he described as wearing new shoes?

[The play allows for an aura of mysticism which is powerful whether Maurya's vision is seen as an actual supernatural event or as a projection of her deeply troubled heart and soul. Since she sees the image before she actually knows Michael is dead, the apparition indicates her profound sense of dread and foreboding, as well as her growing understanding that the deaths in her life have all been connected—father leading son and brother leading brother to the same fate. Perhaps Michael wears new shoes because he is walking a new path; he has already gone to his own death and now he plays a new role as he guides Bartley to the inexorable sea.]

3. Note how Cathleen and Nora react to their brother's clothes as they examine them. Do you find this scene convincing?

[As the sisters look at the clothing, their dialogue reflects both their dread and their struggle to hold on to hope that the drowned body is not their brother Michael. They search for explanations of why the shirt may not be his and only accept the truth when they discover the undeniable evidence of the sock with the telltale dropped stitch. Anyone who has sat waiting for news of someone they love who is in danger will identify painfully with the combination of fear, denial, hope Nora and Cathleen embody as they examine the bundle of clothes.]

4. What is the significance of the comments made by the men who come to the cottage after Bartley's death? How do they compare or contrast with Maurya's speeches?

[While the men think only of the practicality of making Bartley's coffin and wonder aloud why Maurya has not thought of buying nails, the bereaved mother shows herself to be a figure larger than life. Her final speeches create the powerful resolution of the play as she admits her losses and describes her gain. No longer will she worry and fret. The sea has taken from her all that it can. She has nothing to lose and so now can endure life without constant anxiety and fear. Her terrible acceptance of fate provides a model of the courage to endure the unendurable.]

Trifles • *Susan Glaspell (pp. 1264–1274)*

Although *Trifles* was published in 1916, its theme is remarkably timely. The characters play out the traditional roles assigned to men and women, yet the ironic ending issues a strong challenge to those stereotypes.

When she wrote *Trifles*, Glaspell was living in Greenwich Village earning a living through her writing and collaborating with her husband, George Cram Cook, on producing and directing experimental drama. Yet the characters in *Trifles* who assert the rights of women to be respected and to lead productive, dignified lives are not big-city professionals or social rebels. Instead they are farm women, drawn perhaps from Glaspell's memories of her early years in Davenport, Iowa, where she had the opportunity to observe and evaluate the rural characters who appear in many of her writings.

Possible Responses to Questions (p. 1274)

1. The men in Glaspell's play assume that women's work is trivial and far less important then their work. Note, for instance, the exchange over the fruit which ends with Hale commenting that "women are used to worrying over trifles." Of course it is just such "trifles" that lead Mrs. Hale and Mrs. Peters to find the motive for the murder which the men, with their self-important posturing, fail to discover. The men condemn Mrs. Wright because she doesn't have clean towels. They are ready to see what women *do not* do when their own sensibilities are offended, but they fail to ask themselves why. Mrs. Hale and Mrs. Peters, on the other hand, are not quick to judge their neighbor, but wonder instead if one of the sheriff's men might not have soiled the towel. The women notice the "trifles" that make the workload in their lives unnecessarily heavier, whereas the men casually criticize the imprisoned Mrs. Wright's housekeeping skills because in their own minds they have not been properly "taken care of" as they tear apart her house looking for a motive for murder. They are more interested in a clean towel for their hands than they are in trying to understand Mrs. Wright—for whatever reasons, judicial or humane.

   Students' responses will differ regarding the title of the work. Certainly "A Jury of Her Peers" suggests the discrepancies in a system of justice where (especially in 1916 when this play was written) the power rests primarily in the hands of men. Mrs. Hale and Mrs. Peters "try" Mrs. Wright and find her innocent on the grounds of justifiable homicide. Given the evidence of the dead bird, a male jury might well have made a different decision.

2. The country attorney is officious and self-important. He patronizes the women (for example, inviting them up to the fire as though the house is his). Mr. Hale is impressed with the murder investigation and shows himself to be a rather simple man who is none too brave (he wanted his friend to go upstairs with him once Minnie had told him her husband was dead). He shows his attitude toward women when he admits that he was going to appeal to Minnie to get a party telephone line installed. He clearly thinks that as a woman, she would favor the idea of a telephone that would provide communication with her neighbors. Hale also is the character who notes that "women are used to worrying over trifles"; ironically, in his speech he shows that he, in fact is caught up with the trivia of life. The sheriff is busy defending himself and his methods to the county attorney. He looks hurried in the room and pronounces, "Nothing here but kitchen things." Yet it is among the "kitchen things" that the women eventually find the evidence of what happened.

3. Although Mrs. Peters is more reluctant than Mrs. Hale to excuse Minnie Wright, she is willing to hear what Mrs. Hale has to say. As the two discover the evidence together, they also discuss experiences that were typical, especially in their day, for women. Mrs. Hale describes Minnie's pleasure in singing in the choir when she was a young girl and her loss of joy once she was married to Mr. Wright, including her inability even to belong to the Ladies Aid Society because of John Wright's penure. When Mrs. Hale and Mrs. Peters discover the canary and speculate on what its loss must have meant to Minnie, Mrs. Peters says, "I know what stillness is," and she recalls the loss of her first child during the years she and her husband were homesteading. Mrs. Peters also remembers her feelings when her childhood pet, a kitten, was deliberately killed by a bully. The women talk together, opening up their lives and their emotions, as they gather items for Minnie. Although Minnie is not physically present, Mrs. Hale and Mrs. Peters form a community with her, a community from which the men are excluded primarily because they choose not to enter. The men condescend to the women and treat them with jocular teasing. The women never overtly challenge the men or question their comments, but in the end Mrs. Hale and Mrs. Peters hold the power. They could provide the sheriff with his motive, but they choose to close ranks with Minnie and to protect a person they have come to regard as a brutally wounded bird.

4. Certainly the empty birdcage and the sewing box with the dead bird are the most important props. The birdcage suggests the trap Minnie found herself in when she married the dour Mr. Wright, while the bird, killed apparently by the man who could not bear to hear a cheerful sound, symbolizes Minnie herself and also explains her choice of murder method. The quilt, too, is important. It represents the "trifles" of women's work that become so significant in the play, and in addition, when Mrs. Hale at the end answers the county attorney's facetious question by firmly responding, "We call it—knot it," we can imagine Mrs. Wright knotting not only her quilt, but also the noose that strangled her husband.

5. Students' responses will vary widely. Many will suspect from the beginning, but certainly the description of Minnie's life will make them even more suspicious. The discovery of the bird confirms (emotionally if not legally) Mrs. Wright's hand in her husband's death.

6. The wonderful pun on "knot it" ("not it") sums up the irony in the play. The men condescendingly ask about the women's term for working a bedspread, but in her response Mrs. Hale reflects the resolution to the conflict she and Mrs. Peters have been facing. They have discovered what they assume (with good reason) to be the cruel work of Mr. Wright and thus could offer to the sheriff the important motive that he lacks for understanding the crime and the particular way in which it was committed. In analyzing the crime, however, the women have discovered the situation to be more complex than they had imagined. Mrs. Peters agonizes over whether to tell her husband, but perhaps she resents being described as "married to the law" or perhaps the scales are tipped by the condescending question of the county attorney. At any rate, she firmly announces the jury's verdict when she says, "We call it—knot it, Mr. Henderson." The men have *not* discovered *it* (the motive) any more than they have discovered *it* (the truth of Mrs. Wright's life and by extension the lives of all women).

Additional Topics for Writing and Discussion

1. Explain how you might stage this play to best convey its tension.

2. What is the central conflict in the drama? Is there more than one important conflict? Are the conflicts resolved? How?

3. Describe the married life of the Wrights as suggested by Mrs. Hale's comments and by other evidence in the play.

4. What role is played by the setting in this play? How does setting reveal character and suggest the theme of the play?

5. What is the effect of the play's chronology? Why would Glaspell choose to present the murder off stage and simply show the investigation? Would the play's theme be different if, instead, she showed the steps leading up to the murder first and then the murder as the climax? Explain.

Death of a Salesman • *Arthur Miller (pp. 1323–1392)*

Students usually respond well to this play, in part because it portrays a society with which they are familiar and characters with whom they can readily identify. In the opening stage directions the reader is presented with a classic image of postwar America: the city encroaching upon the homestead. Willy himself is presented as the old man who has been broken by a ruthless system that demands constant success, and the extent to which he has deteriorated is clear in the opening scene. He contradicts himself from line to line: immediately after calling Biff "a lazy bum," he muses, "There's one thing about Biff—he's not lazy" (p. 1326). He also talks about driving along with the windshield open, only to realize later that cars aren't made like that any more—he believed he was driving his 1928 Chevy. He even admits that he's confused, telling Linda, "Suddenly I realize I'm goin' sixty miles an hour and I don't remember the last five minutes" (p. 1324).

The first few scenes establish all of the major characters and begin to hint at the central conflict of the play. You may want to ask students to describe the characters based on what they read in the first scenes. What they will discover is that each of the characters revolves around Willy; we understand them only in their relationship to him and his dreams. Through the members of his family we gain a clearer picture of Willy in all of his roles: the husband—loving but quick-tempered and often in need of mothering; the salesman—determined but doomed to failure; the father—proud but unable to understand his sons' needs. In fact, difficult as it is for him to understand, it is Willy who has made his sons what they are: Happy sharing his ambitions, but unable to settle down to a family life, Biff rejecting everything about Willy's world. The conflict between Willy and Biff becomes entwined with the conflict between the salesman and the business world (represented by Howard), revealing in Willy a character who can neither understand nor advise his son because he cannot understand himself. As Biff says in the end, "the man didn't know who he was" (p. 1391).

Students may need to be reminded that Willy is not a great salesman who has hit a slump—the scenes from the past reveal quite clearly that he was never very successful. In fact, he complains to Linda that "people don't seem to take to me" (p. 1337). He tries to keep telling himself that he is successful, but the evidence keeps indicating otherwise. He boasts about breaking sales records, but he can't keep up with his bills. He models himself as a loving husband, but he buys his mistress silk stockings while his wife must mend hers. He prides himself on being a good influence on his boys, but he condones cheating and stealing and ridicules Bernard, who is genuinely concerned about Biff's graduating. Willy is hooked on the American Dream of the postwar era; the rugged individualist has been replaced by the salesman. And by continually striving to succeed in a career he wasn't cut out for, Willy manages to fail everyone in his family.

The plot of this play follows an inevitable path downward. We may share the excitement of Willy and Biff as they set out to change their fortunes, but we also know, from the glimpses of the past that Miller has provided, that these men are fooling themselves. The only real suspense involves wondering when and how Willy will ultimately destroy himself. We know that he will do so because his life is fraught with ironies and contradictions. He is adept at carpentry but scorns it as a trade; he praises American craftsmanship but feels himself imprisoned by machines that don't work; he thinks he has done the best for his sons but fills them with all of the wrong values. Success eludes Willy because, in the ultimate irony, the salesman has been sold a bill of goods.

Possible Responses to Questions (p. 1392)

1. Willy's literal death comes first to mind. The title describes his downward spiral to suicide. In addition, of course, Willy has died many small deaths before he drives his car off the road. He recognizes his lost opportunities and his failed dreams. Happy and especially Biff are the pride of his life, yet he has been unable to "sell" them his vision of monetary success and hard work. Willy's hope for a home that affords some privacy and serenity has been killed by the encroaching suburban sprawl. Perhaps most of all, Willy is unable any longer to sell himself on the American Dream; he recognizes that he will never be—and has never been—a highly successful, admired, self-made man.

2. Loman translates easily to "Low Man," a fitting title not only for Willy, who is currently the "low" salesman at work, but also for Biff and Happy, who are unsure about their lives and who have never become the successes their father had hoped for. Biff's name suggests a strong, rough-and-ready man who has a quarrel with life and goes about solving his troubles with his physical strength. Happy, of course, lives up to his nickname too. He remains cheerfully optimistic in spite of the signs of disintegration in his own life and in the lives of his family members. Willy sounds more like the name of a little boy than that of a grown man, and indeed Willy has remained childlike (and even childish) in many ways. His still dreams of riches from diamond mines; he nurses revenge fantasies, and he believes popularity to be more important than substance. Linda's name means "pretty" in Spanish; while this interpretation may be stretching a point, we do see Linda as a woman who was once attractive but who has now been worn down by her role as the only true adult in the family.

3. As the play opens, Biff is a 34-year-old drifter who has never been able to find his role in life. Throughout his childhood, he was the favored son. Willy encouraged him in every way, even defending his petty thievery as justified. The young Happy stood on the sidelines, admiring his older brother and trying desperately to get his father to notice him. Happy has stayed around and is trying to pursue a career in business which he hopes will please Willy, yet as always Willy's main concern is for Biff. Following the stunning disillusion of discovering his father's Boston affair, Biff gave up his plans for college and has been through a series of jobs where he was either fired or earned too little money to support himself in what he considers a reasonable way. Biff has a more realistic view of Willy than does Happy, and in the course of the play Biff faces both his own and his

father's shortcomings. Happy still holds out hope that the family will somehow become whole and that he will finally be admitted to what he sees as the inner circle, now guarded by the father he grew up adoring and the older brother he idolizes.

4. Willy is a complex character, both as the younger man we see in the flashbacks and as the older man of the present. As a young man he exudes confidence and bravado, spending a great deal of time with his sons, especially Biff. The young Willy expects the best and tries to do what he can for his family. Still, his attitude toward his neighbors, Charley and his son Bernard, shows that he is insecure and somewhat defensive. Willy must constantly denigrate his neighbors, perhaps as a way of building up himself and his family. The older Willy has been forced to face the blighting of his earlier hopes. The scene in Charley's office is particularly poignant. While Happy remains "the assistant to the assistant buyer" and Biff has just been fired for petty thievery, Bernard has been trying a case before the Supreme Court. As Charley offers Willy help, showing that he has succeeded while the "popular" Willy has failed, Willy must also see the contrast between Bernard and his sons. Perhaps worst of all for Willy is Bernard's quiet modesty. Charley comments quietly that his son does not have to brag; his accomplishments speak for themselves.

Is Willy a tragic hero, then, or simply a pathetic failure? Miller himself, in "Tragedy and the Common Man" (text p. 1732), tries to make a case for Willy as a tragic figure. He calls tragedy "the consequence of a man's total compulsion to evaluate himself justly," and considers tragic feeling to be "evoked when we are in the presence of a character who is ready to lay down his life, if need be, to secure one thing—his sense of personal dignity." But does Willy seek to evaluate himself justly? Is his sense of dignity based on an honest assessment of himself? These questions might stimulate discussion among students not just on the question of Willy's character, but on the nature of tragedy as well.

5. Women in this play are cast in fairly stereotyped roles. Linda is the good, strong, caring wife who, although she sees his weaknesses, "stands by her man." She is no pushover and certainly stands up to her sons when they fail to give Willy the respect she believes he deserves. Nevertheless, it is clear that over the years, Linda has been the one to hold the family together, humoring Willy through his fantasies and never questioning him about his activities on the road. She makes do with darned stockings and does not nag Willy for a better way of life. Although she has been a loyal wife, she has not fulfilled the role of ideal mother. She seems to have left the boys' moral rearing to Willy even though she must have known that his moral sense was somewhat skewed. The only other women we see in the play are Miss Francis, Willy's Boston lover, and the prostitute Happy brings to the table in the restaurant. These women represent temptations and loose living that neither Willy nor Happy can resist. In their minds, Linda represents the "good" woman, the kind of woman one marries; Miss Francis and the prostitute are "bad" women who are on earth to provide men with pleasure. Biff, who was shocked to learn of his father's relationship with Miss Francis, seems to have very little connection with women. In the opening scene Biff and Happy reminisce about Biff's connection with "big Betsy" who lived on Bushwick Avenue, yet Biff admits to being shy with women. Also in the restaurant scene, Happy is cheerfully confident with Miss Forsythe, while Biff is hesitant and concerned about Willy, instead of setting himself up for the night.

6. Two interesting characters who appear (or at least enter into) Willy's fantasies are his brother Ben and the salesman he admires, Dave Singleman.

Students will readily recognize the contrast between the adventurer Ben and the more cautious Willy. Ben's scenes provide us with information about Willy's background, revealing that Willy's own father was a dreamer who espoused the old American Dream of the frontier. Ben, in escaping to parts unknown, carries on in the adventurous spirit of the father. In wistfully viewing Ben as a symbol of what he could have been, Willy fails to see the reality of his own situation. Ben chose his path because it suited his nature and talents, not because he was a dreamer. His advice to Biff never to fight fair with a stranger shows a firm grasp of the harsh realities of life; he isn't afraid to admit that he doesn't play by the rules. Willy, on the other hand, pays lip service to the rules, telling the boys not to steal but praising their initiative when they do. Thus, even in his view of Ben, Willy fails to see things as they really are. For example, Ben recognizes that Willy's grand sacrifice will not make Biff respect him: "He'll call you a coward," Ben says to Willy before drifting out of sight. ". . . you've got to be sure you're not making a fool of yourself" (p. 1385). Ben exists in Willy's dreams, and as Biff says over his father's grave, "He had the wrong dreams. All, all, wrong" (p. 1391).

The first reference to the title of the play, the Singleman story (p. 1360), functions in several ways. First, it emphasizes Willy's view of the status of a salesman: "What could be more satisfying than to be able to go, at the age of eighty-four, into twenty or thirty different cities, and pick up a phone, and be remembered and loved and helped by so many different people?" Second, it foreshadows Willy's death. The one thing Willy wants out of life is to be "well-liked." Incapable of distinguishing between love and respect, Willy attributes success to the former. Thus, when he describes Singleman's death, we sense Willy's hope that his own will be as poetic. We will later recognize the irony in Willy's speech. Instead of dying "the death of a salesman, in his green velvet slippers in the smoker of the New York, New Haven and Hartford, going to Boston," Willy dies behind the wheel of a beat-up Studebaker, going nowhere. Willy hopes, too, to have the funeral of a salesman. We recall Singleman's funeral as Willy discusses his suicide plan with Ben, telling him, "That funeral will be massive! They'll come from Maine, Massachusetts, Vermont, New Hampshire! All the old-timers with the strange license plates—that boy will be thunder-struck, Ben, because he never realized—I am known! . . . He'll see what I am, Ben!" (p. 1385). The irony, of course, lies in the fact that the only mourners at Willy's funeral are his family and his only remaining friend, Charley. And Biff's eulogy is equally ironic, "He never knew who he was" (p. 1391). Dave Singleman was just another dream of Willy's.

7. In Miller's play certain musical themes suggest specific characters or circumstances, and lighting is used to suggest dream or memory. *Death of a Salesman* uses scrim and spot-lighting to suggest Willy's fantasies as well as music as a bridge to flashback scenes.

8. In the preface to his fascinating book *Salesman in Beijing*, Miller describes why he himself went to China to supervise the production of *Salesman*. As he contemplated the task ahead of him, he warned himself that "the realities of *Salesman* are . . . culture-bound. Willy Loman has sprung out of a world of business ambition, a society infected with success fever; China was more than ninety percent peasant and most living Chinese had been taught proletarian socialist values, the very antithesis of those Willy strives for. The whole effort might end in calamity."

As a research project, students may want to read more about the Beijing production of *Salesman* and its cultural implications. Miller's book was published by Viking in 1983.

9. Students' responses will vary. Most people see a little of themselves in Willy (or they know someone close to them who is like Willy). His downfall evokes a shiver of identification.

10. Reading and critiquing "Tragedy and the Common Man" make a useful assignment for a formal paper three to five pages long.

Additional Topics for Writing and Discussion

1. Miller is very particular about the way he wants the play staged. Reread the opening stage directions and comment on Miller's purpose in presenting such an unrealistic set.

2. How does Miller help us to know when the action is taking place in the past? Do you find his treatment of these scenes more effective than a more obvious treatment—for example, an actual scene change with characters really appearing younger?

3. In the beginning of Act II, Willy laments, "Once in my life I'd like to own something outright before it's broken! . . . They time those things. They time them so when you finally paid for them, they're used up" (p. 1356). Willy is talking about cars and refrigerators, but how does the statement reflect on his life?

4. Analyze the scene between Willy and his boss. What is the significance, for example, of the tape recorder? How do the two men compare and contrast?

5. Imagine that you are Biff, writing a letter to Willy in order to square things with his memory. Now that the two of you will never again confront one another in anger, try to explain to him who you are, why you are that way, and how you feel about him.

The Glass Menagerie • *Tennessee Williams (p. 1275)*

Tennessee Williams, born Thomas Lanier Williams, was the son of a traveling shoe salesman who prided himself on his years as a lieutenant in the Spanish-American War and on his ancestry of rugged frontiersmen and Indian fighters. His mother had been raised gently as the daughter of an Episcopal clergyman and cherished a romantic view of the antebellum South, with its gracious social life and elegant plantations. Williams was born in Mississippi because his father's occupation kept him away from the family, and thus his mother chose to return to the sheltered, dependable cocoon of the Episcopal rectory. Williams spent his early years there, a favorite of his grandfather, who read to him, told him stories, and recited exciting narrative poetry that delighted the young boy.

In 1918 the family moved to St. Louis to be with Cornelius Williams. The move was most unhappy for Thomas. His father tried to get him interested in sports and found his son's interest in reading a "womanish" trait. Tom hated the shabby apartment they were forced to live in because Cornelius never adequately supported the family. *The Glass Menagerie* reflects, to a modest degree, Williams's home life as a young man during his years in St. Louis. His sister, though shy, was not physically incapacitated and did not collect glass figures. His father evidently did not abandon the family, though he did have a drinking problem. And like Tom Wingfield, the young Tennessee Williams was unhappy at work and south fulfillment in attending movies, writing poetry, and finally in wandering.

A gift of a ten-dollar typewriter from his mother on his twelfth birthday started Williams on his writing career. When he was still in high school, he began to earn money with his fiction, receiving $35 from the magazine *Weird Tales* for his story "The Vengeance of Nitocris." When he finished high school, Williams entered the University of Missouri, where he became a journalism major. After two years, however, his grades were so poor that his father forced him to drop out of school and take a job in the same shoe factory where he was employed. Two years later, suffering from physical and mental exhaustion, Williams left and moved in with this grandparents, who now lived in Memphis. During his stay with them, he developed an interest in drama, and when he returned to St. Louis, he joined a small theatrical group called The Mummers. Although Williams continued to develop this talent in writing drama, his career was set back by his sister Rose's mental illness. In 1937, she was committed to an insane asylum, and Williams was deeply distressed by his inability to help her and by the loss of the family member to whom he had felt closest.

After several failed attempts, Williams completed college and earned his B.A. from the University of Iowa. He refused to go back and work in the shoe factory, so he broke his family ties and moved to New Orleans, adopting as his pen name Tennessee," the label given him by his college classmates. Working at odd jobs to support himself, Williams got his first break when a one-act play won a $100 contest and an agent who liked the play got Williams a grant to continue his writing. *The Glass Menagerie*, which opened in 1945, was his first solidly successful play, followed by *A Streetcar Named Desire* for which he won the Pulitzer Prize in 1947. Other well-known dramas by Williams include *Summer and Smoke* (1948), *The Rose Tattoo* (1951), *Cat on a Hot Tin Roof* (1955), and *Suddenly Last Summer* (1958).

Possible Responses to Questions (p. 1321)

1. The scenes are tied together by the play's major themes. For example, the Wingfields are all isolated and lonely, each in his or her own way. Each has a way of escaping, Amanda by dreaming of past splendor, Tom by drinking and going to the movies, and Laura by staying at home and immersing herself in the world of her glass animal collection. Themes to consider, then, include isolation, loneliness, escape, and fantasy versus reality.

   The scenes are also tied together, of course, by the action of the two plots: Tom's plans to leave the family and join the merchant marines and Amanda's plans to find a husband for Laura. Every scene in some way reveals the hostility and anger Tom Feels about his living and working situation, just as every scene shows something about Laura's fragile nature and the bleak prospects she faces in life.

2. Without the narrator, the play would be entirely changed. Because of the narrator, we see the action as memory, and it takes on the hazy, mythic qualities of all memories. We cannot be sure what actually happened and what the narrator simply things happened. Like memories, the scenes in the play are selective. We remember what we want to remember or what we are forced to remember. Tom is trapped by his memories. He cannot help replay some scenes over and over again, and that is what we are shown in the play. Also, as an older narrator, Tom can provide for us the social context of the play.

   We realize that as the war in the Wingfield household is being played out, the world outside that seems lively, spirited, and music-filled is, in fact, preparing itself for the devastation of World War II. The ironies of the setting would be lost if we had no narrator to place the main action of the play in a larger context. The narrator acts as a guide and interpreter for the reader/viewer, remaining largely outside the action until the end of the play. Then he seems to speak directly to the remembered Laura, urging her to blow out her candles, to erase herself from his memory (or at least to purge the pain from his memory). Since Laura complies, leaning forward and extinguishing the flames on the candelabrum, we can reasonably speculate that the play provides a catharsis for Tom, who has now told his sister's story and can be free from its agony.

3. Laura's collection represents her fantasy world. When Jim talks about the importance of having an interest so that one keeps motivated, he uses as an example his fascination with radio engineering. Laura, however, can offer only her collection as an interest and it is an activity that draws her further away from the world rather than into the world (as does Jim's practical interest). The figures in the menagerie are beautiful and fragile, like Laura herself. They are also, however, frozen, cold, and locked forever in one form. Laura shares these qualities, too. She is unable to cope with normal pressures and situations and so keeps her feelings and fears locked up inside. Like the glass animals, she can never grow and mature emotionally.

The unicorn, of course, is Laura's favorite animal and it most closely resembles her. It is different from all the other horses because it has a horn. Jim notes that unicorns are extinct in the modern world, and, indeed, Laura herself seems to have escaped from some far earlier, imaged time when princesses could stay sheltered and locked up in protected towers. When Laura and Jim dance, the horn is broken from the unicorn. It becomes like the rest of the horse, and Laura seems to recognize that such a move toward the ordinary may, in fact, be positive. When Jim reveals that he is engaged, however, she loses the tiny thread of confidence she had gained and slips back into her glass world. The unicorn must go with Jim because it carries memories of Laura's once special moment and, perhaps, also because it no longer belongs entirely to the fantasy world where Laura will once again retreat.

4. Possibilities abound. Here are some suggestions:

Blue Rose.   Jim's nickname for Laura, suggests once again an unreal, fantasy beauty. Jim unknowingly transforms the name of an ugly disease into a lovely phrase. For Laura, it represents a cherished memory and the possibility of love. For Jim, it represents misunderstanding, which is central to his relationship with Laura.

Blue Mountain Blue.   Blue is also significant in Amanda's life. But her "blue" is a remembered place rather than a name. She thinks of her childhood and young girlhood, and for her it represents a time when she was beautiful and desired. She idealizes Blue Mountain and compares her situation there with her current circumstances. In one sense, Blue Mountain sustains her, but in another, it prevents her from facing the reality of her daughter's desperate isolation.

The Picture of Mr. Wingfield.   In the opening dialogue, Tom introduces his father as "a fifth character." Mr. Wingfield never appears in the play, yet his picture is illuminated at significant moments. For instance, in Scene IV the light glows on the portrait as Tom drunkenly complains to Laura about the confinement of his life. The father's influence over the family is evident throughout the play. Amanda never stops moaning about her wretched choice of husband, yet she advises her son to improve his grooming habits, noting that attention to personal appearance was the one thing his father had plenty of. And, of course, Mr. Wingfield's bolting from the family foreshadows Tom's own escape at the end of the play.

5. The dark walls of the tenement in which the Wingfields live and the darker alleys that surround it suggest the darkness and depression of the family's life. In addition, the tenement seems to be a trap, with the fire escape, where Tom often sits, as the only means of getting free. The transparent fourth wall of the building and the transparent gauze portieres give the scene a hazy, blurred look that suggest the quality of memory. The setting definitely reflects Tom's claim that "[t]he play is memory. Being a memory play, it is dimly lighted, it is sentimental, it is not realistic."

6. Williams himself says that the purpose of the legends is "to give accent to certain values in each scene. Each scene contains a particular point (or several) which is structurally the most important. . . . The legend or image upon the screen will strengthen the effect of what is merely allusion in the writing and allow the primary point to be made more simply and lightly than if the entire responsibility were on spoken lines." Williams chose to omit the screen device from his final acting version, and some critics have found the legends excessive believing them to be distractions that detract from the power of the plays spoken lines.

Additional Topics for Writing and Discussion

1. Consider ways in which the play is both realistic and non-realistic.

   [The hazy quality of memory, along with the stage devices such as the spotlighting of characters and props and the screen device, makes the setting and ambiance of the play unrealistic. The interactions and conflicts of the characters and the poignant quality of their hope and dreams strike a note of realism in the hearts and minds of most readers/viewers.]

2. Of what importance are dreams to Laura, Amanda, and Tom? To what extent are their dreams illusory? To what extent are they based on reality?

   [Laura is the most innocent character in the play, and, her dreams reflect that innocence. She truly believes that she can live in a world as unreal as her glass menagerie, without any need to either support herself financially or to follow her mother's wishes to "find a husband." When Jim arrives at the house, it is easy for Laura to believe that he is the Prince Charming who will enable her to escape from her mother's promptings. Although she suffers a cruel disillusionment, Laura does not move from her original innocence. We have no sense that she has grown or developed. Amanda holds firmly to her romantic dreams of an idealized youth. She denies the nature of the conflicts and problems in her current household and dreams that there are easy, one-step solutions to her problems: Laura needs a husband or a job; Tom should find a career to pursue. Although at the end of the play, Amanda is forced to face the unreality of her hopes of a "gentleman caller" to rescue Laura, she seems unable to truly acknowledge the depth of her self-deception. At the end of scene VI, Amanda accuses Tom of being a "selfish dreamer." Certainly tom does dream of escape and, in some ways, he is selfish. He focuses primarily on his own needs, although he does feel guilty about leaving his sister. While Tom's ambitions may seem like pie-in-the-sky, the irony is that the playwright was able to leave a household very much like the one we see in the play and to become a successful writer.]

3. What is Jim's role in the play? What does he represent?

   [Jim is the most pragmatic character in the play, although, paradoxically, he is also rather naive about relationships with women. Jim does not intentionally hurt Laura, and he is genuinely distressed by her response to their dance. He comes to realize that his simple approach to life may not work for every situation. In some way he represents the "real" world, yet he also learns that the world of dreams and dreamers has its own beauty. And his awkward responses to Laura's fragility suggest that the straightforward approach to life has as many costs and dangers as the wandering approach of the dreamer.]

4. Who is the protagonist in the play? Amanda? Tom? Laura? Explain and defend your choice, using details and examples from the play.

5. Write the letters Tom might leave behind for Amanda, Laura, and his friend Jim when he first leaves St. Louis. Reread the final scene and include details from the narrator's comments to make the letters logical extensions of what we learn about Tom in the play.

A Raisin in the Sun • *Lorraine Hansberry (pp. 1393–1459)*

The play is set in Chicago's South Side in the early 1950s. Students who did not live through this era need to know that the civil rights movement of the 1960s had not yet taken place. In addition, you may want to mention that abortions, illegal in this country, were performed only without the services of legitimate doctors and hospitals.

Hansberry's play reflects her deep concern with human rights, which was triggered when she was eight years old and her father, Carl Augustus Hansberry, a prominent Chicago banker and real estate broker, deliberately decided to move his family into one of Chicago's restricted neighborhoods. The move ultimately resulted in a civil rights case that went all the way to the United States Supreme Court, with Hansberry emerging as the victor. But the fight had not been an easy one, and the "crackers" mentioned in *A Raisin in the Sun* expressed their hatred toward the family with both verbal and physical violence. In a letter written less than one year before her death in 1965, Hansberry still vividly recalled being spat at and cursed daily as she walked to school; at home her mother kept a loaded German Luger to protect her four children. Her family's concept of courage in the face of injustice permeates all of Hansberry's work and is directly reflected in *Raisin*.

Possible Responses to Questions (pp. 1459–1460)

1. In Hansberry's own words, she writes "about people who happen to be Negroes, rather than Negro plays." The universality of the play's theme, the characters' search for personal freedom and a better existence, allows the drama to transcend the categorical boundaries of urban or minority plays.

2. Mama is both the matriarch of the family and the strongest character of the drama. A woman who has endured much and has survived, she has nonetheless neglected to see how dominant a personality she has become. Beneatha's views of religion sharply contrast with her mother's traditional beliefs, and these differences create a strained relationship between the old and the new. Like her mother, Beneatha is a fighter, but unlike Mama, Beneatha sees no need for the role of God in her struggle for survival. Both women agree, however, on the worth of Beneatha's dream to become a doctor, and Mama is willing to sacrifice a share of the inheritance to help her daughter fulfill this goal.

Mama cannot accept Walter's dream as easily as she can Lena's. With her Christian beliefs, Mama doesn't want giving money to set up a liquor store to be on her "ledger." Mama fails to realize that she has become such a dominant force in the family that she has never allowed Walter to become what she most wants him to be, a man. Walter can only become a man when Mama gives him enough emotional space to exercise his manhood.

3. The Younger family is not so distant from many modern families where members vie for their own dreams without concern for the family unit. Walter's conflict with everyone must, of course, be seen in the light of race; his blackness intensifies his struggle. Walter is an angry young man who asks only for the equality due him. He questions why he must be a chauffeur and why he must accept the fact that his wife won't wear pearls around her neck. He vents his anger on Beneatha, who appears to have beaten the system of prejudice because she will be a doctor; on Ruth, whose "small mind" ties him down to a secure but unfulfilling job; and on Mama, whom he sees as too traditional in her concept of a "proper" business.

4. George represents the black man who wants to deny his heritage, as suggested by his hostile response to Beneatha's interest in African culture. Students may discuss the traditions of ethnic heritage, asking whether the melting pot of America can and should allow for the retention of diverse backgrounds within the American Dream. George Murchison attempts to wipe out his roots in favor of the white educational and business values. His negation of his heritage serves to push Beneatha dramatically closer to Asagai and her search for self while she still retains her dream of becoming a physician.

    Beneatha prepares both the reader and Mama for the function of Joseph Asagai as the symbol of black heritage in her wonderful speech on the stereotyped African black (p. 1450). George and Asagai represent the two forces operating on and within the family as they try to fulfill their dreams. The resolution of the drama suggests that blacks must find individual solutions, acting according to their own life's goals and not according to standards set by either the white American or black African cultures.

5. Possible themes include selfish versus unselfish dreams and ambitions; respect and support for one' heritage; the right of all people to equal treatment; the understanding that no matter how small and selfish someone becomes, "There is always something left to love."

6. The plant, as Mama notes,"expresses me." Although it is a "poor raggedy-looking" thing, she returns for it at the end of the play, recognizing that although it has been kept alive for all these years in the cramped apartment, it will now have a chance to grow and thrive in a new environment. The plant's survival reflects the survival of the Younger family. The single window in the apartment also functions symbolically, suggesting the lack of natural sunshine and the corresponding darkness of the Youngers' life within that apartment.

7. Possible scenes include Beneatha's expression of atheism (Act I, Scene I); Asagai presenting the robes and records to Beneatha (Act I, Scene II); Walter's "will somebody please listen to me" scene (Act I, Scene II); Walter's confronting George Murchison (Act II, Scene I); and Mama and Ruth discussing Walter's coming into his manhood (Act III).

8. Responses will vary. Working in groups, students might write a brief scene showing a future meeting of the family members. These scenes could then be read to the class for comparison and discussion.

9. Hansberry addresses a theme common to American drama: the concept of family struggle and search for identity. Walter, for example, has a sense of isolation and erosion of family that can be compared to the experiences of major characters in play by Tennessee Williams, Arthur Miller, and (more recently) Sam Shepard.

10. Like Hughes, Hansberry suggests the danger and conflict inherent in dreams that are always stifled and denied fulfillment.

Additional Topics for Writing and Discussion

1. Evaluate the character of Mr. Linder. Is he merely a plot device? Is he a stereotype, or do you find him believable? Explain.

2. *A Raisin in the Sun* was first produced in 1959. Do you find attitudes, actions, and conflicts in the play outdated, or are they still relevant today? Explain.

3. Compare the parent-child relationship in *A Raisin in the Sun* with the parent-child relationship of *Death of a Salesman*.

4. Describe the Youngers' apartment. In what ways does it reflect the lives of the characters and the themes of the play? How does the apartment contrast with the new house Mama buys? What is the significance of this contrast?

5. Discuss the significance of Ruth's abortion to the play's themes and characterizations.

The Man in a Case • *Wendy Wasserstein (p. 1513)*

In this adaptation, Wendy Wasserstein brings a late-twentieth-century comic ethos to Anton Chekhov's short story. This short play is ideal for reading aloud in class. Students might prepare readings in groups of three with two students to fill the roles of Byelinkov and Varinka while the third acts as a director.

Possible Responses to Questions (p. 1518)

1. Close reading of the dialogue and action shows how different Byelinkov and Varinka are. Varinka rattles on at length using precious words and phrases as she describes her fiancé. She calls him her "little school mouse" and talks about his "perfectly pressed pants" and his "sweet little galoshes." Byelinkov shows himself a master of brevity and understatement when he notes that she is "fond of expletives." Unlike his effusive lover, Byelinkov talks mainly in short sentences and gives advice rather than praise: "Pride can be an imperfect value" he informs her and adds that "being married requires a great deal of responsibility." Varinka uses metaphor and simile freely, comparing Byelinkov to things like a mouse or a dancing bear while he remains almost entirely in the realm of the literal. Varinka believes in taking chances and in challenging the mores of her society. She takes great delight in riding her brother's bicycle, while her staid fiancé frets and fumes about the image she will present to any of his neighbors or students who may see her. Byelinkov may talk about and translate the beautiful poetry of the ancients, but Varinka sees beauty in the world around her. While Byelinkov complains about the beetles in the roses, she sees only the glorious colors and textures of the petals.

2. The tone of the play is primarily comic, but there are poignant moments. For instance when Varinka demands that Byelinkov dance with her, and he pauses to place a lilac in her hair. This gesture suggests that he can, in fact, look beyond the literal, precise world of the scholar. He is capable of a gratuitously romantic action. Yet Varinka cannot simply accept his gift. Instead she questions his intention to place a lilac in her hair each year in remembrance of the moment. He responds with gently self-mocking humor, assuring her that he will write in his notebook to remind himself of "the day a young lady, your bride, entered

232

your garden, your peace, and danced on the roses." Still Varinka is not satisfied, she pursues her quest to get him to acknowledge his love. And so the fragile spell is broken. Byelinkov reverts to short sentences and to mundane topics such as housekeeping and beet soup. The play then continues with primarily comic exchanges, although at the end, Byelinkov's final gesture—ripping up the note about the lilac, and then gathering the pieces—suggests the pain and loneliness he feels.

3. If we are to take Byelinkov and Varinka as representative of their genders, we get a very bleak picture of the relations between men and women. Although the images and actions are often comic the play shows two people who have different view of marriage, different views of love, and different goals in life. Neither is an evil or even bad person, and each seems to care about the other. Yet Varinka's sense of adventure, her warmth and enthusiasm—which attract Byelinkov to her—also frighten and appall him. He is not about to accept her extravagant language, her impulsive gestures, and her carefree actions. Varinka, on the other hand, seems oblivious to Byelinkov's worries. She cannot seem to understand his need for quiet study, his reluctance to declare his love openly, or his concern for public opinion. Rather than listening to what he has to say, she simply talks through him or dismisses him entirely.

   Some students may make the worthy point that Byelinkov and Varinka are exaggerated types. While they may give us opportunity to smile and to look at our own relationships with the opposite sex, they in no way represent a realistic view of the communication that, with thought and sensitivity, can be realized. Byelinkov and Varinka do not represent our fate, but rather an old stereotype to be recognized and challenged.

4. Any life Byelinkov and Varinka may have together will continue to include conflict and misunderstanding unless they both change in some significant ways. An optimist might hope that Varinka would lead Byelinkov to see and experience more joy in life, to be more spontaneous and less worried about the opinions of others. The incident of the lilac suggests some hope. On the other hand, Varinka must recognize Byelinkov's very different view of life and to grant that his need for solitude and quiet study represent a profound inner need and not a whim (as she now seems to think).

   At present both Byelinkov and Varinka seem to be grasping at what they may see as "the last chance." Varinka describes herself as "a pretty girl of thirty," a girl who is does "not deserve [the] honor" of being called a woman because she has not yet become a wife. She says to Byelinkov that they "deserve the life everyone else has"; they "deserve not to be different." So her motive for marriage is not simply because she is in love, but because she wants to have what she sees as a normal life. Byelinkov several times assures Varinka that he "never was a sad man," yet it is clear he felt his life lacking in something and finally mustered the courage to risk entering a relationship with a woman quite different from himself—a woman who would insist on change (one of the things he fears most).

5. This topic would combine well with reading the play aloud. As students meet in groups of three to plan the readings, they may also suggest additional stage directions and cues. To elaborate on this exercise, consider asking students to describe the costumes, hairstyles, and makeup they would plan for each character.

6. Wasserstein's play takes the central incident from Chekhov's story and imagines one encounter within that incident. The story provides far more information about Belikov than does the play, and thus we come to the encounter between him and Varenka with much less sympathy for Belikov than for his counterpart Byelinkov. We already know Belikov to

233

be a fear-ridden boor who foists his own Puritanistic view of the world on the academic community in which he lives and works. Because the story is told retrospectively by Burkin, a colleague of Belikov, we know before the meeting of Varenka and "the man in a case" that they will not marry. Further, we know that he will almost certainly end up disapproving of her as he does of everything that suggests spontaneity, adventure, and joy. While Chekhov's Belikov is almost entirely unsympathetic. Wasserstein suggests a fuller character for her Byelinkov. She shows the yearning for intimacy and pleasure that lies locked behind Belikov's protective case. We finish reading or viewing the play with some sympathy for both characters whereas we come away from Chekhov's story regarding Varenka as merely a means to initiate the downfall of the altogether unpleasant, mean-spirited, rigid Belikov. Any sympathy we feel comes not from the actions of the two would-be lovers, but rather from the philosophical musings of Ivan Ivanich. As he contemplates Burkin's story of Belikov's life and death, Ivan Ivanich notes that we ourselves might in some ways, "live in a case," although Burkin is quite unwilling to take this meaning, insisting that "this is quite another theme."]

Additional Topics for Writing and Discussion

1. Do Varinka and Byelinkov remind you of any modern couples you know? Explain the differences and similarities you see between the conflicts in the lives of the couple or couples you've identified and the conflicts in Varinka's and Byelinkov's courtship.

2. Which character do you find more sympathetic? Or do you find both equally appealing? Explain your reasons for your response.

3. What is the significance of the bicycle? Why is Byelinkov so distressed about Varinka's riding the bicycle? How does this incident relate to the larger themes of the play?

[Just as the case of curtains and quilts symbolizes Byelinkov need for isolation, security, and continuity, the bicycle symbolizes Varinka's love of adventure, her disdain for custom, and her need for change. At some level, Byelinkov recognizes that the bicycle means more than just a momentary inconvenience in his life; his strong response suggests that he recognizes it as representative of all that separates him and his fiancée.]

4. What is the significance of the play's title? Why do you think Chekhov chose—and Wasserstein retained—this title rather than, say, "The Woman on the Bicycle"?

[This question addresses the issue of whether the play focuses primarily on Byelinkov or primarily on Varinka. While many students will find Varinka the more appealing of the two characters, Byelinkov seems to be the character who is central. It is he whom we see at the beginning of the play, anxiously awaiting Varinka's arrival, and it is he whom we see at the end trying to rid himself of the note that reminds him of his romantic moment. The case of quilts and curtains provides a cocoon which Byelinkov uses to protect himself from the outside world. The play focuses on the conflict he feels as he struggles with the possibility of emerging from this cocoon. When he gathers up the torn fragments of the note as the play's final action, some viewers may see the gesture as merely another compulsive response. Others may believe he still feels ambivalence and thus gathers the fragments with the thought of putting them together and of keeping the lilac anniversary still open as a possibility.]

5. Write a short scene showing Varinka's and Byelinkov's meeting a week after the end of the play. What will they talk about? Will the wedding plans still be in progress?

Fences • *August Wilson (pp. 1460–1512)*

Fences is the second in a projected series of ten plays August Wilson is writing to provide a tapestry of the black American experience. Wilson was born in Pittsburgh in 1945, and spent his early years in a family and neighborhood similar to those he depicts in *Fences.* Coming of age in the turbulent 60's, Wilson committed himself to civil rights issues, particularly the fight against racism. In the late 1960's he began writing plays, seeking to challenge stereotypes of blacks, especially black men. Wilson has said that his early experiences in Pittsburgh not only provided him with characters and settings but also with the speech patterns and rhythms (primarily blues) that flow through the dialogue and ambiance of his plays.

Possible Responses to Questions (p. 1512)

1. The stage directions provide background information for the reader of the play, including a capsule of black American history. Contrasting the success stories of white European immigrants with the plight of black Americans whose ancestors were brought forcibly to this country as slaves, Wilson creates a family and neighborhood filled with broken dreams. Both in the specific setting of the Maxson's backyard and in the historic overview, baseball figures as a prominent metaphor. In the yard, a ball made from rags hangs from a tree and a baseball bat leans against the same tree. In describing the larger setting, Wilson notes that the year is 1957, the year "the Milwaukee Braves won the World Series, and the hot winds of change that would make the sixties a turbulent, racing, dangerous, and provocative decade has not yet begun to blow full."

   It's interesting to note that audiences viewing the play would not have the benefit of reading the stage directions. Students might consider the care directors, stage designers, costume designers, and, of course the actors themselves must take to create through props, clothing, sets, actions, gestures, and vocal inflections the atmosphere established by the opening paragraphs. Discussion of these points emphasizes the differences between viewing the reading a play.

2. The central religious symbol is Gabriel, Troy's brother who sustained a head injury in World War II and now believes himself to be the Archangel Gabriel. Throughout the play, Gabriel stands as both an innocent and a scourge of God. He seems not to know what is going on, yet he turns and fights those who have been taunting him, paralleling in some ways Troy's attempt to fight against racial discrimination at work. In the final scene, Gabriel finally raises his horn to his lips and is unable to create the note he has been holding in his head and mind for twenty years. Recognizing the failure of this traditional religious symbol, he breaks into a ritualistic dance, reminiscent of the African roots of the black church. Wilson's final stage direction suggests that Gabriel has accomplished a miracle. He has summoned the power to show grace in Troy's life and death — rather than failure, anger, and loss. As Gabe finishes his dance, "the gates of heaven stand open as wide as God's closet."

3. The main characters live by very different values. Troy believes in the importance of hard work and in supporting his family. His speech to his son Cory in Act I, Scene III sums up those values:

> A man got to take care of his family. You live in my house . . . sleep you behind on my bedclothes . . . fill you belly up with my food . . . cause you may son. You my flesh and blood. Not 'cause I like you! Cause it's my duty to take care of you. I owe a responsibility to you! Let's get this straight right her . . . before it go along any further . . . I ain't got to like you . . . . I done give you everything I had to give you. I gave you your life! Me and your mama worked that out between us. And liking your black ass wasn't part of the bargain. Don't you try and go through life worrying about if somebody like you or not. You best be making sure they doing right by you. You understand what I'm saying, boy?

Troy says that he learned while he was in jail that he did not want a life of stealing. He believes that the ability to work with your hands and to demand your rights (as he does when he seeks a job as a driver) will see you through. While he loves his wife, he also believes that he has a right to take a lover because he deserves joy and laughter which he does not find at home. He does not apologize to Rose after he tells her about his affair nor does he promise to break off his relationship with Alberta. His loyalty to himself seems to outweigh his loyalty to his wife. Nevertheless, when Alberta bears him a daughter and dies in childbirth, he takes the baby home and accepts responsibility for finding a way to raise her.

Rose places great value on both family and church. She tires to help Troy to look more realistically at his life and, especially, at the possibilities for their son Cory. She tells her husband, "Times have changed from when you was young, Troy. People change. The world's changing around you and you can't even see it." Although she is very angry at Troy when he tells her about his affair, she agrees to help him raise Raynell. In the final scene, we see that Rose has found strength in her church and in her commitment to caring for Raynell.

Cory wants more than Troy had in his life. He sees playing football as a way to get out of the drudging life he believes his father leads. Cory is not afraid of work—he has held an after-school job—but he is young and does not always take care of responsibilities as his father wishes. Cory respects his parents and wishes desperately for Troy's love and approval—something Troy can give only through financially supporting Cory, rather than through words or companionable actions. It should be noted that Cory does not fantasize a career in sports as his father fears. Cory earns good grades and sees the scholarship his father denies him as a way of progressing. It's significant that when he is asked at his father's funeral whether he'll stay in the Marines, he replies "I don't know. I got six [years] already, I think that's enough." He seems to be thinking seriously of getting out of the service, now that he has had the opportunity to get away from home. This ability to make a decision to seek change, but not to get stuck in the new mode, suggests that he might well have been able to follow the plan he pleaded with his father to allow: accepting the scholarship, getting the education, and then getting out of sports.

4. The characters are believable because we see so many facets of their personalities and spirits. Troy comes most fully to life because we know the most about him. We learn of his painful childhood—and of his terrified recognition that although he could physically escape his abusive father, he could never be entirely free. As he tells of going off on his own at age fourteen, he says of his father: "I could feel him kicking in my blood and knew that the only thing that separated us was the matter of a few years." Although we

sympathize deeply with Troy's harsh life, he is not depicted as a perfect martyr. He holds on to dreams and prejudices that hurt him and hurt those he loves. He maintains the fiction that he could have been a baseball star if it weren't for discrimination, even though Rose points out that he was forty years old when he got out of prison—too old for anyone to begin a career in baseball. When Cory tries to point out black players on current teams, Troy dismisses whatever his son has to say. Perhaps the most controversial side of Troy's character shows in his decision to have an affair. His obvious love for and devotion to Rose make it hard to accept his claim that he needs Alberta because she provides a place where he doesn't have to worry about getting the roof fixed or paying the bills. Some may sympathize with Troy's need to "be a different man," while others may share Rose's indignation when she describes to Troy how she stayed with him even though she, too, had other "hopes and dreams" and had been tempted to "want to know other men."

5. Troy uses baseball as a metaphor throughout the play. In addition to seeing his failed career in baseball as symbolic of his lost hopes and dreams for a better life, he uses baseball as a way of trying to justify to Rose his decision to have an affair. He talks about being born with two strikes against him and as regarding himself as "safe" when he found Rose and started a family with her. He decided then that he "wasn't gonna strike out no more. [He] wasn't going back to the penitentiary. [He] wasn't gonna lay in the streets with a bottle of wine." Earlier, he chastises Cory by calling "strikes" on him; at the end of Act II, Scene 1, he tells his son, "All right. That's strike two. You stay away from around me, boy. Don't you strike out. You living with a full count. Don't you strike out." Just as Troy saw himself as starting out life with "two strikes against him," he defines his son with the same metaphor.

   Rose, on the other hand, does not see life in terms of a game to be won or lost. In her most moving speech (end of Act II, Scene 1), she compares herself to a gardener:

   > Troy, I took all my feelings, my wants and need, my dreams . . . and I buried them inside you. I planted a seed and watched and prayed over it. I planted myself inside you and waited to bloom. And it didn't take me no eighteen years to find out the soil was hard and rocky, and it wasn't never gonna bloom.

   Rather than striking out as symbolic of losing in life, Rose sees stunted plants and ungerminated seeds as representing the failure of her marriage to help her to grow and to bloom as her full and best self.

6. From the beginning of the play we see the half-finished fence that Troy is building in his yard. This fence represents the relationships of the family. Cory can never please his father as they work together on the fence; it seems to symbolize their separation. Rose wants the fence to serve as a means of protecting her family, and she is always urging Troy to complete it. But the connection and safety Rose longs for is never to be. Troy finishes the fence only after Alberta's death when he challenges Death to stay away from his family and to cross the fence only when ready to claim its maker. Troy, then, sees his fence as keeping out an evil force rather than as keeping in what is good and loving.

   Wilson himself said in an interview with David Savran (from *In Their Own Voices*) that nearly every character in the play is at some point trapped by physical or emotional fences:

   > At the end of *Fences* every person, with the exception of Raynell, is institutionalized. Rose is in a church. Lyons is in a penitentiary. Gabriel's in a mental hospital and Cory's in the marines. The only free person is the girl, Troy's daughter, the hope for the future.

In the past, Troy was in jail (behind fences of a kind) and he also talks about hitting home runs over ballpark fences. All of these walls or fences seem to represent the obstacles these characters face and in nearly every case the fences relate in some way to the efforts of white America to keep blacks "in their place."

7. and 8.   Many scenes and speeches would work well for these topics.

Consider these possibilities:

Troy arguing with Cory at the end of Act I, Scene II; Troy describing his early life to Bono and Lyons (Act I, Scene IV); Troy and Rose discussing the revelation of his affair with Alberta (Act II, Scene 1); Rose and Cory arguing about Cory's attending Troy's funeral (Act II, Scene V); Gabriel's final speech and action.

Additional Topics for Writing and Discussion

1. In an interview with David Savran, Wilson expressed his doubts about athletic scholarship for blacks, calling them a form of exploitation by "universities who made a lot of money off of athletics." He notes that the players "were not getting educated, were taking courses in basketweaving. Some of them could barely read." Research the history of athletic scholarships and respond to Wilson's observation. Do you agree? Disagree? Has the situation changed today?

2. Troy believes that in some way he is doomed to repeat the mistakes of his father. In what ways does this prophecy come true? In what ways is it proved false? What projections can you make for Lyons and Cory. How are they like their father? How are they different?

3. Discuss the role of women in this play. Do you see any gender stereotyping? Explain.

4. Analyze the theme of death in *Fences*. Why does Troy talk to death as though it were a person?

5. Although the play is primarily serious, there are comic moments. Identify some of these moments and discuss their function. How do they contribute to the development of character and theme?

6. What is Jim Bono's function in the play? Does he come to life as a fully developed character, or is he simply a device to allow Troy to reveal various aspects of himself?

Additional Topics for Writing—Drama

1. Compare and contrast the ways Antigonê in Sophocles's *Antigonê* and Nora in *A Doll House* by Ibsen approach their problems.

2. Consider Sophocles's *Oedipus Rex* and Miller's *Death of a Salesman* as exemplary of dramatic tragedy in the fifth century B.C. and the twentieth century, respectively. Discuss the similarities and differences between the two plays, showing how the nature of tragedy has changed.

3. Imagine a discussion between Nora from *A Doll House* and Linda from *Death of a Salesman* on the subject of a woman's role in marriage. The discussion takes place after Nora has left Torvald, but while Linda is still trying to help Willy cope with his failures.

4. What advice would the Sergeant in Lady Gregory's *The Rising of the Moon* give to Antigonê?

5. In what ways is the situation faced by Willy in *Death of a Salesman* like that faced by Mme. Ranevskaya in Chekhov's *The Cherry Orchard*? How do forces beyond the control of the characters shape their fate? How do the characters themselves contribute to their downfall?

6. Watch videotapes of both the 1950s production of *Death of a Salesman* with Lee J. Cobb and the 1980s production with Dustin Hoffman. What are the similarities and differences between the two interpretations of Willy's character? Are there any other significant differences between the two productions? Read Miller's essay "Tragedy and the Common Man." Does either one of the productions fit his concept of modern tragedy better than the other?

7. Read Martin Esslin's *The Theater of the Absurd* and choose two other playwrights to consider in conjunction with Ionesco. After studying several plays by each playwright, write your own analysis of the social, political, and artistic theories behind this genre.

8. Compare Shaw's *Arms and the Man* to Shakespeare's *As You Like It*. What conventions of classical comedy does the Shakespeare play illustrate? How well does Shaw's play conform to these conventions? What are the differences between the two notions of comedy?

9. *Death of a Salesman* shares a common theme with other American plays of the mid-twentieth century, notably Eugene O'Neill's *The Iceman Cometh*. After reading various critical interpretations of the two play, write a paper analyzing the notion of dreams being shattered by an impersonal urban society. How does each of the playwrights portray the dreams of the common person? What does each use to represent society? Do the playwrights share the same conclusion about shattered dreams?

10. In what ways are the characters of Oedipus and Othello similar? Do they believe they are responsible for their own mistakes? For their own downfall? What are the similarities and differences in the way they approach their problems? In the way they react to their mistakes?

11. Compare and contrast the purposeful and manipulative actions of Iago and Molière's Tartuffe. Did either have sufficient motivation? Was one more justified? Was one more corrupt or evil?

12. How would Oedipus have reacted to Creon's decree not to bury the body of Polyneicês?

13. Discuss the nature of complacence in Desdemona (*Othello*), Mariane (*Tartuffe*), and Nora (*A Doll House*), and Linda (*Death of a Salesman*).

14. Compare the relationships between man and woman in any three of the following plays: *Othello, Trifles, Death of a Salesman, Riders to the Sea,* and *The Man in a Case.*

15. Compare the relationship between parents and children in *Death of a Salesman, Raisin in the Sun, Riders to the Sea, The Glass Menagerie,* and *Fences.*

16. Write a dialogue between the women in *Trifles* and Nora in *A Doll House*. Focus the discussion on the roles of women in the nineteenth and early twentieth centuries.

17. Compare Torvald's and Nora's conflicts in *A Doll House* to Varinka's and Byelinkov's conflicts in *The Man in a Case.*

18. Compare the treatment of death in any of the following plays: *A Doll House, Riders to the Sea, Death of a Salesman,* and *Fences.*

19. Compare the theme of romance and marriage in *As You Like It, The Glass Menagerie,* and *the Man in a Case.*

20. Compare the concept of the black American "dream deferred" as presented by *A Raisin in the Sun* and *Fences.*

PART FOUR

The Essay

CHAPTER TWENTY-TWO

Reading Essays

In this chapter, the process of reading an essay is demonstrated and analyzed, just as previous chapters have detailed the process of reading fiction, poetry, and drama. The comments and annotations accompanying the selections are intended to suggest possible paths readers might take; they are not meant to be definitive analyses. Students are urged to make their own decisions about the meaning of the essays, using the commentaries as leads rather than final answers.

Each section of the instructor's guide has provided suggestions for helping students become more sensitive to their own reading and writing processes as they analyze and evaluate the selections. The essay, of course, provides a perfect link between what is commonly called imaginative literature and nonfiction prose. Considering how essayists like E. B. White or Annie Dillard use voice, style, and structure to convey their ideas helps students recognize the essential connections among all forms of writing. Poets use metaphors and conceits, but so do biologists and historians and political scientists. The essays in the text open up possibilities for writing that many students may never have considered, and they may enjoy experimenting with some of the new forms they discover.

You can use the teaching strategies of this chapter by selecting other works from Chapter Twenty-Six, A Collection of Essays, and asking students to read and respond to them along the lines suggested with the three demonstration essays. Short essays, such as Francis Bacon's "Of Love" or E. M. Forster's "Our Graves in Gallipoli," work best for in class analysis. In addition, the reading process suggested in this chapter serves admirably as a first step in writing an essay responding to one of the selections.

Topics for Writing and Discussion

"The Ring of Time" • *E. B. White (pp. 1525–1527)*

1. In what sense is this an essay about the circus? About performance? About time? What does White mean by his suggestion in paragraph 3 that the circus is "the world in microcosm"?

[The essay is only about the circus on the literal level. As suggested in paragraph 3, the circus serves as a metaphor for the world. Each of us, at some point in our lives, is like the young girl—not yet aware that time takes a terrible toll during even the most simple and graceful moments. The girl's performance is particularly meaningful to White because she is unaware of its beauty and power. She seems to exist almost outside of time, which makes White's view of her—juxtaposed with his consciousness of time—especially poignant.]

2. Twice in the essay White refers to his task and responsibility as a writer. What is his point? Has White failed to accomplish what he set out to do (paragraph 8)? What has he set out to do here as a writer?

[In paragraph 3, White says that he is acting as recording secretary for all of us who have "surrendered . . . to the bedazzlement of a circus rider" (p. 1525). He seems, however, to attempt much more. He makes a profound comment on the nature of time and also on the value of the unself-conscious performance, the beauty of the natural connection between performer and performance. White may feel that he has failed, but he has certainly managed to capture images that make us more aware of the themes he addresses. He has not given us final answers, but he has raised evocative questions.]

3. In the opening paragraph, White locates and describes the scene. Later, he moves from that initial description to speculation about what he has seen. He alternates between description and speculation during the remainder of the essay. Which paragraphs are primarily descriptive? Which speculative? What would be gained or lost if the essay were to be reorganized with the paragraphs arranged in the following order: 1, 2, 4, 7, 3, 5, 6, 8?

[Paragraphs 1, 2, 4, and 7 are primarily descriptive. The others have descriptive elements but are primarily speculative. The rearrangement would place all of the descriptive paragraphs first and would make the speculation seem as though it were a reflection on time quite separate from the actual event. By integrating the description of the girl's ride with his speculations, White suggests how action and thought, time and timelessness, mortality and eternity are inextricably intertwined.]

4. Reread the opening paragraphs and underline, circle, or list all the words suggesting circularity. Why does White include so many of them? Look through paragraph 6 for echoes and repetitions of the details of the opening paragraph. What is the effect of such repetitions? How are they related to what White suggests about the girl and about time?

[The circular imagery suggests both the circus with its three rings and the cyclical nature of time. In paragraph 6, White reinforces the cycle-of-time theme by picturing the young rider twenty-five years later, looking like—in fact, actually becoming—the older horse trainer the spectators had watched with such boredom when they arrived. No perfect moment can be contained; it always changes and moves, taking its participants, willing or not, along with it. But time does not necessarily move in a linear way where the changes are unique; rather, those changes can be seen as part of a larger, repetitive pattern.]

5. Paragraph 3 introduces the language of light which burns so brilliantly in the essay's final sentences. List all the "light" words (and "dark" words) you can find in this paragraph. Explain what each of the images means, especially the last one: "out of its preliminary shabbiness comes the final splendor." Then reread the final paragraph and explain how White uses light imagery to make his point.

[Light images include "bedazzlement" and "final splendor." Dark images include "shade" and "preliminary shabbiness." The light and dark words suggest that the circus, which has its tawdry and seamy side, nonetheless also has a miraculous and life-affirming side that is more than outward show. There is a kind of courage and joy which White, in his final paragraph, describes as the "combustion of stars"—a spectacular explosion that contrasts with the dull but steady light of ordinary life which he compares to "planetary light."]

6. The following sentence by White inverts the regular word order of the English sentence—subject, verb, object. How does this alteration compare with the sentence in regular word order?

White   And buried in the familiar boasts of its advance agents lies the modesty of most of its people.

Regular: The modesty of most its people lies buried in the familiar boasts of its advance agents.

Write an imitation of White's sentence.

[White's sentence uses inverted order to emphasize the familiar boasts of advance agents, which then contrast startlingly with the modesty of the people. In the traditional order, the element of the sentence provide no special impact or surprise.]

7. Write an analysis of "The Ring of Time." Explain what White is saying in the essay. Discuss his strategy or organization and his use of language, especially imagery. Summarize his main points, paraphrase the most important paragraphs, and respond to his ideas with your own.

"Marrakech" • *George Orwell (pp. 1529–1535)*

1. What is Orwell's point and where does he make it explicit? Who do you think is his envisioned audience? Why do you think he wrote this essay?

[The next-to-last paragraph makes Orwell's point specific when he describes the though every white man has when seeing a black army march by: "How much longer can we go on kidding these people? How long before they turn their guns in the other direction?" The point of all the examples in this essay is to reveal the effects of racial inequality and to suggest that British oppression cannot last forever. Orwell probably envisioned his audience as either mildly sympathetic or at least open-minded. His appeals are heavily emotional and probably would not convince a diehard Empire supporter of the evils inherent in colonialism.]

2. In the essay overall, Orwell presents a series of scenes—the burial ground, the zoo, the ghetto, the women carrying firewood, the Senegalese troops—all to create his view of Marrakech. What does each scene imply, and how are they all related?

[The burial ground is compared to an abandoned building lot: the grave plots are unmarked; the bodies are dumped in the round. These details indicate the lack of dignity accorded the people of Marrakech. From the burial ground, Orwell's narrative moves to the zoo. His comments seem unrelated to the first scene until we get to the section where the worker asks him for some of the bread he has been feeding the gazelle. Then we recognize the connection: the people are treated like animals when they die, and while they live, they sometimes eat less well than the animals. After the zoo section comes the description of the ghetto. Here people fight bitterly over a few cigarettes, which are looked on as "impossible luxur[ies]." The reader now has one more facet to add to the picture: death, food, no small luxuries. All suggest the anonymity, poverty, and repression of the people. The woman carrying firewood advances these themes further—people see her bundle of sticks, not her. In the final scene, the Senegalese troops support the theme, but at the same time challenge the colonial assumptions. The vision of the black soldiers with guns raises the question of how long they will be willing to live the degraded lives the earlier scenes have depicted.]

3. You might think of the third section (p.1531) as a miniature version of the essay as a whole. This section, like the essay overall, contains a series of vignettes, each of which describes a scene and suggests, by implication, an idea. Identify these vignettes and explain what they have in common.

[Section 3 (p. 1531) shows us the deformed grandfather working with his grandson, then moves to the episode of the narrator passing out cigarettes. We next hear a dialogue revealing the prejudices of both Arabs and Europeans against the Jews. Each episode leads to

245

Orwell's observation at the end of this section in which he equates the Jews of Marrakech with helpless old women who were burned as witches, although they could not even work enough magic to get themselves a square meal.]

4. One of Orwell's strengths as a writer is his use of vivid and precise verbs. The following passage from the second paragraph of the essay has been stripped of its verbs. Before looking back to see what verbs Orwell used, fill in the blanks with your own choices. Try to be as precise as you can.

> When the friends get to the burying-ground they _____ an oblong hole a foot or two deep, _____ the body in it and _____ over it a little of the dried-up, lumpy earth, which is like broken brick.

5. At two different points, Orwell shifts from statements to questions. On both occasions he strings questions together. What is the effect of the accumulated questions, and what are the implied answers? (See paragraphs 3 and 26.)

[In the middle of paragraph 3, Orwell poses the questions Europeans in Marrakech ask themselves: "Are they really the same flesh as yourself? Do they even have names? Or are they merely a kind of undifferentiated brown stuff, about as individual as bees or coral insects?" These questions are answered by his vignettes, which show in painful detail the individuality of the people. And these vignettes lead to his questions in paragraph 26: "How much longer can we go on kidding these people" How long before they turn their guns in the other direction?" The implied answer to those questions is, of course, "Not long."]

6. Twice Orwell uses fragmentary sentences:

   a. No gravestones, no name, no identifying marks of any kind.

   b. Not hostile, not contemptuous, not sullen, not even inquisitive.

What do you gain or lose if you rewrite these fragments as grammatically complete sentences?

[Making these fragments into complete sentences would detract from the power of their brief, direct, parallel phrases.]

7. Orwell also includes an occasional inverted sentence like this one from paragraph 9:

> Down the centre of the street there is generally running a little river of urine.

If you think of this as a three-part sentence, you can separate it like this:

(1)	(2)	(3)
Down the centre or the street /	there is generally running /	a little river of urine.

Move the parts around like this: 3, 2, 1; 1, 3, 2. Which version do you prefer and why? (Look at the sentence in context.)

8. Write an imitation of paragraph 3 including the following: varied lengths of sentences; varied sentence forms; different sentence openers; balanced phrasing.

9. Write an advertisement or travel poster inviting Americans to vacation in Marrakech. You might think of yourself as a representative for public relations for the Moroccan government. Or you might write as a member of the United Nations Committee on World Brotherhood. Or . . .

"The Masked Marvel's Last Toehold" • Richard Selzer (pp. 1536–1539)

1. Selzer begins his essay with a brief description followed by a series of questions. Why do you think he chooses this pattern for his introduction?

    [The dramatic personal image of Elihu Koontz sitting alone in his bed, his leg amputated at the knee, sets the scene. We also learn that the speaker is the surgeon who performed the operation, and the series of questions serves both to establish the speaker's curiosity and to arouse our own. Selzer's poetic sensitivity (imagining, for instance, that Koontz contemplates "his foot's incandescent ghost") encourages readers to think beyond the surface of the situation and to wonder about the complexity of the human body, in sickness and in health.]

2. Why does Selzer find Koontz's contention that he is The Masked Marvel "shocking, unacceptable," something to "be challenged"?

    [At first we are surprised by the speaker's reaction, but as the story unfolds, we realize that Selzer is thrown off guard by the juxtaposition of his image of the powerful wrestler with the reality of the elderly, crippled man who is now his patient. As a young boy, Selzer saw The Masked Marvel wrestle and was amazed by his strength, power, and endurance. Now the fate of the same man lies in his hands. Like most of us, Selzer would probably like to hold the childhood memory intact, to imagine that The Masked Marvel still survives somewhere, wrestling and challenging, as he did that night in Toronto. Instead, Selzer must acknowledge the reality of time passing, of change, of the disabilities and diseases that inevitably accompany growing older.]

3. What is the young Selzer's reaction to the wrestling match? How does this response relate to his later encounter with Koontz?

    [As the ten-year-old Selzer watches the encounter between The Angel and The Marvel, he clearly identifies with the latter's pain and anguish. Selzer is shocked by his uncle's bloodthirsty yell, "Tear off a leg and throw it up here!" The boy has been able to watch the standard wrestling holds (although early on we learn that he was "shocked by [the wrestlers'] ugliness"), but when the ironically named Angel begins twisting The Marvel's toes, he cries out, repeating that such action is "not fair." The older Selzer notes, "The whole of the evil is laid open for me to perceive." At that moment he recognizes fully the fruitless brutality he is witnessing. The boy screams for someone to stop the pain, and he believes that his encouragement was the magic that enabled The Marvel to rally and win the match. Years later, as he is about to perform a second operation to remove Koontz's remaining leg, Selzer thinks back on the night of the match. Now he is the "masked marvel" (behind his surgical drapings), and Koontz once again faces pain and misery. This time, of course, the pain is for a reason, but nevertheless Selzer recognizes the deeply sad irony and as he moves into the operating theater mutters to himself the old words, "It's not fair."]

4. When the ten-year-old Selzer cries out for the fight to be stopped, why does he do so? What is the significance of his motivation?

    [The boy recognizes "the evil" when he sees The Marvel's pain, but he only cries out against it when The Angel attempts to remove his opponent's mask. This invasion of privacy is too much; the older Selzer evaluates his earlier response, saying that The Angel was going to "lay bare an ultimate carnal mystery!" It is the invasion of The Marvel's privacy, of his spirit as well as his body, that seems most upsetting. As an adult surgeon, of

247

course, Selzer must commit just such an act as The Angel's; he must invade the innermost parts of human beings, searching out the body's deepest secrets and often laying "bare an ultimate carnal mystery."]

5. Notice Selzer's sentence structure. What choices does he make to serve his rhetorical purposes?

[Selzer often uses short sentences to emphasize a point, frequently at the beginning or ending of a paragraph or as a separate paragraph. Note, for instance, at the end of the first paragraph, "It is a kind of spying, I know." Another example occurs during the initial conversation between Selzer and Koontz: "He clucks his tongue. He is exasperated." Selzer also uses parallel structure, as well as lists of parallel items, to underscore a point he is making. For example, he describes the wrestlers thus: "They are all haunch and paunch." He explains the wrestlers' actions: "The two men join, twist, jerk, tug, bend, yank, and throw." And in the final section, note these sentences: "I am in the operating room. . . . I amputated the left leg. . . . I have already scrubbed. I stand to one side. . . . And . . . *I am masked*."]

6. Selzer uses dialogue to develop his experience of the wrestling matches. Think of an incident from your childhood that was deeply moving and then describe it using a combination of vivid details and dialogue.

7. Try writing an opening paragraph using an introductory description and then a series of questions. Use Selzer's beginning as a model.

8. Compare the view of medicine and of doctors suggested by Selzer's essay with the view suggested by Eudora Welty's "A Worn Path." Which do you find more similar to your own experience with the medical profession? Explain.

"About Men" • *Gretel Ehrlich (p. 1540)*

Several of the questions here are suggested by the interviews on pp. 1542–1544 of the text.

1. Ehrlich argues against the romanticized image of the American cowboy, but does she herself perhaps also present a distorted and idealized version?

[Ehrlich's cowboys sound too good to be true. Here are gentle, kind men who work hard at brutally demanding labor and who react bravely yet almost automatically in a crisis. Her claims are filled with logical fallacies. For instance, she says "A cowboy is someone who loves his work," and then goes on to offer her proof: "Since the hours are long—then to fifteen hours a day—and the pay is $30, he has to." People work at all kinds of difficult, low-paying jobs for many reasons: they lack the training to do other work; they do not want to relocate to another part of the country; they do not have the initiative to leave known work for the unknown. While it is certainly probable that *some* cowboys love their work, it is highly doubtful that all of them (or even most of them) do. Ehrlich also depicts "her" cowboy as "gruff, handsome, and physically fit on the outside"—certainly as stereotyped as any Hollywood B film of the 1940s. And her picture of the chivalrous ranch hand tipping his hat and saying "Howdy ma'am" must get lots of laughs at the local bars in Wyoming and Colorado (if any of the patrons have read Ehrlich's picture of them).]

2. Which title do you think best fits the essay, "Revisionist Cowboy" (the title used by *Time* magazine) or "About Men," Ehrlich's choice?

[Here is an intriguing question that demonstrates how important titles can be. It's a good guess that the *Time* title was dreamed up by an editor there and was not assigned by Ehrlich herself. *Time* saw the essay as a new look at the Old West, and on the surface, that's what it seems to be. Yet as we look at the final paragraphs, with their emphasis on the relationships between cowboys and women, it's fair to speculate that Ehrlich sees these men as emblematic of the American male (whether he wears a Stetson or a three piece suit, rides to work on a horse or in a BMW, wrangles steers or government contracts).]

3. Where do women figure in the picture of Ehrlich's Western scene?

[Although Ehrlich herself worked at hard physical labor on a ranch, she seems to see herself as an exception to the rule. One sentence in her final paragraph suggests her view of women in the West: "For all the women here who use 'fragileness' to avoid work or as a sexual ploy, there are men who try to hide theirs. . . ." Here she shows the women "avoiding work," by which she apparently means the outdoor work of ranchers, since in the same sentence she describes many of the men as dependent on women to "cook their meals, wash their clothes, and keep the ranch house warm in winter." Apparently Ehrlich does not see these actions (which even "fragile" people can perform) as work. She stereotypes Western women just as she stereotypes Western men. Furthermore, western women, according to Ehrlich, had better not expect any demonstrations of tender feelings. They just need to show more understanding of those deeply "hidden" emotions that run deep inside their men—and if they know what's good for them, they'd better be satisfied with a single caress on the face or an isolated "I love you," which according to Ehrlich "will peal for a long time."]

4. Comment on the quote from Ehrlich's friend Ted Hoagland, "No one is as fragile as a woman but no one is as fragile as a man." What do you think Hoagland meant by this apparent syllogism? Can you give examples to demonstrate or to refute what he says?

5. Compare Ehrlich's view of Western men and women with the views in current films and television programs.

CHAPTER TWENTY-THREE

Types of Essays

This chapter briefly explains four major categories of essays. You may wish to break some of the categories into further subdivisions. For example, you may want to explain forms such as comparison and contrast, cause and effect, or classification and division. The four types of essays described here are intended as a starting point and not as a definitive list of all possible options.

During your discussion of the types of essays, you might ask students to look at some of the suggested examples and have them think about where the authors got their ideas. For example, E. B. White seems to have conceived the premise of "The Ring of Time" while watching a circus rehearsal. He had expected what he saw to be relatively predictable, but instead, as he watched the young girl ride her horse, he found himself speculating on a series of complex ideas that intertwined with unique and remarkable images. Students might keep a writer's notebook for a week or two, jotting down brief descriptions of people, places, or incidents that caused them to think beyond their surface meaning. In the same notebook, they might also write down a memory from the past, then speculate on its significance—just as Loren Eiseley speculates on his response to the pigeons in New York City. They could explore the implications of a childhood ambition as Mark Twain does in " 'Cub' Wants to Be a Pilot." Or they might plan an argument using the strategy of two voices, as E. M. Forster uses the voices of the British and Turkish soldiers in "Our Graves in Gallipoli."

CHAPTER TWENTY-FOUR

Elements of the Essay

In this chapter, four critical terms for analyzing the essay are defined and illustrated. By providing examples for each element from essays in earlier chapters as well as essays in the collection in Chapter Twenty-Six, the commentaries make students aware of how repeated readings (or previews of readings) can illuminate a work. In addition to the references to essays in earlier and later chapters, new examples are introduced at various points and are followed by extensive discussion.

Each element of the essay is explained by emphasizing its primary features. Through discussions of these features, students should be able to enhance their reading skills and, in addition, focus on elements of their own writing that can be improved through greater understanding and control of voice, style, structure, and thought.

VOICE

Considering how voice is established and how voice affects the reader encourages students to think about their own writing voices. Some students may feel that creating a "voice" means presenting a false or manipulative self. You may want to spend some time looking at the examples in the text and discussing this concern. For example, Orwell's voice in "Marrakech" suggests that he feels deep concern and even anger about the colonial situation. His anger, however, is controlled. He does not toss wild accusations around; instead, he presents carefully planned examples to support his view. If he were in a small group of friends who felt exactly a he did, he might have been more strident and accusatory toward the British government. Nonetheless, his voice in "Marrakech" is not false; it is simply an aspect of his personality, one that removes itself a bit from a situation and presents the evidence with only minor intrusive commentary. Obviously he hopes that the audience will draw the same conclusions he has, or at least that they will ask themselves some of the same questions he has posed in the essay. You might point out to students that voice is particularly important in writing arguments or proposals and ask them to discuss their own experiences with these kinds of writing.

"Los Angeles Notebook" • Joan Didion (pp. 1550–1551)

Possible Responses to Questions (p. 1551)

1. Didion's tone could not be called urgent in the sense that she expects people to be able to do very much about the Santa Ana wind, although she does suggest the possibility of making minor changes in everyday living patterns. For example, in paragraph 3, she mentions that some teachers in Los Angeles do not attempt to conduct formal classes during a Santa Ana. On the other hand, the forcefulness of her diction and the ominous tone of her words ("isolated beach," "ominously glossy," "peacocks screaming," "eerie absence of surf," "surreal" heat—all in paragraph 2) tell readers that Didion insists we see and understand her point of view. She is very personal in her tone, including many details from her own

life ("The baby frets. The maid sulks. I rekindle a warning argument with the telephone company"). In addition, she addresses a particular audience: Easterners (paragraph 4) and people who have not lived in Los Angeles (paragraph 6). By identifying the audience so clearly and entreating them so urgently to see her point of view, she comes alive not just as the impassive voice of an author, but as a living person who must survive through at best uncomfortable, and at worst dangerous, weather conditions.

2. The relentless accumulation of facts adds to the insistent, compelling tones. Didion is not going to let readers off the hook. If one set of examples won't convince us, the next paragraph presents us with a new (more disturbing) list of details.

Additional Topics for Writing and Discussion

1. Find as many examples as you can of sensory descriptions of the Santa Ana (words that appeal to your sense of sight, hearing, taste, touch, or smell). What effect do these images have on your response to the Santa Ana?

2. Notice in paragraphs 4 and 5 the many dates and other numbers Didion uses. Why do you think she chooses to tell us exactly when a particular event happened or exactly how fast the wind was blowing? Does she document her evidence? Do you find her sources convincing?

3. Why does Didion compare the Santa Ana with the foreign winds in paragraph 3? Does the Santa Ana seem mild by comparison? In what ways do the comparisons help her make her point? In what ways do the comparisons undermine her insistence on the power of the Santa Ana?

4. At the beginning of paragraph 3, Didion quotes Raymond Chandler. Who was Chandler? Do you find his testimony convincing evidence? Why? Is Didion's choice of Chandler as a witness consistent with her tone in the rest of the essay?

5. Write the description of a weather condition typical of a place where you live or have lived. Imagine an audience similar to Didion's—people who have never experienced the weather condition you are describing and who take a skeptical view of it.

STYLE

Studying the style of various essayists should suggest to students the importance of their own writing style. Many students have only a hazy idea of what "style" means. Before they read this section, you might ask them to write down their definitions of style and then as for volunteers to read responses. Usually the definitions are imprecise and halting. Often you'll hear examples of a particular writer's style rather than an explanation of the elements of style. These responses are particularly significant in light of the frequently heard student complaint, "I got a low grade on my paper because the instructor doesn't like my style." Too often "style" is confused with either content or the minor mechanical aspects (e.g., spelling, punctuation) or writing. While choice of content and use of mechanics may contribute to a writer's style, decisions about diction, syntax, figurative language, rhythm, and sentence and paragraph structure are surely far more important. This section of the text helps students to identify these elements and to recognize their contribution to the essay's meaning.

"The Battle of the Ants" • *Henry David Thoreau (pp. 1556–1557)*

Possible Response to Questions (pp. 1557–1558)

1. Like E. B. White, who sees the circus as a microcosm for the experiences of the greater world, Thoreau sees the ant world as a microcosmic reflection of the greater world. In particular, he compares the ant war to the Trojan War. By making this comparison, he creates a mock-heroic situation. The ants, of course, are considered to be insignificant and bothersome creatures by most humans. Reporting their wars in terms of human wars makes us reassess the true importance of those battles that have long been praised as patterns of patriotic splendor. He must certainly have deflated the pride of the readers in the Concord of his own time who regarded the battles of Concord and Lexington as the most important military events in recorded history. Likening Colonial soldiers to ants creates a bold and shocking comparison. More important than diminishing the splendor of human war, however, is the invitation Thoreau extends to readers to notice more carefully and with more concern the small creatures of the earth, who have their struggles just as we have ours.

2. By quoting these battles cries, which would have been immediately recognized by his readers, Thoreau makes the ants seem even closer to the human world. The ants become small, individual beings rather than mute creatures blindly struggling toward some undefined end.

3. Thoreau's choice of Latin diction reinforces the analogy by which he compares the ants of Concord to the soldiers of Troy. These formal words establish a tone of dignity that reflects Thoreau's belief in the importance of the tiniest, the seemingly most insignificant, part of nature.

Additional Topics for Writing and Discussion

1. "The Battle of the Ants" is sometimes reprinted with the following conclusion. What is added to the essay by including it? Do you read the meaning of the entire piece any differently with this new conclusion? Is anything lost by the omission of this final paragraph?

   Kirby and Spence tell us that the battles of ants have long been celebrated and the date of them recorded, though they say that Huber is the only modern author who appears to have witnessed them. "Aeneas Sylvius," say they, "after giving a very circumstantial account of one contested with great obstinacy by a great and small species on the trunk of a pear tree, adds that 'this action was fought in the pontificate of Eugenius the Fourth, in the presence of Nicholas Pistoriensis, an eminent lawyer, who related the whole history of the battle with the greatest fidelity.' A similar engagement between great and small ants is recorded by Olaus Magnus, in which the small ones, being victorious, are said to have buried the bodies of their own soldiers, but left those of their giant enemies a prey to the birds. This event happened previous to the expulsion of the tyrant Christian the Second from Sweden." The battle which I witnessed took place in the Presidency of Polk, five years before the passage of Webster's Fugitive-Slave Bill.

2. Is Thoreau's subject the ants or is it human war? What is the main point he makes in the essay? How do you respond to his ideas?

3. Compare Thoreau's view of nature as exemplified in this section of *Walden* with Blake's view of nature as suggested in his poem "To see a world in a grain of sand."

4. Write an essay describing your own close observation of some very small aspect of nature. Choose something you found particularly significant and explain your response.

STRUCTURE

The essays in this anthology have been carefully selected to represent many possible rhetorical choices. Students may have learned that essays can be easily classified as "comparison and contrast" or as "narration" or as "definition." The reality, of course, is that these patterns are often intertwined, although sometimes one pattern may dominate. In addition, students who believe that all essays must fall into the precisely defined categories they have learned will be surprised with experimental structures such as E. M. Forster's dialogue in "Our Graves in Gallipoli" or Alice Walker's complex meditation as she goes "In Search of Our Mothers' Gardens." Considering these essays, as well as the other selections, helps students to expand their view of structure. You may want to encourage them to write experimental essays of their own. Or you might have them write a traditional, formal essay and then revise it by using an innovative and less formal structure.

"The Death of the Moth" • Virginia Woolf (pp. 1559–1560)

Possible Responses to Questions (p. 1561)

1. The first paragraph describes the moth, content with his life. He seems a compatible part of the lively harvest activities in the field. In the second paragraph, we learn that the moth is inside the speaker's window. She connects the moth to the harvest activities by comparing their tremendous sense of energy. After the transitional sentence, however, the moth's energy takes on a poignance. He is not toiling to bring in a harvest; he is struggling to escape the trap of the window panes. Woolf opens the third paragraph with reference once again to the energy of the moth, but here she uses it as a means to begin a meditative discussion in which she sees the moth as representative of "the true nature of life." The fourth paragraph focuses once more on the moth itself, this time struggling futilely to survive. In this paragraph, the narrator for the first time interacts physically with the moth, trying first to save it, then recognizing its fate. The final paragraph moves from the dead moth to the scene of the harvest, where the workers have gone for lunch with no notice or knowledge of the scene the narrator has witnessed, and finally to the narrator's mediation on the nature of life and death. She continues to describe the moth, but always as part of the commentary on the strangeness of life and the power of death.

2. Paragraph 3 interrupts the chronology of the story with the narrator's commentary on the moth as a "tiny bead of pure life." Woolf makes the modification to suggest that her narrative is more than just a story or a description; she intends to make a larger point about life and death.

3. By including the details of the harvest in the field, Woolf suggests both the cyclical and linear nature of time. As the moth began its struggles, the field was full of workers, horses, and rooks; when the moth dies, the workers have gone to lunch, the horses stand still, the rooks have flown away. The reader senses real change—the linear progression of

time—yet also, as the the narrator suggest, the essential energy remains, in a different form yet still there. "Yet the power was there all the same, massed outside indifferent, impersonal, not attending to anything in particular." In this sense we are brought back full circle from the scene in the first paragraph to the scene in the last.

Additional Topics for Writing and Discussion

1. Does Woolf imply any resemblances between the moth and human's How are human lives and deaths similar to, or different from, the life and death of the moth described in Woolf's essay?

2. What is the speaker's attitude toward the moth? Consider carefully the words she uses to describe it and her actions toward it. Does her attitude seem similar to Thoreau's attitude toward the ants?

3. Compare Woolf's treatment and presentation of the moth to Whitman's treatment and presentation of the spider in "A noiseless patient spider" (p. 595).

4. Both in paragraph 4 and in paragraph 5 the narrator mentions trying to save the moth with a pencil. What significance might the pencil have?

5. Write an essay commenting on a philosophical issue: love, hate, revenge, jealousy. Use an extended example of an animal, bird, or insect to make your point.

THOUGHT

Asking students to find the thought in an essay—including, of course, feeling as essential to thought—often proves less troublesome and less threatening than asking them to discover the thesis of an essay. For one thing, many writers do not overtly state their thesis in one or two sentences, and students who are accustomed to the "thesis statement" approach to essays become frustrated and confused. In addition, using the term "thought," as it is explained in the text, makes clear that the meaning of an essay does not reside in a pronouncement in the opening paragraph or in a concluding summary. Instead, the central thought or thoughts of an essay pervade every sentence and every paragraph. The thought of the whole cannot be discovered without careful attention to each of its parts.

"Of Revenge" • Francis Bacon (pp. 1563–1564)

Possible Responses to Questions (p. 1564)

1. As Bacon suggests, revenge is "wild" because it is outside of the law. In addition, we think of revenge as wild because it is usually carried out in anger, without calm or careful consideration. Revenge may be seen as "just" because it punishes a wrong, yet the term must be qualified by the word "wild" because revenge does not follow the planned system of retribution dictated by government.

2. Bacon's arguments are primarily moral. For example, he says that we should ignore the wrongs committed against us because, by passing over a wrong, we make ourselves better than, rather than even with, our enemies. In addition, he argues that people do not commit

wrongs for gratuitous reasons, but only to gain profit or pleasure or honor for themselves. This being the case, Bacon says, we should not seek revenge, for how can we blame people for seeking to advance themselves?

3. The historical and biblical allusions would have been familiar to Bacon's audience and would serve as authoritative references to give credence to his theories.

Additional Topics for Writing and Discussion

1. Take any one of the following statements from Bacon's "Of Revenge" and plan a convincing argument either agreeing or disagreeing with it:

   A. Certainly in taking revenge, a man is but even with his enemy, but in passing it over, he is superior, for it is a prince's part to pardon.
   B. There is no man doth a wrong for the wrong's sake, but thereby to purchase himself profit, or pleasure, or the like.
   C. This is certain, that a man that studieth revenge keeps his own wounds green, which otherwise would heal and do well.

2. In the final sentences of "Of Revenge," Bacon differentiates between "public" and "private" revenge. He says, "Public revenges are for the most part fortunate, as that for the death of Caesar, for the death of Pertinax, for the death of Henry the Third of France, and many more." Think of some twentieth-century examples of "public revenge." Then decide whether or not you think Bacon's pronouncement holds true for your example.

3. Compare Bacon's view of revenge with that of the narrator in "The Black Cat" by Edgar Allan Poe (p. 80).

258

CHAPTER TWENTY-FIVE

Approaching an Essay: Guides for Reading and Writing

This chapter summarizes the approaches to reading essays explained in detail in earlier chapters. You may want to work through each step with your class, asking them to respond, either in writing or through discussion, to Annie Dillard's "Living Like Weasels" before they read the commentary that follows the essay.

You might remind students that the guidelines provided on pp. 1565–1566 may be applied not only to the selections in the anthology section but also to any other essays they may read. In addition, students may profitably use the guidelines to become more conscious of the various elements of their own writing as they become more knowledgeable about and familiar with the works of professional authors.

"Living Like Weasels" • Annie Dillard (p. 1566)

Additional Topics For Writing and Discussion

1. As is mentioned in the discussion of style (p. 1569, Dillard uses many short sentences. Notice how many of her paragraphs start with very short sentences or phrases, sometimes with only one word. What effect is created by her use of short sentences in the initial position?

2. Choose one metaphor or simile from "Living Like Weasels" and analyze it in detail. What exactly does it mean? What does it contribute to the essay? (See, for example, the description of the weasel at the end of the first paragraph—"like a stubborn label." Or the definition of the weasel's journal at the end of the third section: "His journal is tracks in clay, a spray of feathers, mouse blood and bone: uncollected, unconnected, loose-leaf, and blown.")

3. How do you think Thoreau would respond to Dillard's view of what she can learn from wild animals?

4. Do you agree with Dillard the "we can live any way we want" (end of Section 5, p. 1568)? What exactly does she mean by living "any way we want"?

CHAPTER TWENTY-SIX

Topics for Writing and Discussion for a Collection of Essay

"Of repentance" • Michel de Montaigne (p. 1574)

1. The title of Montaigne's essay is "Of repentance." Where does he begin discussing repentance? What purpose is served by the paragraphs that precede this starting point?

[Paragraph 10 introduces the first mention of repentance. The section of the essay that precedes this serves to establish Montaigne's larger subject: human nature as reflected through his own experiences and observations. In paragraph 5, he notes that he is the first author to appeal to an audience directly, as a fallible, real person rather than as an abstract authority. He explains that his purpose is not to instruct, but rather to explain: "I do not teach, I tell." His remarkable honesty and directness establishes a believable and sympathetic ethos.]

2. How does Montaigne define "vice"? Why is this definition important?

[Because vice occasions repentance, Montaigne must explain exactly what he means by this term. He considers not only actions that reason and nature would condemn but also actions forbidden by human laws and customs to be vices. To discuss repentance, Montaigne must first establish the circumstances he believes should elicit this response.]

3. What does Montaigne believe motivates people to do good? How does this discussion relate to the subject of repentance?

[Montaigne notes that many people do good because they are gratified by the pride they feel and by the acclaim they win from others. Montaigne warns against reliance on the opinions of others and stresses instead the important of a sustaining inner life. He says, "I have my own laws and court to judge me" (p. 1577). As the essay continues, we see that the private judge evaluates not only good deeds but vices as well.]

4 Throughout the essay, Montaigne quotes other philosophers and authors. Why does he cite these individuals?

[In some cases they are cited as authorities to support a point Montaigne is making. For instance, on p. 1576 Montaigne argues against too heavy reliance on popular opinion and quotes Seneca to explain his warning: "What were vices now are moral acts." Montaigne also uses quotations to echo his own sentiments. See, for instance, the quotation from Cicero on p. 1577, beginning "You must use your own judgment. . . ." Finally, Montaigne uses quotations to expand and develop a point he has made. Note the lines from Lucan on p. 1578.]

5. Find a paragraph developed through the use of examples and a paragraph developed through the use of comparison and contrast.

261

[Montaigne makes use of examples throughout the essay. See, for instance, the paragraph in which Julius Drusus refuses to pay workmen to make his house more private but instead suggests that they make it more easily viewed by the public. Montaigne uses this example to support his contention that the truly moral man will act with the same virtue in private life as he does in public life. He continues to develop this point through his comparison of Socrates (who represents for Montaigne the ideal "private" person) and Alexander the Great (who represents a venerated public person). Montaigne notes that he can imagine Socrates taking Alexander's place but not the reverse. Again he asserts the integrity of the individual who has examined his own life and lives according to honorably conceived inner laws. He finds this individual superior to the "public" man who may act honorably in public situations but about whose interior life we know little.]

6. What does Montaigne believe inclines a person to vice or to virtue?

[Montaigne stands on the side of nature rather than nurture. Although he believes that natural inclinations can be strengthened by education, he does not think essential qualities can be changed. He believes that an honest person identifies his strengths and tries to enhance them, but also that this same honest man must recognize his vices and truly repent. One of the main problems of his time, Montaigne believes, comes from people who recognize neither their own strengths nor their own weaknesses and who can, therefore, have only a "blurred" idea of reformation.]

7. What is the purpose of the anecdote of the thief who lived in Armagnac?

[The thief, who began life as a beggar, soon determined that he would live better if he stole in a clever and sly manner. Because he was never caught, he accrued wealth and came to live well. He claimed to be doing penance by gradually returning what he had stolen to the kinsmen of those from whom he took the means for building his fortune. Montaigne points to this case as an example of false repentance. The thief saw steeling as morally repugnant, yet not so repugnant as living in poverty. He was unwilling to sacrifice for his values and could not be deemed truly repentant simply by returning some of what he stole.]

8. What does Montaigne mean by "accidental repentance"?

[Montaigne calls the artificially forced virtue of old age "accidental repentance." Those who are no longer able to perform sexually or to enjoy nights of carousing often condemn such activities and claim to despise them. Montaigne sees such people as hypocrites who repent the sins of their youth only because they can no longer commit them.]

9. How does Montaigne differentiate between regret and repentance?

[One feels regret for negative consequences over which one had no control, repentance for negative actions which one could have stopped but chose not to do so.]

10. Montaigne says, "When my friends apply to me for advice, I give it freely and clearly, and without hesitating as nearly everyone else does because, the affair being hazardous, it may come out contrary to my expectations, wherefore they may have caused to reproach me for my advice; that does not worry me." Do you act as does Montaigne when friends ask for advice? Do you agree with his approach? Explain.

"Of Love" • *Francis Bacon (p. 1583)*

1. Is Bacon's purpose to warn us of the dangers of love? To encourage us to devote ourselves to love? Something else?

   [The contradictions and playful tone of the essay suggest that Bacon simply wants us to think about the ramifications of love. This is an essay that opens many doors and closes only one: the entry for wanton love.]

2. Why does Bacon quote the statement "That it is impossible to love and to be wise"? Why does he associate love with flattery? Do you agree?

   [Using a quotation usually lends authority to an argument. It is interesting to note here that Bacon does not document his source. He associates love with flattery because in this part of the essay he is speaking of romantic love where the lover is completely obsessed with the beloved to whom he pays extravagant compliments.]

3. Reread the essay, noting how many times Bacon makes an assertion only to qualify or even contradict it. What happens to his assertions in light of his qualifications? Look, for example, at the criticism he levels against love, then at his qualification of that criticism.

   [The essay is based on a series of assertions that are then qualified or contradicted. For example, in the first few sentences Bacon says that not one great and worthy person has been "transported to the mad degree of love." Then he immediately gives two examples of great and worthy men who have loved in exactly this way. The essay balances positive aspects of love against many negative aspects and finally leads to the conclusion that some types of love are worthy while others should be condemned.]

4. What is the relationship of the final sentence to the rest of the essay? Has Bacon discussed the three kinds of love?

   [Bacon does not present dearly defined discussions of each type of love, but we can assume that his constant re-examination and qualification of generalizations has led to this final classification.]

5. Reorganize Bacon's one-paragraph essay into a multiparagraph one. Explain why you divide it as you do. Explain also what is gained and what lost in the reorganization.

6. You might argue that this essay is a kind of rough draft in which Bacon is working out his ideas about love. You might think of it as an unfinished essay, one in which contradictory ideas are vying for consideration. Suppose Bacon had rewritten the essay to eliminate the contradictions and qualifications. How would your experience of the essay be different? Would you gain or lose more? Why?

"Meditation XVII: For Whom the Bell Tolls" • *John Donne (pp. 1585–1586)*

1. Dorine begins and ends this meditation with the image of the bell ringing. Why does the bell ring at the beginning and end? How is the bell used throughout the essay to present Donne's main idea?

   [The bell at the beginning is the church bell, apparently tolling to mark the death of another but heard by the speaker as possibly meant for him. Throughout the essay, bells represent beginnings and endings (the start and close of day; the start and close of religious ceremonies) and the connection of all human beings (the connection of the evening and morning bells). At the end, the bell has clearly become a symbol of the interconnection of all life and of the necessity of human connection with God. Donne sees the bell as warning him—and all of us—to contemplate not only our neighbor's death but also our own, and thus to make our peace with God.]

2. Compare the style and form of any of Donne's poems on pp. 549–553 with the style and form of "Meditation XVII."

[Donne uses the extended metaphor in both his poetry and his prose. Note, for example, his comparison of the Catholic church and its members to the human race and its members; also the well-known comparison of humanity to a continent, with each individual a part of the main.]

3. Is Donne's "Mediation XVII" an argument? Is he trying to convince us of anything? Is he trying to persuade us to take a certain course of action?

[By focusing the meditation on himself and his own need to contemplate death and make his peace with God, Donne establishes a tone of explanation rather than persuasion. The careful marshaling of so many extended examples, on the other hand, suggests that Donne wants the reader to see his view of the human condition. He is not trying to lead readers toward a course of action, but rather urges them to understand the validity of his thesis.]

4 Compare John Donne's "Mediation XVII" to Matthew Arnold's "To Marguerite—Continued" (reprinted below). Consider what each writer says about human relationships as well as the imagery each uses to convey his idea.

TO MARGUERITE—CONTINUED
Matthew Arnold

Yes! in the sea of life enisled,
With echoing straights between us thrown,
Dotting the shoreless watery wild,
We mortal millions live *alone*.
The islands feel the enclasping flow,
And then their endless bounds they know.

But when the moon their hollows lights,
And they are swept by balms of spring,
And in their glens, on starry nights,
The nightingales divinely sing;
And lovely notes, from shore to shore
Across the sounds and channels pour—

Oh! then a longing like despair
Is to their farthest caverns sent;
For surely once, they feel, we were
Parts of a single continent!
Now round us spreads the watery plain—
Oh might our marges meet again!

264

> Who ordered, that their longing's fire
> Should be, as soon as kindled, cooled?
> Who renders vain their deep desire?—
> A God, a God their severance ruled!
> And bade betwixt their shores to be
> The unplumbed, salt, estranging sea.

"A Modest Proposal" • Jonathan Swift (pp. 1586–1591)

1. When do you first realize that this proposal could not possibly be serious?

   [Answers will vary greatly because many students have difficulty recognizing irony. Certainly the animal imagery in paragraph 4 should offer a clue: "a child just dropped from its dam" is not the way most concerned citizens would describe a newborn infant and its mother. Paragraph 7 refers to boys and girls over the age of twelve as "salable" commodities, which should signal a clear discrepancy between the narrator's apparent altruism and his real attitude. Most students will see the irony when they get to paragraph 9, which suggests a long list of possible ways to cook a child. Some students, however, will read the entire essay and still think that Swift and his narrator are one and the same. You'll need to point out the accumulating detail that makes clear this could not possibly be a serious proposal.]

2. Who is the speaker in the essay? What does he tell us about himself?

   [The speaker is an eighteenth-century "projector," as he tells us in paragraph 4. We also learn in this paragraph that there were many other projectors during this period who brought forth their own proposals for solving the "Irish problem." At the end of the essay we learn that the proposer is married, but his wife is past child-bearing age and his youngest child is nine years old. These personal details are intended as evidence that he himself would not benefit from the scheme of selling babies for food; of course, the irony should be clear: his family would not suffer the loss of their children.]

3. Consider the images of the opening paragraph. How do you respond to them? What purpose does this paragraph serve?

   [The picture of the desperate mothers and children should certainly arouse readers' sympathy. The picture given here contrasts violently with the "proposal" in paragraph 9, which shocks and sickens us.]

4. Why do paragraphs 4 through 7 provide so many statistics and explanations of the beneficial effects of the proposal? And why does the speaker return to more statistics in paragraphs 11, 12, 14, and 15?

   [The first group of statistics seems to be simply part of the proposer's building his case logically and reasonably. Then he outrages readers with his proposal in paragraph 9. His quick return to statistics is an attempt to assure the reader that the proposal is really nothing out of the ordinary, simply another proposition that can be supported by carefully worked-out figures.]

5. The proposer seems to appeal primarily to "reason" by using statistics and quoting "authorities" such as the American who gave him the recipes for cooking babies. Does Swift make *his* argument through appeal to reason or to emotion?

[Swift's appeal is mainly emotional. We are meant to be astounded and outraged at the supposedly rational appeal not just of this proposer, but of all unfeeling proposers who do not stop to think—or who do not care—about the effects of their grandiose plans.]

6. Where does Swift peek through the mask of his proposer to suggest his real beliefs about possible solutions to the problems of Irish poverty and hunger?

[Paragraph 29 offers several options which the proposer says he does not want to hear about. The qualification in paragraph 30, however, is interesting, and here Swift speaks for himself as well as his persona: "Let no man talk to me of these and the like expedients, till he hath at least some glimpse of hope that there will be ever some hearty and sincere attempt to put them into practice."]

7. Research some of the solutions that have been proposed for feeding the hungry here and abroad. Do any of them seem like the kind of proposal Swift is making fun of in "A Modest Proposal"? Explain.

8. Write your own "Modest Proposal" suggesting an outrageous solution to a problem you feel strongly about. Create a persona (like Swift's projector) and be sure to let the audience know who your speaker is. Remember that you are writing ironically—saying the opposite of what you really mean.

"Cub' Wants to Be a Pilot" • Mark Twain (p. 1591)

1. What is Twain's main goal in "'Cub' Wants to Be a Pilot"? Is he arguing for a particular way of leading one's life? Is he simply telling a story? Is he presenting episodes to lead to a central point? Or is he presenting a speculative meditation?

[While the essay's structure is primarily narrative, with Twain recounting events from his own life, it has a highly speculative quality. See, for example, the beginning of paragraph 3, where he comments on the implications of his father's position as justice of the peace, or the end paragraph (p. 1596), where he reflects on the discovery that the night watchman was not a displaced nobleman.]

2. Compare Twain's description of his hometown friend who becomes a "striker" on a steamboat (paragraph 3) with his description of himself when he becomes a "traveler" (paragraph 7). What is the effect of these two paragraphs? How would your response to them change if they had appeared right next to each other instead of being separated by several other paragraphs? How would your response have changed if Twain had provided an explanatory statement suggesting the connection between the two descriptions?

[In paragraph 7, Twain becomes very much like the "striker' he describes as outrageously boastful in paragraph 3. We have to see the striker in a somewhat more sympathetic light when we recognize that the appealing narrator of the essay cannot resist the same swaggering postures once he has become associated with steamboats. If the paragraphs had immediately followed one another, or if Twain had made an intrusive commentary on the similarity between his behavior and the behavior of the striker, the essay might have taken on a didactic, preaching tone. As it is, readers are gently led to the comparison and allowed to chuckle at the folly of both the striker and the traveler (as well as that of human nature).]

3. Find examples of understatement and overstatement and explain what they contribute to the essay.

[At the beginning of paragraph 3, Twain suggests that being the son of a man who had "the power of death over all men and could hang anybody that offended him" was in general "distinction enough" for the young Twain. Here the overstatement of the father's power, contrasted with the understatement of the son's response to what he believes to be within his father's control, helps to establish the essay's tone of gentle, ironic humor. For another ironic overstatement, see the last sentence of paragraph 5. Twain's greatly exaggerated daydream humorously suggests the propensity of the young to see and express emotions through large, sweeping, absolute images.]

4. Compare the final sentence in the next-to-last paragraph and the first sentence in the final paragraph. How are they structured? What is their effect? Try writing two sentences that use a similar structure for a similar purpose. For example:

When I first _____ , I felt _____ , _____ , _____ , _____ . Now, however, when I _____ , I feel _____ , _____ , _____ , _____ .

[Twain makes wonderful use of a long series of parallel adverbs in the next-to-last paragraph and parallel adjective in the final paragraph to emphasize the dramatic change in his feelings. You might also note that the two sentences serve as strong transitions between the two paragraphs.]

5. Read Chapter 19 of *Huckleberry Finn*, where the Duke of Bridgewater and the Dauphin are introduced. Compare the descriptions there with the description of the watchman in the last two paragraphs of " 'Cub' Wants to be A Pilot."

6. Write an essay describing one of your own childhood ambitions. Explain how far you pursued the ambition and whether or not you have any regrets.

"Our Graves in Gallipoli" • *E. M. Forster (pp. 1596–1597)*

1. Although "Our Graves in Gallipoli" presents a persuasive argument, its structure is dramatic. Considering the processes of actively reading drama and actively reading essays, what elements of this work might you profitably evaluate?

[While evaluating the usual elements of an essay (voice, style, structure, and thought) will be useful, students should also consider such elements of drama as character, setting, and dialogue.]

2. Characterize the two soldiers. Are they alike? Do they agree on most points? How are they different, and why is this difference significant?

[The characters seem very much alike, although they play different roles. The first soldier does most of the speaking and is clearly angry. The second soldier asks short questions or makes brief comments about the first soldier's remarks: he supports the points made by the first soldier, but he is more controlled and resigned in what he says than is his companion. We learn, of course, near the very end of the dialogue that the second soldier is a Turk, while the first soldier, who has been railing against the policies and leaders of Britain, is English. By having soldiers from two different sides participate in this dialogue of agreement, Forster points out not only the absurdity of war but also the universality of blame for war. The English soldier may hold his own country to blame, but the responses of the Turkish soldier suggest that he also holds the leaders of his country accountable.]

3. How do the setting and the first soldier's references to Homer contribute to the meaning of the dialogue/essay?

[Gallipoli, a place which lies between East and West, suggests the division between those cultures. The classical references insist that readers recognize the long history of war and the endless misery that it has brought. In addition, both the site of the graves and the classical references suggest the universality of the originators of wars; the blame can be placed on no one nation or time period.]

4. Sometimes this essay is reprinted with an opening dialogue that sets the scene as a "spot looking out across the Dardanelles"; the graves are unmarked by any monument because "they escaped notice during the official survey." Do these introductory details change your reading?

[The Dardanelles, of course, divides East and West and thus emphasizes both the difference and the similarity of the two soldiers. The strait may divide two cultures, but in a sense it also unites them because its margins touch both banks. In like manner, the two soldiers are divided by their cultures but united by their deaths in war and their realization of the brotherhood of humanity. Learning that both soldiers escaped official notice suggests the impersonal treatment governments accord the individual; as "unknown soldiers" the two speakers are particularly closely connected.]

5. In addition to the opening commentary printed above, a closing commentary is sometimes also included with Forster's essay. The narrator notes that the second soldier cannot answer the first soldier's final question and then describes the "warlike preparations" that can be seen on the opposite coast as long as there is light. Then the sun sets and "through the general veil thus formed the stars become apparent." How would your reading differ if this ending were included?

[The narrator's comment underlines the rhetorical nature of the final question and also underlines the fact that the first soldier, who has been the one with the answers throughout the dialogue, now finds himself faced with the true conclusion of his deliberations—the unanswerable madness of war. Warlike preparations reflect the reality of the concerns voiced by the two soldiers throughout the dialogue, and the veil of stars which covers them suggests that all peoples, all nations, all wars are eventually covered by the same end—the peaceful night of death.]

6. Write a dialogue between two graves based on Forster's essay. Have them discuss a different topic. One voice should pose questions, while the other should give responses that indicate your point of view.

Once More to the Lake" • E. B. White (pp. 1598–1602)

1. What is White's attitude toward time in the essay? Does his attitude stay the same throughout the essay? If not, where does it change?

[White at first thinks that time has pretty much stood still at his old lakeside vacation spot. Yet the longer he stays, the more he recognizes that the patterns stay the same while the details differ. For instance, the girls who wait on tables look the same—but now they have gone to the movies and thus have learned that they should wash their hair in imitation of glamorous film stars. The motorboats are noisier now, and there is more Coca-Cola than Moxie when he and his son stop at the store for a drink. Still, White continues to document the similarities and to try to stop the hands of time. He does not emphasize for us the implications of the changes he notes: the way media have changed the world, the way modern technology and the advertising of products have modified our lives. He does not describe the pain of time's passage until the final paragraph where, seeing his son go through the ritual of pulling on a wet bathing suit while he prefers to sit warm and dry, he recognizes that he has changed, that time has passed, and that each change he has documented throughout the essay brings him one step closer to his own death.]

2. How does White's son remind him of himself? Note specific details. Why is this comparison significant?

[The significance is first suggested in paragraph 4, where White tells us that he "began to sustain the illusion that [his son] was I," and that he (White) was his father. The son fishes exactly the way the father remembers himself doing (paragraph 5) and loves the rented outboard the same way the father had loved his old one-cylinder engine. In the end, of course, White is forced to recognize that his son is *not* he and that he (White) has, in fact, taken the place of his own father. He too, like the lake, is the same but infinitely changed.]

3. Why does White say in the last paragraph that his groin "felt the chill of death"?

[His contemplation and gradual acknowledgment of the passage of time has forced him to recognize his own mortality. Even in the midst of joy and life—perhaps because of the joy of life—there is the ever-present reality of finite time and eventual death.]

4. Write an essay describing a place you have been to both as a child and as an adult. Explain what has changed and what has stayed the same. What are your responses to both the changed and unchanged aspects?

5. Compare White's view of time in "Once More to the Lake" to his view of time in "The Ring of Time" (p. 1525).

6. Compare White's view of his relationship with his son to Donald Hall's view in "My son, my executioner" (p. 715).

"Shooting an Elephant" • *George Orwell (pp. 1602–1606)*

1. Where does the action of this essay begin? How do the first two paragraphs prepare us for the action? Where does Orwell interrupt the action to explain his idea? What is the idea, and how does the final paragraph reinforce it?

[The first two paragraphs set the scene and establish the narrator as a sympathetic character who, although he serves the British Raj, is really on the side of the Burmese. We also see him as humanly fallible when he admits that his sympathy with the Burmese is theoretical rather than practical. In reality he has a hard time thinking of the natives as anything other than "evil-spirited little beasts" who try to make his job difficult. These details are essential for us to understand the implication of the action that begins in paragraph 3. In the middle of paragraph 6, the narrator interrupts his narrative to tell the readers that as he stood facing the crowd, he suddenly realized "the hollowness, the futility of the white man's dominion in the East." The final paragraph underlines the futility as we see the younger officers arguing that a coolie is worth less than an elephant. We have to recognize the impossible situation the British Empire is in; the failure of the British rulers to see the Burmese as fully human will surely cause their downfall.]

2. Examine the description of the dead man in paragraph 4. What picture does Orwell draw in that description? What does it add to the essay? Is it essential?

[The description of the coolie as "crucified" certainly suggests a relationship with Christ. And the graphic description of his look of "unendurable agony" indicates that, although the narrator claims to have killed the elephant only to please the crowd, he also might have had unacknowledged feelings that revenging the coolie's death was morally right. This complexity would not be suggested without the gory details of paragraph 4. In addition, paragraph 4 shows us that coolie as a suffering, real, human individual, and that makes the young officers' callous remarks in the final paragraph even more horrifying.]

3. Throughout the essay Orwell uses comparisons. How does the imagery of acting and theater reinforce the point Orwell makes in paragraph 7? What is the purpose of the comparisons used in paragraphs 11 and 12? What impression of the elephant do you come away with after reading those paragraphs? How is it accomplished?

[The theater imagery in paragraph 7 suggests the role reversal of the Burmese and the British. The narrator finds himself as a puppet of the mob rather than the lead actor he had previously imagined himself to be; the British will soon discover that they are all puppets and not masters. In paragraph 11, the crowd is described as though they were happy theatergoers, anticipating an exciting show. What is important to the narrator is merely an amusing illusion to the onlookers. In paragraph 12, the audience lets out a "devilish roar of glee," just as spectators would at a play or sporting event. They do not care at all for the agony of the elephant who has become symbolic of the large and powerful who are brought down in response to the pressure of the apparently weak and subservient. Without reaching too far, the elephant can be seen as a symbol of the British Raj.]

4. In paragraphs 7, 8, and 9, many sentences begin with "and" or "but." Rewrite one of these paragraphs so that no sentence begins this way. Which version do you prefer and why?

5. In explaining his feelings about his job in Burma, Orwell uses balanced sentence forms to contain and heighten his meaning:

> "All I knew was that I was struck between
> my hatred of the empire I served and
> my rage against the evil-spirited little beasts
> who tried to make my job impossible."

> "With one part of my mind I thought of the British Raj
> as an unbreakable tyranny,
> as something clamped down, in *saecula saeculorum*,
> upon the will of prostrate peoples;
> with another part I thought that the greatest joy in the
> world would be to drive a bayonet into a Buddhist
> priest's guts."

Try to write an imitation of each quotation.

6. The following sentences contain interrupters—words and phrases which break into the initial thought of the sentence. Look carefully at the interrupting words. Can they be eliminated? Try reading the sentences both with and without them. What do the interpolated words contribute to the sentences?

> "When I pulled the trigger I did not hear the bang or feel the kick—one never does when a shot goes home—but I heard the devilish roar of glee that went up from the crowd."

> "It is a serious matter to shoot a working elephant—it is comparable to destroying a huge an costly piece of machinery—and obviously one ought not to do it if it can possibly be avoided."

Write an imitation of each quotation.

7. In the two sentences below, the interrupting words are set off by commas rather than by dashes. Repunctuate the sentences, once with dashes and once with parentheses. Is there any difference?

> "In that instant, in too short a time, one would have thought, even for the bullet to get there, a mysterious, terrible change had come over the elephant."

> "And my whole life, every white man's life in the East, was one long struggle not to be laughed at."

Write imitations of both quotations.

8. Paraphrase paragraph 7, adding your own responses to Orwell's ideas.

"Notes of a Native Son" • James Baldwin (pp. 1612–1625)

1. In Section 1, Baldwin describes his father, characterizing him. How does this characterization compare with what Baldwin says about him in Section 3? In these descriptions of his father, Baldwin reveals things about himself. What does he reveal, and why is it important?

[In Section 1, Baldwin describes his father's cruelty, anger, and paranoia, while in Section 3 he remembers some early examples of his father's love and concern. By showing both sides of his father—by forcing himself to acknowledge the complexity of his father's actions and motives—Baldwin demonstrates his ability to overcome bitterness and to let go of hatred. He cannot forget his father's cruelties, but he is no longer entrapped by rage.]

2. Throughout the essay, Baldwin uses description and narration in the service of argumentation. What point does Baldwin make via the restaurant incident at the end of Section 1? What point does he make by his description of Harlem as he rides through its streets on the day of his father's funeral?

[The restaurant indicates Baldwin's growing awareness of the evils of discrimination and his recognition of just how powerful his anger is. The description of Harlem in the midst of race riots connects his father's life, and his father's predictions of doom, to the world in which Baldwin must live. As Baldwin watches the looting and burning, he recognizes that all of Harlem feels the same need to smash something that he had felt in the restaurant—and for the same reason.]

3. What ironies of circumstance does Baldwin indicate in the first paragraph of Section 3? What other ironies do you detect in the essay? What is the point, for example, of mentioning who attended the funeral? What does Baldwin mean when he suggests that his aunt was one of the few people in the world who had loved his father, and that "their incessant quarreling proved precisely the strength of [their] tie"?

[The first paragraph of Section 3 suggests the irony of Baldwin's worrying what to wear to the funeral. In addition, his birthday falling on the day of his father's funeral ironically juxtaposes life and death. Baldwin mentions who attended the funeral to underscore his father's inability to make strong human connections. "The chapel was full, but not packed . . .," and most of the mourners were relatives or "one-time friends." The aunt's willingness to pay attention to the father's ranting suggests that she cared about him. Most other family members simply stayed silent and tried to keep out of his way.]

4. In paragraph 45, Baldwin brings together the personal and the social, the private and public, his father and Harlem. What conclusion does he draw about his relation to his father? About the hatred and rage and bitterness that sparked the riots? Explain the final sentence of the paragraph: "Hatred, which could destroy so much, never failed to destroy the man who hated and this was an immutable law."

[Baldwin has seen his father destroyed by his uncontrolled hatred and rage. He sees himself and all black people (represented by the race riots in Harlem) as in danger of being destroyed in the same way.]

5. The essay ends with a pair of apparently contradictory impulses, with two irreconcilable ideas. What are they, and how does Baldwin both emphasize them and tie them in with what has gone before, especially with what he suggests at the end of Section 1?

[The first idea is accepting people as they are; the second idea is never accepting injustice as commonplace. Baldwin suggests that there must be a balance between the two commitments. Otherwise, he fears, all black people will be in danger of being destroyed—as he felt he was after the incident at the restaurant—by their own rage and hatred.]

6. "Notes of a Native Son" is divided into three major sections. Provide a title for each, explain the main point of each, and comment on the relationship among them. Take any one of the three parts and examine its structure. Explain how it begins, where it goes, and how it ends. Explain how each of its parts fits into the whole section and into the essay overall. You might look, for example, at Section 3, specifically at the third paragraph which splits into two parts. Explain also how Baldwin manages the shift from the preacher's sermon to happier memories of his childhood (consider paragraph 34).

7. Discuss the following poem in relation to what Baldwin says about himself in the final paragraphs of sections 1 and 3.

A MAN FEARED
Stephen Crane

A man feared that he might find an assassin;
Another that he might find a victim.
One was more wise than the other.

"The Right Stuff" • Tom Wolfe (pp. 1625–1635)

1. In paragraph 2, Wolfe names the subject of his essay "the right stuff." How does he develop his definition of "the right stuff"? Does he ever give a simple summary of the definition? How does his method of definition particularly suit the picture he gives of the fighter pilots and the way they talk to each other?

   [Wolfe never comes right out with a definition; instead he piles example upon example, carefully steering away from assigning one label or term to "the right stuff." His method of definition ironically reflects the young pilots as they talk to one another about the possibility of death; they pile example upon example, but they never use the word. Their "code" requires an avoidance of any real confrontation of what flying fighter planes demands from them.]

2. Wolfe's essay is filled with vivid comparisons. List several comparisons which describe the carriers the pilots are expected to land on. Who apparently uses these metaphors to describe the ship? What effect is created by the point of view and description?

   [The carrier is described in paragraph 5 as "a great beast" that rolls and tosses, "a *skillet*! —a frying pan!—a short-order grill," and "a heaving barbeque." When these images begin (about twenty lines into the paragraph), the voice becomes that of the young trainees. The images suggest danger and extreme difficulty. In addition, we hear the bravado and braggadocio of the neophyte pilots who both fear landing on the small, slippery deck and long for the status they will gain by doing so.]

3. What attitude does Wolfe take toward the men he describes?

   [Wolfe is certainly not sympathetic, even though he is able to get inside the heads of the men to show their views and reactions. He pictures them as gigantic egos who are willing to risk their own lives and the lives of the people who work with them in order to prove their manhood. Their leisure time is spent drinking and then driving around in fast cars, their work hours in "hot dogging" and figuring ways to break the rules while they are flying.]

4. This essay comes from a book Wolfe wrote about astronauts. What kind of audience do you think Wolfe was writing for?

   [Wolfe addresses a relatively educated and well-informed audience. He's expects his readers to be able to understand complex metaphors like "gyroscope of the soul" (paragraph 5) and allusions such as "Gideon's warriors" (paragraph 7). In addition, his book will probably appeal most to readers who take a skeptical view of the military, the space program, and the macho flyers' code. His ironic undercutting of the fighter-pilot training program would not convert a staunch supporter to question its validity; instead, such a reader would likely be angry and annoyed. On the other hand, a friendly or neutral reader will almost certainly find Wolfe's extended comparisons of the trainees with raucous fraternity boys amusing, convincing, and at the same time frightening.]

5. In paragraph 1, Wolfe compares the young men at military flight-training school to fraternity members. What are the similarities between the two groups as suggested by the essay? What are the differences? Does Wolfe's essay convince you that the analogy is accurate? Explain.

6. In paragraph 8, Wolfe suggests that the trainees continue in spite of fears and difficulties because they believe that becoming fighter pilots will prove that they are manly—that they have achieved manhood. Does the process Wolfe describes reflect qualities you believe to be an essential part of becoming a man? Explain.

7. Rewrite one paragraph of this essay from the point of view of the pilot being described. Wolfe takes on the voice of the pilots in many paragraphs but, of course, the point of view that comes through is his. Create a different voice for your pilot to use; try to make your pilot a sympathetic character.

"No Name Woman" • Maxine Hong Kingston (pp. 1636–1643)

1. What was the occasion that prompted Kingston's mother to tell the story that opens the essay? Why does Kingston wait until the end of the mother's story to reveal the occasion?

[Kingston's mother tells her the horrifying story of her aunt's illegitimate pregnancy on the day the young girl began to menstruate. After learning the details of the marauding neighbors, birth in the pigsty, and the subsequent suicide and infanticide, the reader is appalled to discover the mother's purpose in telling her daughter. We imagine the young girl, just moving into her womanhood, frightened, fascinated, and revolted by the threats inherent in adult sexuality. We see that the story has not been told to encourage sympathy for the aunt, but rather to terrify Kingston into what her mother considers proper behavior.]

2. How do the examples of New Year's Day movies and melting ice-cream cones relate to the story of the no-name aunt?

[As Kingston seeks to define the values of the Chinese immigrant, she thinks of the childhood pleasures that were sparingly doled out. She says, "After the one carnival ride each, we paid in guilt." Even the smallest luxury was given grudgingly. Kingston introduces the paragraph following these examples of childhood pleasures with a startling transition: "Adultery is extravagance" (p. 1638). She theorizes, then, that her aunt did not voluntarily engage in sexual intercourse because she would have understood the impossibility of any support from her family should she become pregnant. Instead, Kingston projects a possible scenario, picturing her aunt as the victim of rape, probably by one of the same villagers who later raided the family home.]

3. Why did the villagers react so strongly to the illegitimate pregnancy?

[Kingston reports the rituals of Chinese marriage customs and explains that by her action, the aunt declared herself an individual rather than part of a group. Whether or not she chose to have sex with the man who impregnated her, she was a visible symbol of a break in the wilderness, the "roundness" of Chinese village life. Because she represented the disturbance of natural order, she threatened not only her own family's existence, but also the structure of the lives of their neighbors. To restore the balance and unity they believed the aunt had upset, the villages reacted violently, thinking they had to exorcise the spirit of the "broken house."]

4. How does Kingston justify and explain the aunt's taking her newborn with her in her suicide jump?

[In her attempt to understand her aunt and to create a believable, even admirable character, Kingston shows painfully loving details of the imagined birth. The mother nurses her baby and holds it close to her. Taking the child to the well was her way of assuring that the baby

274

would not be mistreated or neglected. As a final poignant note, Kingston comments that the baby "was probably a girl"; a boy, she surmises, could have expected better treatment, and his distraught mother might have left him behind. In this observation, Kingston underlines once again the motif that runs throughout the essay: women were valued only as commodities in China, not as human beings.]

5. What is ironic about Kingston's writing the story of her aunt?

[The family wanted to punish the aunt by denying her existence, by disowning her. Kingston's mother tells her to forget the aunt ever lived. Yet by telling the story, Kingston gives her aunt the dignity and acknowledgment she never received during the difficult days of her life. Kingston's mother, by trying to silence and inhibit her daughter, has in fact given voice and credence to the aunt, who would otherwise have been forgotten.]

6. Compare Kingston's picture of her aunt and her mother with Alice Walker's picture of her mother in "In Search of Our Mothers' Gardens."

"In Search of Our Mothers' Gardens" • Alice Walker (pp. 1644–1650)

1. Walker combines many different structures and approaches in writing this essay. Point out examples of definition, comparison and contrast, and narrative.

[Walker plays with the definitions of "saint" in the first paragraphs and redefines "artist" as she moves through each example and story in the essay. She compares Toomer's view of "saints" to her own view of "artists." And she compares the experiences of black American women to the suppressed English women described by Virginia Woolf. She tells narratives of Jean Toomer, Phillis Wheatley, and several vignettes from her mother's life.]

2. How would you describe the tone of the essay? Is it formal or informal? Angry? Loving? Objective? Subjective?

[The essay's tone is particularly interesting because Walker breaks the rule that tone should be consistent. She cites formal, academic references such as Woolf and Toomer and intersperses her careful analyses of those references with anecdotes and informal diction. The combination of the formal and the informal works particularly well in this essay because Walker makes the point that, for black women, art cannot be formally separated off from the informality of their day-to-day life. In some passages Walker is angry; in others she is optimistic and affirming.]

3. What are the main sections of this essay? How are the sections related?

[The essay can be divided into two parts, the first ending after the phrase the *notion of song* (bottom of p. 1647). The first section explores the black woman's history in this country, focusing on the example of Phillis Wheatley. Walker emphasizes the spiritual quality of the black women's art, which resulted, at least in part, from the extreme difficulties these artists faced trying to keep their creativity alive at a time when it was a crime for a black person to read or write. The second section moves from the primary example of Wheatley to the primary example of Walker's mother. Her art, the narrator explains, was in the love and care she put into her gardening. The two sections are clearly united in the final paragraph, when Walker compares her mother's gift to her—live of beauty, love of creating—with the gift of poetry that she speculates Phillis Wheatley's mother may have passed to her.]

4. Choose one of the poems Walker quotes and show how it relates to the man thought of her essay.

5. Reread the epigraph by Jean Toomer at the beginning of the essay. Why do you think Walker chose this quotation to open her essay? How does it relate to what Walker says?

6. Compare Walker's view of her heritage from her mother to Baldwin's view of his heritage from his father ("Notes of a Native Son," p. 1612).

Additional Topics for Writing—The Essay

1. Compare the minority experience as described by Orwell in "Marrakech" (p. 1529) with the minority experience described by Baldwin in "Notes of a Native Son" (p. 1612).

2. Read the essays listed below and then write an analysis of the way writers use the creatures of nature to explain their ideas:

   The Battle of the Ants..1556
   The Death of the Moth 1559
   Living Like Weasels 1566

3. What lessons can one generation learn from another? What do parents gain (and lose) by virtue of their parenthood? How are children helped (and hindered) by their parents? Read the essays listed below to suggest ways you might approach this writing topic:

   Once More to the Lake 1598
   Notes of a Native Son..1612
   No Name Woman..1636
   In Search of Our Mothers' Gardens 1644

4. Read Thoreau's "The Battle of the Ants" (p. 1556) and Forster's "Our Graves in Gallipoli" (p. 1596). How do you think Thoreau would respond if he could overhear the conversation between the two graves? Write a new dialogue using Thoreau as the third voice.

5. Compare Orwell's description of suffering and death in "Marrakech" (p. 1529) with Donne's metaphor for the relationship of humankind ("Mediation XVII: For Whom the Bell Tolls" (p. 1525). How does Donne's picture of humanity differ from the scenes Orwell shows us?

6. What are the similarities and differences among Francis Bacon's three essays?

   Of Revenge 1563
   Of Love..1583
   Of Youth and Age 1677

7. What aspects of style are common to all three? What generalizations can you make about Bacon's approach to argument?

PART FIVE

Writing about Literature

CHAPTER TWENTY-SEVEN

An Approach to Writing about Literature

This chapter provides extensive treatment of writing about literature. If the course you are teaching emphasizes writing, you may want to assign this chapter early in the term. Logical times to teach "An Approach to Writing about Literature" include the first class following the course introduction; immediately following "Reading Stories"; two weeks prior to the due date of the first writing assignment.

Just as text Chapter One, Six, Twelve, and Twenty-Two emphasize the process of active, engaged reading of literature, so does Chapter Twenty-Seven explain the process of active, engaged writing about literature. Students especially appreciate the sample writings—for instance, the response statements of p. 1654 and p. 1656–1658. The response statement by Carol Holt (p. 1661) and the essay that grew from it (p. 1662) demonstrate a discovery process that works well for many writers. Annotating (pp. 1658–1667) and writing double-entry journals encourages both summarizing and reacting to what has been read. The model (pp. 1666–1667) shows how such journals encourage creative, critical thinking. Sample outlines on pp. 1686–1687 suggest possibilities for writing comparisons, and the final student paper, "Has the Prodigal Daughter Really Returned?" (pp. 1692–1696), leads students through the process of reading a scholar's response to a work and then evaluating that response. Considering this paper leads logically to a discussion of MLA documentation and format.

In addition to the suggestions offered in Chapter Twenty-Seven, the following projects offer possibilities for writing experiences that can supplement or replace some of the traditional out-of-class formal papers:

1. *Warm-Up Writing*: You can use any of the questions in the text or in this guide (or, of course, your own) as topics for brief writing assignments at the beginning of class. Students can write for ten or fifteen minutes and then discuss their responses either in small groups or as a full class. If you do warm-up writings fairly often, students tend to come to class prepared. In addition, the discussions that follow warm-ups are usually focused and lively. Students come to understand what Flannery O'Connor was talking about when she said, "I write because I don't know what I think until I read what I say."

2. *In-Class Essay Series*: The in-class essay series requires some organization, but the results are usually worth the trouble. Students write a series of essays (three seems about right) on various topics, using one class period for each essay. After the essays are passed in, they should be alphabetized and stored in a folder, large envelope, etc. After all three essays have been written and collected (but not corrected by the instructor), they are redistributed during another class period to the students who wrote them. Meeting in small groups, they share the results of the writing and choose which of the three essays they will rewrite and submit for a grade. If you ask them to submit the original essay along with the final copy, you'll have a chance to observe and comment on their revision process. This project promotes a great deal of writing, yet the correcting load is manageable.

3. *Collaborative Projects*: You might have groups of students work on some of the extended projects suggested on manual pp. 76–77, pp. 155–156, pp. 239–240, and p 277. They might start work in class when they can make arrangements for further out-of-class meetings. The final presentation works well as a panel discussion with each panelist submitting a one-page précis of his or her remarks.

4. *End-of-the-Term Review Reports*: Each student may prepare a three-minute commentary on a story, poem, play, or essay the class has read during the term. The focus of the commentary might be a particularly strong negative or positive response or, even better, an explanation of a changing response. If these reports are given as part of each class during the final two weeks of the term, they serve as a good basis for review. You might ask for volunteers to cover certain works so that you don't have seventeen reports on the same short story. Each students might be asked to submit a one-page summary of his or her commentary.

You probably would not want to use all of these writing projects in one term, but we would be interested to hear your responses to any you do use. In addition, we'd be grateful for descriptions of writing projects you have originated and used successfully with your classes.

Topics for Writing and Discussion for Works Included in Chapter Twenty-Seven

"Symptoms of Love" • *Robert Graves (p. 1655)*

1. List the words that specifically suggest and sustain the medical metaphor Graves uses in the poem. Explain how they contribute to the poem's theme.

2. Try writing your own poem beginning with the line "_____ is a _____." Make an abstract term concrete as does Graves. (You might consider such an emotion as hate, jealousy, fear, anger, or sorrow.)

"Magic" • *Katherine Anne Porter (p. 1659)*

1. Madame Blanchard speaks only twice. Do her words or her gestures indicate in any way her reaction to the story she hears? What effect do you image that tale of Ninette might have on Madame Blanchard?

2. Characterize the narrator. What is her position in the Blanchard household? Why do you think she tells this story to her new mistress? What connections do you see between the act the narrator performs as she tells the story and the details of the charm the madam in the story used to lure Ninette back to the house of prostitution?

3. What is the significance of the story's title? What kind of magic is worked in the tale of Ninette? In the relationship between the narrator and Madame Blanchard?

"Theme for English B" • *Langston Hughes (p. 1663)*

1. Notice the sound devices in this poem (rhyme, rhythm, alliteration, and assonance, for instance). What do these sound devices contribute to the meaning of the poem?

2. Read the instructor's directions given in lines 2-5. Do you think the piece that follows fulfills those directions? Explain. If you were the instructor how would you grade this "theme," and what comments would you write to your students? (Try to imagine that you do not know that the poem's author is a famous poet; instead, picture that you are the middle-aged white instructor and Hughes is your young black student.)

3. What do you think Hughes means in line 31-32 when he tells the instructor, "You are white—/yet a part of me, as I am a part of you." What is your response to these lines?

"How It Feels to Be Colored Me" • Zora Neale Hurston (p. 1668)

1. Hurston writes about coming to the realization in her childhood that she was black. Describe an incident in your childhood when you realized that you were different in some way from some or many of your peers. How does your response to this discovery compare with Hurston's?

2. Hurston says that during her childhood other black people never gave her money for dancing or speaking pieces. At the time, she saw their unwillingness to reward her a evidence that "they deplored any joyful tendencies in [her]. . . ." Can you think of any other reasons they may have refused to give her their "small silver" as the white people did?

3. In the third section of the essay, Hurston describes a scene in a jazz club. Her reaction is entirely different from her companion's. Write a description of the scene, including personal responses, from the point of view of Hurston's friend.

"Of Youth and Age" • Francis Bacon (p. 1677–1678)

1. Complete the following diagram as an aid in analyzing Francis Bacon's views of youth and age:

Qualities/Actions	Youth	Age
Positive	Invention is more lively Fitter to invent Fitter to execute (carry out)	Generally wiser Fitter to judge Fitter to counsel (give advice)
Negative	More likely to ruin business The young embrace more than they can hold	Might have done more sooner The aged object too much

How did Bacon organize his essay? What other ways could Bacon have chosen to present the comparisons and contrasts? Use the chart you have made to rewrite the essay in modern English, using a simpler structure. What are the advantages of your rewriting? What has been lost from the original? Explain.

2. Choose one or two of Bacon's points about either youth or age and write an essay explaining why you agree or disagree with his observations.

3. Why does Bacon quote the statement "Your young men shall see visions, and your old men shall dream dreams"? Check the quotation in the Bible (Joel 2:28).

"Aunt Jennifer's Tigers" • Adrienne Rich (p. 1679)

See instructor's manual p. 183.

"War Is Kind" • Stephen Crane (p. 1685)

See instructor's manual pp. 87–88.

Appendix A

Critical Comments About Literature

These critical comments about literature, new to the third edition of *Literature: Reading Fiction, Poetry, Drama, and the Essay*, open many options for lively classroom discussion as well as for writing assignments. Many of the selections suggest new ways for students to think about their own writing processes. In addition, they show a side of literature many students have never seen, providing an open door through which students can see and hear men and women discussing literature as a passionate, essential part of their spiritual and intellectual lives. If students choose, they can pass through that door and join the conversation themselves, viewing fiction, drama, and poetry not simply as subjects to be taught in school but as an ongoing, vital part of their own lives.

As you integrate this new section into your syllabus, consider the following options:

1. Assign several readings on a genre before you introduce or while you are teaching that genre. (See the listing on page 286 of this manual for an indication of which selections work well with each genre). As students learn more about the genre, ask them to respond to any one (or more) of the readings. They might question or challenge the author of the critical comment. Or they might support a point he or she makes with evidence they have discovered.

2. Use selected examples from the critical comments to encourage an atmosphere of literary conversation in the classroom. You might, for instance, as students to watch for differences in point of view among the comments. It's often reassuring for students to know that not all literary commentators agree on definitions or even on judgments. For instance, you might note that Plato argues that poetry is the work of God with the poet simply the medium (page 1704) while Wallace Stevens claims that "after one has abandoned a belief in God, poetry is that essence which takes its place as life's redemption."

3. Ask students to read several comments that focus on a particular literary theme, issue, or concept and ask them to compare these views and then, based on their own reading, to evaluate the commentators' views. For instance, Sir Philip Sidney (p. 1707), William Blake (p. 1709), William Wordsworth (pp. 1709–1710), and Anton Chekhov (pp. 1715–1716) all talk about Nature. What do they mean by this term? Why the capital "N"? Can students discover other readings that expand the range of possibiiities for the concept of nature in the literary world?

4. Choose several comments you find particularly though-provoking or important to the way you structure your course and ask students to read more critical observations by one or more of these scholars, authors, or critics. You might ask students to work in groups on this project and then to present their findings on, say, Aristotle's view of literature or theories on writing.

5. Ask students to use one or more of the comments (perhaps from a list you compile) as models from which to develop their own critical comment about literature. Ask that they refer to works in the text as examples to support the points they remaking. If students are asked to keep these comments brief, you might then have each students read his or her manifesto as a springboard for discussion or for further writing assignments.

List by Genre

The Essay

Topics for Writing and Discussion

Poetry and Inspiration • *Plato (p. 1704)*

1. Read the first paragraph of this selection. Then read Samuel Taylor Coleridge's "Kubla Khan" (p. 572) and comment on the similarities you see. Research Coleridge's process in writing this poem to develop the comparison further.

2. Plato suggests that poetry is pure feeling rather than reason. After reading several selections from this text, do you agree that poems appeal primarily to your emotions rather than to your intellect? Are there poems that do both? Explain.

On Tragedy • *Aristotle (p. 1705)*

1. Aristotle says that "a tragedy cannot exist without a plot, but it can without characters." What does he mean by this? Do you agree? Can you think of any poem or song that has a plot but no characters and that also fits Aristotle's definition?

2. Aristotle believes *peripety* and *recognition* (the turning-about of fortune and the tragic hero's recognition of the truth) to be the heart of the tragic plot. He also says that in the best tragedies these two occur simultaneously and provides an analysis of *Oedipus* to demonstrate his point. Choose any other tragic plays in this anthology and write an analysis of the peripety and recognition, using the pattern Aristotle provides here.

An Apology for Poetry • *Sir Philip Sidney (p. 1707)*

1. In the first paragraph, Sidney provides an etymological definition of poet. Using poems from this book as examples of the poet's work, explain why you do or do not find this definition apt and fitting.

2. In the long second paragraph, Sidney provides a series of examples describing what scholars in various disciplines do. He uses these examples to contrast with his definition of a poet. Following this pattern, develop your own definition of a practitioner of an art, science, or sport you admire.

The Metaphysical Poets • *Samuel Johnson (p. 1708)*

1. Samuel Johnson, an eighteenth-century writer, criticizes the metaphysical school of poets who wrote in the seventeenth century. John Donne, the best known of the metaphysical poets, frequently used the "combination of dissimilar images" against which Johnson rails. Read several of Donne's poems (pp. 427, 548–552), and then explain how you might defend his work against Johnson's charges.

2. In the third paragraph, Johnson quotes his contemporary Pope. Read the selection from Pope's "Essay on Man" (p. 560) and then explain the differences you see between his poetry and the poetry of John Donne. Do you see any similarities? Given what Johnson says in this essay, why do you think he admired Pope's work?

Art and Imagination • *William Blake (p. 1710)*

1. Look at William Blake's watercolor painting "The Sick Rose" (p. 503) and read his poem by the same name. What does this critical comment add to the way you look at, react to, and think about these works.

2. Blake says, "I see Every thing I paint in This World, but Every body does not see alike." Give your own series of examples to support this statement. Use these examples to help you define your own unique way of seeing the world.

Poetry and Feeling • William Wordsworth (p. 1709)

1. Read carefully the first long series of connected sentences in this comment. Then write a paraphrase, putting Wordsworth's ideas in your own mind. Note in the sentence that follows he says "successful composition generally begins" as a result of the process described. Try this strategy yourself. Begin by recalling a strong feeling or reaction you have had ("emotion recollected in tranquillity"). Try to focus on the specific image that evoked this feeling or reaction. Then write about what you have discovered.

2. Wordsworth claims in the final sentence that of "two descriptions . . . equally well executed, the one in prose and the other in verse, the verse will be read a hundred times where the prose is read once." Whether or not you agree with this observation, explain why for some readers it might be true.

The Authenticity of the Imagination • *John Keats (p. 1710)*

1. Compare Keats's observations on truth and beauty in this comment with his exploration of the same theme in "Ode on a Grecian Urn."

2. What does Keats describe as a possible vision of the afterlife? If you could create your ideal vision of the afterlife, how would it be similar or different from his? Give specific details.

Poets and Language • *Percy Bysshe Shelley (p. 1712)*

1. In what way does Shelley believe poets to be prophets? Why would this belief lead him to see poets as also particularly fit to be legislators? Do you agree with him? Explain why or why not.

2. Shelley says, "Poets are the hierophants of an unapprehended inspiration." With the help of a dictionary where needed, explain and response to this definition.

True Poetry • *Edgar Allan Poe (p. 1713)*

1. List long poems you have read (possibly parts of Chaucer's *Canterbury Tales* or the old English epic *Beowulf*). Then consider whether or not you agree with Poe's statement that any long work cannot legitimately be considered a poem.

2. Poe also believes that very short poems can never produce "a profound or enduring effect." Read several examples of Japanese haiku poetry (easily found at any bookstore or library). Note the birth and death dates of the poets. Clearly these poems have lasted through centuries and have, therefore, had an enduring effect. How might Poe respond to this example that challenges his thesis?

The Single Effect • *Edgar Allan Poe (p. 1713)*

1. Read Poe's evaluation of Hawthorne's work and then read Hawthorne's story "Young Goodman Brown" (p. 96). Would you agree that it has a single effect? If so, define that effect and explain how it is achieved. If not, explain the elements that prevent your seeing a single effect in this work.

2. Using the same process Poe uses to evaluate Hawthorne, read and evaluate Poe's story "The Black Cat."

Technique in Writing the Short Story • *Anton Chekhov (p. 1715)*

1. Following the process described in the first letter, write a paragraph revealing your view of a part of Nature you particularly value. Remember to "seize upon the little particulars" and combine them "in such a way that, in reading, when you shut your eyes, you get a picture."

2. Does Chekhov follow his own advice? Read "The Man in a Case," and then explain your evaluation.

Notes for the Modern Tragedy • *Henrik Ibsen (p. 1716)*

1. Read this comment as a companion piece to Susan Glaspell's *Trifles* (p. 1264). How do the two relate to each other?

2. Writing in the nineteenth century, Ibsen defines what he sees as the feminine point of view and the masculine point of view. What has changed or remained the same about these definitions today. Do men and women still have trouble communicating their view of the world to each other? Do men and women, in general, have different goals and values?

Sprung Rhythm • *Gerard Manley Hopkins (p. 1717)*

1. Try reading a prose passage applying the principles of sprung rhythm as described here. Does paying attention to the rhythm change the way you hear the message as well as the sound of the passage? Explain.

2. Read several of Hopkins' poems (pp. 611–612). Then read Anthony Brode's "Breakfast with Gerard Manley Hopkins." Write the response you think Brode might make to Hopkins's explanation of sprung rhythm.

The Scene • *August Strindberg (p. 1718)*

1. Compare Strindberg's view of "the scene" with Poe's explanation of "single effect" (p. 1713).

2. By "a scene," Strindberg apparently means what we would call a one-act play. How does his observation relate to your own experience of viewing films. In general, do you prefer short films to long films? List several films you would consider short and several you would consider long. How would you compare your enjoyment of the films on each list?

The Interpreter of Life • *Bernard Shaw (p. 1718)*

1. Consider any of the plays you have read in this book. Explain how the playwright's choices make him or her an "interpreter of life." Then discuss what you believe his or her interpretation to be.

2. Take a scene from a play you enjoyed reading. Rewrite the scene from a different point of view to provide your own "interpretation of life." Consider Shaw's observations as you plan your revision of the action, characters, and setting.

Poetry, Delight, and Wisdom • *Robert Frost (p. 1719)*

1. Rewrite the first sentence of this comment to explain its meaning. Then choose any poem you have enjoyed and evaluate whether or not it meets Frost's criterion.

2. In the second paragraph, Frost describes a moment of inspiration as "the glad recognition of the long lost . . . ." Think of a time when this has happened to you. Describe both the original event and your recovery, and later assessment, of the memory. Remember, this assignment calls for *glad* recognition—you are not being asked to dredge up misery and pain.

Observations on Poetry • *Wallace Stevens (p. 1720)*

1. Compare Wallace Steven's view of the spiritual aspect of poetry with William Blake's observations (p. 1709).

2. Choose one of these statements that interest you or evokes a strong response. Then copy the statement several times (handwritten, not typed). Finally, write your response to the statement.

The Poet and the Tradition • *T. S. Elliot (p. 1721)*

1. Elliot claims that to write poetry well, one must understand the tradition of poetry that has been written in the past. Consider a field with which you are familiar to see if you agree with this principle. For example, to write good modern music, should one be familiar with traditional music? To become a great athlete, should one understand the history and development of the sport he or she pursues? Explain the reasons for your response.

2. Read the final paragraph of this comment and explain Eliot's view of how understanding old art (including, of course, literature) leads not to boring repetition, but rather to new discoveries.

Theatre Notes • *Bertoit Brecht (p. 1722)*

1. Compare Brecht's view of pleasure and entertainment as a goal of theatre with Bernard Shaw's view (p. 1718). With whom do you agree? Explain.

2. Choose your favorite play in this book. Does it conform more to Brecht's definition or to Shaw's? Explain.

The Essayist • *E. B. White (p. 1723)*

1. In the opening paragraph, White describes essay writing as a liberating experience. Have you ever done any writing that made you feel this way? If so, explain the circumstances and your process. If you have never experienced a sense of freedom through writing, imagine a situation in which you might. Describe the subject you might write about and explain why writing about it would make you feel "self-liberated."

2. White describes the essay as standing "a short distance down the line" from fiction, drama, or poetry. Read several selections from the essay section and then explain whether and why you share this judgment.

Poetry and Human Living • *Georg Seferis (p. 1724)*

1. Seferis notes that "a poem written from a purely erotic impulse may become in another era the expression of the feeling of human humiliation, of deceit, of degradation. . . ." Read some of the oldest poems in this book. (Poems in the "Collection of Poetry" appear in chronological order). Then explain how you think today's view of them might differ from the view of their original readers.

2. Seferis suggests that "petty details" are not what makes great poetry, but rather the ability of the poet to represent universal human experience. Choose several of your favorite poems and evaluate them, using Seferis's guidelines.

Lyric Poetry and the Short Story • *Frank O'Connor (p. 1725)*

1. O'Connor says that a novel requires "far more logic and far more knowledge of circumstances" than a short story. Do you agree? Use examples of stories from this book and of novels you have read to explain your responses. As part of your responses, explain whether you prefer to read novels or short stories. (Do you enjoy and seek them out equally?)

2. In the second paragraph, "O'Connor describes his method of writing as "getting black on white." Once he has his rough sketch, then he shapes an polishes. To try an experiment in "getting black on white," think about your first hour on a college campus (as a visitor or a student). Focus on one image you recall from that hour. Write the image at the top of a sheet of paper, then "get black on white" for ten minutes without stopping. If you lose steam, just rewrite the previous sentence until you get going again. Later, try shaping what you've done into the kind of prose O'Connor describes.

"The Word" • *Pablo Neruda (p. 1726)*

1. Is this piece a critical comment or a poem or something else? Develop your own definition, using examples from the work to defend your ideas.

2. What are your own favorite words? For the next week or so, keep a list of words that catch your interest and imagination. Then write a response in Neruda's style explaining your own relationship with language.

The Origin of a Story • *Eudora Welty (p. 1727)*

1. Before you read this comment, read "A Worn Path" (p. 71). Then read Welty's observations and explain how they affect your response to and understanding of the story.

2. Think of a person you have seen who caught your attention (someone you do not know—perhaps at a shopping mall or an airport). Write a description of the person and then create a story to go with the description. Make a rough outline so you'll have a sense of where you want your character to go and how you want him or her to get there. Most of all, keep in mind that the story is not about "its circumstances but its *subject*." Every detail should in some way develop and reveal that subject, just as "A Worn Path" shows us "the deep-grained habit of love."

Folklore and Fiction • *Ralph Ellison (p. 1728)*

1. Read the first two paragraphs in this comment. Then reread "Battle Royal" (p. 286) and identify specific details and images that suggest Ellison's conscious use of myth, folklore, and ritual. Finally, read the rest of this comment and see whether your observations were in any way similar to the analysis Ellison provides in the final paragraph.

2. What examples of myth, folklore, and ritual do you see enacted on campus, at your job, or within your family? Explain. Use the final paragraph in this comment as a pattern for your evaluation.

The Power of Poetry • *Octavio Paz (p. 1729)*

1. Compare Paz's definition of the power of poetry with Samuel Johnson's view (p. 1708). Do you think Paz finds the poetry of the metaphysical poets (like John Donne) powerful? Explain.

2. What do you think Paz means when he says, "The first hunters and gatherers looked at themselves in astonishment one day, for an interminable instant, in the still waters of a poem"? Speculate on as many possible meanings of this sentence as you can. How would you create this instant if it were to be part of a film you were directing?

Production Notes for The Glass Menagerie • *Tennessee Williams (p. 1730)*

1. Before reading these notes, read the play (p. 1275). How does reading these notes change your response to the play?

2. If you were staging the play, how would you use these directions? For example, what music would you choose? Explain your reasons.

Tragedy and the Common Man • *Arthur Miller (p. 1732)*

1. Miller says, "As a general rule . . . I think the tragic feeling is evoked in us when we are in the presence of a character who is ready to lay down his life, if need be, to secure one thing—his sense of personal dignity." Using this general rule, evaluate any of the following plays: *A Doll House; Riders to the Sea; The Glass Menagerie; Death of a Salesman; A Raisin in the Sun; Fences.* Do you think the play (or plays) you are evaluating "evoke the tragic feeling"? Explain your reasons.

2. Miller claims that "in truth, tragedy implies more optimism in its author than does comedy, and that its final result ought to be the reinforcement of the onlooker's brightest opinion of the human animal." How does Miller's view compare to your own responses to viewing tragic plays?

The Theater of the Absurd • *Martin Esslin (p. 1734)*

1. How might Esslin's comments serve to illuminate not only theater of the absurd, but also many late twentieth-century stories such as "The Garden of Forking Paths (p. 265), "Continuity of Parks" (p. 296), or "A Very Old Man with Enormous Wings" (p. 310).

2. Esslin says that "Theater of the Absurd is the true theater of our time" because it reflects our real world, one that he defines as "without faith, meaning, and genuine freedom of will." Do you agree with this assertion? Explain.

Poetry and Song • *Wendell Berry (p. 1735)*

1. Berry says that song is "a force opposed to specialty and to isolation." Explain what he means by this statement; use a favorite song or poem to illustrate.

2. What do you see as the difference between poetry and song? Try reading the lyrics of a favorite song aloud; what is lost? Is anything gained?

Poems are Not Luxuries • *Audre Lorde (p. 1736)*

1. Read several of the poems in the anthology that are written by women. How do they affirm (or challenge) Lorde's claim that for women "poetry is a vital necessity."

2. Why does Lorde specify women when she says that poetry is a necessity? Does she seem to think poetry is not necessary for men? What is your response to this implied contrast?

Poetry, Language, and Meaning • *Mark Strand (p. 1736)*

1. Compare Frank O'Connor's view of poetry and fiction (p. 1725) with Strand's view.

2. Strand says that poetry invites readers, yet at the same time wards them off; poetry remains in some way impenetrable and "will always resist all but partial meanings." Do you agree? If so, do you find yourself drawn to poems by this mysterious power or do you find yourself put off by the lack of a quick, complete "answer"? Explore the implications of your response.

Our First Stories • *Margaret Atwood (p. 1737)*

1. Margaret Atwood describes the process by which children first encounter stories. Think about stories that came to you "through the air" which you were a child. Retell your favorite and explain why you think it remains in your memory today.

2. Comment on Atwood's observations that most people's family stories come from the mother (or other female relatives). Does this concur with your own experiences? Can you think of any stories told by your father, grandfather, or other male relative?

Feelings into Words • *Seamus Heaney (p. 1738)*

1. Before you read this comment, read the poem "Digging" (p. 737). Then write your own response. Next read the comment. How is your response changed by knowing Heaney's process?

2. Heaney says people advised him to stay in school because "the pen's lighter than the spade." What did they mean by this? Do you agree with this bit of folk wisdom?

Stories are Letters (To Robby) • *John Edgar Wideman (p. 1740)*

1. Compare Wideman's observations about the watermelon to Ralph Ellison's observations about the interconnection of folklore and fiction.

2. Think about Wideman's analysis of the watermelon. What is your own equivalent "letter from home?" What are some of the stories that "letter" evokes?

What a Poem Knows • *Diane Ackerman (p. 1740)*

1. Read Ackerman's explanation of what a poem can do. Then choose one of your own favorite poems and explain how it compares to her definition.

2. Write your own critical comment entitled "What a Song Knows." Use Ackerman's pattern to develop your definition.

What Essays Can Do • *Annie Dillard (p 1741)*

1. Compare Dillard's view of the essay with E. B. White's view. Whose view is closer to your own? Explain.

2. To explore Dillard's claim that an essay is often a superior form to fiction, choose one of the essays in this text and try writing it as a short story. Remember that you are attempting to preserve the thesis of the essay in the short story's theme. (Essays that might work well for this topic include " 'Cub' Wants to Be a Pilot," "Our Graves in Gallipoli," "Once more to the Lake," and "No Name Woman.")

APPENDIX B

Text: A Program about Literature

A new feature of the second edition of *Literature* is an IBM-compatible computer program called "TEXT: A Program about Literature," keyed to selected works in the anthology and providing word-processing capability. The program consists of two parts, DIALOGUE and DISCOURSE.

DISCOURSE allows for essay-type answers to questions concerning selected works from all four genres in *Literature*. The program displays the questions in one area of the screen and provides space for the student to write in another. The environment for this is the Plain Vanilla word process—a powerful and flexible part of the Discourse program. Plain Vanilla is so simple that most students are up and running in less than an a hour without classroom instruction.

DIALOGUE uses multiple-choice questions about selected poems and stories to teach students how to unlock meanings. Imagine the Dialogue program as a Socratic conversation between teacher and student. After a student answers, the program explains the reasoning behind its own answer. The program has plenty of time and infinite patience. It can cover works that there is no time for in class, or help with review. The computer, of course, will not replace class discussion; it is one more tool, one more way of getting the student's attention. Many students find each study intensely involving; the computer speaks, then keeps quiet until the user makes an intelligible response—for the student an engaging pattern of behavior indeed!

English teachers will of course be skeptical about any attempt to develop understanding of literature through multiple-choice questions. We hope that curiosity will overcome skepticism sufficiently to get them to sample the program, try it out on at least a few students, and draw their own conclusions.

Dialogue

We suggest that teachers encourage students to use Dialogue's multiple-choice questions as jumping off points for essay responses. A Notepad feature within the program is quickly accessible as space for jotting down ideas and paragraphs or even stating disagreements the student has with the program's answers. These notes can be printed out on the spot or later revised into larger essays, using the Plain Vanilla word processor. The teacher can supplement the program by giving out topics for essays prior to an assignment in Dialogue, allowing the computer to do the preliminary work of clearing up a few points of interpretation as the student begins to write on the Notepad.

The Dialogue program attempts to teach more than the "answers" to a few questions about selected poems and stories. It tries to teach reading techniques, more by example than by precept. The student learns by the program's example that a key to unlocking a text is to ask questions, to proceed systematically from the obvious to the less obvious. The key to the matter is the word "systematically." For example, the program points out ways in which words, images, scenes, characters, and ideas in a given work "resonate" against each other in patterns for parallelism and contrast. The larger questions of experience, interpretation, and evaluation are left for the Discourse program and for class discussion.

Some teachers may wish to use selections of the program for group or individual testing. Students' scores are automatically calculated and preserved and can be printed out for each user and each session. The Dialogue program can also be given to students who need individual help, to those who want to do extra work and receive credit for it, or to those who have missed classes because of an illness. Teachers who use the program for testing purposes can advise students to use the Notepad or a piece of paper to defend answers scored wrong by the program but that are debatable, permitting the teacher to override a "wrong" answer if the defense is good. The scores can be printed out by the students upon exiting the program.

Dialogue has many options. Scores are always available, but their display can be turned on and off at will, as can the musical notes that salute correct answers. Students can skip around from one story or poem to another instead of following the predetermined order. At the end of a series of questions on a work, users can return to review the questions and comments, but cannot change their scores. The student can quit at any time without losing scores. The score record will show what sections were covered for that day, how many questions were answered, and the percentage score.

Discourse

Some teachers will want to use the Plain Vanilla word processor to write additional lessons for essay-type responses, fill-in-the-blank homework, quizzes, and other exercises. Such material can either be printed out or copied to the students' disks. (It takes less than five minutes to save a file to twenty different disks.) On the computer the student can see the questions in one "window" and simultaneously write essay answers in another (or the same) window. Most students will appreciate the ease of revising and turning out their work with less manual labor than typewriting or handwriting requires. Many teachers will like the improvement in legibility compared with handwritten or even some typewritten papers.

Teachers who have their own computers may wish to receive student essays on disk, reducing paper clutter and making it easier for teachers who are fast typists to write (and erase!) comments. Discourse can thus be turned into dialogue, with the comments inserted directly into the student's file. Plain Vanilla's macro capability makes it possible to insert up to nine different marginal comments, created by the teacher, with a single keystroke for each comment. A whole library of macro files can be maintained, each file containing nine macros to automate repetitious tasks.

The word processor automatically preserves a backup file (with a .bak extension added to the file name) of the version that existed just prior to the last "save" command. This is important in case of power failure or accidental erasure. Students can often use this feature to recover lost text.

Dialogue and Discourse

<u>Works covered on each disk</u>

Dialogue

Poems: I taste a liquor never brewed; I dread that first robin so; I like to see it lap the miles; A route of evanescence; Apparently with no surprise; Further in summer than the birds; Acquainted with the Night; Meeting at Night; Design; The Windhover

Short Stories: Araby; Astronomer's Wife; Bliss; Young Goodman Brown; A Worn Path; The Short Happy life of Francis Macomber; The Metamorphosis; Everyday Use; The Yellow Wallpaper; Gimpel the Fool

Discourse

Short Stories: Astronomer's Wife; The Blind Man; Bliss; Young Goodman Brown; A Worn Path; Everyday Use; The Metamorphosis; Battle Royal; Bad Characters; The Yellow Wallpaper; Gimpel the Fool

Poems: The Eve of Saint Agnes; Ode to a Nightingale; The Waking; The Dance; The Windhover; Design; Apparently with no surprise

Plays: Oedipus Rex; Death of a Salesman

Essays: The Right Stuff; About Men; Once More to the Lake; The Judgment of the Birds

<u>What you need to run Dialogue and Discourse</u>

Dialogue and Discourse will run on an IBM PC, PC/XT, AT, PS2, or close compatible computer with a minimum of 256K memory and at least one 5¼" floppy disk drive. DOS version 2.0 or higher is required; generally the higher the version of DOS, the less space will be available on disks for student files. The programs can be copied to and run from a hard disk, if your computer is equipped with one. With an optional printer, student essays and scores can be printed out.

Getting Started

1. Floppy disk systems—Follow the instructions in your DOS manual to format a blank diskette that contains DOS (usually this command is FORMAT B:/S). This process is often referred to as creating "bootable" or "system" disks. Then copy all of the files on your Dialogue disk to this new disk. Label this disk "Dialogue" and put the original in a safe place. Format a second disk in the same way, copy all of the Discourse disk files to the second disk, label it "Discourse," and put the Discourse original disk in a safe place. If your working disks every get damaged, new copies can be made from the originals as necessary.

2. Hard disk systems—Follow the instructions in your DOS manual to create a new subdirectory. Copy all of the files on the Dialogue disk to this subdirectory. Put the original distribution disk away in a safe place. Then copy all of the files on the Discourse disk to this subdirectory and put the original disk in a safe place.

To begin the Dialogue program:

Floppy disk systems: place the Dialogue working disk in the A: drive. Type DL and strike the Enter (Return) key.
    Hard disk systems: go to the new directory. Type DL and strike the Enter (Return) key.

To being the Discourse program:

Floppy disk systems: place the Discourse working disk in the A: drive. Type DC and strike the Enter (Return) key.
    Hard disk systems: go to the new subdirectory. Type DC and strike the Enter (Return) key.
    You can use the Plain Vanilla word processor without the Discourse program by typing PV (instead of DC) and striking the Enter key. Experienced users not needing an initial Help file on screen can start up by typing MS followed by a space and then a filename.

A brief summary of some Plain Vanilla commands:

F1 = Create/call up file	F2 = Save file cursor is in
F3 = Open a window	F4 = Zoom window (on/off)
F5 = (or Ctrl N) = Next windows	F6 = Rebuild paragraph
F7 = Begin block	F8 = End block
F9 = Move block	F10 = Rename file cursor is in; save it

Ctrl K Q = Quit. Exit from program, with option of saving or abandoning files.

Notes on Plain Vanilla

1. Complete information on all Plain Vanilla functions and commands is contained in the HELP and HELPSUPP files on the Discourse disk. These files can be loaded, viewed on screen, and printed out like any other file. When Discourse is started by typing DC, the complete HELP file will be displayed at the bottom of the screen. Use the arrow keys and the pag up and pag down keys to scroll through the file. Use the printing commands described there to print out the file.

2. When typing an essay, you must press the Enter key twice at the end of each paragraph. blank line must separate paragraphs.

3. After insertions or deletions, use F6 (Rebuild paragraph) to make paragraphs fit margins. Rebuilding begins at the cursor and ends at the next blank line.

4. Some operations described in the help files require more than one key press. With Alt key combinations, HOLD DOWN the Alt key while striking BOTH character keys, one after the other. With the Ctrl key two-character combinations, release the Ctrl key before striking the second character. For cursor movement, both keys are held down simultaneously.

5. Note especially CTRL + O and Ctrl + P for moving rapidly by sentence units.